Organizing Professionals

Organizing Professionals
••••••••••••••••••••••••••••••••
Academic Employees Negotiating a New Academy

GARY RHOADES

Rutgers University Press
New Brunswick, Camden, and Newark, New Jersey
London and Oxford

Rutgers University Press is a department of Rutgers, The State University of New Jersey, one of the leading public research universities in the nation. By publishing worldwide, it furthers the University's mission of dedication to excellence in teaching, scholarship, research, and clinical care.

Library of Congress Cataloging-in-Publication Data

Names: Rhoades, Gary, author.
Title: Organizing professionals : academic employees negotiating a new academy / Gary Rhoades.
Description: New Brunswick, New Jersey : Rutgers University Press, [2025] | Includes bibliographical references and index.
Identifiers: LCCN 2024040291 | ISBN 9781978844230 (paperback) | ISBN 9781978844247 (hardcover) | ISBN 9781978844254 (epub) | ISBN 9781978844261 (pdf)
Subjects: LCSH: College teachers—United States. | College teachers' unions—United States. | Collective bargaining—College teachers—United States. | Universities and colleges—United States—Administration.
Classification: LCC LB2335.865.U6 R46 2025 | DDC 378.1/22—dc23/eng/20241126
LC record available at https://lccn.loc.gov/2024040291

A British Cataloging-in-Publication record for this book is available from the British Library.

Copyright © 2025 by Gary Rhoades
All rights reserved

No part of this book may be reproduced or utilized in any form or by any means, electronic or mechanical, or by any information storage and retrieval system, without written permission from the publisher. Please contact Rutgers University Press, 106 Somerset Street, New Brunswick, NJ 08901. The only exception to this prohibition is "fair use" as defined by U.S. copyright law.

References to internet websites (URLs) were accurate at the time of writing. Neither the author nor Rutgers University Press is responsible for URLs that may have expired or changed since the manuscript was prepared.

♾ The paper used in this publication meets the requirements of the American National Standard for Information Sciences—Permanence of Paper for Printed Library Materials, ANSI Z39.48–1992.

rutgersuniversitypress.org

To all those from whom I've learned that small groups of people can organize and catalyze larger movements and moments of negotiating meaningful, progressive change, and that, everything is negotiable . . .

Contents

1 Now Is the Time   1

2 A Critical Juncture and a Distinctive Dynamism   12

Part I   From the Margins to the Center: Contingent Academic Employees Organizing and Negotiating a New Academy   35

3 Bread and Roses, and a Labor-Based Conception of Quality: A New Faculty Majority Organizing a New Academy   39

4 Negotiating Bread and Roses and Labor-Based Quality into Part-Time-Only and Combined Bargaining Unit Contracts   62

5 More than Would-Be Apprentices: Graduate Student and Postdoc Employees Organizing and Negotiating amid New Forms of Contingency in an Aging, Changing Academy   87

Part II   Faculty Negotiating Retrenchment and Technology amid Management's Austerity Agenda   119

6 Challenging Management's Austerity Practices: Organizing amid and Negotiating Furloughs   123

7 Negotiating Management's Austerity Practices: Retrenchment for Financial Exigency and Other Reasons in the Contracts   144

8 Protections and Possibilities in Negotiating a Progressive Academy amid New Circuits of Production   168

9 Organizing and Negotiating for Respect and Public Purpose:
Toward a New Progressive Normal   191

Acknowledgments   215
Notes   219
References   243
Index   271

Organizing Professionals

1

Now Is the Time

• •

Now is the time.

"NOW IS THE RIGHT TIME." So reads a "Thank You" card from a faculty group I spoke to over a decade ago, in Big, Black, BLOCK letters. Propped up on my desk, it reminds me to write and to connect that writing to collective action.

Over two decades ago, I wrote *Managed Professionals: Unionized Faculty and Restructuring Academic Labor* (Rhoades, 1998a). Utilizing a national database of 212 collective bargaining agreements (CBAs), I analyzed the formal terms and conditions of faculty work in what remains the most comprehensive analysis of faculty CBAs in the literature. The title expressed my findings about a power (im)balance between managerial discretion and professorial rights and autonomy. Faculty are "managed professionals." Their employment conditions and their role in shaping the academy are defined, delimited, undermined, and superseded by management.

The book's subtitle reinforced that theme. Academe's workforce is being restructured. Tenure-stream faculty are declining as a share of the workforce. Managers have more discretion over the growth segments of part- and full-time nontenure-track faculty who have limited to no due process rights in their employment and voice in the academy's trajectory.

Now is the time to update that analysis. I do so with a much larger database (506 CBAs) covering a much larger proportion of all faculty CBAs (82 percent, versus 45 percent in 1998).

Now is also the time to extend that 1998 work empirically and conceptually. The last two decades have seen extraordinary levels of organizing by academic employees, forming new bargaining units in new realms and mobilizing existing units. That has happened despite extraordinary levels of political assault against academic employees' collective bargaining efforts and rights. Multiple possibilities are being negotiated, with new questions to ask.

It makes sense to revisit questions posed in 1998. What is the (im)balance of power between managerial discretion and employees' rights in the formal terms and conditions of employment? And, what are the dimensions of professorial stratification between tenure-track faculty and the "new faculty majority" (Maisto, 2012) of part- and full-time contingent faculty?

It also now makes sense to ask new questions and variations of old ones. It especially makes sense given the limited opportunity structure of tenure-track careers for contingent faculty as well as graduate and postdoc employees aspiring to them. And it makes sense given that the lower-paid, lower-status, most precarious types of academic positions are disproportionately held by more demographically diverse employees. Contingent faculty are more diverse than tenure-track faculty by gender and ethnicity (Finkelstein, Conley, & Schuster, 2016). That is even more true for graduate and postdoc employees, who are also more diverse by nation of origin. How might these reduced career opportunities and social inequities play out in identities and issues in organizing campaigns for new units and in contract negotiations?

The 2000s have seen more organizing of academic employees in new bargaining units than higher education has experienced since the 1970s (Herbert, 2016b; Herbert, Apkarian, & Van der Naald, 2020). And that activity has been most extensive, by far, among three categories of contingent employees. So, I have expanded this book's empirical focus beyond (but including) tenure-stream faculty, devoting its first half to foreground contingent employees' organizing and contract campaigns, considering the identities, issues, and ideologies that animate them.

One category of such employees is adjunct (part-time) faculty, who constitute nearly half the instructional workforce. They are in the vanguard of organizing, advocacy efforts and unionizing (Rhoades, 2015a, 2015b, 2015c, 2024). Sometimes they have organized with full-time nontenure-track faculty (FTNTT), who have also organized their own units. Disproportionately, new adjunct and contingent faculty unionizing has been in private universities (Herbert, 2016b).

Organizing among a second category—graduate employees (Herbert, 2016b; Herbert et al., 2020; Rhoades & Rhoads, 2003)—has also been particularly strong in the previously uncharted waters of major private research universities. Graduate assistant unions already existed in major public research universities, and have expanded and mobilized there, too.

Finally, for the first time, there have been union campaigns and new, stand-alone bargaining units among a third contingent category—postdoc employees. With one exception, these have been in public research universities (Camacho & Rhoads, 2015; Herbert et al., 2020).

At the same time, there has also been much organizing among full-time, tenure-stream (and FTNTT) faculty. That has involved the emergence of new bargaining units, often in settings that had previously experienced less unionization. And it has involved faculty bargaining units organizing to expand and mobilize, and to include new categories of members.

Given these developments, I have extended my empirical and conceptual focus in this book, evidenced in the title, *Organizing "Professionals"* (for reasons I will explain, I've put the second word in quotation marks here, but not on the book's cover or its title page). The first word emphasizes the action of the times. I conceptualize and analyze the organizing and contract campaigns in terms of the identities, issues, and ideologies that drive the campaigns and are embedded in the contracts.

In this chapter, I've put quotation marks around the book title's second word to trouble it for three reasons. First, my focus is not only on faculty but also on graduate and postdoctoral employees, who, in the eyes of some (and themselves), are professionals/professors-in-training (Bauer, 2017).[1] Second, some adjunct faculty leaders frame themselves and their campaigns more as exploited, low-wage employees, and less as "special" "professionals" apart from and above other workers (Berry, 2005; Berry & Worthen, 2021). Third, for some tenure-stream faculty, the individualistic, "special" identity of "professional" leads them to oppose unions or undermines them in forming a common cause with "non-professional" employees both within and outside academe. The quotation marks around "professional" were not included on the cover and title page also for three reasons: to mirror my 1998 book title, to facilitate searchability, and so as not to be perceived as mocking or demeaning the qualifications of academic employees.

My book's expanded empirical and conceptual focus is also evident in its subtitle, *Academic Employees Negotiating a New Academy*. Tenure-track and contingent faculty, graduate assistants, and postdocs are all academic employees.[2] Their union/contract campaigns, often in coalitions with groups in and outside the academy, are negotiating a new academy. That includes renegotiating their jurisdictions and relations to one another. I study their identities, the issues they organize around, and their ideologies regarding how and with what visions they are reshaping their place within the academy, and the public space and purposes of the academy.

When I shared my book title with Joe Berry, a longtime leader in and analyst of the contingent faculty labor movement, he wrote,

> I like the new title . . . ; [It] has two verbs in it . . . and you picked the right verbs, organizing and negotiating. Easier to use un-self-consciously now since the movement in both these areas is bigger and stronger than it was when you wrote *Managed professionals*. (personal communication, June 26, 2016)

4 • Organizing Professionals

That is true. When I wrote *Managed Professionals*, I was asked by some colleagues, "Are there any unionized faculty?" (1998a, p. 9). Now I am asked, "Why are so many faculty, and other academic employees unionizing, and what are they negotiating for?"

Answering such questions about organizing and negotiating requires backstories. So, let me start with mine regarding this academic (and activist, union) work.

At the core of this book are my identities and purposes. I am a professor and a member of United Campus Workers, Arizona, Local 7065 of the Communications Workers of America, a wall-to-wall union.[3] My nephew affectionately and playfully calls me "Professor." That is not just my occupational identity, it is a part of who I am.[4] Yet, I am also the son of a seminary professor who came from the working class, was the first in his family to go to college, and was as comfortable under the hood of a car as in a classroom. My dad (as do I) identified as an employee, never losing his affinity for working people or his hostility to the self-importance of those who see themselves as special because they are professors or administrators.

Like my dad, I worked in a unionized factory (in my case—a paper mill, in his—a tire factory) in my postsecondary education years. Indeed, as a college student, from working summers in a unionized paper mill as a utility worker I learned about the power of a union. The wages were superb, as was the overtime. But what I remember most viscerally is learning early on that a union is about collective power and about respect for workers and their safety. On one of my first days on the job a foreman told me to operate an overhead crane (with a hand-held device on the ground) to move a several-ton roll of paper over the factory floor, above equipment and people below. "I can't do that," I replied. "I haven't been checked out on the equipment." The foreman (I still remember his name—Mike Hawkins) was a wiry six feet two inches tall with a crew cut. He started reaming me out, telling me to take the device and operate the "goddamn crane." Again, I refused. Before I knew it, a shop steward came charging up. Though much smaller than Hawkins, he got between us, physically and metaphorically, and told "the Hawk" to get out of my face, that I hadn't been trained on the crane. Hawkins, red-faced, walked away. At that moment, I felt to my core the power of a union, of a collective that protected my safety and commanded respect from management.

I have experienced and witnessed that same visceral sense of efficacy and force in union campaigns in higher education, confronting academic capitalism's embodiment and enactment of capitalist practices toward employees (Slaughter & Rhoades, 2004). And I have experienced and witnessed the same stemming from being part of a re-energized academic labor movement.

On the latter point, from both of my parents, who were civil rights and antiwar activists in the 1960s, when my political consciousness was forged, I learned the importance and possibilities of social movements and collective struggle. And the crucible of those times helped define my purposes, which for me are fundamentally less about "succeeding" in the system than being part of effecting progressive change to bend it more toward justice.

Of course, I am more than simply my work identities of professor, employee, and union member. Like most tenured and full professors, I am a White, cisgender male, in an academic capitalist university that, like capitalism, embodies systems of classism interwoven with racism, genderism, and settler colonialism. It is important to intersect and embody work identities with the racial/ethnic and gender/orientation identities that are so central to so many of the social movements of my formative years and today, and to so much of the academic literature over the decades. Such identities are connected to organizing academic employees, who, in doing so, are intersecting workplace and social justice. It is especially important to foreground such identities and issues given organized labor's troubled history with marginalized populations, and given critical scholars' relative lack of attention to labor issues.

The above considerations can enhance and embody the analysis of organizing campaigns (and CBAs), helping us understand what drives them, even if they don't (at first) succeed. For example, as noted in the opening, the "NOW IS THE RIGHT TIME" thank-you card came from members of Washington State University's "chapter" of the American Association of University Professors (AAUP). At their invitation, in February 2010, I had visited their campus as AAUP's "General Secretary."[5] My presentation to and conversations with WSU chapter members were largely about general issues confronting faculty. They felt the university had become too top-down, too little informed by respect for meaningful faculty input, and that the "professional" structure of a faculty senate was not, on its own, sufficient for realizing the faculty's goals. So, in part, the conversations were their initial questions about possibly forming a union, to counter their sense that the university was becoming too corporatized in its practice and purposes at the expense of academic, educational, and public interest considerations.

Although WSU faculty have not thus far launched a unionization drive, the Associated Student Employees of WSU have, negotiating their first contract on February 1, 2024 (WSUCASE, 2024). At the center of the unionization campaign and contract gains, as for nearly all graduate and postdoc employees, were independent external arbitration for sexual harassment and racial discrimination, as well as family leave. Such issues are animated by social movements, and are contributing to employees negotiating new, expanded versions of issues at the center of union organizing, mobilizing, and negotiating.

Therein lies another reason why "NOW IS THE RIGHT TIME" to write this book. It is the right time to not simply replicate the analysis of *Managed Professionals*, but also to extend it empirically and conceptually. It is time to push a rethinking and retheorizing in analyzing union campaigns and hundreds more CBAs to understand the catalysts and consequences of the academy's unprecedented level of organizing. Indeed, the ongoing time we are in is ripe for analysis of and contribution to the academic labor movement.

Throughout my two-and-a-half years as general secretary, I often articulated the message that "Now is the right time [to organize/unionize]; now is OUR time." Despite my association role, that mantra referred to not only the AAUP but also the larger academic labor movement. It was framed to encompass tenure-stream and nontenure-track faculty as well as graduate employees, postdocs, and nonacademic professionals in various institutions, and affiliated with various (inter)national unions.[6] And it spoke to the need not just to form new bargaining units but also to energize and mobilize existing bargaining units around three sets of issues animating so many campaigns across the country: traditional "bread and butter" issues (e.g., pay, benefits, working conditions, and due process); "professional" issues (e.g., for faculty, shared governance and academic freedom, and for graduate and postdoc employees, academic support); and "social justice" issues. All three are underlain by matters of respect.

Given the time I have spent since 1998 engaging leaders and members of the academic labor movement, before, during, and after my years with the AAUP, I can offer insight into organizing strategies and contract negotiation. I can speak to the iterative process by which union leaders lay the foundation for current campaigns and contracts for future ones.[7] To accomplish this, I interweave backstage insights and stories (often in endnotes) as to what plays out on the public front stage in organizing campaigns and CBAs.

Three research questions drive my analysis: (1) What identities, issues, and ideologies of social critique and approaches to effecting change are expressed in the organizing and CBAs of academic employees?; (2) what is the (im)balance of power between managers' discretion and employees' due process rights, and voice in the collectively negotiated formal terms and conditions of labor that define the latter and delimit the former?; and (3) what are the ways that professional stratification is being (re)negotiated and reduced, as well as sometimes (perhaps inadvertently) reinscribed in organizing campaigns and in contract provisions?[8] For all three, I am interested in whether and how conceptions of public benefit and justice are invoked. That can include labor-based conceptions of quality working conditions that benefit the students, communities, and society we serve (Rhoades, 2020).[9] It can also include larger framings of higher education's public purposes as well as critiques of systemic inequities that entail intersecting workplace justice with issues of social (in)justice.

My principal theses are as follows. First, respect is at the core of the organizing and the contract negotiations related to the identities, issues, and ideologies of academic employees—respect for the workers in their full humanity, for their work, and for the academy's public purposes. Second, academic employees continue to be "managed professionals," but they have succeeded through organizing and contract negotiations in establishing and extending greater jurisdictional, due process rights and voice within and in shaping the new academy. Third, there is continued stratification within the academic workforce, but academic employees have reduced some of this through their collective action, the configuration of their bargaining units, and the CBAs they have collectively negotiated. Finally, academic employees' have foregrounded the centrality of their work and working conditions to the benefit of the students, communities, and society they serve, as well as to the larger public purposes of higher education that management is compromising with its broken priorities. The new academy they are negotiating is connected to social critiques of the academy and to intersecting larger social justice movements and issues.

As shall be seen, the particulars of how the above theses have played out vary by categories of academic employees. As well, there is variation within and among categories of employees in the general patterns and in the specifics. Moreover, the organizing and contract negotiations are contested and in flux. What will play out in the future is to be negotiated. The stories and analyses I offer here are but single acts in an ongoing (inter)play of negotiations between academic labor and higher education management.

The Study

The Contract Data Base

The database at the heart of much of this book's CBA analyses is the Higher Education Contract Analysis System (HECAS), a national collection of collective bargaining agreements (CBAs). Although HECAS is compiled by the National Education Association (NEA), it includes CBAs negotiated by bargaining units affiliated with various (inter)national academic (i.e., the American Federation of Teachers [AFT], AAUP, and NEA) and non-academic unions (e.g., Service Employees International Union [SEIU] and United Autoworkers [UAW]), as well as by independent locals representing academic employees. The 506 CBAs in the database are 82 percent of all contracts in a national directory (Berry & Savarese, 2012). Especially for graduate and postdoc employee contracts (far smaller in number and not as present in HECAS), I supplemented the database with contracts found online.

CBAs constitute formal terms and conditions of employment that are central in defining academic employees' working conditions bearing directly on my research questions.[10] And HECAS is the most significant, searchable data source of CBAs.[11]

Of course, all databases have limitations. One limitation of CBAs is that contractual provisions may be violated (and the union may file a grievance—which may be ruled on by an independent arbitrator—to effect enforcement). The formal terms do not always translate into (in)formal practice. Contracts tell us an important but incomplete story.

Moreover, contractual provisions do not always (and in some cases almost never) reflect the initial proposals of the two parties at the table. They are the product of negotiation. A cautionary caveat I offer in presenting exemplary contractual provision data to labor groups is that the suggested language should not be your original proposal because you may not get what you first ask for. Experienced negotiators know this, as with a SEIU staff leader and negotiator who emailed me for my PowerPoint slides with contract language. He responded to my caution with this—"My opening proposal is usually to launch the provost into the sun."

Further, contract negotiation is an iterative and forward-looking process (and backward-looking, too, to past practice). CBAs have backstories of strategies about making trade-offs, keeping future negotiations in mind. Smart negotiators lay the foundation for negotiating the next contract. Faculty leaders have told me of trade-offs they made in putting one sort of provision on the table as a bargaining chip for other language that was more important to members or more achievable at that time. They do this with the next contract in mind. For example, a community college faculty leader told me in reference to a presentation I'd done at a previous conference that she had tried to get a class cancellation fee clause in the CBA to provide adjunct faculty with some remuneration if their class was canceled. Although she hadn't succeeded, the bargaining team utilized that clause as a trade-off for getting pay equity language for adjunct faculty in prorated salaries. In the next contract, the union successfully negotiated class cancellation fees. There is a long game to contract negotiation.[12]

A final caveat about analyzing contractual language is warranted. It is one thing to sit in the comfort of my office, listen to music, and analyze provisions in a database, tracking patterns and offering suggestions. It is quite another matter to sit with a bargaining team across the table from a management team and to successfully negotiate language into the CBA. That takes savvy and discipline at the table, and it helps for that savvy to be backed up by the support and strength of union membership. There is a performative aspect to bargaining (e.g., each party asks for more than they are likely to get, each presents data and rationales supporting their case, there is back and forth, there may be impasses and threats of strike), and yet there are also implicit and explicit exercises of force on both sides (e.g., picketing, strike votes, and public communications to the press, politicians, and employees) that surround the formal, legal bargaining process. A curmudgeonly, longtime local academic labor leader once expressed to me his frustration about too many faculty believing that to "persuade" management at the bargaining table, one simply needed a good argument based on data: "Collective bargaining is not a goddamn seminar," he said. "It's about power." It's about management believing (or not) labor can exercise that power.

Yet, my contractual analyses are not just academic exercises. My intent is for them to inform and strengthen labor negotiations. Over the years, academic labor leaders have asked for advice about provisions or related that my work helped inform negotiations. That is why I do this work, for "I came in to the academy to change it" (Rhoades, 2018, p. 58).

Participant and Observer in the Academic Labor Movement

For three decades, I have been an observer of and a participant in the academic labor movement (Rhoades, 2018). The roles I have played inform and enhance my analysis of organizing and contract campaigns with what I have learned from working with people in the field.

My most longstanding role is that of a scholar writing and presenting about these matters to union leaders and members. From 1994 to 2018, I wrote an annual chapter for the *NEA's Higher Education Almanac*, analyzing contractual provisions, presenting the findings at the NEA's annual Higher Education conferences, and talking there with those in the field (as I did again in 2022 and 2023). So, too, for over two decades, I have been speaking at national- and state-level AFT and AAUP meetings, and to system-wide and institutional locals about trends, enabling me to learn from faculty leaders and staff involved in organizing and bargaining.

During my two and a half years (from January 2009 to June 2011) as general secretary of the AAUP, I became a more direct participant in the academic labor movement. Partly, that took the form of speaking to and with faculty groups at the campus and state level—in my second year, I made fifty-nine plane trips (and numerous train trips) to institutions. Most trips were made in response to requests from local chapters, bargaining units, and state conferences (groups of AAUP chapters and bargaining units) to speak as well as listen to members' concerns and aspirations.[13] Some invitations were from independent faculty activists forming advocacy groups. Others were from organizing committees of faculty seeking to unionize.

My time at the AAUP also afforded insight into the concrete work of organizing, as well as the operations and issues in existing bargaining units, including negotiating CBAs. In relation to organizing, much of that came from experience in union campaigns that were initiated and conducted during my time. As for contract negotiation, insight came from conversations with leaders and locals with deep experience and expertise in these matters, which was invaluable.

Invaluable as well was the experience, perspective, and insight I gained at the AAUP regarding the national academic labor movement and policy environment. Although I had relationships with staff and leaders in the major national education unions prior to the AAUP, my time as general secretary constituted an extended, intensive seminar and workshop in inter- and intra-union competition and politics, as well as in the national higher education policy arena.

My role and work at the AAUP also catalyzed my involvement at the national and local levels with other entities. One was the Campaign for the Future of Higher Education, a national coalition of academic labor groups launched in

May 2011, which held conferences, organized actions, and produced white papers to shape public discourse and policy (a recent iteration of such a coalition is Higher Education Labor United). Similarly, for many years I worked with the New Faculty Majority, an advocacy group of contingent faculty leaders from various unions. I have also worked with national and local staff and faculty leaders affiliated with SEIU in organizing adjunct and FTNTT faculty nationally, speaking at the launches of six "metro campaigns" of "Faculty Forward" (connected to SEIU), aimed at organizing faculty within a metro region. At those launches, I talked with, listened to, and learned from adjunct faculty organizing new bargaining units as well as staff leaders strategizing about such campaigns and negotiating CBAs, yielding stories of contingent faculty organizing and bargaining. During and after my time at the AAUP, I also began attending (and speaking at) the annual conference of the National Center for the Study of Collective Bargaining in Higher Education and the Professions (NCSCBHEP), which brings together players from management and labor, affording insight into the strategies and mechanics of collective bargaining (e.g., the conference sometimes includes panels of faculty and management from the same institution discussing new contracts).

Documentary and Archival Sources
Finally, I have also drawn on documentary sources other than CBAs. For instance, in chapter 5, I draw on the websites of graduate and postdoc employee groups, as well as on amicus briefs surrounding these employees' rights to unionize. And in chapter 7, I draw on policy documents, emails, and other documentary records surrounding matters of retrenchment.

Organization

After two introductory chapters, with chapter 2, "A Critical Juncture and Distinctive Dynamism," outlining attacks on collective bargaining rights, organizing campaigns, and the academic literature, the book is organized into two parts of three chapters each, plus a conclusion. Part I, "From the Margins to the Center: Contingent Academic Employees Organizing and Negotiating a New Academy," focuses on segments of the academic workforce that have re-energized the academic labor movement. Chapter 3, "Bread and Roses, and a Labor-Based Conception of Quality: A New Faculty Majority Organizing a New Academy," traces the combination of identities, issues, and ideologies that are expressed in the respect-based organizing of adjunct faculty. And it explores the creative strategies employed by these employees in their organizing campaigns. Chapter 4, "Negotiating Bread and Roses and Labor-Based Quality into Part-Time-Only and Combined Bargaining Unit Contracts," reviews first contract gains in salaries, benefits, and pay parity, and then examines contractual provisions surrounding class cancellation fees as well as access to instructional resources and professional development. It addresses how adjunct faculty are renegotiating their rights and jurisdiction relative to management and internal stratification relative to tenure-stream faculty. Chapter 5, "More than Would-Be Apprentices: Graduate Student and Postdoc Employees Organizing and Negotiating amid New Forms of Contingency in an Aging, Changing Academy," focuses on graduate and postdoc employees, mapping and intersecting organizing campaigns and contract gains in respect-based and social movement-connected identities, issues, and ideologies.

Part II, "Faculty Negotiating Retrenchment and Technology amid Management's Austerity Agenda," foregrounds tenure-stream faculty, with some attention devoted to contingent faculty. It focuses on realms addressed in *Managed Professionals*. Chapter 6, "Challenging Management's Austerity Practices: Organizing amid and Negotiating Furloughs," explores organizing and mobilizing, as well as contract provisions regarding furloughs. Chapter 7, "Negotiating Management's Austerity Practices: Retrenchment for Financial Exigency And Other Reasons in the Contracts," shifts the focus largely to established bargaining units and to contractual provisions regarding financial exigency and retrenchment of faculty for other rationales such as program reorganization. Chapter 8, "Protections and Possibilities in Negotiating a Progressive Academy amid New Circuits of Production," addresses instructional technology matters in collective bargaining agreements. It explores defensive and proactive approaches to negotiating new ways of delivering education, and what can be learned from the COVID-19 pandemic experience of shifting to remote learning.

The book closes with chapter 9, "Organizing and Negotiating for Respect and Public Purpose: Toward a New Progressive Normal." I summarize the findings and review implications for the academic literature. Finally, I offer a counternarrative to the policy, managerial, and, too often, academic austerity discourses about so-called new realities, which are, in fact, decades old. I speak to sets of principles for negotiating a new progressive normal, in the form of what I call "activist funds of knowledge."

Much organizing and negotiating in higher education is understandably from a reactive posture of defending academic employees' rights, core academic missions, and the academy's public purposes, which are under assault. But the dynamism of the times is about more than that. As a Washington State University faculty member during my 2010 visit said to me, something that I've heard from others over the years, "I feel like we are always in the position of fighting against a constant litany of attacks. I want to be FOR something." Now is the right time to articulate and negotiate progressive possibilities for academe.

2

A Critical Juncture and
a Distinctive Dynamism

• • • • • • • • • • • • • • • • • • • •

In 2010, a recently hired AAUP governmental relations staff professional, Nsé Ufot, warned that Republican governors (at the fall Governor's Association meeting) were planning to assault public employees' collective bargaining rights. The veteran AAUP national staff were dismissive—it seemed inconceivable. But Nsé was right.[1]

In the fall of 2009, I attended a Chicago meeting of representatives of the AAUP, the American Federation of Teachers (AFT), and the Illinois Federation of Teachers (IFT) to discuss a possible unionizing campaign at the University of Illinois, Chicago. It would be the first major research university tenure-track faculty to unionize in decades, and it involved a coalition of unions with troubled relations. It seemed like long odds. Yet, it succeeded.

The 2000s have been the worst and the best of times for unionized and unionizing academic employees. Academic labor has been experiencing a critical juncture and a distinctive dynamism. A critical juncture does not refer to the times' multiple, dramatic economic downturns (dot.com bust, Wall Street crash, and pandemic-driven recession), although such matters are addressed in chapters 6 and 7. Nor does it refer to technological changes and/or the pandemic, although those are addressed in chapter 8. It refers to academic employees' hotly contested collective bargaining rights.

A distinctive dynamism refers to remarkable levels of unionizing and mobilizing of existing bargaining units. Some of the unionizing included tenure-track faculty, organizing in distinctive settings, bargaining unit affiliations, and configurations. Far more extended beyond tenure-track faculty, mostly with new organizing by nonacademic unions, in less unionized institutional sectors, and around progressive issues. Such patterns were most evident among adjunct and full-time nontenure-track faculty (FTNTTF) and graduate and postdoc employees, as is discussed in chapters 3 through 5. Yet, there was also a distinctive dynamism characterizing existing bargaining units.

On the latter point, in September 2023, I spoke to the all-faculty meeting of the Lane Community College Education Association (LCCEA, the full- and part-time faculty union). Adrienne Mitchell, the president, asked me to provide a national perspective about trends in higher education and faculty work, and how academic employees are organizing around and negotiating them. Trends included austerity budgets, increased use and exploitation of adjunct faculty, and challenges to meaningful shared governance.

A quarter century earlier, in November 1999, I presented a similar sort of talk to the California Faculty Association's State Assembly at the request of Susan Meisenhelder, CFA's newly elected reform coalition President. The title was, "Managed Professionals: Unionized Faculty and Restructuring Academic Labor."

In both of the above cases, the issues being addressed reflected progressive goals. My CFA talk was centered on enhancing contingent faculty working conditions (CFA is an exemplar for adjunct faculty in negotiating pay parity and central involvement of contingent faculty in union governance). That was also a focus in my LCCEA talk on issues such as pay parity for adjunct faculty. Reflecting the times, however, at LCCEA I also focused on social justice issues, a focus that also came to characterize the CFA's work (Rhoades, Canton, & Toombs, 2023). In both talks, I highlighted the possibility of exercising collective power as part of a national labor movement.

In setting the stage for the book, this chapter details the critical juncture we are at and the distinctive dynamism of organizing in these times. It closes by bringing academic labor and academic literature together.

A Critical Juncture

The 2000s are a critical juncture. Not since the 1970s and the initial expansion of unionization in higher education has there been such animus toward and energy for academic employees collectively bargaining. On the one hand, there has been ongoing partisan bifurcation regarding workers' rights (and relatedly, reproductive, civil, and voting rights), with Republicans seeking to roll back rights established a half century ago. On the other hand, there has been dramatic growth in bargaining units and activity.

The 2000s have witnessed unprecedented challenges to and reductions in the rights of faculty and graduate employees to collectively bargain. Such challenges have played out at the federal and state level, in different ways for different employees in different higher education sectors. For example, as detailed in chapter 5, the rights of graduate assistants working in private universities are governed by the National Labor Relations Board's (NLRB) reading of the National Labor Relations Act. Changes in federal administrations have resulted in shifting NLRB rulings on these employees' rights (and on occasion of other academic employees) in private universities. Similarly, shifting party control of state government has led to shifts in public sector bargaining rights.[2]

State-Level Assaults

The threat that AAUP staffer Nsé Ufot identified emerged after the 2010 midterm elections and the ascension/expansion of Republican governors and state legislative (super) majorities. Targeting public sector unions, new legislation asserted public employees' "right to work" without joining a union or paying "agency fees" (lower than union dues, for the bargaining and services from which employees not in the union benefited), reduced the issues on which unions could bargain, and sometimes required them to hold annual elections for recertification.

Two of the most prominent examples of such legislation were in Wisconsin and Ohio, states that had historically been at the heart of organized labor. Wisconsin was the first state (in 1959) with enabling legislation establishing public sector employees' right to collectively bargain. Yet, Governor Walker signed a budget bill on March 11, 2011 (Act 10), with "right to work" provisions that undermined union representation for public sector employees (excepting police, firefighters, and state troopers). The law limited contracts to one year, delimited bargaining to salary increases capped by inflation, and required unions to take annual votes to maintain certification.[3] It led to a dramatic decline in union representation (Nack, Childers, Kulwiec, & Ibarra, 2020), and effectively stopped union organizing at the state's public universities.[4] Although Walker was defeated in 2018, and a major issue was education, the state legislature continued to be dominated in both houses by Republicans (after 2022 as well).

In Ohio, a related piece of legislation, Senate Bill 5, was signed into law by Governor Kasich on March 31, 2011. It restricted the scope of bargaining to wages (not benefits). It prevented unions from charging nonmembers agency fees. And a provision targeted faculty, indicating that full-time faculty, due to their role in curriculum, hiring, and tenure, were managers and ineligible for collective bargaining (part-time faculty already lacked bargaining rights). Yet, the law did not exempt police and firefighters.[5]

Partly due to the battles fought in Wisconsin, partly due to the inclusion of police and firefighters, there was a strong countermobilization against SB 5. A "We Are Ohio" coalition gathered petitions to put a referendum (Issue 2) on the ballot. Ohio is a base of strength for the AAUP, and its state conference (formed by chapters and bargaining units in the state to influence policy) and local faculty leaders were involved in gathering petitions—the future AAUP president,

Rudy Fichtenbaum, also testified in state legislative hearings. Over 61 percent of the November 8, 2011, vote was "no," repealing the legislation (McNay, 2013). Yet, four years later, the state's House Finance Committee considered, then decided against similar restrictive legislation (Flaherty, 2015, "Anti-Faculty Union"). And in the 2018 elections, the Republican nominee, DeWine, won.

A few years later, also in the Midwest, Governor Branstad of Iowa signed House Study Bill 84 and Senate File 213 on February 17, 2017. Modeled after the Wisconsin law, the Iowa bill exempted "public safety employees," restricted bargaining to wages, with a cap of 3 percent, prohibited unions from negotiating payroll dues deductions by employers, and required annual recertification. And the law prohibited unions from negotiating grievance procedures.[6] As testimony to the long-term nature of the struggle over collective bargaining rights, Branstad was one of the few Republican state legislators in 1974 who opposed the bipartisan collective bargaining legislation (Noble, 2017). Forty-three years later, he signed legislation reversing much of that law.

Federal Rulings on Collective Bargaining

At the federal level too, there has been an assault on unions. In a "right to work" *Janus v. AFSCME* ruling, the Supreme Court eliminated "agency fee," the practice that employees who are covered by a collective bargaining agreement and derive benefits from it must pay a fee even if they are not union members (Flaherty, 2018, "Supreme Court Rules").

In response, national unions and local bargaining units have adjusted their practices to become more proactive with members and nonmembers. That is part of unions' shift from a service orientation and culture to one of organizing and mobilizing, which may strengthen unions (see Nissen & Churchill, 2020, on United Faculty of Florida's transformation). Consider this message from a new faculty local: The day after the ruling, United Academics of the University of Oregon (UAUO) posted this on its website: "When Michigan became a right-to-work state in 2013, union membership actually increased; we can do the same here in Oregon. You can help by remaining involved with United Academics, or becoming active if you have not already. (Hammond, 2018, para. 9).[7]

Such mobilizing can mitigate and even overcome the adverse impact of *Janus* on unions' membership and monies. In their article, "Unions Fend off Membership Exodus in 2 Years since Janus Ruling," Kullgren and Kessler (2020) drew on Labor Department data and found that of the unions that organize academic employees, AFT and the United Steelworkers (USW) had realized net gains in membership by converting fee-payers to union members (Kullgren & Kessler, 2020).

The contest over bargaining rights will continue. As is discussed in chapter 5, Biden's election in 2020 had an immediate, dramatic effect on private university graduate employees' rights to unionize. Moreover, an August 25, 2023, ruling by the NLRB in *Cemex Construction Materials, LLC*, provides a new framework for union representation that "disincentivizes" management's unfair labor practices in union elections by ensuring that in the case of such practices, the employer will be required to recognize the union without rerunning the election (Sainato, 2023).

A Distinctive Dynamism

The distinctive dynamism of the times is expressed not only in the growth of new bargaining units, but also in who is organizing, where, and why. Here, I discuss three of the campaigns in which I was involved at the AAUP, highlighting these developments even among tenure-stream faculty. I also briefly address how dynamism does not equal success. Further, I note that the dynamism is centered beyond tenure-track faculty, as chapters 3 through 5 detail, among contingent faculty, graduate employees, and postdocs.

Before turning to the campaigns, consider this. In the first half of the 2000s, seventy-eight new bargaining units were formed, an increase of 15.7 percent.[8] Union representation among faculty and graduate employees reached all-time highs by the mid-2000s—for faculty, one-third of all universities and 42 percent of two-year colleges, and for graduate employees, more than 500 institutions (Sproul, Bucklew, & Houghton, 2014). New campaigns and bargaining units continued to emerge throughout the Great Recession and beyond. Since 2012, there has been a 25.9 percent increase in private sector bargaining units (over a quarter of it in part-time faculty units). On a far bigger baseline, the growth of new faculty units in the public sector was much smaller (2.1 percent), but 73.5 percent of faculty voting in those elections supported unionization (Herbert, 2016b, Table 3, p. 7).

Moreover, from 2013 to 2019, there have been 118 newly certified or recognized faculty collective bargaining units (sixty-five in private, not-for-profit institutions, fifty at publics, and three at private for-profit institutions), covering 36,264 employees (Herbert, Apkarian, & Van der Naald, 2020, p. 13). In addition, four new stand-alone postdoctoral units were certified, with another four new faculty units that included postdocs. Finally, there were an additional sixteen bargaining units of graduate employees (three-quarters exclusive graduate and one-quarter including undergraduate employees), covering 19,627 academic employees, a 50 percent increase of such units (Herbert et al., 2020, p. 20).

The dynamism has continued into the 2020s. Among graduate student employees, the growth of new bargaining units has been explosive—thirty-one of eighty such units were formed since 2020 (as of 2023). Additionally, two new postdoc units, as well as eleven new faculty units were formed in 2022/2023 (Herbert, Apkarian, & Van der Naald, 2023). And in April 2024, a new faculty unit at the University of Kansas, including tenure-track, nontenure-track, full- and part-time faculty was certified in an overwhelming vote of 850 to 132 (Lawhorn, 2024). That dramatically high election margin (87 percent) characterized graduate employee elections too, which in 2022/2023 averaged 91 percent, versus 75 percent in elections between 2013 and 2019 (Herbert et al., 2023, p. 8). Another marker of dynamism is the number of strikes. Nearly a third of strikes in the last decade occurred in 2022 and the first half of 2023 (Herbert et al., 2023). In short, there has been extraordinary expansion in academic employees signing on to (literally) a collective bargaining identity.

The three campaigns discussed below are emblematic of the distinctive dynamism in which tenure-stream faculty are organizing in public higher education—a public university medical center, a science-heavy public research university, and a member of the Association of American Universities (AAU). They are also emblematic of distinctive types and coalitions/configurations of academic employees stretching across segments of a stratified workforce—clinical and basic science faculty at a university health center, full-time nontenure-track and tenure-stream faculty, and a bargaining unit including tenure-stream, full- and part-time contingent faculty, and postdoc employees. Finally, the campaigns are emblematic of the wide-ranging, consistent issues and ideologies that animated organizing: respect for faculty voice and the public aspects of a university health center; respect for faculty voice and commitment to an urban public university mission as well as outrage at furloughs and misplaced financial priorities; and respect for the voice and work of faculty and postdocs, concern about privatization in athletics, academics, and funding, and a commitment to progressive views of equity.

The University of Connecticut Health Center (UCHC)

The first union campaign I authorized as AAUP's General Secretary was for a group of physicians, dentists, and basic science faculty at the University of Connecticut Health Center (UCHC).[9] It would be the first stand-alone unit of faculty at an academic health center to unionize.[10] Two previous organizing efforts had failed. In June 1999, faculty voted 250 to 169 against forming a union (affiliated with the American Federation of State, County, and Municipal Employees— AFSCME). Eighteen months later, the vote failed again by 261 to 147 (Pennington, 2009). Making matters more challenging for an AAUP campaign, it had been involved in but then pulled out of a previous campaign.[11]

In the summer of 2009, there was little interest among the AAUP's Department of Organizing and Services (DOS) staff in launching a campaign. As one responded to my question of whether he'd be interested in going to UCHC to assess the situation, "I'd rather die than go back there again and have to deal with some of the same people."[12]

The AAUP had not had a major successful union campaign in nearly a decade. It had suffered a lost election (by twenty-six votes) at the University of Minnesota in 1997 (after two earlier failed efforts in 1978 and 1981, as noted by Chaduvula, 2016). Moreover, DOS had limited staff and resources, and their campaign at Bowling Green State University (BGSU) had stalled.

However, times had changed at UCHC. There was a new head of the Health Center and a major new issue galvanizing faculty. Hired as the Vice President for Health Affairs, starting August 11, 2008, Dr. Cato Laurencin oversaw an effort to "integrate" the Health Center's hospital with a private entity, the Hartford Health Care Corporation. Beyond concerns about privatization, basic science faculty were unhappy with the lack of consultation, and clinicians were unhappy about a "non-compete" provision that would impede their ability to practice elsewhere in Connecticut.[13]

The situation unfolded rapidly. On July 16, 2009, I was called by Ed Marth, longtime executive director of the University of Connecticut main campus faculty union.[14] He wanted me to consider an AAUP union campaign and to provide some material support ($5,000) for that. Marth felt there was new energy and a chance for success.[15] Two faculty leaders from past campaigns were involved, but new folks had also emerged.

Judging from the email strings that Marth forwarded to me, faculty were deeply unhappy with developments at UCHC. Beyond the merger, issues included a proposed "productivity" plan (that would squeeze clinicians, undervalue teaching, and increase administrative costs) and a proposed mandate that basic science faculty bring in half of their salaries in external grants. On the latter issue, as one basic science faculty member (a new activist) wrote, "It has been for some time now that we have been asked to support our research time and effort on our grants as salary support. . . . However, never before have we been set with a mandate and threats that salaries will wax and wane with granting tides. . . . What I see . . . is that this is the administration's way of forcing an overall 25 percent pay cut on its faculty" (personal communication, July 17, 2009).

Her email captured a collective sense of frustration with a new chief administrator acting like he was managing a business.

As one faculty member emailed to the organizers (July 17, 2009), "Faculty have no representation, voice, or recourse." The faculty council had been dissolved earlier that year. At the core of faculty organizing was anger that "academic medicine is now reduced to a metric and relative value units" (personal email, July 18, 2009).

After talking with Marth, I met that afternoon with the AAUP's head of organizing, who briefed me on the situation, players, and challenges.[16] One big challenge was the differences between clinical and basic science faculty. Previous campaigns had failed in part because of broad opposition from the former. As a UCHC faculty member involved in the earlier drive wrote to me in an email on July 31, 2009, "I paid dearly for being very visible during UCHC's previous faculty unionization effort. I've made it clear to my colleagues that this time there must be broad support, including clinician support." Such support was essential given that a rough count of the possible bargaining unit revealed that 36 percent were basic science and 64 percent were clinical faculty (email communication, July 31, 2009, from local faculty leader).[17]

Still, it seemed worth a visit to explore a possible union campaign. The faculty's sentiments spoke to what I had been studying and seeing in universities' move to academic capitalism (Slaughter & Rhoades, 2004), and nowhere more so than in medical schools. And if the campaign succeeded, it could re-energize the AAUP.

A month later, on August 13, 2009, I visited UCHC. Marth had organized a panel with Charlie Parrish, faculty union president at Wayne State University, and me where medical school faculty were in the bargaining unit. I would convey the national office's support and provide a national perspective on academic medicine's corporatization. Parrish would explain to the medical school faculty that there were peers elsewhere who were unionized. Employees always want to know if there are others like them who have unionized and fared well. The turnout was pretty good, and the energy was impressive.

Subsequently, after consultation with the national executive committee, I authorized a union campaign at UCHC. The campaign broke many conventions of organizing. First, UCHC faculty leaders did few face-to-face office visits with colleagues that organizers see as a key to successful campaigns.[18] Thus, in an October 29, 2009, email to me conveying a report from Bunsis about his visit to UCHC just three weeks before the election, the DOS head wrote, "Between now and the election, they're doing emailings and distribution of literature; no office visits because those didn't work when they tried them." Local leaders built support through virtual leafleting, secure listservs, and small cells of faculty, organizing in ways they felt were best attuned to medical school faculty's work lives.[19]

A second break with convention was that organizing committee members were not representative of UCHC's academic units; all organizers I've known believe it essential to map/build representation across departments.[20] Only a few clinical faculty were involved, but not in proportion to their numbers.

Third, conventional wisdom is that you do not file for a union election with less than 60 percent of union authorization cards signed (in most cases, 30 percent of the employees in the unit must sign in order for the state board to approve an election). But at UCHC, with less than a month to go before the election, only 38 percent of the potential unit had signed cards.[21]

The election, held just four months after Ed Marth first called me, an extremely short time for a campaign, could not have been closer. On November 18, 2009, the results were announced. Of 444 (out of 519 eligible) voters, 223 supported and 221 voted against forming a union affiliated with the AAUP (Pennington, 2009). What a difference a decade makes.[22]

As Bunsis wrote to the CBC Executive Committee, "This is a great victory for the AAUP, and it proves we can organize a unit." Similarly, I wrote to UCHC faculty, Ed Marth, and national AAUP staff, leaders, and members, "The election is a testimony to the possibility of challenging the current patterns in American higher education, which . . . are nowhere worse than in university health science centers. You are redefining what is possible for faculty in the academy."

That is a central point of this book—academic employees are redefining what is possible in a new academy.

Winning a union election was important. What followed—negotiating a first contract—took more time. Over a year and a half after the election, UCHC faculty's bargaining unit signed its first collective bargaining agreement on June 13, 2011.

The UCHC story begins to flesh out the book's narrative about organizing. It is about what academic employees are organizing against (privatization) and for (respect for their voice and work), and about internal professorial stratification. It speaks to what it takes to organize—time, leadership, and taking risks. And it highlights the sustained, collective efforts of employees over time, and the distinctive dynamism of the moment.

University of Illinois at Chicago (UIC)

The second union campaign I authorized, at the University of Illinois at Chicago (UIC), also speaks to the dynamism of the times in who is organizing, where, and what for (and in how vigorously management fights unionization). Although I authorized the AAUP's participation, it was a joint campaign with the AFT (under the organizations' 2008 joint organizing agreement) and the Illinois Federation of Teachers (IFT), with those bodies following their governance structure in undertaking the campaign.

UIC would be the first large, science/engineering-heavy, public research university in decades in which tenure-stream faculty would vote to unionize. The campaign was a compelling case of tenure-stream and full-time, nontenure-track faculty (FTNTTF) working in coalition. The issues were corporatization and faculty voice, privatization, and the university's trajectory away from its urban mission and students.

On September 9, 2009, AAUP, AFT, and IFT representatives had their first meeting in Chicago. We discussed the prospect of a joint campaign. Within two months, with the work of Troy Brazell (AFT) and Lorenzo McDonald (IFT), who worked full-time on the campaign, the UIC United Faculty (UICUF) organizing committee had its first meeting, attended by nine faculty from eight academic units.

Two years later, on September 15, 2011, the Illinois Labor Relations Board certified the union, a ruling the university contested in court, claiming that tenure-stream and FTNTT faculty should not be in the same bargaining unit. The faculty eventually chose to form two unions—and the tenure-stream unit was certified on June 28, 2012. It took another two years to negotiate the first contract, signed in May 2014. The time entailed is testimony to academic employees' extraordinary persistence.

The campaign had four challenges beyond management's resistance. UIC is a research university. It is science heavy. The campaign included tenure-stream and full-time, nontenure-track (FTNTT) faculty. And it was a joint AAUP/AFT/IFT campaign.

UIC is a major research university (at the time, among the top fifty in research funding). Faculty's status sensibilities made it likely some would be hostile to unionizing, for they associate unions with less prestigious occupations. During the campaign, I encountered faculty who said they had family members who were union members (e.g., of trade or teacher unions) but felt a union was not appropriate for research university faculty. Two key players in the UICUF campaign later spoke to this issue:

> One of the original points of the whole concept of the professional—as it applied to ministers, doctors, lawyers, and professors—was to distinguish them from workers. But ... in the 21st century that distinction is pure ideology. Professionals ... and professors are workers. ... In organizing our union[,] ... many (especially tenure-track) professors were reluctant to join, seeing themselves the way the administration wants us to see ourselves: as professionals who shouldn't be lumped together with public school teachers, university staff, fast food workers, even our own non-tenure track colleagues. (Davis & Benn Michaels, 2014, para. 19)

The identity of and ideology about being professionals, experts grounded in competitive individualism and meritocracy, can be an obstacle to employees identifying as union members. At the heart of the AAUP's failed union effort a decade earlier at the University of Minnesota (Twin Cities) was a letter circulated by twenty-six regents professors opposing unionization and invoking "excellence" (Rhoades, 1998a, p. 3). As a Duluth campus faculty leader (where faculty are unionized) familiar with the situation wrote, "Too many faculty couldn't marry their self-image as professionals with the idea of carrying a union card, just like Teamsters" (McClure, 1999, p. 100).

That is why I put "professionals" in quotation marks in chapter 1, and shifted to "employees" in the book's subtitle to problematize the former term.[23] That is also why AFT signed an agreement with AAUP to organize in public research universities.[24] Their polling of faculty indicated support for a union reached a tipping point for unionization if the bargaining agent was not just AFT but also AAUP.[25]

Moreover, many faculty in research universities believe they can negotiate better deals as individuals on the external market than the union can do collectively. In a session on organizing in "Tier 1 Research Universities" at an NEA Higher Education conference, a University of Florida United Faculty of Florida leader indicated that one challenge in organizing at tier 1 research universities is many faculty members' choice of "flight versus fight." If they are not happy, they can leverage their expertise and marketability for a raise or to move (Trainor, 2022). They also may mistakenly believe that a union contract would eliminate their ability to negotiate this way, not knowing that contracts often have provisions for such individually negotiated retention raises.

A second, related challenge for the campaign was that many UIC faculty were in STEM fields, related professional schools, and the Business School (the Colleges of Dentistry and Medicine were not included in the bargaining unit). They were higher salaried, with many running labs dependent on external grants and institutional resources. So, they are less likely to be amenable to unionization.[26] And such higher-paid faculty sometimes mistakenly associate unions with standardized (to the lowest common denominator) salaries, a concern heightened in research universities, where salary differences across departments are dramatic. Faculty do not always understand that unions negotiate percentage increases on an existing (differentiated) base.

A third challenge at UIC was that originally the campaign included tenure-stream and FTNTT faculty. There were internal dynamics within the organizing committee, in relations between and solidarity among tenure-track and FTNTT faculty. A protracted set of legal challenges by management to the unit's configuration significantly delayed holding a union election.[27] Nevertheless, the faculty organizing committee's choice of the name, "United Faculty" reflected more than an aspiration; it spoke to an ongoing reality of tenure-stream and FTNTT faculty working through the tensions together and coordinating their demands even in separate units (see Rhoades, 2021).

A fourth challenge was that the campaign included the AAUP, AFT, and IFT (as a state affiliate, the IFT was subordinate to the national affiliate). AAUP and AFT have different histories, identities, and members. Although the same age, the former came to collective bargaining long after the latter did, in a contentious decision that some would suggest (and that was my experience) still plays out in intraorganizational politics and competing identities (see Hutcheson, 2000). Moreover, far more AFT members are community college and/or contingent faculty and graduate employees than in the AAUP, whose members are overwhelmingly tenure-stream faculty in four-year institutions.[28]

A further complication in the joint campaign was the organizations' distinctive cultures in organizing, partly related to their size. Given its small membership (45,000) and national organizing staff (five), the AAUP lacked the people to provide the "boots on the ground" that the AFT (with over one million members and vastly larger national and regional staffs and resources) and IFT had. Relatedly, AAUP staff and faculty leaders took pride in an organizing model driven by local faculty (they lacked the staff to do otherwise). That translated into different communication strategies. AFT's model involved the lead staff member on the ground being pressured to obtain approvals for campaign communications up the chain of command to the national office. The AFT also had a preference for campaign materials being produced by national office professionals (who mostly worked with K–12 units/campaigns), with a standard look. By contrast, the AAUP model was more that communications and materials be generated by local faculty (through an organizing or communications committee).[29] Further, AFT's preference was to run an under-the-radar "stealth" campaign until the organizing committee was strong enough to go public, whereas AAUP staff, leaders, and I preferred publicly leveraging local issues earlier on to galvanize support and strengthen the organizing committee.

Finally, the two organizations had (and have, even as they affiliate) competing interests and resource levels. They have vastly different resource levels and different capacities to commit personnel and monies to the campaign. For all the effort of AAUP leaders and staff (e.g., Howard Bunsis made at least fifteen campus visits in the campaign's first year, and I made ten), the AFT and IFT had full-time staff on the campaign, in an office just off campus. Over 90 percent of the campaign's financial/material resources came from the AFT and IFT. That played out in contested campaign decisions.[30]

More than that, though, as in the case of UCHC (and subsequently, the University of Oregon), there was resistance among AAUP's organizing staff.[31] No doubt, doing a joint campaign with the AFT was hard because for years AFT had been raiding some AAUP units. Plus, the AAUP was engaged in a solo campaign at BGSU.

At the heart of the staff's reluctance, though, is what is at the heart of organizing—taking a risk, being willing to fail, and persisting amid and after setbacks, as has been seen. At the time, AAUP's organizing staff, perhaps because of past failed campaigns seemed to be looking less for ways to succeed than for ways to explain why a campaign would fail, and they were behaving accordingly. Once, when relating the situation to my wife, Janet, she said, "It's like the Circumlocution Office." She then read me a passage from *Little Dorrit*: "Whatever was required to be done, the Circumlocution Office was beforehand with all public departments in the art of perceiving—HOW NOT TO DO IT. . . . The Circumlocution Office was down upon any ill-advised public servant who was going to do it, or who appeared to be by any surprising accident in remote danger of doing it, with a minute, and a memorandum, and a letter of instructions, that extinguished him" (Dickens, 1998, pp. 119–120).

"That's it!" I exclaimed.

Organizing is a risk, taking people out of their comfort zones and offices. At the time, AAUP's organizing staff were risk-averse, ensconced in their office-focused routines.[32]

At UIC, as with UCHC, my feeling was the time was ripe, and it was worth the risk. Having studied and lived in research universities, I sensed a deep reservoir of dissatisfaction about their trajectory, about operating increasingly like businesses, moving them away from educational and public purposes, with deteriorating faculty working conditions and voice. And I felt a victory would open up more possibilities.

However, the opportunity to unionize UIC came because of the AFT's sense of possibilities. Its Organizing Director (Phil Kugler, now retired) and its

Director of the Higher Education Department (Larry Gold, now deceased) strategically targeted tenure-stream faculty in public research universities, a sector where union representation was less dense than in two- and four-year teaching-oriented institutions. That initiative led to the subsequent organizing of over 11,000 faculty and laid the foundation for the 2022 AAUP/AFT affiliation agreement (AAUP, 2021).

Four issues were at the heart of the UIC campaign—furloughs, institutional trajectory, faculty voice, and reducing professorial stratification. The campaign was catalyzed by the University of Illinois system's furloughing of faculty (see chapter 6).

In addition, the UICUF organizing committee faculty objected to ongoing patterns of privatization that were taking UIC away from its public purposes, its urban mission, and prioritizing local, lower-income students (disproportionately of color). The first of the four principles the United Faculty put on its "About Us" webpage at the time (it's now on the home page's first bullet under "Who we are"; https://uicunitedfaculty.org) was, "Realizing the mission of the University of Illinois at Chicago (UIC) as a public research university in a democratic society."

UICUF also felt faculty's governance role was being disrespected/undermined by corporate-like decision making. Principles 2 and 3 on its "About Us" webpage (and now on the home page) were about faculty voice in decision making— "Making the promise of shared governance a reality by backing it with the power of collective bargaining," and, "Making sure that every member of the faculty has an individual voice and that the faculty as a whole has a collective voice in determining our future."

Finally, reducing professorial stratification was at the campaign's core. The organizing committee was committed to respect for and solidarity among different segments of faculty, renegotiating relations between full-time tenure- and nontenure-track faculty, whereas management argued they did not share a community of interest. If management won the legal battle, contractually reinscribing the faculty's stratification, the two full-time faculty segments won the war, continuing to coordinate their activities.

The UICUF victory again redefined possibilities for organizing. It was the first large public research university in a quarter century in which tenure-stream faculty unionized. It spoke to the power of coalitions between union affiliates (and of working through the challenges to leverage the coalitions' combined resources and strengths) and of cooperation among tenure-track and FTNTT faculty. Finally, it spoke to another theme of the book: the importance of public good and social justice issues.

The University of Oregon

Notwithstanding UIC's prominence, it was neither a member of the Association of American Universities (AAU) nor its state's flagship university.[33] Only four of the thirty-four public AAU institutions in the U.S. at the time (Rutgers,

Stony Brook, University at Buffalo, and University of Florida) had unionized tenure-stream faculty.[34] And those faculty had unionized in 1970, 1973, 1973, and 1976.

That is partly why a third successful union campaign in which I was involved at the AAUP at the University of Oregon (UO) was so important. The UO would be the first AAU university to unionize in three decades. UO faculty asked whether any other AAU institutions had unionized tenure-stream faculty, and the argument of some faculty and management was that unionization was inimical to quality and could compromise the UO's national standing.[35] A counter-argument was that all four unionized AAU institutions became AAU members more than a decade *after* the tenure-stream faculty unionized.[36]

The AAUP/AFT campaign at UO took five years. It was launched in December 2008, just before I joined AAUP. Over three years later (March 13, 2012), the Oregon Employment Relations Board certified the bargaining unit. The first contract was signed in October 2013.

The campaign's length was partly due to it stalling after a year. On March 30, 2010, national AFT and AAUP leaders (including me) met with organizing committee members, who had several concerns. One was a gender-related disconnect between the AFT's lead organizer (again, the AFT was committing almost all the on-the-ground resources) and key faculty leaders, who were progressive women. Another concern was the AAUP organizer on the campaign, who lived in the San Francisco area and was spending little time in Eugene.

Moreover, the senior person overseeing AAUP's work was former AAUP general secretary Ernst Benjamin (2015), who was openly skeptical about the campaign's chances. He was following AAUP's risk-averse organizing strategy of building an "advocacy chapter" (not an organizing committee, with AFT) as a step to perhaps developing a union and as a fallback in case the union campaign failed. AFT and organizing committee faculty were unhappy about people being recruited to an AAUP chapter that was not addressing union issues amid a joint unionizing campaign.

AFT's leaders were not alone in their discontent. AAUP's leaders were also frustrated by AAUP organizers' relative inattention and strategy. To them, it was a path of not really trying, of settling for a small "chapter" of few to several dozen members, compared to a bargaining unit that would be about 1,700. So, leading up to the meeting, I took on oversight of the campaign for AAUP.

The campaign also changed who would be in the bargaining unit. Initially, support professionals were to be included. But when polling suggested they were less supportive of a union, the decision was made to not include them. The campaign was centered on academic employees—tenure-stream faculty, contingent faculty (full-time and adjunct), and postdoctoral employees. The organizing committee chose its name, United Academics, accordingly.

Two interrelated issues driving the campaign were finances and faculty voice, amid privatization. The UO was at the bottom of the AAU in faculty salaries and institutional funding, and academic employees saw unionization as a remedy. Also, faculty had a sense of having lost voice relative to management and donors (i.e., Phil Knight, investing in UO athletics) in influencing the institution's trajectory. Identified in AFT's early polling of faculty, the issues continued to be important throughout and were further exacerbated by UO's president proposing a privatization plan that the university be funded not by state appropriations but by an endowment that would receive state monies for a set period of time.

With the replacement of the lead AFT organizer (three months after the March meeting) and the AAUP's commitment to refocusing campaign activity and providing more on-the-ground staff support, the campaign was re-energized. The AAUP began to help run a more open, aggressive campaign.[37]

The challenges of a joint campaign played out again. The question of card check arose but was less of an issue given its resolution in the UIC campaign.[38] Also, early on, the biggest issue was whether to organize at both the University of Oregon and Oregon State University and in what sequence. My first visit to Oregon in March 2009 was to OSU, where AAUP organizing staff were working to build a local advocacy chapter. But AFT leaders saw UO as the first target in a sequenced, two-university campaign. When I took over leadership of the AAUP part of the campaign, that is what we moved to, and the sequence played out several years later.[39]

Dynamism Does Not Always Equal Success

Despite the successful campaigns discussed above and other successes in unionizing public research university tenure-stream faculty, there were also false starts and failed organizing efforts. Four cases are illustrative.

The successful union drive at UIC led to a comparable effort at the University of Illinois, Urbana-Champaign (UIUC), after I left the AAUP. The campus's forty-plus-year-old Campus Faculty Association was supportive. But an anti-union drive among tenured faculty, with a "No Faculty Union" blog emerging, along with a short statement entitled "Preserving Excellence at Illinois: Joint Statement of Concern about Faculty Unionization." The latter was first circulated to named or endowed chairs (see Prochaska, 2014), and the list of signatories grew by June 2014 to 334.[40] The campaign among tenure-stream faculty failed. Yet, a full-time, nontenure-track faculty union was certified by the Illinois Labor Relations Board on July 9, 2014. Two years and two strikes later Local 6546 signed its first contract (Gilmore, 2018).

During the successful BGSU campaign, the AAUP also explored a possible solo drive at Ohio University. After several exploratory visits from staff, the initiative died. What remained was a small AAUP advocacy chapter. Yet, in March 2024, United Academics of Ohio University (affiliated with the AAUP/ AFT) filed cards with the State Employee Relations Board for a union election; OU's management responded by challenging the configuration of the bargaining unit (Hendrix, 2024; Ohio University, 2024). It is another example of academic employees' persistence and of management's resistance.

Another research university campaign that faltered around my time at the AAUP was at New Mexico State University (NMSU). Initial steps involved visits, talks with, and presentations to faculty members. The issues were, again, university finances, faculty voice, and a commitment to higher education's public purposes. DOS's head led this solo AAUP campaign and characteristically pursued building an advocacy chapter on the way to a possible union campaign. The campaign failed.[41] In 2022, another union drive emerged with the NEA, and in March 2024 faculty filed a petition for union recognition with the state's Public Employees Labor Relations Board (D'Ammassa, 2024).

Finally, one of the more activist and larger AAUP advocacy chapters in the 2000s has been at the University of Washington (UW). During my time at the AAUP, that did not translate into a union drive. But subsequently, some UW faculty approached SEIU (after meeting with AAUP leaders, who expressed no interest), which launched a drive. That effort stalled, partly due to a faculty anti-union campaign and website—"UW Excellence" (EW Excellence, n.d.). Yet, postdocs have unionized at the university.

Dynamism beyond Tenure-Stream Faculty

The greatest organizing dynamism, as will be discussed in chapters 3 through 5, has been among contingent faculty and graduate and postdoc employees who are now at the vanguard of organizing (Rhoades, 2021, 2024). The primary unions in these efforts have been nonacademic ones, particularly SEIU, United Autoworkers (UAW), United Electrical Workers (UE), and the United Steelworkers (USW). Counter to conventional wisdom, union competition is re-energizing the academic labor movement, as has happened in other sectors (Stepan-Norris & Southworth, 2010; Milkman, 2006).[42]

Now is the right time.

The 2000s, then, are a time of distinctive dynamism in the academic labor movement. Now is the right time to analyze that organizing and the negotiated collective bargaining agreements coming out of it in ways I hope will frame the academic literature and inform the academic labor movement.

Academic Labor and the Academic Literature: Bringing Professors, Academic Employees, and Organized Labor Together

Unions see higher education as a site for much organizing. Yet, few scholars see it as a site for studying unions. If the data and sites for studying academic unionization and collective bargaining are extensive, the academic literature is exiguous. Scholarship on organized labor disproportionately concentrates on blue-collar workers in private-sector employment. Studies of faculty overwhelmingly frame them as individual, white-collar professionals (or as aggregated workforces studied longitudinally) in not-for-profit settings, not as collective actors (Rhoades, 2014a). And studies of graduate and postdoc employees frame them as individuals and/or in relation to socialization and career paths.

It is long past time to change such patterns. Far higher proportions of faculty are unionized (25 percent, see Berry & Savarese, 2012) than of the general workforce (9 percent)—for graduate employees, the percentage is 20 percent, and growing (Berry & Savarese, 2012). So, too, public sector employees are a more unionized workforce (32.5 percent) than are private sector ones (6 percent; see U.S. Bureau of Labor Statistics, 2024). The intersection of academe and organized labor is a fruitful ground for study.

Part of what informs my analysis of academic labor is the increased precariousness of all work, including professional and academic work, over the past five decades amid the increased demographic diversity of the (academic) workforce. A leading scholar of that expansion of precarious work in the broader economy has spoken to that pattern in the professoriate, too, noting dramatic growth in the 1970s, 1980s, and 1990s of part- and full-time contingent faculty (Kalleberg, 2009, Figure 3, p. 9).

Central to Kalleberg's argument was that occupations/sectors that were once in primary labor markets in their job security, wages, and benefits have seen significant segments of their ranks become secondary labor markets. That pattern applies even in the relatively privileged STEM fields of academe (Rhoades & Torres-Olave, 2015). This shifting context of academics' work as "gig" work is detailed by Kezar, DePaola, and Scott (2019) and by Tolley (2018).

The changing structure of the academic profession has been a subject of much study, historically and currently. Much of that work has concentrated on the growing ranks of contingent faculty. Early on, scholars wrote of the "invisible faculty" (Gappa, 1984; Gappa & Leslie, 1993) and "contingent" employment in higher education (Barker, 1998). Later, as the ranks of full-time nontenure-track grew, scholars wrote about the working conditions of faculty who were "teaching without tenure" (Baldwin & Chronister, 2001). Subsequently, some have embraced the terminology of contingent faculty leaders, of "the new faculty majority" (e.g., see Kezar, 2012), as an "adjunct underclass" (Childress, 2019), and more inclusively of contingent graduate and postdoc employees (Kezar et al., 2019).

Much work has focused on the professoriate and the pipeline into it. That has mostly consisted of analyzing shifting patterns such that, as one study phrased it, faculty were *"A National Resource Imperiled"* (Bowen & Schuster, 1986). Two leading scholars over the years have been Martin Finkelstein and Jack Schuster. An early review of national trends in *The American Academic Profession* (Finkelstein, 1984) was followed by an analyses of *A Profession in Transition* (Finkelstein, Seal, & Schuster, 1998), with the increased hiring of nontenure-track faculty in "the new academic generation" of hires, and then of "the restructuring of academic work and careers" (Schuster & Finkelstein, 2006). Most recently, they have "reassessed" academe "in a turbulent era" (Finkelstein, Conley, & Schuster, 2016), finding that as academic employment has become more contingent, the most precarious segments of the academic workforce are those whose members are most likely to be women and people of color (Finkelstein et al., 2016).

Yet, except for brief mentions in Finkelstein's first and last books, and in Kezar, DePaola, and Scott's 2019 book, unionization is unaddressed. Finkelstein (1984) briefly addressed governance and economic issues related to unionization. Finkelstein, Conley, and Schuster (2016) briefly addressed its effects on salaries. Kezar et al. (2019) devoted one chapter to the topic.

It is time to explore how academic employees have collectively organized for and negotiated better jobs, working conditions, and higher education futures (Kezar et al., 2019; Rhoades, 2014a). Here, I go beyond the sociology of the professions. Amid the rise of academic unionism in the 1970s, "professionalization" studies analyzed how occupations collectively mobilize and negotiate monopolies over domains of work, by defining them as "professions" (e.g., Abbott, 1988; Freidson, 1984; Larson, 1977). But they largely overlooked both academic employees and unionization, as did the subsequent body of work that examined expert work in large organizations (Brint, 1994; Gorman & Sandefur, 2011: for an exception, see Park, Sine, & Tolbert, 2011).

It is time to bring the study of academic employees together with the study of organized labor. Here, I ground political sociological sensitivities in organizational-level analysis. I study academic employees' collective organizing and negotiating of the terms and conditions of their labor within higher education. I analyze their negotiation of their jurisdictions (Abbott, 1988) in relation to management and to other segments of the academic workforce. I explore their collective projects.

In doing so, I draw on a key focus of the sociology of work—workers' desire for dignity, as in Hodson (2001)—so as to bring workers back in (Simpson, 1989) to the study of workplaces. Like Hodson, I focus on labor versus management, and on relations between segments of the academic workforce negotiating jurisdiction and dignity. Unlike Hodson, I analyze workers' collective agency, exploring the indignities that animate their organizing and their negotiations in CBAs, as they seek to advance respect for workers, their academic work, and the academy's public purposes. Sennett and Cobb's (1972) classic study explored indignities experienced by workers as individuals. My aim here is to give voice to how academic employees translate those individually experienced indignities into collective action in organizing campaigns and at the bargaining table.

Sociological Studies of Unions and (De)Unionization

Most sociological scholarship on unions focuses on blue-collar workers. Perhaps that made sense historically, given the rise and prominence of blue-collar craft and trade unions. But for at least thirty years, given the decline of manufacturing and of the private sector, blue-collar unionization, and the rise of public, white-collar unionization, it has made little sense. As Abbott (1993) noted, "The identity of the union literature with manufacturing is curious, since unionization in that sector has plunged in the United States, to be replaced by public sector unionism (AFSCME and NEA) that is relatively more female" (p. 195). Such unions have also been defined by more members of color, making it even more important in scholarly work to intersect workplace and social justice.

Nevertheless, the historical academic focus on blue-collar labor continues for many to frame scholarly analysis of the challenges facing organized labor. Some such analyses center craft sectors of employment, such as manufacturing and building, mining, and transportation (e.g., see Kimmeldorf, 2013). Others focus on AFL-CIO blue-collar workers or on low-wage service occupations (Bronfenbrenner, 1998; Getman, 2010).

A similar slant defines many studies of the decline of unionization. Some have traced that to economic restructuring as well as to a post-industrial political economy that has embedded anti-union government policies (Clark, 1989). Others have focused more fully on political factors and addressed the Republican party's influence on reduced union recognition elections. A defining moment was President Reagan's victory over the Professional Air Traffic Controllers Organization (PATCO) strikers—white-collar federal employees (Tope & Jacobs, 2009, p. 842, 858).

What is overlooked, though, in such research is a similarly consequential decision point at the federal level that suppressed faculty unionizing in independent colleges and universities, and that led to decertification campaigns of twenty-six bargaining units of full-time faculty. At a time of rapid growth in faculty unionization, the Supreme Court's 1980 ruling in *NLRB v. Yeshiva University* determined that the full-time faculty at Yeshiva University were managers and not covered by the National Labor Relations Act, and therefore not eligible to form a union (Douglas, 1990; Saltzman, 1998, p. 50). In the ensuing two decades, only two private colleges had successful faculty union drives. That decision effectively stalled the unionization of tenure-stream faculty in private institutions.[43] It makes the dramatic rise in organizing in these settings of contingent faculty and graduate employees all the more striking.

Along related lines, Tope and Jacobs's (2009) reference to the importance of political appointments to the National Labor Relations Board has affected organizing in higher education as well. As will be discussed in chapter 5, the NLRB's shifting composition has led to different rulings and reversals regarding graduate teaching and research assistants' right to collectively bargain under the National Labor Relations Act.

Consequential political decisions have been taken at the state level as well, as discussed earlier in this chapter (see also, Jacobs & Dixon, 2010; Saltzman, 2012).

That is particularly important for public sector unionism, the major sector of unionization for some time.[44]

For some time, the growth sector of unionization has been white-collar unions (Press, 2018; Semuels, 2018). For perspective, in 1910, the largest union in the U.S. was the United Mine Workers (UMW), which has long since been eclipsed in numbers and power by the "United Mind Workers" (Kerchner, Koppich, & Weeres, 1997), unionized schoolteachers (in the AFT and NEA).[45]

Still, far less sociology focuses on white- than on blue-collar unionized workers. Even less addresses faculty or other academic employees. Yet, important exceptions can inform the study of unions and academe. For example, a classic study (Murphy, 1990) addressed the strategies, governance structure, and democracy of teacher unions, which I speak to in the relations between union staff, leaders, and members. An enduring line of work addresses variations among contracts across the country and within districts (Strunk et al., 2018), as I do in some regards in my contract analysis. Some scholars, relevant to my discussion of organizing, articulate the view that teacher unions need to focus on "professional matters" of quality more than on "bread and butter" issues of wages and benefits, as well as working conditions and due process (Kerchner et al., 1997).

Some scholarship on other public sector workforces, of nurses and other health care workers, also informs my analysis. Silver's (2013) book on the California Nurses Association's successful challenging of established structures of power pointed to the significance of strategies oriented to public debate and the public good for white-collar, public-sector professionals. The latter point was at the heart of Johnston's (1994) book on "social movement unionism," which is at the core of my analysis of organizing around respect for higher education's public purposes. For public sector unions' success lies in the public legitimacy of their claims and the strategic alliances they form. Nurses' unions persuasively connected their working conditions (e.g., nurse-to-patient ratio) to the quality of medical care. That has clear parallels to adjunct faculty's mantra about faculty working conditions being students' learning conditions. At stake in public sector organizing and negotiating are public interest issues and beneficiaries beyond the two parties at the table.

Important lessons can also be drawn from the historical rise of a healthcare sector union that has been particularly prominent and successful in organizing adjunct faculty—SEIU. In tracing the story of SEIU's powerful Local 1199, Fink and Greenberg (1989) detail "upheaval in the quiet zone," a combination of elements that are evident in my work on contingent faculty. Nurses' deteriorating working conditions were important in giving rise to unionizing. Important as well in organizing and negotiating were internal tensions among different segments of health care workers, including along gender and racial lines, as well as governance tension between (inter)nationals and locals, and between union staff and members.

Studies of Unionized Academic Employees

Faculty are one of the more unionized workforces in the country: over one quarter (27 percent) of all faculty nationally are represented by a collective bargaining unit (Herbert, 2016b). Yet, despite an explosion of organizing campaigns by academic employees, there is limited literature on the topic, conducted by a limited number of scholars and activists. Some scholarship addresses unions and the working conditions of adjunct and contingent faculty (Baldwin & Chronister, 2001; Berry, 2005; Kezar, 2012; Kezar & Sam, 2013; Rhoades, 2013b, 2013c; Tolley, 2018). Some addresses graduate employees and postdocs (Camacho & Rhoads, 2015; Kezar et al., 2019; Rhoades & Rhoads, 2003). Even less scholarship addresses tenure-stream faculty and/or organizing that combines segments of the academic workforce (Flaherty, 2016, "Notre Dame"; Tolley, 2018).

Faculty unionization emerged a century ago (Cain, 2010a, 2010b). The modern form of academic unions, however, with collective bargaining agreements, can be traced to the 1960s and 1970s. Some of the issues today are similar to those of earlier times, centered on faculty voice, respect, and dignity. Of the earlier time, Cain (2010b) quotes an anonymous letter to the editor from a union member: "That is the precise reason why members of the faculty have banded together and have united themselves with the American Federation of Labor; they wish their profession to have those things that will restore to it the dignity that it has lost" (p. 560). Similarly, Ladd and Lipset (1973) found faculty voice in governance was a key factor explaining support for unionization. And Arnold's (2000) study of three New England universities found that a sense of eroding faculty power underlay union campaigns.

Moreover, another matter that I explore in this book historically centered on professional identity and stratification in tension with a collective bargaining identity and solidarity. Thus, a historical study of faculty unionization at the University of Illinois found "conflicted notions of professionalism and labor, division within the faculty, [and] barriers between educators and other laborers" (Cain, 2010b, p. 543).

More recent literature reviews of faculty and other academic employee unionization map the contours of the limited research on the topic (Cain, 2017, 2018; Rhoades & Torres-Olave, 2015). In Cain's (2017) words, "the great scholarly interest in the topic in the early years of widespread bargaining" has been followed by years of neglect in the post-*Yeshiva* years (p. 7).[46] A few exceptions prove the rule. One study of 341 public universities (S. Porter, 2013) found that unions positively affected faculty voice in governance. Three by me (2017a, 2017b, 2020) analyzed contract language nationally in four-year institutions as well as in contracts covering contingent faculty. And Kezar et al. (2019) provide a chapter on academic employees' unionization.

Part of this book's contribution, then, is combining an analysis of the resurgence of academic employee organizing with comprehensive contract analyses.

Key Takeaways

In the 1990s, after the ascendance of academic capitalism (Slaughter & Rhoades, 2004) and its attendant restructuring of academic labor, a defining feature of the times that centered my analysis was that tenure-track faculty and the rising numbers of contingent faculty were "managed professionals" in increasingly corporatized higher education institutions (Rhoades, 1998a). Now, a quarter century later, a defining feature of the times is the critical juncture and distinctive dynamism of academic employees organizing and negotiating challenging and articulating alternatives to that old normal.

As established professional structures have failed to ensure quality working conditions and higher education's public purposes and promise, leaving various categories of employees feeling exploited and disrespected, more of them are collectively organizing. At the center of this explosion of organizing, as is discussed in the next three chapters, are marginalized categories of academic employees. Even so, as detailed in this chapter, increasing numbers of tenure-stream faculty, too, as a marker of the distinctive dynamism of the moment, have become "organizing 'professionals,'" increasingly forming common cause with other academic employees in negotiating a new academy.

Part 1

From the Margins to the Center

• •

Contingent Academic Employees Organizing and Negotiating a New Academy

Like many tenure-track faculty, my academic career path started with a graduate assistantship and then a postdoc, both at UCLA. Then, neither workforce was unionized at UCLA. Now, both are with UAW. That is part of this chapter's story—contingent academic employees' organizing. If graduate assistants and postdocs were once part of a temporary apprenticeship path to the professoriate, increasing proportions of this workforce now identify as exploited employees and are unionized and unionizing.

So, too, when I started my academic career, adjunct and full-time contingent faculty were on the margins of the academic workforce. By the time I entered a tight academic market for tenure-track jobs, contingent faculty numbers were growing. In my academic lifetime, contingent faculty, like the graduate and postdoc employee categories of contingent academic employees, have moved from the margins to the center, not just numerically and proportionally, but also as leaders in the academic labor movement. That is remarkable given the "temporary," dispersed, and low-wage nature of contingent academic employment, which makes these faculty harder to organize. That is also part of this chapter's story—how these least secure faculty members have reflected and effected enduring changes in organizing academic employees.

What has also changed in my academic lifetime is what contingent academic employees are organizing and negotiating for. Sexual harassment and racial discrimination issues were centered in the union my younger daughter, Olivia, belonged to in the mid-2000s as a graduate teaching assistant at the University of California, Davis, along with other social justice issues that animated my older daughter, Elizabeth (and their generation at large). These were not so widely present in graduate employees' negotiations even a few years earlier, let alone in my day. Further, contingent faculty bargaining units have increasingly centered educational quality and the public interest in their negotiations. From the mid-2000s on, contingent academic employees have consistently intersected workplace and social justice and addressed the public interest in organizing and negotiating for a new academy.

Thus, I intentionally focus this first section of the book on the organizing and contract campaigns of contingent academic employees—contingent faculty, graduate employees, and postdoc employees. Their impact is most evident in the explosion of organizing and establishing new bargaining units, which have expanded at a rate not seen in four decades. Yet, it is also quite evident in the contract gains of new locals. First contracts for contingent employees can entail quantum shifts in the balance of power between them and management. Moreover, the terms and conditions of their employment in those initial CBAs are also a basis and foundation for subsequent, incremental improvements through an iterative process of negotiating successive contracts. Contingent academic employees have moved from being largely victims of/in the academy to being agents collectively working to reshape it.

The first two chapters in this section address contingent faculty. Chapter 3 maps the dynamism of adjunct and full-time contingent faculty re-energizing the academic labor movement in the 2000s. It draws parallels between the organizing since 2000 and a defining moment in the industrial labor union movement 100 years ago, the "Bread and Roses" strike of textile mill workers. It traces the distinctive institutional settings, union affiliates, and strategies of adjunct and contingent faculty's organizing, as well as the issues, including the distinctive labor take on educational quality that animated them. Chapter 4 analyzes the translation of this organizing into collective bargaining agreements. It focuses on gains in wages and benefits (i.e., "bread"), as well as on provisions regarding job security, access to instructional resources, and access to professional development (i.e., "roses," aka respect and educational quality).

Graduate and postdoc employees are addressed in chapter 5, which tracks the organizing campaigns and contractual gains of these once would-be individual "apprentices" (to tenure-track positions) who are increasingly collectively asserting their rights and advancing claims through collective bargaining. And, as noted above, these negotiations for graduate and postdoc employees are systematically and aggressively centering broader social justice issues in their contract campaigns, negotiations, and strikes to realize their aims.

Perhaps what is most impactful about the collective bargaining identity and work of these contingent academic employees is what is least materially tangible. The scope, strength, and focus of their mobilization, the quality of their fights (not least of their strikes), and the public interest and social justice focus of their demands are ongoing catalytic forces in labor activism and agitation. Contingent academic employees have front and centered issues intersecting broad social justice issues and movements of the day. They have featured the interests of students and the public, as well as of marginalized populations, such as women, BIPOC (Black, Indigenous, and people of color), LGBTQ+ (lesbian, gay, bisexual, transgender, queer), and international or DACA (Deferred Action for Childhood Arrivals—aka "dreamers") students. Their agitation keeps employees, the academy, and society vigilant and critically hopeful with regard to building a more progressive academy. Contingent academic employees are re-emphasizing, re-envisioning, and expanding the public functions and trajectory of the academy. As a colleague, Ben Baez, has pointed out to me, that can arguably be the labor movement's (like any social movement's) most significant effect.

3

Bread and Roses, and a Labor-Based Conception of Quality

• •

A New Faculty Majority Organizing a New Academy

Hearts starve as well as bodies[;] . . . yes, it is bread we fight for, but we fight for roses too. (Oppenheim, 1911)

We need to go from awfulizing to organizing. (Caprice Lawless, an adjunct faculty activist, presenting to an AAUP state conference meeting on shared governance, Fort Lewis College, September 2014)

Our operative principle [as the New Faculty Majority] is that "faculty working conditions are student learning conditions" (Maisto, 2012, p. 201)

"Education First." This became our rallying cry and part of our public image, which we worked to establish over our first couple of years—clarifying who we

> were, why we unionized, and what we
> were fighting for. (Gilmore, 2018, p. 146)

Over 100 years ago saw a defining moment in labor organizing. In 1912, in a major low-wage, at-will sector experiencing restructuring and deskilling amid industrialization, textile workers in Lawrence, Massachusetts, walked out in the "Bread and Roses" strike. The title of a poem (see epigram one), the mantra was said to have been articulated by a female striker who, when asked to explain the workers' demands, replied, "bread and roses" (Vallas, 2004, p. 13). Those words, used by labor activists since, express a desire for "a living wage and a little respect" (Watson, 2005, p. 3).[1]

Now, adjunct faculty members are academe's twenty-first-century version of low-wage, at-will academic employees, demanding better wages and more respect (for themselves and the work they do).[2] In a major sector of the postindustrial economy experiencing restructuring and deskilling, they are like growing ranks of precarious workers throughout society with no security and little to no benefits (Kalleberg, 2009, 2011, 2018). Working semester to semester in part-time positions, and often listed in course schedules as "professor staff" (Street, Maisto, Merves, & Rhoades, 2012), adjunct faculty can be nonrenewed without cause, even when they have taught for decades. The median $2,700 per-course wage, mostly without health benefits (Coalition on the Academic Workforce, 2012), makes these professors, many of whom also carry student debt, part of academia's working poor (Rhoades, 2013a).[3]

Adjunct faculty are part of an expanding, contingent faculty workforce that includes full-time, nontenure-track faculty (Baldwin & Chronister, 2001; Finkelstein et al., 2016). Both segments have grown steadily over four decades, with adjunct faculty consisting of 43 to 49 percent of faculty, and FTNTTTF another 16 to 20 percent. They are "the new faculty majority" (Maisto, 2012, 2024). Most women and/or people of color who are faculty are employed in these contingent positions, where they experience multiple contingencies, semester after semester, and multiple marginalities.[4]

In a defining time and shift for academic labor, adjunct (and contingent) faculty have gone from "awfulizing" to "organizing," (see epigram two). They have increasingly taken on a collective bargaining identity, organizing to improve their working conditions. In demanding respect, they have taken on and owned the term "adjunct" as a badge of pride—embodied, for example, in a national campaign amid a national day of action—"Wear the [Scarlet] Letter 'A' for Adjunct with Pride, Not Shame" (Rojas, 2015).

More than that, adjunct and FTNTT faculty (sometimes in joint, sometimes separate organizing campaigns) are now at the vanguard of and are re-energizing the academic labor movement (Rhoades, 2024). They are often organizing in new settings (private universities), with nonacademic union affiliates, largely with SEIU (Herbert, 2016a), but also with the United Autoworkers (UAW) and the United Steelworkers (USW), and in broad configurations of bargaining units as well as in wall-to-wall units in United Campus Worker locals of the Communications Workers of America. They have organized national advocacy groups (e.g., the New Faculty Majority—see Maisto, 2012, 2024) to leverage change in national unions, local bargaining units, and nonunionized settings, as well as in the public visibility and perception of contingency.

Adjunct and contingent faculty are redefining what is possible for them, for other academic employees, and for the academy in a social movement that is organizing a new academy. Beyond their success in negotiating better working conditions and beginning to rebalance power relationships in the academic workplace, their impact lies in the ongoing collective sense of agency and urgency that drives organizing and contract campaigns.

The one-hundred-year-old "bread and roses" rallying cry of labor could be the clarion call of adjunct and contingent faculty today. Their organizing similarly centers issues of respect for the worker and their work.

Yet, contingent faculty have added a public interest dimension, linking their working conditions to quality education. Often, managerial and policy discourses of excellence label faculty as the problem and increased accountability measures as the answer (Rhoades, 2020). By contrast, adjunct professors have taken the stance that faculty's working conditions are students' learning conditions (see epigram three—Maisto, 2012, 2024), in a labor-based conceptualization of quality (Rhoades, 2020).[5] That mantra rejects the neoliberal pitting and prioritizing of consumers/customers against and over workers. It reconnects workers' interests to students and the public, establishing "common ground for the common good" (Maisto, 2024), juxtaposed against misplaced managerial priorities.

Underlying the slogans of contingent faculty organizing campaigns is a call to reorder higher education's priorities. As articulated in epigram four, a contingent faculty activist at UIUC's FTNTTF unit detailed the mantra underlying why his union mobilized two strikes to gain a good contract: "'Education First' centered the "systemic issues affecting the employment of NTTF," centering educational considerations and mission—"Our primary concerns were not economic" (Gilmore, 2018, pp. 144, 145). It involved negotiating respect for workers, their work, and the public purposes of higher education.

This chapter maps the emergence, energy, and dynamics of post-2000 organizing by adjunct and contingent faculty. Returning to the 1912 Bread and Roses strike, I draw parallels between then and now, between that strike and George Washington University adjunct faculty organizing with SEIU Local 500, one hundred years later. Subsequently, I review adjunct and contingent faculty's organizing strategies and tactics and consider the whys that drive their respect-based organizing.

"Bread and Roses": Then and Now, How and Why

The parallels between the Bread and Roses textile workers' strike in 1912 and adjunct faculty union drives in the 2000s offer insights into the hows and whys of organizing precarious workers. They speak to how, in the face of powerful adversaries and long odds, precarious workers can successfully negotiate improved working conditions. And they speak to whys of equitable remuneration (bread), and of (dis)respect for workers and their work (roses). Both then and now, precarious workers utilized creative strategies and foregrounded key issues to gain public support and (re)define workplace (in)justice.

Then

Within the world's largest textile mills, on Massachusetts' Merrimack River, there was a distinctive strike in 1912 of over 15,000 textile workers, mostly immigrant women. The monumental strike drew a dramatic response. "Starting on a Friday morning of January 12, 1912, with workers pouring into the streets leaving the Lawrence mills' massive industrial era machines silent, the strike lasted for two months and two days and captured the nation's attention. On that Friday morning 'city officials sounded a riot call on the bells of City Hall in Lawrence for the first time in the city's history'" (Cahn, 1977, p. 98).

Local government responded by supporting mill owners. By Monday, the mayor called in three companies of militia (by the strike's end, over ten times that were called), "the first time in Massachusetts that the militia was used in a labor dispute" (Cahn, 1977, p. 112). One was of students from Harvard, excused from midterms by a president who was the grandson of Abbott Lawrence, city founder and one of the region's textile industry founders. Workers faced the interlocking forces of industry, government, and higher education elites.

Soon, reporters from across the nation descended on Lawrence, from prominent outlets like the *New York Times* and the *Los Angeles Times*, and less prominent ones such as the *Topeka Capital*. Their coverage helped mobilize public opinion in support of the strikers. For as sometimes happens in collective action, authorities' (heavy-handed) response backfired. Reports were filed of standoffs between militia and women strikers and of bayonet charges. The optics, conveyed in text, pictures, and political cartoons of strikers being confronted by overwhelming force contributed to the public's sense that strikers were being abused (Cahn, 1977; Watson, 2005).

National attention and presence also came from organized labor. By the end of January, a national labor leader, "Big Bill" Haywood, of the Industrial Workers of the World (IWW) was on site. Greeted by more than 15,000 people, Haywood spoke to and advised the strikers (IWW sent other organizers too).

Part of the Bread and Roses strike's importance lay in the creative tactics workers employed to garner public support. Lawrence saw the first marching picket line (with women) in American labor history (Watson, 2005). Moreover, workers utilized another tactic never seen in the U.S. Reflecting their international visibility and connections, and of IWW's scope, strikers adopted a tactic utilized in Europe. To dramatize the plight of their working conditions and situation in a prolonged strike, mothers (and fathers) took their children to the Lawrence train station to send them to families in New York City (and elsewhere), where the children were marched down Fifth Avenue.

The first "children's exodus" on February 12 got much sympathetic coverage. A second one was planned for February 24, but police were at the train station in force and tried to prevent women from boarding their children. Press coverage featured police dragging and beating mothers, generating national public outcry, and further galvanizing public pressure to resolve the strike.

Within a week, Congressional hearings on the strike began. Attended by the First Lady, Helen Taft, testimony was heard, including from a delegation of child strikers.[6]

Two weeks later, textile workers voted for a settlement that met their demands for overtime pay for overtime work, an increase in the minimum hourly wage, an overall flat increase, and no discrimination against the strikers.[7] The strike's larger importance was that these low-wage, largely immigrant workers won public support and helped change the national conversation and policy about organized labor.[8]

Now, Circa 2004–GW

Now, fast forward to early twenty-first century Washington, DC. At George Washington University (GW), adjunct faculty filed not out of the workplace on strike but with the National Labor Relations Board (NLRB) to form a union affiliated with SEIU Local 500, which was certified in May 2005. Their struggle with GW management would take not three months but rather three years to be resolved. In January 2008, adjunct faculty signed their first CBA with GW (Ahmad, 2004; Gravois, 2008).

The eventual success of the GW adjunct faculty was preceded by earlier failed efforts. There had been a UAW-affiliated drive to organize a bargaining unit of adjunct faculty and graduate teaching assistants that went public in 1999 (Chernow, 2013). But UAW eventually withdrew resources. Adjunct faculty persisted.

Years later, having met three times with a representative at AFT's offices, as one of the GW adjunct faculty leaders said, "We felt like we weren't getting anywhere, and one of us said, 'That's it, we're not going there again'" (personal interview, September 24, 2015). Then, in contrast to AFT, a young organizer from SEIU Local 500 came to the GW adjunct faculty's site/space and worked with them on their data. Moreover, SEIU was willing to file with the NLRB with a smaller percentage of signed authorization cards than was true for AFT.[9] The adjunct faculty chose to affiliate with SEIU's Local 500.

But when they filed for an election in the spring of 2003, they lacked the necessary 30 percent of the proposed bargaining unit required by the NLRB.[10]

44 • From the Margins to the Center

That led the faculty to employ a creative tactic adapted to the distinctive semester-by-semester employment patterns of adjunct faculty. "'We realized we could give it one more go,' said Anne McLeer, an adjunct professor of women's studies and one of the leaders of the union movement. 'We sat down and thought if there was anything we hadn't tried, and one thing we hadn't done was file just for the Spring semester'" (Ahmad, 2004, para. 4).

That tactic facilitated SEIU Local 500 filing cards in October 2004.[11]

Adjunct faculty at GW were facing an extraordinarily well-resourced, powerful employer. George Washington University, as the second largest (only to the federal government) property owner in the District of Columbia, was no less formidable an adversary for part-time faculty than the American Woolen Company (the Lawrence mill was the largest in the world) had been for textile workers.

Adjunct faculty at GW also were facing a seemingly inhospitable national political environment. In 2004, as in 1912, there was a Republican president, whose NLRB appointments led to its 2004 *Brown* decision (reversing a 2000 NLRB decision) defining graduate student teaching assistants as primarily being students, denying them the rights of statutory employees under the National Labor Relations Act (NLRA) (Saltzman, 2006). Yet, in May 2005, that same NLRB certified the fall 2004 adjunct faculty election results (341 to 331), supporting a union affiliated with SEIU Local 500. And it rejected management's challenge of those results, ordering GW to negotiate (Jaschik, 2006, "NLRB Orders").

Prior to the election, GW's administration did not run an active anti-union campaign (in contrast to several other private university administrations in later years). One adjunct faculty leader has written that management did not initially take the union drive seriously, underestimating faculty's "animus" toward management, and overestimating faculty's sense of "privilege" in teaching at a prestigious university (McLeer, 2024, p. 211). Moreover, the drive had stalled before, falling short in spring 2004 of obtaining the requisite percentage of cards.

However, from the time of the NLRB's certification, GW's administration was deeply resistant to recognizing the union. They filed an objection to the election, calling for an extension of voting rights to all adjunct faculty hired through third parties (i.e., contracted-out employees—see Levy, 2005). Despite the NLRB's rejection of that objection, they continued refusing to work with the union, and the NLRB charged GW with an unfair labor practice (Levy, 2005). The university appealed to the U.S. Court of Appeals, DC. After losing in a unanimous ruling, management agreed to negotiate (Wozobski, 2006, "Web Update"; 2006, "GW Concedes") but then hired a renowned "union avoidance" firm to lead management's bargaining team.[12] GW's president, Steven Joel Trachtenberg was, in a word, intractable.

How were adjunct faculty able to successfully battle such a powerful adversary? As at-will employees who could be nonrenewed or have their classes canceled even after the semester started, they were extremely vulnerable. Although highly educated, adjunct faculty lacked a workplace like the textile mills that physically brought them together in a "community of interest" (McLeer, 2024). They were isolated from one another, lacking offices and often teaching at more than one campus. They also lacked high profile labor leaders to come and support them.

How, then, did they build their union and gain and sustain visibility and support in drawn-out negotiations? The answers lay in creative tactics and strategies for organizing and building (imagined) community (McLeer, 2024). Rather than relying primarily or solely on one-on-one organizing conversations (hard to arrange with a dispersed workforce), organizers developed "big picture" research to educate potential members about the structural exploitation of part-time faculty in the university, region, and nationally (McLeer, 2024), a standard practice now in contingent faculty campaigns.

Relatedly, rather than running (as was done before with UAW), a "stealth campaign" (under management's radar), union activists developed a public face to make workers aware of their peers' activities and build an "imagined community" (McLeer, 2024).[13] That was also part of a strategy for building coalitions on (and beyond) campus.

Key players in campus coalitions were students. As an adjunct faculty leader explained (personal interview, September 25, 2014), students were important in generating support and sustaining interest throughout the campaign. Their voices carried moral force. And they could be "connectors" who leveraged support from other groups on and beyond campus.

Student support for GW adjunct faculty's union campaign took various forms. Early on, the Progressive Student Union and Students for Peace and Justice organized an event at which Senator Edward Kennedy spoke (Okolski, 2004), with the focus being inclusive of adjunct faculty and custodial employees' rights.[14]

In another example of students' direct action, the Progressive Student Union worked with adjunct faculty and union staff in the fall of 2005, leafletting parents on family weekend with pro-union literature (Kigner, 2005). One campaign theme was GW's misplaced priorities, evident in adjunct faculty's low wages at a high-tuition institution: "Kip Lornell, an adjunct music professor and lead union organizer, said the main purpose . . . was to educate students and their parents about the University's treatment of adjunct professors, and [about] where tuition money is going. 'If GW students realized that they provide 85 percent of the budget money for the University, they would be asking where the money was going'" (Kigner, 2005, para. 3–4).

At high-tuition institutions, it is hard for management to justify the disjuncture between students' tuition and adjunct faculty's low wages. "GW's economic wealth is part of what made it vulnerable to the organizing efforts of faculty being paid poverty-level wages to teach country club-level fee-paying students" (Rhoades, 2015b, p. 438).

More than simply the low wages, the percentage of courses adjunct faculty teach versus the percentage of the budget going to their salaries is a framing consistently used in organizing campaigns.[15] As a GW adjunct faculty leader put it, "Part-time faculty taught 46 percent of courses offered last fall, . . . [but] part-time salaries accounted for only 1 percent of the University's total budget" (Phillips, 2007, para. 6). That disjuncture speaks to misplaced priorities in an unjust system. It strengthens adjunct faculty's identity as exploited workers. And it connects their exploitation to a pattern of (dis)investment that disrespects the work of education and students' investment in it. Such connections are all the more powerful when students see and articulate them in a labor-based framing of educational quality that centers faculty working conditions.[16]

A key source of student support for the union was the student newspaper. Consider this staff editorial lead for the *GW Hatchet*, "Stop the Foot-Dragging with Part-Time Union," followed by "Our view: GW's underhanded tactics to block the formation of an adjunct union must stop" (Staff Editorial, 2006). The paper provided consistently sympathetic coverage (Phillips, 2007) and a readily accessible forum to adjunct faculty for sharing their views with the campus community (Larson, 2004).

The issues that animated adjunct faculty in the GW campaign, and that are explored later in other adjunct faculty organizing campaigns, were bread and roses issues, for instance, of a livable wage as a step toward pay equity relative to full-time faculty and quality working conditions expressing respect for workers and their work, although respect and professionalism can be double-edged swords in organizing (McLeer, 2024).

The close vote in the union election (341 to 331) spoke to a challenge in organizing (adjunct) faculty—the idea of professors being "professionals." In its individualistic and "apolitical" form, that identity carries ideological baggage that can be hostile to unions, sometimes playing out in universities, as noted in chapter 2, in anti-union faculty websites and messaging claiming unions threaten excellence, merit, and collegiality. So, too, with some GW adjunct faculty, where one of the organizers spoke of the challenge of persuading faculty with PhDs and a commitment to being professionals to support the union (anonymous personal communication, September 25, 2014; see also McLeer, 2024). Recognizing this, organizers' strategy was to leverage that commitment to being professionals by focusing on how their work had been de-professionalization.

Remarkably, like the textile workers, GW adjunct faculty won. In August 2007, GW transitioned to a new university president (Steven Knapp), and to a new law firm (Morgan, Lewis, and Bockius) to lead negotiations for management. Then, in a creative show of strength, the union issued a statement of principles signed by 400 faculty (anonymous personal communication, September 25, 2014). Months later, the university and adjunct faculty union ratified a collective bargaining agreement. The union indicated that the contract would bring "substantial pay improvements, long-sought job security, and a joint commitment to professional development" (Gravois, 2008, para. 6).[17]

Post-GW "Metro Campaign" Strategy

One (SEIU) "Metro Campaign" Strategy

The GW adjunct faculty's victory was an important step in advancing a "metro campaign" strategy aiming to represent the vast majority of adjunct faculty in a metropolitan area (Berry, 2005). Such a strategy is structured by the metropolitan region in which adjunct faculty work and often commute to (part-time) positions at different institutions (Berry & Worthen, 2018). It was in the GW faculty and SEIU Local 500 organizers' minds from the start (McLeer, 2024, p. 213). It later expanded to other metro areas and states with SEIU (and catalyzed other unions' metro strategies).

After the GW victory, SEIU Local 500 organized adjunct faculty in separate units in the DC metro area at Montgomery Community College (2008), American University (2012), and Georgetown University (2013). With subsequent victories at Howard and the University of District of Columbia (both Historically Black Colleges and Universities or HBCUs) in 2014 and 2015, as well as others, it now represents the vast majority of adjunct faculty across the DC metro area. That extends the imagined community beyond the campus, reflecting the lived reality of many adjunct faculty members' work across multiple institutions.

SEIU Local 500 is far from the idea of one metro contract, or of a "[metrowide] hiring hall [for adjunct faculty in the area], professional development support, curricular commons, [and] peer-to-peer evaluation" (McLeer, 2024, p. 214) As David Rodich (now retired) SEIU Local 500 Executive Director has put it, "The time is now, the question is how, and probably the first step is in professional development" (Rodich, 2017) The current higher education director has more recently written that, "Uniting all adjunct faculty under a citywide contract is less pressing than uniting all workers on campus," advocating for a wall-to-wall approach within institutions (McLeer, 2024, p. 214).

In suggesting professional development (PD) as the first step, Rodich was identifying an issue over which there could be shared interest among multiple institutions and framing quality enhancement in labor-based terms (i.e., institutional support for faculty versus in managerial terms of individual faculty performance). Institutions and SEIU Local 500 could pool funds to support faculty learning communities to enhance instruction and establish a metro-wide PD/resource center.

One could also imagine another labor and locally based conception of quality—metro-relevant courses produced by a metro-curricular cooperative (MCC). Such courses could be owned by the adjunct faculty (and/or their local). Local relevance and control are key to enhancing educational quality and service to (and learning from) local communities, preferable to the standardized, mass-produced, mass-marketed curricula promoted by policymakers, publishing companies, and managers, which are not tailored to local realities (Rhoades, 2013b).[18]

Multiple Metro Campaign Models

Various models of metro campaigns have been imagined and developed (Berry, 2005; Berry & Worthen, 2018). Across models, the strategy is to foster a connection and flow in democratic movement building beyond a single institution to enhance collective bargaining metro-wide. Possibilities range from coalitions of existing unions to expansion of local advocacy organizations to independent locals (e.g., SEIU Local 500). Several examples can be found under affiliation with three major unions. Each is a variation on SEIU Local 500's theme.

One model has been undertaken by the United Steelworkers in Pittsburgh, their headquarters. New bargaining units and first contracts for adjunct faculty have been negotiated for individual campuses in the metro area—at Point Park University in 2015 and Robert Morris University in 2017 (at the University of Pittsburgh, the bargaining unit, which signed its first contract in May 2024, includes adjunct, FTNTT, and tenure-stream faculty).[19] USW's model includes organizing full-time faculty and graduate employees.[20] The organizing approach, led by Robin Sowards, has been to set up a metro-wide organizing committee and then a local one. The aim of what was known as the Metro Volunteer Organizing Committee (MVOC) was "to make sure there was a worker-controlled organization to set the strategy until they reached the stage at which they have their own local union" (personal email, January 22, 2019). Subsequently, Local 1088 was established.[21] It included and connected members from campus organizing committees in a forum for discussing local and metro-wide strategies. It reflected a grassroots model combining movement and organization building.

Another metro model has been pursued in Philadelphia. An AFT local was set up in 2013—United Academics of Philadelphia (UAP): "Local 9608 is an organization that seeks to unify and support the nearly 16,000 adjunct instructors working in Philadelphia-area colleges" (http://uap.pa.aft.org/about-us). It involved a commitment to pay dues once a union election was won at a campus. The first election was at Temple University, where adjunct faculty voted to affiliate with the existing full-time and tenure-track faculty unit (another, at Acadia University was signed in April 2019).[22] UAP's idea was explained by Zoe Cohen, one of UAP's leaders: "'There are two goals,' Cohen said. 'One is to build community and support among adjuncts in the region. The other is to create bargaining units, to actually set up adjuncts at Philly universities that have a bargaining unit at each school. If we were just doing one or . . . the other it wouldn't be as impactful'" (Scott, 2017, para. 13).

Yet, there was also a broader democratic aim, related to students and society: "Education is a public good, so we need to provide our students with a secure, respected faculty" (http://uap.pa.aft.org/about-us).

As at GW, UAP campaign adjunct faculty employed creative tactics to garner public support. As Jennie Shanker, labor activist, adjunct professor in fine arts, and Vice-President of the Temple Association of University Professionals (TAUP) said:

> During our campaign to get into TAUP, and during our first contract campaign, we engaged with our creative members in a number of ways: doing theater during rallies, we printed a banner with 1300 people on it—60 yards long representing the number of adjuncts on campus. We built a pop-up "Adjunct Office" based on Lucy's psychiatry booth from *Peanuts* (the adjunct is in!), at graduation we created a "path" where students could write a thank you on a "brick" (drawn on a long plastic table cover) under the name of the teacher who helped them the most along their "path." (personal email, December 16, 2018)

Adjunct faculty organizing has re-energized the academic labor movement, engaging members to mobilize student and public support for building a more equitable academy.

Other SEIU Campaigns/Organizing

Notwithstanding the significance of other unions' metro campaigns, SEIU campaigns have eclipsed them in numbers. In just the first three quarters of 2016, SEIU organized 90 percent of the new bargaining units of contingent faculty in private universities (Herbert, 2016b, Table 2). From 2013 through 2015, most of the sixty-six new bargaining units organized were of part-time faculty, and thirty-eight of those were organized by SEIU (Herbert, 2016b). The trend has continued. From 2013 to 2019, 86.2 percent of new faculty bargaining units in private higher education were SEIU affiliated (Herbert, et al., 2020, Chart 3, p. 16), representing 90.3 percent of newly organized faculty (Herbert et al., 2020, Chart 4, p. 17). SEIU's organizing has not been exclusive to private universities. From 2013 to 2019, although accounting for only 13.6 percent of new faculty units in public institutions, SEIU units accounted for 71 percent of newly represented non-tenure track (NTT) faculty in stand-alone units (Herbert et al., 2020, Chart 7, p. 19).[23]

SEIU Local 500's success led other SEIU locals to urge the international union to invest in other metro campaigns (Rhoades, 2017a). Boston, the site of an earlier failed AAUP metro initiative in the late 1990s (Berry & Worthen, 2018), was the first subsequent launch, with Local 509. Other campaigns emerged nationwide under the umbrella of "Faculty Forward" campaigns.[24]

The metro campaigns have varied in their particulars. Some have been in delimited metro regions, as with Boston, Chicago, Los Angeles, Oakland, and St. Louis. Others have encompassed larger regions, as with Miami/Ft. Lauderdale, and with Local 925, the state of Washington. So, too, the bargaining units' configurations can vary. At local faculty members' insistence, Local 925's campaign included full-time contingent faculty with adjuncts (in some other regions, FTNTTF have unionized within metro campaign institutions separate from adjuncts, as at Tufts). And they have been connected to organizing graduate employees and professional staff. In addition, the prominence of the targeted institutions has varied. In Boston, the targets were leading universities such as Tufts. At some other sites, such as Seattle and Oakland/Bay area, that was not the case. Further, campaigns have varied as to whether the targets were primarily private universities. In St. Louis, the targets were publics as well as privates, whereas in Miami, they were all publics, including community colleges.[25]

Although the metro campaigns have been partially driven by local contexts and activists, they are part of a national contingent faculty movement. Local activism has been informed by adjunct activists and labor leaders nationally—for example, local launches consistently included activist speakers from other places, putting the local campaign in the context of a national movement. The mantras and messaging of local campaigns are drawn from the national movement, as are tactics like the "big picture research" done in Local 500 regarding the conditions of contingent faculty labor. And the union affiliates provide national connections and resources.

By way of another example of national influence, some Faculty Forward metro settings intersected SEIU's "Fight for 15" national campaign (to raise the minimum wage). Thus, at the Miami launch, faculty leaders talked with me about the origins of their campus organizing. One, at Highline Community College, had a friend who had invited her to a "Fight for 15" event. That was what got her engaged with other activists and led to her and others working on a collective bargaining campaign at their campus. Another person, at the University of South Florida, said that the first event he went to with a friend was a "Fight for 15" one. After that, while sharing beers, their conversation turned to unionizing. Later, an SEIU organizer called them based on their participation in the Fight for 15 event. So, there can be interconnections between and spillover effects of such non-collective bargaining campaigns on unionization and on worker solidarity.[26]

Before and Beyond Metro Campaign Strategies: Inside/Outside Strategies

Before and beyond the proliferation of metro organizing campaigns, adjunct (and contingent) faculty have been employing other organizing strategies. That is evident in two examples of an "inside/outside strategy," which consists of activists working from within existing structures (e.g., local bargaining units and/or national unions) and at the same time forming independent organizations outside the structures to leverage fuller representation of their interests (Berry, 2005; Berry & Worthen, 2018, 2021). Utilizing this strategy, around 2000, adjunct and contingent faculty worked to transform two system-wide and citywide bargaining units on the West and East Coasts that have since been leaders in enhancing contingent faculty working conditions and central players in the national academic labor movement. Subsequently, in the 2010s, contingent faculty activists formed a national advocacy group that included key members of various locals and unions, coordinating efforts in their unions and in the national media to energize and frame the contingent faculty movement.

Before the Metro Campaigns

The California Faculty Association (CFA) is now regarded as a particularly progressive faculty union, especially in terms of contingent faculty voice and rights. That was not always so. It was re-energized in the late 1990s by "lecturers" (their designation for full- and part-time nontenure-track faculty) over a decade after the CFA had formed in 1983. In a union in which lecturers had been marginalized, a reform coalition of newly elected leaders worked to ensure lecturer representation and participation in union governance (Berry & Worthen, 2021; Geron & Reevy, 2018; Hoffman & Hess, 2014).[27] That eventually played out in contingent faculty gaining representation in leadership positions, on committees, and on the bargaining team. That, in turn, led to the CFA negotiating contractual provisions enhancing contingent faculty working conditions.

The "inside/outside" strategy was evident within and beyond the CFA. Within, the new leaders and lecturers re-energized the existing statewide Lecturer's Council to be an independent "center of power within the union" (Hoffman & Hess, 2014, p. 19; see also Berry & Worthen, 2021) from which contingent faculty could make increased demands for fuller representation in union operations and governance. To leverage change within and beyond the CFA, lecturers worked through state and national groups, including the California Part-Time Faculty Association, the Coalition of Contingent Academic Labor (COCAL), and later, the New Faculty Majority. They also brought in national labor activists to speak to and mobilize lecturers (Hoffman & Hess, 2014, p. 22) and to intersect the national academic labor movement.

The ascendance of adjunct faculty representation and interests was part of another reform coalition re-energizing another union, the Professional Staff Congress (PSC) of the City University of New York (CUNY). The union's transformation, also around 2000, resulted in a local that has consistently negotiated improvements in contingent faculty working conditions (though not always to internal activists' satisfaction).

Divisions between CUNY's contingent and tenure-stream faculty had been longstanding. Formed in 1972, the PSC combined two organizations—a full-time faculty and staff organization (the NEA-affiliated Legislative Conference) and a local of part-time faculty, lecturers (full-time but temporary), and staff (the AFT-affiliated United Federation of College Teachers). In the mid-1980s, it survived part-time faculty's efforts to decertify the unit as their bargaining agent (Negri, 2018). In the late 1990s, a progressive "New Caucus" emerged, first at the campus level and then citywide in the multi-institutional PSC. Its victory in 2000 (following a 1997 loss) was on a platform calling for parity for adjuncts.[28]

Still, some adjunct faculty formed CUNY Adjuncts Unite, working outside and within PSC to leverage more change and respect. In one adjunct activist leader's words: "We [adjuncts] met up with the New Caucus to try to ally. At some point, we felt dissed and formed our own [organization.] We didn't go away from them, but didn't [stay close]" (Negri, 2018, p. 158). From that position, adjunct activists pushed the local's fuller treatment of their issues in bargaining, including "conversion" lines for long-serving adjunct faculty and health care.

In both the PSC and CFA, presidents, as well as contingent activists, have effected changes at the national level. Given AFT's governance structure and PSC's powerful position in it, Barbara Bowen (PSC's president for twenty-five years) exerted pressure on the national AFT to more actively serve contingent faculty. As a major affiliate at the time of the NEA and (still) of the AAUP, CFA presidents and lecturer activists have also foregrounded contingent faculty issues in these nationals.[29]

Another mechanism for pursuing an "inside/outside" strategy has been the involvement of lecturers of both locals in COCAL, an important organization in the contingent faculty labor movement. Moreover, a CFA lecturer activist has played a major role in the New Faculty Majority.

Beyond the Metro Campaigns

In 2009, the New Faculty Majority (NFM) was formed and soon came to be a prominent national advocate for contingent faculty. The "inside-outside" strategy was very much at play in its work. In the words of its president, "The idea is that NFM needs to be an organization that works within institutional structures, be they unions or colleges and universities, to effect change from within, while also exerting pressure from outside when necessary" (Maisto, 2012, p. 198).

Several NFM officers and board members have been active in their unions (e.g., AFT, NEA, SEIU, and USW). The effectiveness of their inside/outside strategy lies in the prominence of the locals in which they have been members, including CFA, SEIU Local 500, USW Local 1088, and United University Professions, among others.

Within a relatively short period, and for the better part of a decade, NFM, and particularly its then-president, Maria Maisto, became the go-to place for reporters doing stories on contingent faculty. That was a central NFM strategy, making contingent faculty's lives visible, "conquering stereotypes," and "refocusing the conversation" around the operative principle and mantra that "faculty working conditions are student learning conditions" (Maisto, 2012, pp. 199–201, 2024). Maisto and NFM were important spokespersons/advocates for contingent faculty, with groups that included disciplinary associations such as the Modern Languages Association (MLA), sometimes seeking NFM's imprimatur for their initiatives and work.[30]

The organization's public image and legitimacy facilitated NFM leaders' work in their respective unions, encouraging more focus on contingent faculty. And that has played out in organizing in the big three academic unions and in joint campaigns among them. For example, from 2013 to 2019, in public institutions, AAUPP/AFT units in public institutions accounted for 10 percent of faculty in NTT units, and for 84 percent of joint NTT and tenure track units (Herbert et al., 2020, Chart 7, p. 19).

As Maisto (2024) indicates, NFM translated that public advocacy into lobbying as well, which is remarkable for such a small entity with limited resources. In 2014, Representative George Miller of the House Education and Workforce Committee produced a report that "largely endorses previous studies on the subject; 'The Just-In-Time Professor' document marks the first time Congress has so formally acknowledged a situation that adjunct activists have long deemed exploitative" (Flaherty, 2014, "Congress Takes Note," para. 1). NFM briefed congressional staffers, encouraged contingent faculty participation in the committee's e-forum, and produced the study cited in the congressional report, which largely adopted its "just-in-time" language and a critique of employment practices and working conditions compromising educational quality (Street, Maisto, Merves, & Rhoades, 2012).[31]

Further, NFM had gained the moral (and political) suasion to be both an initiator and a "connector" (Rhoades, 2015b), facilitating cooperation among competing unions in lobbying the federal government.[32] One of NFM's national initiatives was to change the federal government's guidance on unemployment insurance so adjunct faculty would be eligible. Various unions were involved in leveraging the Labor Department (and the Education Department and IRS) to change its guidance, which excluded education, denying adjunct faculty access to unemployment in the summer. They succeeded: "The document [now] mentions adjuncts specifically, saying that their numbers have increased significantly and that many 'have contracts or offers to perform services in subsequent years or terms that are contingent on factors such as funding, enrollment, and program changes.' The New Faculty Majority, a national adjunct advocacy organization that campaigned for the updated letter, called it 'long-overdue guidance to address the new reality of contingent academic employment in higher education'" (Flaherty, 2017, "Adjuncts Included," para. 2–3). As an insider in one of the unions said to me, "There is no way the unions would have all come together on their own, without Maria" (personal interview, September 25, 2014). They all had internal issues with adjunct faculty and could not afford to not cooperate.[33]

Animating Issues and Ideologies across Campaigns

Having analyzed contingent faculty's organizing strategies, I turn now to the issues and ideologies that animated the organizing. These center on respect for workers, their work, and for higher education's public purposes.

Issues and ideologies articulated by adjunct faculty have resonated broadly, enhancing their ability to build coalitions with students and other workers and to gain public support (also see Moser, 2014). They involve "bread and roses" issues and a labor-based conception of quality that challenges the management's neoliberal employment practices and priorities.

Pay and benefits are central in adjunct faculty organizing, but more is involved than (incremental) pay raises (bread). What catalyzed organizing and galvanized student/public support was/is incredulity and outrage at adjunct professors' poverty-level wages. In 2012, the national average was $2700 per course (CAW, 2012); almost a decade later, most respondents to a national AFT survey made less than $3500 per course, a substantial improvement, but still poverty level (Flaherty, 2020, "Barely Getting By"). So, too, with adjunct faculty's lack of health care mobilizing adjunct faculty and galvanizing public support. For example, Miami Dade College's email to its adjunct faculty in 2019, indicating that they should apply for Medicaid if they could not afford health care for themselves and their family, triggered greater support for the union drive there, which subsequently succeeded, and garnered attention in the national press. (Schlaerth, 2022) Sympathetic news coverage in major national news outlets (e.g., *The Atlantic* and *The Washington Post*) over the years, in headlines like "Adjunct Professors Get Poverty-Level Wages" (DePillis, 2015), "There Is No Excuse for How Universities Treat Adjuncts" (Fredrickson, 2015), "'It Keeps You Nice and Disposable': The Plight of Adjunct Professors" (Douglas-Gabriel, 2019), essentially characterized adjuncts as "the New Working Poor" (Rhoades, 2013a), like other low-wage workers in the fast food, child care, and home care industries (Weissman, 2015). The discourse moved to an ideological framing of adjunct faculty members' plight and mistreatment.

At each of the six metro campaign "launches" in which I have participated, SEIU has conducted and publicized studies showing that adjunct pay is not a living wage in the metro area. The ability of adjunct faculty activists to frame their wages and benefits as unjust in the public eye is ideologically powerful in both lower-tuition, broad-access public institutions and high-tuition private universities. At the former, it is jarring to first-generation students in view of higher education's claim that advanced education will ensure students' economic security. At the latter, it is a jarring indictment of how wealthy institutions treat their employees, who are teaching many or most undergraduates, and how they spend students'/families' tuition monies. At both, it enhances student support. At Tufts University, for example, in discussing the adjunct faculty union campaign, a dean related the story of receiving a student delegation on the issue: "Tufts has a strong activist history among students. Students were very supportive of adjuncts. It mattered that the 'consumers' wanted this" (Glaser, 2015).

So, too, at Georgetown, students were vocally supportive, including in the student newspaper (Wertsch & McCartin, 2018). The foundation for this support had been laid by earlier student activism around establishing a "Just Employment

Policy" with regard to janitorial workers, followed by student support for their unionizing efforts (Wertsch & McCartin, 2018).[34]

More than "bread" (pay and benefits), contingent faculty organizing has also been about "roses"—respect. As Rebecca Gibson, an adjunct faculty member on the negotiating committee at Tufts said on a conference panel: "We were fairly well paid, and we had benefits, so why did we jump in to this movement? It started with the 2008 salary freeze. Fine, we thought, a necessary move in the recession. But in 2010–2011 the salaries were unfrozen for tenure-track and for full-time, non-tenure-track faculty. Yet the salaries of part-time faculty remained frozen" (Gibson, 2015). This adjunct faculty member and two other faculty members on the panel spoke about how they came to realize that "even though we were loyal to and respected the work of the University, WE were not respected by the University." Organizing was driven by a sense of being invisible, in a pattern overlaid by gender.

On structured disrespect, consider the case of an adjunct faculty leader in the Point Park University union campaign, who felt unionization made him happier and more productive in making life better for students. He had been nominated for a Distinguished Teaching Award by students, but administration indicated that as a part-timer he was not eligible. (Fuschino, 2019). Management treats this part-time faculty member and his colleagues as adjunct to the institution's core work and reward system, But they are not adjunct to their students. That has been part of my message when speaking at metro campaign launches. Part-time faculty are not "adjunct" to their students. They are central to students' education. Disrespecting adjunct faculty is disrespecting higher education's students and the institution's core educational mission.

Managerial disrespect is often palpable, not just materially but discursively, in managers' comments, which can facilitate organizing. A University of South Florida faculty activist provided a telling story (personal exchange, February 17, 2018): "It's easy to organize faculty here. Because the university lawyer and senior academic administrator publicly say things like, 'The fact that you are an adjunct with these working conditions is the result of a poor life choice.' They say stuff like this all the time. So, when I start talking with an adjunct faculty member about organizing, although I have my whole spiel ready, I never have to use it, because the faculty member almost immediately says, 'Hell yeah.'"

At the core of the indignity, beyond the statements, is the material reality and cyclical communication surrounding semester-by-semester or year-by-year renewal of employment. Management can nonrenew contingent faculty (and for adjuncts, cancel their courses up to and through the first week of class) with no cause. As in so many organizing (and contract) campaigns, in St. Louis, job security and class cancellation fees were major issues identified in a survey of potential bargaining unit members as key (Ramirez, 2018).

Such respect-based issues hold true as well in full-time contingent faculty campaigns. On the home page of Local 6546 at UIUC was a placard held by a nontenure-track faculty member that read, "Recognition, raises, and respect" (www.local6546.org). Two issues that drove their campaign were job security (contract length) and voice (governance): "The two primary concerns centered on the contingent nature of our employment and our lack of shared governance. Non-tenure-track faculty expressed concern over UIUC's one-year contracts and how those contracts were or were not renewed. They were also concerned about the limited roles [including in evaluation] that NTTF played in their respective departments and units. . . . Our primary concerns were not economic" (Gilmore, 2018, p. 145).

Such respect-based themes are consistent with Berry's (2005) observation that "as one old union organizer said, ultimately all organizing revolves around a demand for respect: respect for the people who are doing the work and respect for the work that they are doing" (p. 27). In higher education, that translates into respect for quality working conditions and education.

Although an overriding focus of organizing campaigns is respect in relation to management, there are also deep undercurrents of resentment about professorial stratification and regular disrespect from tenure-track faculty (e.g., in departmental interactions). That can translate into hostility toward tenure and the "two-tier" system. (see Hoeller, 2014, and calling for legislating separate bargaining units for adjunct and contingent faculty because they have a separate "community of interest," Longmate, 2014). In units that combine tenure-track and contingent faculty, one resolution of the tension can be working toward pay parity (equal pay for equal work) for part- and full-time faculty in their teaching, toward "regularizing" part-time faculty after a defined period, with accompanying rights, a potential path of conversion to full-time positions, and equitable access to professional development and more, partly through pro rata calculations (e.g., see Cosco, 2014).

Tensions surrounding professorial stratification have contributed to internal strains that academic unions have experienced and increasingly addressed in organizing campaigns and bargaining units.[35] As discussed earlier, NFM was key in moving unions, often through contingent faculty caucuses, to address contingent faculty issues more consistently. That has led to national campaigns, such as the AAUP's "One Faculty" campaign. It has also yielded public colleges and universities union campaigns, including contingent and tenure-track faculty, as exemplified in chapter 2 with the UICUF and UAUO campaigns (see also Herbert et al., 2020—about 20 percent of faculty represented in new bargaining units between 2013 and 2019 being in combined units).[36]

One factor overriding resentment about stratification is the "faculty working conditions are students' learning conditions" mantra, which re-centers education.

Consider the following exchange among three adjunct faculty activists at a national conference in 2015. One said, "My life has been oppressed for decades by the tenure system and by tenured faculty." The two others (both NFM leaders) stressed a common ground among all faculty in transforming working conditions for contingent faculty that adversely impact students' learning conditions. The first activist suggested that the others did not understand. To which one replied, "Don't tell me I don't understand. I *know* what poverty is. I know what it means to drive the freeways day after day among several teaching jobs, just trying to piece a living together to pay the rent and put food on the table. Don't tell me I don't understand. . . . But I am an activist because I care about higher education." The other NFM leader spoke to what animated her involvement, cajoling the first activist, who had fought by her side for years against many tenured faculty in MLA: "I am not interested in focusing on old resentments between faculty in part- and full-time positions. We need to move forward together. I care about my students because my working conditions affect their learning conditions. And I care about the higher education my children will confront and experience. That is what motivates me to try to change the academy."

The above exchange embodied the problems and possibilities of organizing adjunct faculty. The NFM leaders' centering of education is evident in the movement, as in this faculty member's words after the adjunct faculty's UAP victory at Temple. "In the words of an adjunct professor at Temple, 'This win at Temple University is a victory for teachers who value quality education and believe in fairness in the workplace'" (American Federation of Teachers [AFT], 2015). Similarly, it was clear in the UIUC campaign's "Education First" rallying cry (see the chapter's fourth epigram). It was explicit in a Miami adjunct faculty leader's phrasing: "Mike Ruso, an adjunct instructor at the University of South Florida, says when schools continuously fail to pay instructors a living wage, everyone suffers. 'The adjunct professors suffer, students suffer, and higher education as a whole suffers,' he stresses. 'The only one who is benefiting is the administrator who is trying to cut cost'" (Gomes, 2017, para. 3–4). And it was evident in media coverage, as in this subheading, "Students are paying higher tuition than ever. Why can't more of the revenue go to the people teaching them?" (Fredrickson, 2015).

In their organizing campaigns, adjunct faculty have centered public interest issues (Rhoades, 2015c) and "bargaining for the common good" (Maisto, 2024; Sneiderman & McCartin, 2018). They have successfully challenged neoliberal managerial priorities and practices that disinvest in and compromise higher education's instructional and public missions. And their critique of management ideology about excellence has centered and replaced it with labor-based conceptions of educational quality and public purpose (Maisto, 2012, p. 201). They are challenging the idea that institutional prestige is enough to justify/counterbalance adverse working conditions (and high tuition). As a member of the newly certified Harvard Academic Workers UAW-affiliated unit (including lecturers, researchers, postdocs, and teaching assistants) said, "'Prestige is not enough'" (Quinn, 2024, "Nontenure Track Harvard," para. 2), recalling the GW campaign. So, too, at New York University (NYU), where the largest private university FTNTT faculty unit in the nation, Contract Faculty United, affiliated with UAW was certified (Quinn, 2024, "Full-Time, Non-Tenure"). As one leader said, "'Our work powers NYU's educational mission—but too many of us face unpredictable salaries that routinely shortchange women and people of color. We look forward to negotiating a strong first contract that allows us to live in New York City, protects our job security and academic freedom, and makes NYU an equitable place to work. Our working conditions are our students' learning conditions'" (UAW, 2024, para. 2).

In short, the issues that have framed contingent faculty's organizing campaigns link a bread and roses, social justice framing of respect for workers and work to (student/public) beneficiaries beyond labor and management in building a new academy.

Uncovered by COVID: Organizing against Disaster Academic Capitalism

As with students and communities, so with adjunct faculty. COVID-19 uncovered, resurfaced, and heightened existing stratification and inequity. For adjunct and contingent faculty, it has done so in working conditions and employment security, in access to health care, and in disparate impacts expressing institutionalized patterns of systemic oppression. So, too, the pandemic and recession have further clarified and amplified respect issues that animate organizing. And they have contributed to a recognition of the common cause shared by academic employees, and their connection to economic and social justice on campus and beyond. Such recognition has been fostered by the broader political context. Our politics have exposed and made even more raw longstanding workplace, social, and racial justice issues.

The recognition of common cause has been further realized in the face of local institutional pursuit of what I call "disaster academic capitalism" (Rhoades, 2021, p. 2). That refers to the tendency of colleges/universities amid tumultuous times to double down on academic capitalism's inherent dual logic of aspiring to accumulation amid claimed austerity. Those logics play out through exploitation of employees and extraction of wealth from students in ways that are disrespectful of and disastrous for employees, students, and the communities in which they are situated and that we serve.

The transition to remote learning in the spring of 2020 and into the fall semester and the 2020–2021 academic year contributed to multiple levels of hardship for contingent faculty. It further clarified their limited access to institutional resources and technical training/support and was evident in their nonrenewals and loss of jobs and health care.[37] Accordingly, on March 8, 2020, AFT's Adjunct/Contingent Caucus issued a statement on the COVID-19 outbreak. Two of the eleven bullets in the statement connected directly to quality working conditions: "It is essential [adjunct faculty] . . . be compensated for additional training needed for the transition to a remote format . . . [and be], when lacking the proper tools to provide online education, loaned tools by their respective institutions for no charge" (email circulated to NFM Foundation Board, March 29, 2020). Many of the other bullets addressed the importance of contingent faculty maintaining employment, health care, and when non-renewed, retaining recall rights and eligibility for unemployment compensation.

The pandemic and recession have, in many cases, increased solidarity among academic employees. That has played out in the actions of existing academic units. The economic threat of COVID is disproportionately experienced by adjunct and contingent faculty relative to tenure-track faculty. Yet, there are examples of bargaining units that include the latter prioritizing the former's job security (Rhoades, 2024). At UIC, where the tenure-track and full-time nontenure-track faculty had separate contracts, the tenure-stream faculty union pushed to ensure continuity of employment for contingent faculty (UIC United Faculty, 2020c, filing an Unfair Labor Practice against the administration on this issue. Existing bargaining units have also mobilized around unemployment compensation, demanding this benefit during the pandemic and recession. SEIU Local 500 and TAUP, among other locals, have featured resources on their websites for adjunct faculty regarding unemployment (and underemployment) benefits (Service Employees International Union Local 500, 2020; Temple Association of University Professors, 2020).[38]

Arguably one of the most dramatic developments in organizing during the pandemic and recession has been the rapid rise/expansion of United Campus Workers (UCW) locals affiliated with the Communications Workers of America (CWA). Most such locals (nine nationally) predated the pandemic, as at UCW Tennessee (Local 3865) and UCW Georgia (Local 3265). Yet, amid the pandemic, they have been quite active, and the solidarity among workers has grown. For example, a facilities worker member of UCW Georgia wrote a piece published in the *Chronicle of Higher Education* on August 27 and posted on the union website. "At Risk, All Day, Every Day" by David Nickel (2020) points to how the pandemic has facilitated solidarity among the local's workers:

> But the crisis has also given rise to unexpectedly positive developments for the university as a whole. I have been a member of the United Campus Workers UGA chapter for more than two years. The chapter is a "wall to wall" union, which means that our membership is open to anyone who receives a paycheck from the University System of Georgia, from facilities and clerical staffers to faculty members and graduate students. While our segments of the campus work force don't always face the same struggles or share aspirations, this pandemic has made us brothers and sisters in arms. (para. 5)

UCWs around the country are affiliated with the Communications Workers of America, a linkage between this local and larger social movements of the day.

The CWA's national website for the UCWs has a newsletter, the tab for which defines CWA's purpose as "building a movement for economic justice and democracy every day" (https://www.ucw-cwa.org). Along these lines, the UCW Tennessee website features on its home page a Juneteenth event on "Labor and Black Struggle in the South," alongside a report on "Exploitation at ETSU: How the Adjunctification of Instruction Harms Faculty and Students at East Tennessee State University" (https://www.ucw-cwa.org).

As these locals have been established in Southern states that have public sector employment laws particularly hostile to unions, they are not collective bargaining units. Thus, they are unconstrained by labor board interpretations of "a community of interest." That leaves them freer to establish "wall-to-wall" locals that include various segments of faculty, graduate (and undergraduate) employees, and staff (including custodial, hospitality, and grounds workers, for instance).

Two such UCW locals emerged amid the pandemic through technology-mediated organizing in Colorado (Local 7799) in the spring of 2020 and in Arizona (Local 7065) in August 2020. The one at Arizona is particularly distinctive in the prominence of faculty, including contingent faculty, in its formation. And the issues driving the United Campus Works of Arizona (UCWAZ) intersect with the issues and ideologies that surfaced and were heightened by the pandemic and recession, as well as the racial/social justice struggles of the day. "We mobilize around the shared issues we care about, such as stopping unnecessary pay cuts and layoffs, ensuring our health and safety, dismantling structural racism and other forms of oppression on our campus, as well as protecting public higher education from private and corporate entities" (https://www.cajuarizona.com/union).

Born of an activist movement and organization, the Coalition for Academic Justice, University of Arizona (CAJUA), the local, of which I am a member, is, in the words of one of its posters, "Embodied in our people and our place." That phrasing speaks to honoring the gifts of our varied identities and fulfilling what a public university can and should be in the borderlands, honoring occupied tribal lands and Indigenous peoples/nations. For all this physical embodiment, however, virtually (pun intended) all the organizing and mobilizing was done in technology-mediated (generally Zoom) space. As with organizing adjunct faculty at GW in an imagined community (McLeer, 2024), perhaps it is, in some ways, easier to organize and construct communities that cut across the workplace and social stratification in virtual space.[39]

Key Takeaways

In closing this chapter, I turn back to its opening, to the striking Lawrence textile workers and the organizing GW adjunct faculty. Through creative strategies and around issues that galvanized worker and public support, those low-wage, under-resourced members of the key industrial and postindustrial sectors helped catalyze and re-energize the labor movement. They organized around a shared sense of injustice and exploitation at the hands of management and a broader (academic) capitalist system.

Although adjunct and full-time contingent faculty are the "new faculty majority," it has been small groups of activists with quite limited to no material resources who have contributed to the emergence of a collective bargaining identity and the explosion of organizing activity among their peers. They have moved to the center of the academic labor movement with their creative, public-facing tactics, metro campaigns, and inside/outside strategies.

More than that, their respect-based organizing centers bread and roses issues, as well as labor-based conceptions of educational quality and public purpose that challenge prevailing managerial practices and undergird neoliberal ideology. The mantras and messaging of contingent faculty activists have resonated widely (including with tenure-track faculty) and, particularly importantly, with student groups and the media. With limited resources, they have won the discursive struggle in the public eye, surfacing and revealing prior to, during, and after the pandemic the moral bankruptcy of disaster academic capitalism and its agenda, which is disastrous for employees, students, and higher education's public purposes.

Remarkably, these faculty have also consistently been winning the material struggle with well-resourced management in forming collective bargaining units and gaining first contracts. Part of that winning is evidenced by the certification electoral results, which have been quite extraordinary (over 70 percent in private and in public institutions—see Herbert, 2016b). Adjunct faculty elections are overwhelmingly successful. Part of the winning is also evidenced in the sustained level of agitation and organizing of contingent faculty. That has substantially reshaped the terms of negotiation between contingent faculty and management. It has also contributed to reducing stratification among segments of the faculty, as will be discussed in the next chapter's analysis of CBAs for part-time only and combined bargaining units. It is in both those (often iterative) gains in improved working conditions in contractual provisions, as well as in the larger, discursive framing of alternatives and possibilities, that contingent faculty are both imagining and implementing a new academy.

4

Negotiating Bread and Roses and Labor-Based Quality into Part-Time-Only and Combined Bargaining Unit Contracts

• • • • • • • • • • • • • • • • • • • •

> What have they gained? (question from reporters about contingent faculty unionizing)

In talking with reporters (and colleagues) about contingent faculty unionization, variations of the same question arise—"What have they gained?" Similarly, many contingent faculty in organizing conversations ask, "What are the benefits of having a union?"

Here, I answer these and other questions by examining first contract gains, organizing/negotiating campaigns, and collective bargaining agreements of part-time-only (PTO) and combined (COMB—full and part-time) bargaining units. Underlying the questions and interwoven into the analyses are the core matters of respect for workers and their work, and the public purposes of the academy that drive contingent faculty's growing collective identity and collective agitation and action in organizing a new academy.

The chapter opens by exploring adjunct and contingent faculty's first contract gains in wages and benefits (i.e., "bread"). But adjunct faculty organizing is about more than more money/benefits and a living wage. It is about pay injustice and inequity (i.e., respect—"roses"), which I explore next. A subsequent section focuses on class cancellation fees (embodying respect, job insecurity, and quality) in the contractual provisions of adjunct faculty (in PTO and COMB units). Then I focus on a labor-based conception of quality working conditions embedded in contract language about access to instructional resources and professional development for contingent faculty in PTO and COMB units. The issues reflect the organizing and contract campaigns of recent times and the explosive organizing of the 2000s in which a contingent faculty mantra has been that faculty's working conditions are students' learning conditions.[1]

The contract analysis utilized the HECAS database (see chapter 1), consisting of 506 collective bargaining agreements (CBA's). Of those, sixty-six (twenty in four-year and forty-six in two-year institutions) were in PTO units, and 188 (fifty-five in four-year and 133 in two-year institutions) were for COMB units covering at least some categories of adjunct faculty.[2]

Salaries/Benefits in First Contracts

"Bread and butter" (in classic labor language) issues of salaries and benefits have been at the forefront of contingent faculty organizing/contract campaigns. Campaigns also entail demands for "roses"—as in respect for workers and their work's value. As a Clemson lecturer said, "I would just say that the work we do has dignity. And the wage does not match that dignity. . . . We are not paid a dignified wage" (Flaherty, 2020, "Clemson English Lecturers," para. 1)

Do contingent faculty realize salary and benefits gains with unionization? Managements' "informational" websites that are posted during unionizing campaigns commonly claim that the answer is "Not necessarily" or "No." Consider this example:

Q Will I get more money if there's a union?
A No. Voting in a union only requires a negotiation. That does not mean more money. The results of that negotiation could be the same, worse, or better than what contingent faculty have now (p. 4). (Pacific Lutheran University, 2014)

Seriously?

A national study of salary/benefits gains in contingent faculty units' first contracts offers a clear, contrary answer (Tolley & Edwards, 2018). Analysis of thirty-five CBAs of mostly new bargaining units between 2010 and 2016 found "adjunct faculty winning salary increases at every institution" and that "89 percent of the contracts include provisions allowing part-time faculty to receive health insurance" (Tolley & Edwards, 2018, p. 188). Moreover, the increase levels were striking. At Point Park University, for example, adjunct faculty "gained a 23 percent increase" (Tolley & Edwards, 2018, p. 188). At Washington University, St. Louis, "adjuncts won a 26 percent increase over the subsequent four years"

(Tolley & Edwards, 2018, p. 188). And at Boston University, "adjuncts won pay raises between 29 percent and 68 percent over the three-year period covered by their contract" (Tolley & Edwards, 2018, p. 188). Not all increases were at these levels, but they were substantial.

In 2017, the pattern continued, as announcements in *InsideHigherEd* about new contracts demonstrated. For example, part- and full-time contingent faculty signed their first contract with Barnard College, averting a threatened strike. It set a new minimum per course salary of $7,000, which by 2021 would increase 43 percent to $10,000 (Jaschik, 2017). Similarly, the first contract signed by adjunct faculty in the College of Arts and Sciences and the School of Education at Saint Louis University raised the salary floor and ensured increases in two subsequent years of up to 8.5 percent (Saint Louis University, n.d.). On July 12, 2017, Duke University adjuncts' part- and full-time faculty unit (the first unit at a major private Southern university) signed a contract that included "pay increases of up to 46 percent for the lowest-paid instructors," with the average increases in per-course pay of 14 percent over three years and 12 percent for salaried instructors" (Flaherty, 2017, "Union Contract Includes Gains," para. 2). They also won benefits. Also, adjunct faculty at Tufts University signed a second contract (the first had up to 40 percent increases), that included "pay raises of 22.5 percent over five years for half the part-time faculty, and a 12.5 percent pay increase for others" (Flaherty, 2017, "Tufts Adjuncts," para. 1).

A few examples from 2018 show the continuing trend amid the height of contingent faculty organizing. In April, University of Chicago adjunct faculty approved a first contract that included "up to a 49 percent pay increase for some instructors" (Flaherty, 2018, "U Chicago Adjuncts," para. 1). The gains also included paid parental leave. On April 27, 2018, Loyola Chicago nontenure-track faculty (part- and full-time in the College of Arts and Sciences) signed a first contract that included "wage increases as high as 51 percent" (Pratt, 2018, para. 8).

And the wins have continued into the 2020s. Consider the contract of University of California lecturers (COMB, but of full- and part-time nontenure-track faculty) settled in 2021 in the early morning hours before an impending strike (CFT, 2021). It raised the salary floor, included a bonus, and assured salary increases for all lecturers of at least 30 percent over the contract's five years. It also assured four weeks of paid family leave for all lecturers. In February 2024, the University of the Arts in Philadelphia, an affiliate of the metro local United Academics of Philadelphia, won a first contract (Schrader, 2024) that established 13 and 11 percent raises on average for adjunct and full-time-nontenure track faculty, as well as a new minimum salary for full-time faculty, and healthcare stipends for adjunct faculty with seniority.[3] In May 2024, the USW-affiliated COMB unit at the University of Pittsburgh ratified a first contract that raised average salaries for FTNTT faculty by 15 percent and part-time faculty by 32 percent over the life of the contract. Per-course payment increased for adjunct faculty up to threefold.

One of the major strategies of bargaining units has been to raise the floor/ minimum salary for adjunct and full-time contingent faculty. Others are to bargain increases for faculty who have taught a certain number of terms. There are also often across-the-board increases. And there have been consistent and significant gains in some benefits, especially key for adjunct faculty who generally have had limited-to-no benefits.

Pay Parity

Word choice matters.

Much of the media's public discourse and academics' writing about adjunct faculty pay refers to them seeking a "living wage." Certainly, that is an issue. Such phrasing is often embedded in stories about professors receiving public assistance or being the "working poor" without health care (Rhoades, 2013a). There is a sense of injustice about the poverty level wages and lack of benefits.

But I have been rightly schooled by adjunct activists about this discourse, including once in a Twitter string about the need for pay parity, not just a living wage. Thus, in the paraphrased words of an organizer for the United Steelworkers, Robin Sowards, "All these first contracts make significant improvements but none have ensured equal pay for equal work on a pro rata basis, meaning that an adjunct would get paid the same to teach a course as would any other faculty member. That's a goal of many part-time instructors" (Flaherty, 2016, "Big Gains," para. 23). Adjunct faculty are organizing and negotiating against the inequity of unequal pay for equal work. They are demanding not just bread but roses too.

Pay parity with full-time faculty, calculated pro rata, is a key goal of the adjunct faculty movement. These faculty are taking on management and the two-tiered professorial stratification system (Hoeller, 2014). They are seeking to "regularize" adjunct faculty (Cosco, 2014).

Parity can be defined in different ways. For example, it can mean full pro rata of adjunct faculty salaries in relation to full-time and tenure-track faculty, or, as in the cases of Clark College, it can be iterative steps toward full pro rata (i.e., it can mean negotiating for nearly 60 percent pro rata, on the way to 80 percent—see Southerland & Kamara, 2023). Or it can mean equal pay for equal instructional work—that is, the same pay for classes.

Although not common, important examples of pay parity language exist. One example also highlights the iterative nature of bargaining. If gains are iterative, the long game and goals need not be. Sometimes, faculty bargaining teams make trade-offs, trading off one provision to get another, laying the foundation for the next contract negotiation. That played out at Dutchess Community College in negotiating the 2017–2020 CBA for adjunct faculty.[4] Dr. Laura Murphy, at the time of the negotiations a member of the faculty bargaining team and a former union vice president, approached me at a national conference about my research presentation analyzing contractual provisions on class cancellation fees for adjunct faculty. She talked about the CBA at Dutchess, and we communicated afterward by email about that negotiation, which related to pay parity and class cancellation provisions. "Regarding the course cancellation fees, I do think our fee proposal, backed by your research, did help us to get more in the area of how quickly the new proportional pay model would advance toward an equity percentage of a full-timer's salary (personnel email, April 2, 2017).

Trying to get a class cancellation fee provision paid off in getting pay parity language. The contract's Appendix B, which is on pay equity, read: "Part-time faculty contact hour wages are directly tied to the salary of full-time faculty by using a negotiated rate of full time salaries." The plan was also to implement four part-time faculty ranks, instituting an "Equity Percentage" compensation schedule with steps, "to move toward the goal of equal pay for part-time and full-time faculty for comparable instructional work."

Exemplifying the intersection among bread and roses issues, in the subsequent 2020–2025 contract negotiation, faculty succeeded in embedding a class cancellation fee in the CBA. Further, the DCC example also speaks to the increased focus on quality working conditions and of solidarity among full- and part-time faculty (e.g., by centering pay equity). The faculty leader spoke of how negotiating faculty evaluation helped protect adjunct faculty—who are too often one or two student complaints away from nonrenewal—and connected this protection to academic freedom as well as faculty from marginalized populations (Murphy & Atkins, 2019).[5]

A number of COMB bargaining units had pay-parity-related language. For example, for many adjunct activists, the California Faculty Association contract is an exemplar here (and in other regards as well—e.g., see Berry & Worthen, 2021). Lecturers (part- and full-time) are on the same salary schedule as tenure-track faculty and receive the same general salary percentage and the same percentage of Service Salary Increases (see CFA, 2019–2020). Another contract that is sometimes cited is the (COMB) unit of APSCUF (Association of Pennsylvania State College and University Faculties). Part-time faculty are paid on a pro-rata basis of a full-time academic year salary for their workload hours. Yet another example is the University of Massachusetts, Amherst's (COMB) contract: "The salary minima in Article 26.4 shall apply to all full-time and, on a pro-rata basis, all part-time NTT faculty."

Distinctively, a bargaining unit of adjunct and FTNTT faculty at Fordham University proposed a new conception of pay parity, negotiating for parity among colleges within the university in contingent faculty pay (Hertzler-McCain, 2023). Such parity was framed as a broader social justice issue in that adjunct faculty in the lowest paying colleges (Religion and Social Work) are more demographically diverse than in other colleges. On the eve of an impending strike, the university settled, agreeing to increases that were a step toward parity and a step toward health benefits (Hertzler-McCain, 2023).[6]

Thus, although PTO units have successfully negotiated significant gains in salaries and benefits, the exemplary contracts for pay equity are in COMB units. One longtime activist wrote, "For the majority of contingent faculty, the best contracts and working conditions have been the result of combined bargaining units" (Moser, 2014, p. 89).[7] However, I have also heard another longtime activist say that "some of the worst contracts are also in COMB bargaining units."

Now, I turn to findings regarding contract provisions, first for class cancellation fees.

Contractual Provisions: Class Cancellation Fees

At the center of adjunct faculty organizing are employment practices that provide them with neither job security nor respect. For adjunct faculty, "Respect is expressed in more stability of employment and adequate notice of work and assignment" (Berry, 2005, p. 123), much as is, for private sector precarious workers, where "predictability of hours" due to employers' rescheduling practices are key (Milkman & Ott, 2014, p. 12).

Class cancellation fees are a step toward establishing such predictability and security. But they are more than that. In the pre-existing "just-in-time" employment model, adjunct faculty are often listed as "Professor Staff" on the course schedule (Street et al., 2012). They are not just disrespected but are invisible. Moreover, the model is not just in time, for faculty or students. Many adjunct faculty have their courses (re)assigned up to a week before class or after classes start. That leaves faculty uncertain about classes (Street et al., 2012; Rhoades, 2013b, 2013c), and undermines students' continuity of education and their access to particular faculty. The evidence is clear. Adjunct faculty's poor working conditions are inversely correlated with good educational outcomes (Bettinger & Long, 2010; Kezar & DePaola, 2018; Rhoades, 2017a).

Most organizing and contract campaigns focus on getting contingent faculty longer-term contracts.[8] An important step toward that, and to establishing faculty's claims to classes lies is negotiating fees they will be paid if or when their classes are canceled. If it seems like a small step, it is a quantum leap in management's acknowledging adjunct faculty's employment claims on assigned classes. And it is an important baseline from which to negotiate multi-year contracts. For bargaining is an iterative process of building on earlier contracts.[9]

Some locals have pursued other strategies for increasing job security, namely what a new COMB USW-affiliated unit at the University of Pittsburgh calls "presumptive renewal," which is essentially automatic renewal except in specified circumstances (e.g., lack of work, program change or elimination, curricular change). For adjunct faculty, it applies to those who have two academic terms of employment, after which they receive one-year contracts with presumptive renewal. Relatedly, the University of California Lecturers' union (AFT-affiliated) contract broke down the stratification between "pre-6" (faculty within the first six years of service) and "continuing" faculty, with lecturers getting multi-year contracts after the first year (CFT, 2021).

If much has been written about the growth of adjunct faculty employment, much less has addressed their working conditions, and even less their collective agency.[10] Faculty in part-time positions have more than doubled in proportion since the 1970s and are nearly half of the instructional workforce (Bowen & Schuster, 1986; Finkelstein, Conley, & Schuster, 2016; Finkelstein, Seal, & Schuster, 1998; Rhoades, 2013c; Schuster & Finkelstein, 2006).

Notwithstanding that long, steady trend line of growth, the burst of organizing by adjunct and contingent faculty has been in the last two decades (Rhoades, 2014a, 2014b). Most new bargaining units in the 2000s have been organized by adjunct faculty (Berry & Savarese, 2012; Herbert, 2016a). Adjunct and contingent faculty are winning in many settings, most notably in (well-resourced) private universities. And they are re-energizing and focusing existing COMB bargaining units on contingent faculty issues.

Here, I consider how class cancellation fee provisions shift the (im)balance between adjunct faculty members' due process rights (and remuneration) versus managerial discretion in making and breaking course assignments. I also consider how provisions reinforce or reduce stratification between adjunct and full-time faculty, tracking any patterns by institutional type (four- versus two-year) or type of unit (PTO versus COMB). And, given SEIU's prominence in organizing adjunct faculty, I first explored such provisions in nine of the SEIU PTO units (the contracts of which I downloaded) versus others in the HECAS database.

Faculty due process rights were evident in provisions' incidence—absent a provision, adjunct faculty lack them. Rights were also evident in specified conditions or rationales for class cancellation, the amount of notice required, and the fee. Also important was language giving managers discretion and making the faculty member's right conditional, such as, "in its sole discretion" or "as the University deems" (see Rhoades, 1998a, p. 326 on "deem clauses").

Professorial stratification was determined in two ways. Considering the incidence of provisions in COMB or PTO units, if they were more prevalent in the latter, that would suggest leaders in COMB units (generally full-time faculty) were less likely to prioritize adjunct faculty's interests. In addition, I looked for content regarding assignment priority for part- versus full-time faculty—for example, if adjunct faculty can be "bumped" from their class by a full-time faculty member filling out their load. Such competition over claims to assignments is a case of "bump chains" (Abbott, 1988), wherein one group's standing and "jurisdiction" in the work takes priority over another. Here, that contest is "collectively negotiated jurisdiction" by adjunct faculty in CBAs (Rhoades, 2017a), which are good vehicles for analyzing "active claims put forth [by groups] in the public, legal, and workplace arenas" (Abbott, 1988, p. 86). On the matter of juris-diction, post-2000, a union (SEIU) new to organizing academic employees laid claim to, in Abbott's (1988) terms, a relatively vacant domain (adjunct faculty in private universities) in which academic unions had for decades chosen mostly not to tread.

SEIU Contracts and Class Cancellation Fees

The nine PTO contracts of SEIU-affiliated units on which I focused were all but one in well-resourced private universities in the first two (DC and Boston) metro campaigns (five in the earlier and four in the subsequent metro campaigns).[11] All but one had class cancellation fee provisions, in contrast to CBOs in most other PTO units.

All nine SEIU metro campaign contracts spoke to conditions surrounding cancellation. The most specific provisions were in the American, Georgetown, and Northeastern contracts. Each had at least a page of conditions justifying class cancellation. They included restrictive phrasing of "elimination or downsizing of a department or program" (American), or the somewhat less restrictive lan-guage of the latter two contracts: "elimination, decrease, or substantial modifi-cation of courses due to changes in curriculum or program offerings." The strongest was GW's: "Cancellation of a course(s) due to under enrollment, based on a predetermined University, School or Department standard for minimum enrollment." That restricted managerial discretion, as faculty had a role in set-ting the unit's standards.

Still, there was much managerial discretion built into the CBAs. For exam-ple, Tufts' language of "insufficient enrollment or other reasons" left those deter-minations to managers. American and Northeastern's CBAs included a deem clause: "Availability of an alternate faculty member who, in the University's dis-cretion [American's contract reads "reasonable discretion"] has better creden-tials, qualifications, and/or performance."

Professorial stratification was also built in to some CBAs. American, George-town, Northeastern, and Trinity Washington's contracts had language justify-ing class cancellation when part-time are bumped by full-time faculty. The phrasing in Georgetown's and Trinity Washington's contract was, "or any other circumstance in which the course will be taught by a full-time faculty member."

Yet, the SEIU contracts provided longer notice and larger cancellation fees than did other contracts, as shall be seen below. Typically, three weeks' notice before classes was required (Northeastern's contract called for forty-five days). Otherwise, a cancellation fee had to be paid. Some contracts had fees that were flat dollar amounts (Howard's was just $300). Others had percentages. For GW and Brandeis, the fee was 20 percent of the faculty member's salary. For BU, it ranged from 15 to 30 percent, depending on the circumstances and timing. For American, it was 75 percent. At Northeastern, "If the faculty member has not been offered an alternate assignment, . . . [they] shall be given full compensation for the course(s) cancelled after the course was assigned and accepted by the faculty member."

HECAS Contract Provisions on Class Cancellation Fees

Incidence. Class cancellation fee provisions were found in 25 percent of the HECAS contracts covering adjunct faculty. That means in three-quarters of the CBAs managers had full discretion to reassign or cancel adjunct faculty's classes without due process or compensation.

Provisions were far more common in PTO CBAs (39 percent) than in COMB CBAs (20 percent). Yet, in four-year settings, they were far more likely in PTO units (two-thirds of them had provisions), whereas in two-year institutions, they were far more likely in COMB units (over two-thirds had provisions).

Content. Managerial discretion was quite extensive, and professorial stratification quite evident. In the CBAs of both four- and two-year institutions, "The rationales provided for cancelling classes are quite broad and undefined, the notice of cancellation that triggers a fee is quite late, and the compensation is quite limited" (Rhoades, 2017a, p. 658). But there was some variation.

A substantial minority of CBAs specified conditions required to cancel a class, particularly in four-year institution contracts. Even then, language was either undefined or left much discretion to managers. In two-year institutions' CBAs, the most invoked rationale, found in fourteen (of forty-six) CBAs, was enrollment. But mostly, the contract language was vague, with terms such as "low" or "insufficient," providing no specific parameters.

Yet, there were important exceptions and exemplars in two-year institutions' contracts of strong language specifying the enrollment that would justify cancellation. For example, "Within the timeframe of 4 weeks to 15 calendar days prior to the first day of a term, a class will not be canceled if it is 50% enrolled of an assignable class size or has at least 12 students. Within the timeframe of two weeks before the beginning of a term and the first day of the term a class will not be canceled if it is at least 70% enrolled of an assignable class size or has at least 15 students" (Lane Community College). Four other Oregon community college CBAs specified enrollment thresholds for cancellation and gave faculty the option of teaching a low-enrolled course for a pro-rated salary.[12]

Moreover, Mt. Hood Community College's (PTO) contract provided much detail on cancellation conditions for different types of classes, and an option for faculty.

> The College retains the right to cancel low-enrolled courses. 1. A required program class, a sequence class, a first-time offering, a non-sequential prerequisite class, in traditional or web format and other classes approved by the appropriate Vice President will be paid at one hundred percent (100%) of the ILC (term FTE) rate. . . . For all other classes, if any lecture class has fewer

than 12 students or a laboratory class has fewer than 9 students, the College will determine whether the class will be continued. If continued, the instructor . . . will be paid a pro-rated ILC rate.

Rogue Community College's (COMB) contract read, "Classes with enrollment below 10 students . . . will be paid at 100% if the College mandates that the class be continued."

Less such language was found in the fifteen four-year institutions' contracts. All but one of those cases were vague. In Portland State University's (PTO) contract, the language was, "The University reserves the right to cancel one or all of the courses listed, should enrollment, in the judgment of the University, be insufficient" (Columbia College's PTO contract identified "lack of sufficient enrollment" as a rationale).

One exception was Saginaw Valley State's (COMB) contract, which referred to student enrollment as a rationale, defining the terms surrounding that: "A course scheduled . . . which ends up after open registration with nine (9) or fewer students may be canceled, but no such class will be canceled unless all of the same size and smaller classes are also canceled."

However, the CBA then provided another rationale for cancellation: "Full-time faculty whose classes are canceled because of low enrollment shall at their option displace part-time faculty teaching classes for which the full-time faculty is qualified." The language established a "bump chain" between segments of academe, hardly a way to build solidarity.

In contrast, Rider University's (COMB) CBA provided protection for some adjunct faculty against such bumping. Adjunct faculty with "priority status" (having taught at least thirty-six credit hours in the previous six consecutive years) had some protection against bumping: "Sections assigned to an adjunct member . . . holding Priority Appointment status shall not be reassigned to a full-time member of the faculty to accommodate a request from the full-time member of the faculty for an overload assignment . . . if such a request was not made by the deadline set by the department chair during the workload planning process." Yet, "Priority Appointment" adjunct faculty could bump other adjunct faculty, structuring stratification among segments of adjunct faculty.

Language about bumping was also found in some CBAs of two-year institutions, as with Sussex County Community College's (PTO) contract: "In the event that the College has issued a letter of intent to employ and the bargaining unit member's assigned class is cancelled due to under-enrollment or displacement by a full-time faculty member, the affected bargaining unit member shall receive pro-rated compensation for actual classroom contact hours rendered."

A few other contracts provided due process protections for adjunct faculty in some circumstances against being bumped. For example, "The Dean may not cancel the assignment of any part-time faculty member for the purpose of providing a full-time faculty member with overload" (South Orange County

Community College District, COMB). The language accords an important right to the adjunct faculty relative to not just department and/or college administrators but also to full-time faculty.

An unintentionally ironic rationale for class cancellation was "lack of funds" (Clatsop Community College, PTO): "The College maintains the right to cancel a class for low enrollment or lack of funds." Considering adjunct faculty's pay, such a claim is hard to credit.

In the contracts of both four- and two-year institutions, the timing and notice required after which a class being cancelled triggered a fee was quite limited. In four-year institutions' contracts, the longest notice required was in Cornell's (PTO) contract: "If a course is cancelled or withdrawn within (60) sixty days before the trimester or semester begins, but after the unit member has agreed to teach the course, the unit member shall receive payment." That was way outside the norm of a few weeks.

Several contracts had language about fees for cancellation after classes had started, a practice involving another level of disrespect for adjunct faculty and their work. For example, "If a class is canceled prior to the third class meeting, the temporary employee shall be paid for class hours taught. If a class is canceled after the third class meeting, the temporary employee shall either be paid for the remaining portion of the class assignment or provided an alternate work assignment" (California State University, COMB). And, "If a cancellation occurs, the University will pay a prorata amount for the number of classes held before cancellation and will pay for one class meeting if the cancellation occurs before the first class meeting" (Portland State University, PTO). Such language clarifies the after-the-last-minute reality of "just-in-time" employment.

In two–year institutions, most contracts had less notice, ranging from two weeks before class (Lane Community College, COMB) to after classes started. Mostly, the notice was seven days before class. Some CBAs specified a time period of less than a week. For instance, it was ninety-six hours before the first class in Mt. Hood Community College's (PTO) contract, and "48 hours prior to the first meeting of the class" at Shoreline Community College (COMB).

As limited as it was, notice and timing mattered for adjunct faculty, for contract provisions linked that notice to compensation at a very specific level: "If the College cancels a course after the first or second class hour, the Adjunct will be paid 10% of what he/she would have received if the entire course was taught. If the College cancels a course after the third or fourth class hour, the Adjunct will be paid 20% of the money receivable for the entire course. If the College cancels a course after the fifth class hour, the Adjunct will be paid 30% of the money receivable for the entire course" (Onondaga Community College, COMB).

Limited though they were, class cancellation fees represented an important recognition of adjunct faculty's time, work, and claims. And they provided some small disincentive to canceling classes. How small that could be was evident in the following two examples. "A faculty member who has accepted an assignment to teach a credit-bearing course in accordance with the processes outlined in Sections 10–13 of this Article shall receive a cancellation fee of 5% (gross) of the established salary" (University of Vermont, PTO). In Rutgers' PTO contract, it was one-sixteenth of the salary for the semester. Some contracts provided flat amounts, which were somewhat higher. In Roosevelt University's CBA, it was $250, and in Connecticut State University's contract, it was $300.

Two-year institutions' contracts generally had even lower class cancellation fees. Again, some provisions were for percentages (5 percent at Tacoma Community College—COMB—and 8 percent at Seattle Community College—COMB), and others were for flat amounts. Some of the flat amounts were incredibly low, as for Flathead Valley Community College (PTO) which provided a $30 "stipend." In two cases (Clatsop Community College and Chemeketa Community College), the compensation was for one hour. And Portland Community College's contract read, "Part-time Faculty shall be paid for contact hours scheduled for the first class session."

Such piece-rate calculations only recognized in-class "contact hours," leaving adjunct faculty's out-of-class instructional work (e.g., preparation, advising, grading) unrecognized and uncompensated. In an exception, Rider University's (COMB) contract recognized this work: "The University shall provide adjunct faculty with as much advance notice as practicable of their next term's workload assignments so as to allow them reasonable time to prepare course materials and to order books and supplies at the same time as full-time faculty." But there was no compensation for that work. In another exception, William Rainey Harper College's PTO contract acknowledged and compensated the work. "The College recognizes that a class contingently assigned but then withdrawn from an adjunct faculty member may be a class for which the adjunct faculty member has prepared." It provided $50 to the adjunct faculty member, and $250 if it was their only class.

Finally, several contracts provided low-enrollment pay options for adjunct faculty, as an alternative to class cancellation (fees).

Discussion

The one-quarter of the 250 COMB and PTO contracts that had class cancellation fee provisions show that adjunct faculty have realized important gains from unionization in negotiating respect and remuneration through due process rights and claims on their assigned classes. Those gains were all the more evident in the SEIU metro contracts of DC and Boston, all of which had provisions, stronger due process rights, and more remuneration than did other contracts. For all their limitations, class cancellation provisions are markers of contingent faculty's collective counter-mobilization.

Clearly, SEIU's entry into organizing contingent faculty has re-energized the academic labor movement. This "competitive unionism" (Berry, 2005) has led to organizing in new sectors of higher education (private universities), with new tactics (e.g., metro campaigns), and stronger contracts. That has spilled over into contingent faculty organizing and negotiating in public colleges/universities. For example, in 2022, Arcadia University adjunct faculty, affiliated with the United Academics of Philadelphia (metro) local, signed a contract that expanded class cancellation fees by 10 and 20 percent, depending on notice. Also, in this second contract, they won the expansion of year-long contracts from six in the previous contract to a total of twenty senior adjuncts (defined by a period of continuous appointment and performance).

Adjunct faculty's collective agency has also been evident in their organizing stand-alone bargaining units, a source of extraordinary growth in new bargaining units. The importance of that in advancing adjunct faculty's interests is clear. In the HECAS database, PTO units were twice as likely as COMB ones to have class cancellation fee provisions (39 versus 20 percent).

Yet, some class cancellation fee provisions point to an ongoing structure of professorial stratification. Contract language identified "bump chains," enabling full-time faculty to "displace" part-time faculty and take their class assignments.[13] The situation is in flux, amid "jurisdictional fluidity" (McPherson & Sauder, 2013). Although that concept has referred to the micro-level negotiation of individual actors' discretion and rights, I utilize it here to refer to the collective negotiation of adjunct faculty's claims on course assignments and due process.

Each negotiation is a baseline from which adjunct (and contingent) faculty collectively work to renegotiate a less stratified academy. Consider the following possibilities in providing adjunct faculty whose classes have been canceled with nonteaching work supporting students. Jackson Community College's (COMB) contract does this for full-time faculty: "If a faculty member has a class canceled he/she may . . . accept assignment of other non-teaching work as assigned by the supervising Dean." Why not provide that opportunity to adjunct faculty? Along related lines, Southwestern College's (COMB) contract had paid office hours for part-time faculty, including for advising students other than those in their classes. Why not provide such responsibilities, then, for adjunct faculty with a canceled class? The same shifting of responsibilities could apply to adjunct faculty whose courses have been canceled.

CUNY's (COMB) contract offers an "other duties" alternative to a class cancellation fee. It indicates that "the appointment provides the assurance of at least six contact hours of work per semester, or its equivalent." If the department has no available course, the adjunct will perform other duties for which they are qualified (Flaherty, 2017, "Some 1,500 Adjuncts"). That is a strong strategy for ensuring adjunct faculty's employment security.

Bargaining Access to Instructional Resources and Professional Development

The adjunct faculty movement's core mantra is a labor-based conception of quality (Worthen & Berry, 2002) that faculty's working conditions are students' learning conditions (Maisto, 2012, 2024). To workers' demands for bread and roses have been added quality, too. That has translated into contract negotiations, with adjunct faculty bargaining for access to basic instructional resources and professional development (PD) that are connected to quality education. The key to quality is less in the content of faculty's individual practices than in the context of adjunct faculty's employment structures and rights, and in the contest between labor and management in negotiating those employment structures and rights. And that contest is also the jurisdictional (re)negotiation between part- and full-time faculty in their rights of access to quality working conditions (Rhoades, 2020), as with class cancellation bump chains.

Such working conditions have been the focus of part- and full-time faculty's advocacy for equitable policies linked to quality (Kezar, 2013; Kezar & Sam, 2013). That has included having a workspace to meet with students and a role in departmental curricular deliberations.[14]

The contrast between a labor-based conception of quality and that of management is nicely captured in Worthen and Berry's (2002) case study of a dispute between an adjunct professor and union activist and administration. In a memo to the faculty member, the Acting Dean charged him with "negligence" and "lack of [professional] responsibility" for allegedly filing attendance reports and grades two weeks late. The letter threatened "disciplinary action" in the future if such behavior continued (the warning was part of the "progressive discipline" policy embedded in the CBA). Timeliness and compliance here were centered as proxies of professional responsibility and quality, arbitrarily applied by a manager. In addition to disputing the accuracy of the charges and the "inflammatory" tone of the memo, the instructor, who was also on the union bargaining team, noted that among the matters currently being negotiated were paid time for paperwork, and access to offices, instructional support, and PD.

Two national surveys have documented adjunct faculty's problematic working conditions regarding access to instructional facilities and resources and PD. Street, Maisto, Merves, and Rhoades (2012, p. 10) found that adjunct faculty had "late and limited access" to office space, course management systems, departmental syllabi, and library privileges. Similarly, the largest survey ever of adjunct faculty found that faculty with, "the presence of a union on at least one of the campuses where they teach were consistently more likely to receive resources and support" including for PD, though the overall percentages were low in absolute terms (CAW, 2012, p. 12).

Academic studies further confirm the situation. Included among the working conditions identified by Baldwin and Chronister (2001) as being related to quality and yet largely lacking, even for full-time nontenure-track faculty, were access to their department's educational culture and practices, as well as to PD. So, too, as Xu (2019) pointed out, "adjunct [faculty] are typically not compensated for participating in professional development, and even if they are interested, campus workshops or programs are often offered during regular working hours or when many . . . adjuncts are not available" (p. 35). Also lacking is what Drake, Struve, Meghani, and Bukosk (2019) underscored as important—meaningful participation in departments' curriculum development. Finally, as Austin and Trice (2016) have said regarding various working conditions' importance (e.g., library privileges and access to instructional facilities/supports): "The lack of office space for part-time faculty . . . diminishes the institution's commitment to educational quality when students cannot easily meet and discuss their work in a confidential setting with their teachers" (pp. 64, 66).

The empirical research is also overwhelmingly clear about faculty working conditions' impact on student outcomes. From community college persistence and transfer to persistence and graduation rates in four-year institutions to performance in key gatekeeper courses, the consistent findings are of an inverse correlation between percentages of part-time faculty and student outcomes because of these faculty's working conditions (Chingos, 2016; Eagan & Jaeger, 2008, 2009; Ehrenberg & Zhang, 2005; Jaeger & Eagan, 2011a, 2011b; Ran & Xu, 2018; Umbach, 2007; Xu, 2019). For instance, without access to offices and with teaching sometimes at multiple institutions to make ends meet, a large percentage of part-time faculty in community colleges do not meet with students outside of class (CCSSE, 2009).

As important as office space is, symbolically and in educational practice, it is worth noting, as will be explored in chapter 8, that there is a gendered and generational shift in preferences favoring technology-mediated instruction and advising. That makes adjunct faculty's access to (and/or reimbursement for) all sorts of materials and resources for technology-mediated educational work all the more important.

Remarkably, despite the evidence, policy and managerial discourse devotes little attention to working condition "inputs" to educational quality. Instead, the prevailing neoliberal framing constructs the "problem" as faculty deficiencies and inefficiencies. The "solution" is increased accountability mechanisms fixated on "outputs," on performance metrics such as graduation rates and student learning outcomes, without regard for faculty working conditions.[15]

Here, I consider what adjunct faculty's access to instructional resources and PD reflects about the (im)balance between their professorial rights of access versus managerial discretion. I also explore what the provisions reveal about stratification between full- and part-time faculty. And I also address whether and how provisions explicitly refer to educational quality and/or public benefits/beneficiaries.

To address the first issue, I analyzed patterns of incidence, types of provisions, and connections between contract language and the re(pro)duction of larger systems of power. Provisions' incidence gave a sense of the (im)balance of power between adjunct faculty's professorial rights and managers' discretion regarding access to instructional resources (facilities such as office space or materials such as syllabi and curriculum guides) and PD. I also analyzed types and extent of access (e.g., for PD, was it available only through competitive funds, or was it available to all?). Moreover, I looked for "deem language" that gave managers discretion by making access conditional—for example, in phrases such as "subject to availability." Finally, I looked for language ensuring adjunct faculty involvement in departments' curricular decision-making and for whether adjunct faculty played a role in organizing/providing PD.

To address the second issue, I tracked the incidence of provisions in PTO versus COMB unit contracts. Also important was whether language provided adjunct faculty parity with full-time faculty in access to instructional resources and PD.

Finally, to address matters of quality (and the public interest), I looked for explicit language that included a modifier like "effective," which went beyond a general statement that something was needed for faculty to perform their duties.

Professorial Rights/Voice vs. Managerial Discretion

Incidence. A little less than half (113 or 44 percent) of the 254 CBAs included adjunct faculty access to instructional resources provisions. Three-quarters or 75 percent (a total of 190) had access to PD provisions.

Content—Type and Scope of Resources. All but four of the 113 contracts with access to resources provisions referred to facilities. Only twenty-seven (25 percent) referred to materials. Mostly, the access was limited (eighty-one contracts), typically to computers and email or text(books); only sixteen each had "broad" or "limited" access to instructional facilities and materials. An example of broad access was in American University's PTO contract: "access to computer workstations; access to printing and photocopying services for class related purposes; access to administrative support services for standard and reasonable requests during normal work hours; access to space (but not necessarily office space) to meet with and advise students; access to departmental guidelines or procedures relevant to adjunct faculty; and access, upon request, to and the use of standard instructional software and computer programs used to teach the assigned course(s)."

Some provisions had detail that included facilities and materials. Thus, in addition to facilities such as shared office space, "equipment, technology and resources to assist them in attaining their teaching goals," Triton College's (PTO) contract also detailed materials such as the faculty handbook and copies of "the instructional media and of any related material such as a workbook or exercise book" and "access to available instructional material, labs and other departmental resources." The City College of Chicago's (PTO) contract detailed over several pages "teaching materials"—texts, workbooks, a part-time faculty handbook, departmental policies, printed materials, and academic and student policy manuals.

A very few CBAs (three) extended such rights of access between academic terms: "A non-tenure track faculty member whose appointment has ended but whose Department Chair indicates, in writing, that the faculty member is likely to be given a new appointment that will take effect within one year . . . shall be accorded, for a period of one year, all library and e-mail privileges to which they would have been entitled had their appointments not terminated (University of Massachusetts, both Amherst and Boston COMB).

A clear example of the labor-based conception of quality was as follows: "It is the College's goal to support adjunct faculty in these efforts [to be accessible to students] through improved office and meeting facilities and increased compensation when sufficient . . . funds become available" (Olympic College, COMB). Though limited and provisional, the language acknowledged the need for the institution to provide working conditions to facilitate faculty engagement with students.

Provisional language was far more common than the declarative "will provide" phrasing of American University's (PTO) contract. Typically, much discretion was provided in (very) limited provisions: "The parties recognize that it is common for the demand for office and work space to exceed supply. When possible, the University will provide bargaining unit members with access to office or workspace" (University of Alaska, PTO).

Some contracts detailed expectations for adjunct faculty but offered no rights to working conditions facilitating fulfillment of those duties, as at the University of Rhode Island (COMB): "Faculty members shall adhere to University policies and procedures for: class attendance, course scheduling, final examinations, course expectations and grading policies, development and distribution of course syllabi, availability for student conferences and advising, the timely submission of grades." Note the reference to timeliness. The management framing was about compliance, not providing working conditions that would enhance quality.

Very few (nine) contracts afforded adjunct faculty a role in the life of their academic unit. Yet, the exceptions are noteworthy. The University of Vermont's (PTO) CBA gave adjunct faculty the right to participate in faculty meetings if departmental bylaws allowed. And Eastern Michigan University's (PTO) contract similarly indicated, "To the extent that . . . department Faculty procedures permit . . . employee participation on curriculum and instruction committees will be allowed." Such language spoke clearly to how far adjunct faculty had to go in gaining respect from tenure-track faculty and a voice in basic departmental decision-making. More progressively, Howard University's (PTO) contract had an "Access to the Academic Community" provision that afforded adjunct faculty access to, among other matters, "participate in departmental committee meetings."

Content—Type and Control of PD. Unlike access to instructional resources provisions, most contracts (75 percent or 190) had access to PD provisions. Still, that access was limited. Provisions allocating monies for every adjunct faculty member in the unit were found in only fourteen contracts. Although typically, the allocation was smaller for part- than full-time faculty, Bellingham Technical College's (COMB) contract established prorated parity: "The pooled dollars will be available to part-time faculty working less than 50% at a rate consistent with their percentage of full-time."

The most common provisions, in eighty contracts, were for a competitive fund with limited monies for which faculty had to apply. There was much variance, connected to institutional wealth and size, in the fund amounts and the activities those funds could support. Thus, in NYU's (PTO) and CUNY's (COMB) contract, the professional development fund for adjunct faculty was respectively $100,000 and $500,000 annually (for BU, it was $27,000, and for Brandeis, $25,000). Contrast that with $5,000 and $3,000 annually for adjunct faculty PD, respectively, in Morton College's (PTO) and Raritan College's (PTO) CBAs.

Adjunct faculty gained access in twenty-nine contracts to PD days and in twenty-six to locally provided PD. Moreover, twenty-four contracts indicated that adjunct faculty would be paid for required PD. Typical examples of each were:

> With prior approval of the appropriate Division Chair and Dean, Adjunct Faculty may be absent from class with pay to attend workshops, conferences, or seminars directly related to their work at the College. (Heartland Community College District, PTO)
>
> The University agrees to provide adjuncts with equal access to University-sponsored professional development workshops or seminars. (Wayne State University, PTO)
>
> When the Employer requires the Employee to attend and/or participate in any type of external training or professional development as a requirement of his/her employment, associated actual costs will be paid by the Employer. (Western Michigan University, COMB)

Significantly, there were many examples of faculty having a voice in PD decisions. A substantial minority of CBAs (40 percent or seventy-six) had such language. Among the strongest examples were the following contracts, all in COMB units in community colleges. One provided for three .20 FTE "Faculty Development Liaison" positions "to support instructional improvement efforts to include . . . professional development" (Gavilan Joint Community College District). Similarly, Lane Community College's contract provided for a .20 to .50 position for a faculty member to be "Faculty Professional Development Coordinator" and "to coordinate faculty professional development activities and chair the Faculty Professional Development Committee." Finally, Seattle Community

College's (COMB) contract provided for a unit member to receive 100 percent release time to be "District Faculty Development Program Coordinator." But tellingly, that person would be "a full-time tenured faculty member."

More typically, contracts provided for faculty involvement in decision-making about competitive funds. Adjunct faculty were sometimes included, as at Parkland College (PTO): "All requests for [PD] funds will be forwarded by the department chair to a committee appointed by the PTFO" (Part-Time Faculty Organization]. In some contracts, a faculty committee administered the monies: "The District shall budget an amount of $10,000 for each instructional year of this Agreement to be used for curriculum projects initiated by part-time faculty and for part-time-faculty professional development. Such funds shall be administered by the Curriculum Grants Committee" (Seattle Community College, COMB). Still others had provision for a committee of faculty and administrators selected by the respective parties. Keene State College's (PTO) contract is an example in an adjunct unit: "This fund will be administered by three members of the adjunct unit and will include participation by a faculty... or staff member designated by the Provost." Again, the prominent examples were in two-year college contracts.

Intra-Professorial Stratification

One gauge of stratification between part- and full-time faculty lay in the incidence of access to instructional resources and PD provisions in PTO and COMB unit contracts. Another was the incidence of provisions that differentiate access for part- and full-time faculty or that provide parity. A third was in whether and what access was differentiated.

Incidence. Slightly less than two-thirds (62 percent) of PTO units had access to instructional resources provisions (forty-one), whereas slightly more than one-third (38 percent) of COMB units had them (seventy-two). By contrast, equal proportions of PTO (76 percent) and COMB (74 percent) units had access to PD provisions (fifty and 140, respectively).

Provision for parity was quite limited, though somewhat less so in access to PD. Of the 190 PD provisions, 22 percent (forty-two) afforded parity, compared to 10 percent (eleven) of the 113 access to instructional resources provisions. Parity was far more common in COMB than in PTO units (all but five of the forty-two PD and eight of the eleven resources provisions). Still, a strong example was in Pace University's (PTO) CBA. The phrasing was "provided this benefit is made available to full-time faculty." It applied to a broad range of facilities, including voicemail, listing in the online University directory, email accounts, a Blackboard account, library privileges, intercampus transportation, photocopying, and Internet access. And denial of access could be grieved.

Stratified Rights in Access to Resources. Few contracts (eleven) provided adjunct faculty some parity with full-time faculty in access to instructional resources.

Two of those were in recently formed PTO units. For Prairie State College (PTO), "All adjunct faculty . . . shall be provided with the textbooks and materials for the courses they are teaching as soon as they are available and shall be provided the same access to technical and clerical support as given to full-time faculty." The language in the Eastern Michigan University PTO CBA accorded adjunct faculty access to "the Employer's IT services on the same basis they are provided to other instructional faculty."

Yet, most of the contracts (eight of eleven) with parity language were in COMB units, as in the case of the University of Michigan's (COMB) contract: "Classroom facilities, technology, technological support and the training necessary for the use of said facilities and technology, shall be provided at no cost to the Employee on the same basis as the tenure-track faculty." See also the City College of San Francisco's (COMB) contract: "Part-time faculty should be considered to be an integral part of their departments and given all the rights normally afforded to full-time faculty in the areas of book selection, participation in department activities, and the use of college resources, including, but not necessarily limited to, telephones, copy machines, supplies, office space, mail boxes, clerical staff, library, and professional development."

The norm, though, was for the access to be differentiated. No contract made clearer the source and doubly dependent nature of that access than this one: "Each division dean/supervisor shall strive to make office/work space available to adjunct faculty by encouraging full-time faculty to share office space with adjunct faculty" (Antelope Valley Community College's contract, COMB). "As if," as the saying goes.

Differential access to instructional resources was found in fifteen CBAs, all in COMB units, that provided at least some access to office space. For example, the University of Florida's (COMB) contract read, "Each tenured or tenure-accruing full-time faculty member shall be provided with an enclosed individual office," whereas "Non-tenure-accruing faculty members and part-time faculty members . . . may be provided office space on a shared basis." Similarly, Hofstra University's (COMB) contract read, "Each full-time faculty member shall have a computer for his/her use available in his/her office," whereas "reasonable effort shall be made to provide office space and computer access for the use of adjunct faculty." For the most part, though, adjunct faculty simply lacked access.

Stratified Rights in Access to PD. A little more than one-fourth of contracts (27 percent—all in COMB units) explicitly stratified access to PD. In some cases, that stratification was severe, as in Minnesota State College and Universities' (COMB) contract: "All faculty except adjunct faculty shall be eligible for professional improvement funds." Wenatchee Valley Community College's (COMB) contract provided $1200 per year for PD only to full-time faculty "for specialized equipment, books or teaching materials that enhance the teaching/learning environment."

In some contracts, the stratification of access was less severe, but no less explicit. Thus, Highline Community College's (COMB) contract gave full-time faculty $1500 every other year of the contract for PD but only gave adjunct faculty the right to compete for access to a total fund of $3,000 each year for PD. Olympic had a less unequal but similarly differentiated model of access: full-time faculty received $200 per year, and adjunct faculty had the right to compete for monies from a competitive fund totaling $5,000 annually.

Another form stratification took was among categories of part-time faculty. Thus, Central Washington University's (COMB) contract accorded rights to PD only for "regular part-time faculty" (typically above a certain FTE), excluding "temporary" part-time faculty. The same was true in Lake Superior State University's (COMB) contract and for the University of Oregon's (COMB) "Professional Development Opportunity Fund." As a contrast, and model, The University of Pittsburgh's new contract (ratified in 2024) with a USW-affiliated COMB unit defined "regular part-time" as those employed over two of three semesters.

Notably, 22 percent of contracts provided adjunct faculty pro-rated parity in access to PD. Some of the strongest were in PTO units. "Any professional development opportunities that are provided by EMU . . . such as workshops, institutes, training sessions, or other professional development opportunities shall be made available to Employees on the same basis as they are available to tenured and tenure-track faculty" (Eastern Michigan University, PTO). And "Unit members are eligible for support funds through the Center for Innovation in Teaching Excellence. These funds include faculty grants and various fellowships for which Unit members and full-time faculty and staff may apply" (Columbia College, PTO). So, too, Wayne State University's (PTO) contract provided adjuncts "equal access to University-sponsored professional development workshops or seminars."

Quality/Public Benefits/Beneficiaries

A little over 22 percent of access to resources or to PD provisions (twenty-five and forty-one respectively) had references to quality/public interest. For the former, there were fourteen contracts, each with references to quality (fourteen) and to public benefits (eleven). By contrast, all of the forty-one PD provisions referred to quality (six also were coded as public interest).

Broad reference beyond the parties at the bargaining table to community beneficiaries of adjunct faculty access to resources was found in one contract. "Technological advances need to be accessible to faculty. . . . Access for the faculty is important because it leads to utilization by the students and the community as a whole" (Governor's State University, COMB).

Typically, though, the provisions were narrower in scope and about office space. A number, as with Montana Community College's (COMB) contract were about the value of adjunct faculty having space for confidential conversations to serve students' needs: "The employer recognizes the need for employees to have access to space for conducting student counseling or other sensitive situations in private." Some connected that space and other resources to fulfilling the institution's mission: "The parties recognize the importance of adequate space and facilities in accomplishing the educational mission of the University. Adjunct faculty teaching credit courses in degree-granting programs shall have reasonable access to desk and file space and computers. Such faculty also shall have access to University e-mail accounts and voice mail. Adjunct faculty shall not be required to conduct classes or instruction in his/her private residence or office" (NYU, PTO).

Some provisions referenced facilities other than office space: "Part-time faculty will have access to all campus resources necessary to effectively deliver course materials to their classes and to facilitate appropriate communication between the part-time faculty member and his/her students. This includes, but is not limited to, duplication resources, supplies, private conference space, texts, and other materials" (Clackamas Community College, PTO).

It is ironic and telling that one of the strongest quality statements was in a contract that provided no access to instructional resources. The Maine Community College System's (COMB) contract enumerated "multiple positive outcomes" of "Faculty-student professional contact in and out of classes" that "can be an important factor in student motivation and involvement," including, "1) retention/persistence to graduation, and 2) academic achievement/performance," among others. Similarly, the Community College of Philadelphia's (PTO) contract provided access only to mailboxes and email "to the extent possible." Still, it invoked the college's "mission to serve all of the citizens in the community" and referred to faculty's "participation in the life of the college" and to the academic community formed between faculty and students as being essential to the college achieving the highest standards of educational excellence and of ensuring access. It was not so essential, apparently, to warrant access for adjunct faculty beyond email and mailboxes.

Yet there were important exceptions. Thus, Eastern Michigan University's (PTO) contract spoke to professional responsibilities that were important "to ensure high quality education for their students." Accordingly, it provided adjunct faculty access to extensive instructional facilities and materials and involvement in the unit's life.

Quality was a theme in forty-one access to PD provisions. Of these, six also addressed public benefits. The focus was on quality teaching and institutional mission. Thus, "the criteria for selecting proposals shall include the potential of the course or seminar for a. improving teaching or learning. b. enhancing interpersonal relationships with students or other staff. c. teaching new instructional methodology" (Community College District #10 in Green River, COMB).

Once more, ironically, a contract with a strong quality statement lacked any provision of PD support for adjunct faculty. Clover Technical College's (COMB) contract read, "In order for the College to become a world-class technical college, all faculty must be lifelong learners. It is expected that every faculty member will continually participate in training activities that will hone and update his or her professional skills." The contract allocated to full-time faculty $1,000 per year for PD but nothing to adjunct faculty.

Some contracts provided PD access that accorded with expansive statements of quality and/or invocations of larger public benefits and purposes. Bellevue Community College's (COMB) contract spoke to the need for PD that addressed "ethnic awareness related activities." In Seattle Community College's (COMB) contract, the reference was to the local community's distinctive needs (though from a deficit model): "The Board and the AFT are dedicated to the ... improvement of a comprehensive community college. ... Essential to this end is the development of a competent, student-oriented, secure and dedicated faculty who are uniquely qualified to meet the challenge of the Seattle metropolitan area." In Massachusetts State College's (COMB) contract, PD was linked to changes in and responsiveness to the larger society (versus to the "challenge" of the metro area): "The purpose of the program of professional development shall comprise the following several ... goals through ... appropriate professional activities: 1. to improve teaching and student advising and to relate those to a changing curriculum that is itself responsive to the larger needs of society." In each case, what followed was a detailed set of PD programs.

Relatedly, Joliet Community College's (PTO) contract read, "The parties acknowledge the value of professional development of Adjunct Faculty in the pursuit of academic excellence, quality teaching and service to the students and the community." Morton College's (PTO) contract also had such phrasing, as did one other: "Peninsula College affirms the need for professional development of its academic employees as an important way of improving instruction, morale, and the effectiveness of the College as a whole in serving both students and community members" (Peninsula College, COMB).

Another step in addressing the public interest was evident at Henry Ford Community College. The PTO unit's contract had much provision for PD. It did not, but could ideally have included a provision that was in the FT unit's contract for a "Community Service Fund" to support part-time faculty's involvement in community organizations.

Discussion

Adjunct faculty's gains in access to instructional resources (44 percent of contracts) and PD (75 percent of contracts) were greater than what was found for class cancellation fees. Yet, there were real limits to these gains and room for expanded provision. The access to resources was more to facilities (e.g., offices) than to materials. And what we know is so important to individual faculty and collective programmatic quality, adjunct faculty's involvement in their departments' life and curricular deliberations, was largely absent. Moreover, although access to PD provisions was prevalent, the dominant model was access to competitive funds rather than per-faculty allocations. Nevertheless, impressively, 40 percent of the contracts had provisions that accorded adjunct faculty a role in deliberations about PD.

As for professorial stratification, there was ongoing differential access of adjunct faculty to instructional resources and PD compared to full-time faculty. Yet, the level of stratification was surprisingly limited—in resources being mostly to office space and in PD being in lesser types and amounts of allocations. Moreover, a notable number of contracts provided parity in prorated access to resources and to PD.

Although their success has been limited, in some contracts, adjunct faculty have negotiated explicit references to students and the public's benefits of their access to instructional resources and PD. Overwhelmingly, the references were to students and quality education, for instance, from an individualistic frame of improving pedagogy. But there were some references to external public beneficiaries, invoking institutions' responsibilities to local communities.

Key Takeaways

Returning to the chapter's epigram, "What have they [adjunct and contingent faculty] gained?" Beyond the considerable benefit of gaining respect and a sense of collective efficacy by being at the bargaining table, the first (and subsequent) contract gains in wages and benefits have been remarkable. Amid widespread institutional relative disinvestment in higher education's instructional function, contingent faculty have negotiated increased investment in the instructional workforce and work. Moreover, adjunct faculty have put pay parity on the bargaining table, demanding an equitable, not just a living wage, and in the process challenging and somewhat reducing professorial stratification.

Further, amid managerial discourse and practices that either ignore or define faculty as a problem and cost, contingent faculty have translated their mantra of faculty's working conditions being students' learning conditions into CBAs. They have negotiated class cancellation fees, greater job security, and access to instructional resources and professional development. Doing so has connected them to the interests of students and broader communities. It has also involved some additional reductions in professorial stratification.

Thus, contingent faculty have gained, relative to management and tenure-track faculty, increased visibility, support for, and investment in them, their work, and the educational mission. They have embedded bread and roses and a labor-based conception of quality into CBAs.

In some regards, the gains have been limited. But the fact that contingent faculty are at the bargaining table and are negotiating subsequent contracts affords them the opportunity to build on the foundation of their first contract gains. As articulated in an article that paraphrases and quotes Robin Sowards, a USW organizer, in commenting on contract gains in first contracts: "Such contracts are platforms on which to build. It's not reasonable to expect that all a union's problems would be solved in its first contract, . . . but this crop of [first] agreements 'represent strong steps in the right direction'" (Flaherty, 2016, "Big Gains for Adjuncts," para. 25).

In another sense, though, the (organizing and) negotiating gains represent a seismic shift in the higher education landscape. Adjunct faculty's claims and conceptions are not only on the map now publicly, they are on the bargaining table in negotiating a new academy. In those and larger negotiations, adjunct and contingent faculty have become central players in the academic labor movement (Rhoades, 2024), as has happened with precarious workers in the larger society and labor movement (Kalleberg, 2011; Milkman and Ott, 2014). Adjunct and contingent faculty have leveraged gains in new sectors (e.g., private universities) with service and industrial unions, which has stimulated more aggressive organizing within the three academic unions.

Impressively as well, adjunct faculty have realized contract gains in reducing intra-professorial stratification in their working conditions relative to full-time faculty. For example, in some cases, adjunct faculty have put significant pay parity language that forms a foundation for subsequent advances on the bargaining table and into the CBAs. In a handful of important cases, contingent faculty have negotiated job security language into CBAs. And, in far more, adjunct and contingent faculty have negotiated reduced professorial stratification in access to instructional resources and professional development. Some of that has come through the gains of PTO units organized largely by SEIU.[16] Yet, COMB units have provided the most prominent examples of contracts with pay parity and job security provisions and of significant expansion of professional development for adjunct faculty. One takeaway is that whatever the bargaining unit configurations, cooperation among part- and full-time faculty and bargaining units is key.[17]

Finally, contingent faculty's demands for and gains in both bread and roses and quality may optimally be framed in the context of the gendered and raced (and classed) academic workforce in which if one is a member of a marginalized community and a faculty member, one is most likely to have a contingent position. That adds important layers to the demands for respect. It would make sense for more contingent faculty to more publicly take another step in connecting their struggle for workplace equity and justice to larger social movements advancing social justice, as was highlighted in the previous chapter, in the words of an NYU contingent faculty member: "too many of us face unpredictable salaries that routinely shortchange women and people of color" (UAW, 2024, para. 2). As shall be seen in the next chapter, graduate and postdoc employee organizing and negotiating are making those justice-centered connections.

5

More than Would-Be Apprentices

• •

Graduate Student and Postdoc Employees Organizing and Negotiating amid New Forms of Contingency in an Aging, Changing Academy

I am a future contingent faculty member. (Marisa Allison, advanced doctoral student in Sociology and member of the New Faculty Majority, introducing herself at an academic conference in 2014)

I am a STEM scientist and have a wife and young kids, but I get no real health care and my salary is very low, less than a high school teacher. (Rutgers University international postdoc interviewed in 2011 in a membership drive, explaining why he would join the union)

CGE wins paid family leave, COLA, salary raise, expanded gender-neutral restrooms and locker rooms. (Coalition of Graduate Employees, 2019–2020 Bargaining Blog)

Salaries up by 34 percent making UC postdocs the highest paid of any public university. (United Autoworkers 5810 infographic, April 2018)

Adam Caparco, a UCSD postdoc in chemical engineering and union executive board member, said, "There is an extreme imbalance of power between postdocs and their supervisors, especially when a supervisor can exert control over a postdoc's visa status. And it's all too common for supervisors to exploit that power." (Flaherty, 2022, "Seeking Protections," para. 9)

"Why do teaching and research assistants want to unionize," a staff member of National Public Radio's *Marketplace* asked, and "What are they bargaining for?"[1] She was taping an interview on August 23, 2016, for a "Morning Report" on the day's ruling of the National Labor Relations Board (NLRB) that graduate student employees at Columbia University are employees with collective bargaining rights under the National Labor Relations Act (NLRA).

The questions are even more pertinent now than they were then, given the dramatic expansion of organizing in the 2020s (Herbert, Apkarian, & Van der Naald, 2023). Now, though, they would be supplemented by, "Why are so many bargaining units striking, given the explosion of strike activity among these workers?" (See Herbert et al., 2023, on increased strike activity.)

I responded to the questions about graduate assistants by also speaking about postdoctoral employees, for they, too, are experiencing new forms of contingency in the old (and aging) academy and are organizing. Both are more than would-be apprentices in having temporary employment and preparation leading to the master's job. Both see themselves not so much just as "professors-in-training" but also as precarious, exploited employees, an identity underlying their pursuit of unionization (Bauer, 2017).

At the core of my answer to the first question were the quotes in this chapter's epigrams. Unionizing graduate (and postdoc) employees see themselves as disrespected, highly qualified, low-wage employees with reduced paths to tenure-track faculty jobs. They are translating the conviction that they are employees as well as students and/or advanced trainees into demands around "bread and roses" issues that attach to both statuses (related to Rhoades & Rhoads's 2003 "bread and butter" and "professional," academic career issues). Both are demanding wages and benefits befitting the value of their work and their life circumstances. Both are demanding delineated work hours and employment periods that respect their rights as employees and as trainees needing to make progress in their careers. Both are demanding opportunities for mentoring and professional development. And both are articulating demands that navigate their dual dependency on their professors and/or principal investigators (PI) as well as on the hiring institution (and department).

Moreover, graduate and postdoc employees are articulating demands to respect their full humanity, reflecting larger social justice issues (see Herbert et al., 2023, p. 7). That has included demanding independent external arbitration in sexual misconduct and racial discrimination cases, as well as support around various marginalized identities (e.g., LGBTQ+ and international), reflecting the larger proportions of such members than among tenure-track faculty. In these respects, graduate and postdoc employees are leading the academic labor movement, intersecting workplace justice and social justice.

Graduate and postdoc employees are realizing major gains. Their demands and gains bear directly on this book's framing questions about the identities, issues, and ideologies that are expressed in academic employees' organizing and negotiating; the (im)balance of power between managerial discretion and employees' rights; the renegotiation of contingent academic employees' "jurisdictional" claims (i.e., a domain of work over which they have legal claims and rights—Abbott, 1988; Rhoades, 2017a, 2020) and professional stratification (here, vis-à-vis professors and/or principal investigators); and the incorporation of broader social movement and public interest issues into organizing and contract campaigns.

Graduate and postdoc employees are "organizing and negotiating new forms of contingency in an aging, changing academy" in two senses. First, the new contingency is more precarious and longer term than what existed previously. Second, the tenure-track workforce has aged (Flaherty, 2020, "The Aging Faculty"), and their share of the academic workforce has declined relative to contingent faculty. So, notwithstanding the eventual retirement of tenure-stream professors,[2] the prospects of tenure-track positions for new generations of prospective faculty have declined.[3] Graduate and postdoc employees have become less temporary, would-be apprentices on their way up the academic ladder than semi-permanent, low-wage employees mostly headed to contingent faculty, (additional) postdoc, or other employment positions.

As will be seen below, graduate and postdoc employees have different chronologies by time and place (and legal histories) of unionizing. Although university hiring practices can contribute to competition for work between them (and contingent faculty), there has been much commonality and solidarity among them in organizing and contract campaigns, and in strikes.[4] And for both, much of the organizing has been done by a non-academic union, the UAW. So, I consider them in this chapter together.

I turn now to a brief chronology and background of graduate employee organizing, to exploring the public discourse and debate about them and unionization, and to analyzing their collective bargaining agreements. Then, I do the same for postdocs.

Chronology and Background of Graduate Employee Unionizing in the 2000s: Workplace Pressures, Academic Restructuring, and Legal Shifts

Graduate employee unionizing dates back to the 1960s in public and the 1970s in private universities. The earliest effort to establish a stand-alone graduate employee bargaining unit was in 1964 at the University of California, Berkeley, where graduate teaching assistants struck in December and were then chartered as an AFT local, only to die out later (Cain, 2018).[5] At the University of Wisconsin, Madison, the Teaching Assistants Association formed in 1966 was voluntarily recognized by the university in 1969, and after a strike, the local's first contract was signed in 1970 (Cain, 2018). Yet, despite unionizing efforts in the 1970s, not until 2002 would the first graduate employee union contract be signed at a private university, NYU (Cain, 2018).[6]

Early graduate student unionizing efforts corresponded to increased workplace pressures on graduate teaching assistants, as enrollments doubled nationally in the 1960s (Snyder, 1993), including at Berkeley and the University of Wisconsin, Madison, where graduate assistants taught significant proportions of undergraduate classes. Subsequent related financial pressures in the 1970s and beyond led to a systemic decline in tenure-track faculty's share of the instructional workforce, with a corresponding increased share of contingent faculty positions, growing from less than one-quarter in the early 1970s to more than two-thirds by the 2010s (Finkelstein, Conley, & Schuster, 2016).

A graduate assistantship was no longer a relatively reliable step to a tenure-track position, even in STEM fields (Rhoades & Torres-Olave, 2015) and elite private universities. At the heart of graduate employee organizing, then, is that these assistants have come to see themselves as exploited employees pursuing an increasingly elusive tenure-track dream. Relatedly, as Herbert et al. (2023) have noted, "The upsurge in student worker unionization [and strikes] reflects a wider labor awakening [and support for unions] among younger workers" (p. 7).

Yet, there have been ongoing legal shifts at the federal level, affecting private universities (also, though less so at the state level, affecting public universities) regarding graduate assistants' statutory right to bargain collectively.[7] A 2000 unanimous NLRB ruling regarding NYU that supported graduate teaching assistants' statutory rights was reversed in 2004 in a three to two ruling along party lines, under a Republican administration, regarding Brown University, that "graduate assistants were primarily students, and therefore not statutory employees for the purposes of the NLRA" (Saltzman, 2006, p. 51). Those rights were restored in the 2016 Columbia University case, three to one along party lines (Flaherty, 2016, "NLRB: Graduate Students"). A post-2016 NLRB with a Republican majority sought to rescind that right, an attack that was aborted in 2021 under the subsequent Democrat-dominated NLRB.

Throughout, managerial resistance and graduate employee persistence played out. In reaction to the 2004 ruling, after years of resistance, NYU's administration signed a collective bargaining agreement with the Graduate Student Organizing Committee (GSOC-UAW). It then chose not to negotiate a subsequent CBA, leading to busting the union legally (Krause, Nolan, Palm, & Ross, 2008; Valentine, 2008). GSOC persisted. In the fall of 2013, NYU's administration agreed to recognize the union voluntarily.[8] After protracted bargaining and mediation, the first contract was signed in April 2015.

Subsequently, within three months after the 2016 Columbia University ruling of the NLRB, the political landscape shifted.[9] Faced with an NLRB whose new members would tip the majority to those hostile to defining graduate assistants as employees, private university graduate employees changed strategy.[10] Bringing a case to the NLRB would enable it to reverse the 2016 ruling. In a remarkable show of national coordination and discipline, graduate employee unionizing campaigns in private universities (e.g., the University of Chicago and Yale) chose not to seek recognition through the NLRB, shifting to organizing outside the NLRA, seeking voluntary recognition from administrations (Flaherty, 2018, "Realities of Trump-Era"; McFetridge, 2018).

Nevertheless, in September 2019, the NLRB announced a proposed rule change entitled, "Non-employee status of university and college students working in connection with their student studies" (Flaherty, 2019, "Ruling Out Grad Unions"). As Risa Lieberwitz, AAUP General Counsel, explained, the NLRB's step departed from the standard practice of rendering rulings in response to a case brought before it (Langin, 2019). There was no case before the NLRB, which simply restated the *Brown* ruling that graduate assistants are "primarily students."

Supporters of graduate employees mobilized to submit large numbers of public comments (which must be reviewed by the NLRB before it takes action). The comments totaled in the thousands (Burton, 2020). The hope was to stall the decision and/or provide a foundation for reversal.

Despite a hostile NLRB, four private universities (American, Brown, Georgetown, and Harvard) that had been fighting union campaigns decided amid the pandemic to voluntarily recognize graduate employee unions (Marcus, 2020). Perhaps the cumulative impact of graduate employees' public name and shame tactics (maybe especially effective in "blue" regional contexts) contributed to management's decisions.

With the November 2020 election came another shift federally (and now with the 2024 election, there will almost certainly be another shift). The first half hour of the new administration brought change, with the firing of the NLRB's general counsel, who had led the proposed rule change and whose anti-union record dated back to work with President Reagan to bust the air traffic controller union (Stern, 2021). President Biden also appointed Lauren McFarren (the lone dissenter on the proposed rule change) as NLRB chair. Two months later, the NLRB issued a public announcement that it was withdrawing the proposed rule change (Flaherty, 2021, "Green Light"; National Labor Relations Board, 2021). Chair McFerran tweeted, "The withdrawal of this proposed rule will ensure that student workers can continue to join together to pursue better wages and working conditions" (McFerran, 2021).

In the public sector, too, the long history and recent story of graduate employee unionizing has had some fluidity. For example, the oldest such union, the University of Wisconsin Madison's Teaching Assistants Association, did not seek recertification after Wisconsin's Act 10 in 2011 essentially outlawed public sector collective bargaining in universities. Relatedly, rulings in 2012 and 2014 by the Michigan Employment Relations Commission and a 2012 change to the state's Public Employment Relations Act signed by Republican Governor Rick Snyder barred graduate research assistants from unionizing because they are not "employees" (Gantert, 2014). Yet, in 2023, Democratic Governor Gretchen Whitmer signed a series of prolabor bills of the now-Democratic controlled state legislature to repeal Michigan's "right-to-work" laws of a decade earlier, including repealing the ban on graduate research assistants unionizing (Eggert, 2023).

Over time, the success of graduate employees in unionizing has been impressive. In the 2010s and 2020s, it has been unprecedented in several regards. The scale and sites of expansion represent dramatic shifts. The greatest growth of graduate employee unions since 2012 has been in the private sector, but there has been growth in the public sector too. From 2013 to 2019, over two-thirds (69 percent) of new bargaining units were in private institutions. Units in the private sector went from none to eleven. Units in the public sector went from twenty-three to twenty-eight (Herbert, Apkarian, & Van der Naald, 2020). Subsequent growth was even greater—with nineteen new graduate student worker units in 2022 and 2023 (Herbert et al., 2023).[11]

The shift in affiliates with whom graduate workers were organizing has been even more dramatic. The dominant player from 2013 to 2019 was UAW—such that one-quarter of all UAW members are now higher education employees (Herbert et al., 2020; Herbert et al., 2023).[12] In 2022 and 2023, UE (United Electrical, Radio, and Machine Workers of America) organized the most new units (seven). UAW and SEIU continued to organize new units. Only one academic union (AFT) was active in this worker realm.

Moreover, it is not just new organizing that has been dramatic. Strike activity has been at unparalleled levels for graduate employees since 2017 (Herbert et al., 2023).[13]

Public Discourse about Graduate Employees and Unionizing

At the core of the public discourse about graduate assistants is their identity (Rhoades & Rhoads, 2003). Are they cast primarily as students and "professors-in-training" (Bauer, 2017), or as employees? Also central are what issues are framed and how. And discourse centers on ideologies of processes by which issues should be resolved, which turns on how higher education institutions and society are characterized. In the ensuing pages, I briefly explore public discourse on these dimensions by the AAUP (in policy statements), management (in NLRB cases/actions), and graduate employees (in NLRB cases and actions and in union and contract campaigns).

AAUP Recommended Institutional Regulation #14

The AAUP has helped define much public discourse (and institutional practice) about faculty regarding academic freedom, shared governance, and tenure. Two mechanisms have been its policy statements and "Recommended Institutional Regulations" (RIRs—the basis for its institutional investigations). Although it has not been a player in organizing graduate employees, its public positions in the 2000s have supported graduate employee organizing, serving as a sort of marker of public support for these employees unionizing from an academic union whose General Secretary from 1994 to 2004 (Mary Burgan) was unsupportive of organizing graduate employees.

In 2000, the AAUP adopted a "Statement on Graduate Students," supporting, among other matters, their right to unionize (American Association of University Professors, 2001, p. 268). In 2004, in response to the NLRB *Brown* decision, the AAUP's Council adopted a "Resolution on Graduate Employee Organizing Rights," reasserting the position that graduate assistants should have the right to collective bargaining rights.

Yet, the AAUP's relevant RIR (#13) referenced "graduate student academic staff" and provided limited due process guidelines in four one-sentence bullets. In 2010, based on a Committee A Task Force report, those regulations were re-titled (RIR #14, Graduate Student Employees) and extended to eight detailed paragraphs of due process guidelines. One hotly contested issue even then was the term "employee" (versus graduate assistant), which would appear fourteen times in the new RIR, whereas before, it was absent.[14]

Amicus Brief of the Ivies Plus Two

The amicus briefs to the NLRB surrounding graduate assistant unionization offer a clear, consistent reading of public positions regarding their identity, professional and other issues in their working conditions, and ideological claims about universities and unions. On February 29, 2016, on behalf of the Trustees of Columbia University and seven other Ivy League universities plus MIT and

Stanford, Joseph W. Ambash (of Fisher & Phillips LLP) filed an amicus brief in Case 02-RC-143-012 regarding the Graduate Workers of Columbia.[15] A core theme was that graduate student assistantships are an "integral" part of their education, that they are first and foremost students: "Graduate assistants perform teaching and research as an integral part of their degree program" (National Association of Graduate Professionals, 2016, p. 8); "The roles [of student and employee] are inseparable parts of the educational experience" (p. 11). The word "employee" was only utilized when the brief argued against it (see p. 32).

Another theme and claim was that graduate students' work "is supervised by experienced faculty members" (p. 2). It is education, not employment, "typically conducted under the supervision of a faculty advisor" (p. 3). Assistantships were framed as part of a careful, professional socialization process, not as work.[16]

The brief further claimed that unionization adversely affects the academic mentoring relationship between graduate assistants and professors, invoking ideological claims about the special nature of higher education institutions. It supported this argument by underscoring that such employees at NYU can file grievances, claiming that this compromises the university's autonomy and academic freedom, ignoring the experience of these unions in public Ivies and alleging that elite private universities are totally different.

Graduate Workers of Columbia's Reply to Columbia's Brief

The Graduate Workers of Columbia's brief emphasized the reality that while these employees are admitted as students, the Human Resources office is involved in the formal selection process for them to be university employees. Moreover, the petitioners pointed out that contrary to the claim that graduate assistants are not apprentices, the students receive upon admission a communication from the university stating, "Your fellowship includes participation in your department's professional apprenticeship, which includes some teaching and research responsibilities" (Graduate Workers of Columbia, 2016, p. 6).

In response to the universities' claim that unionization would compromise faculty/student relationships, the petitioners emphasized that "The amicus briefs submitted by organizations that represent students and those speaking for faculty are uniformly supportive of the Petitioner's position" (p. 1). And they rejected the claim that graduate assistants in private universities are unlike those in publics, noting essential similarities between assistants at Columbia and those unionized assistants at SUNY.

Amicus Brief of the NAGPS

As the national body representing (at the time) over 144,000 graduate and professional student governments and advocating for them in dozens of member institutions, the National Association of Graduate-Professional Students filed an amicus brief in the *Columbia* case (NAGPS, 2016), opening with this: "We continue to hold the position that graduate students are employees . . . and deserve the right to collectively bargain. NAGPS disagrees with the claim asserted in *Brown* that collective bargaining would damage academic relationships and we argue that there is empirical evidence to contradict the majority opinion in that case" (p. 2). It cited three studies' findings that were contrary to Columbia's claims in its brief about the adverse effects of graduate employee unions (Julius and Gumport, 2003; Hewitt, 2000; Rogers, Eaton, & Voos, 2013). And it invoked feedback from its membership institutions and graduate students it had consulted at universities with graduate employee unions. "'[They] have repeatedly stated that unionization at their universities has not negatively impacted their academic relationships. . . . Unionized graduate students have not reported negative impact on their academic or professional lives'" (p. 4).

The NAGPS brief emphasized, like the common mantras of graduate employee unions' websites, that "[university name] works because we do." It detailed how graduate student employees are "fundamental to the ongoing functioning of the institution. Indeed, at several of our NAGPS member institutions, graduate students take on more than 30% of the teaching load" (p. 3).

Management Response to the NLRB Columbia Ruling

On the management side, when asked by *Politico* for a comment on the NLRB ruling on *Columbia*, three of the Ivies (and MIT) did not respond (Skelding, 2016), and institutional spokespersons of the others reiterated the brief's themes. More broadly, several universities put up or updated websites providing "information" about unionization that graduate employees found problematic and hostile (Flaherty, 2016, "Crop of 'Anti-Union'"): "'What's frustrating is . . . under the guise of making information available, what's actually being presented is a partisan argument against unionization,' Paul Katz, a PhD candidate at Columbia University, said about his institution's new website" (para. 2).

Perhaps unsurprisingly, there were similarities among such websites. Joseph Ambash suggested that such websites should be "standard operating procedure" (Flaherty, 2016, "For Your Anti-Union," Nothing New section, para. 11). And the slant that could be expected on those sites can be gleaned from the fact that Ambash's law firm marketed its expertise in "union avoidance." In the "Overview" section on the firm's website, Ambash was described as having expertise in "preventive labor relations."

As two scholars indicated in the early 2000s, management's strategy was very much like that of private sector companies: "By and large, the responses of American universities to organizing drives of graduate and research personnel, particularly where the full-time faculty are not organized (e.g., Yale), resemble companies fighting industrial unions" (Julius & Gumport, 2003, p. 199). The corporatization universities claimed was threatened by unionization then was enacted in the practices of these institutions as they fought graduate employee organizing.

The most common university response to graduate employee union campaigns has been to resist them in various ways, with various degrees of aggressiveness.

Whatever the specific tactic, the claims are generally that unionization threatens academe's collegial environment and special relations between graduate students and faculty.

Judging from the subsequent proliferation of graduate employee unions, the claims of university management about graduate assistants' identity and about unions' threat to the specialness of academic relationships do not seem to have been persuasive. In some cases, administrators' actions may have had the opposite effect. "'I never thought I was someone who would be organizing strikes,' said Noah Rauschkolb, a PhD candidate in mechanical engineering. 'The ways that the university has acted have made people who were originally suspicious about the union far more frustrated with the university'" (Moattar, 2018, From Striking to Bargaining section, para. 5). In the words of another doctoral student and union organizer, Kate McIntyre: "'They have a lot of money and they're able to afford slicker websites, but the fact is that they've consistently been losing the P.R. battle,' she said of the university. 'Every time the provost would send out an anti-union email, we would gain support. When they were arguing about whether we were workers, it was an argument that was so patently untrue'" (Moattar, 2018, From Striking to Bargaining section, para. 4).

ACE on 2019 NLRB Proposed Rule Change

In response to the NLRB's proposed rule change, the lead DuPont Circle umbrella association of management entities, the American Council on Education (ACE), filed a supportive comment. Trumpeting the NLRB's pretext that "uncertainty" surrounding the question due to partisan NLRB shifts was problematic, the ACE, without irony, and ignoring the longstanding reality of graduate employee unionization in elite public universities, called for a partisan reversal of NLRB rulings in 2000 and 2016, speaking of "long-established precedent" about graduate employees' identity in private universities. Speaking of "disruptions" stemming from unionization, the public comment then restated, without data, unionization's threat to academic relationships and encroachment on universities' autonomy (i.e., discretion).

ASHE on Proposed Rule Change

The Association for the Study of Higher Education (ASHE) is a professional association of scholars, scholar-practitioners, and graduate and professional students. The research conducted (and lived) by members includes the experience of graduate students, organizational and workforce restructuring, faculty-student relations, and graduate employee unionization. ASHE's public comment submitted to the NLRB (for which I was the lead author) drew on data and research to inform its position supporting graduate employees' rights under the NLRA to collectively bargain. It countered the unsubstantiated arguments made by managers and institutional associations.

On whether graduate assistants are employees, ASHE's public comment pointed to the official positions of multiple federal entities (Association for the Study of Higher Education, 2020). The IRS treats graduate assistants' wages as taxable income, with universities withholding those taxes (and, in several cases, making this point about graduate assistants' tax status on their websites). The Department of Labor classifies them as employees, as does the Department of Education in its National Center for Education Statistics, as well as in identifying graduate assistants as "mandatory reporters" as "responsible employees" under its Title IX statute (and universities generally require mandatory employee training of them accordingly).

ASHE's public comment also countered management's claims about graduate assistants' academic relationships with faculty and universities' academic autonomy being compromised by unionization. A survey of graduate students in eight public universities (four in which they were unionized) found that "Union-represented graduate student employees reported higher levels of personal and professional support" (Rogers et al., 2013, p. 487). Similarly, a study of faculty members' views at five universities with graduate employee unions found that professors did not believe collective bargaining had adversely affected their advising, mentoring, and academic relationships with students (Hewitt, 2000). Indeed, CBAs often have clauses like the following for Stony Brook's research assistants: "The parties understand and agree that the relationship between a Principal Investigator and a bargaining unit member is both academic and supervisory in nature. Academic issues are outside the scope of this agreement." Moreover, universities' autonomy over academic matters is not compromised by unions and arbitration procedures, which are process, not academic judgment focused.

Finally, ASHE's public comment challenged management's unsubstantiated assumption that faculty-graduate student relations are special and unproblematic. For example, it referenced consistent evidence of profoundly problematic sexual misconduct issues, which institutions have not effectively handled.

What Grad Employees Are Organizing/Bargaining For

Graduate employees have been quite consistent in what they are demanding in their organizing and contract campaigns. Here, I concentrate on private university settings because that is where most new organizing and first contract negotiating is taking place. But the issues crosscut private and public university settings and address not only bread and butter wages and benefits issues but also professional support, development, and workplace issues that have long been the focus of graduate employee organizing (see Rhoades & Rhoads, 2003).

An example of what graduate employees are bargaining for can be found in the first CBA at Brandeis University: "The three-year deal increases teaching assistants' per-course pay by up to 56 percent over the period of the contract.... [It] also guarantees graduate student workers access to the same on-campus professional development opportunities offered to faculty members [and] academic freedom.... Caps on workloads also are included.... Graduate students are now guaranteed access to teaching materials needed for a course.... The contract includes assurances of improved access to mental health care" (Flaherty, 2018, "A TA Union Contract," para. 6–9). As with adjunct faculty, graduate employees have adopted quality working conditions language. In the CBA, that involved ensuring access to class materials. And the union negotiated social justice issues, including independent arbitration for discrimination and harassment cases.

Among graduate employees, there have been consistent social justice demands on matters such as stronger provisions surrounding universities' (mis)handling of sexual misconduct (see Herbert et al., 2023). Such matters were at the center of the protracted, decade-plus mobilization (including three strikes, one for eight weeks) of the Student Workers of Columbia to win recognition and negotiate a first contract.[17] The demands were wide-ranging, from wages, a childcare credit, and partial dental coverage, to neutral arbitration in discrimination and harassment cases (Patel, Kanrar, & Yumeen, 2022).

In an op-ed in the *Columbia Daily Spectator* (Coatsworth, 2018), Columbia's provost restated concern that unionization might compromise student-faculty relations, claiming that. "The model in place today has succeeded in launching the careers of successive generations of scholars" (para. 7). That claim ignored graduate employees' vulnerability and the consistently weak response of many universities to discrimination and harassment claims, as the newly named Student Workers of Columbia indicated:

> Our careers often rely entirely on the goodwill of one or two faculty members who can offer us research and employment opportunities.... We cannot easily find a new workplace if one of our advisors acts inappropriately or is abusive to us. The immense power faculty holdover us makes it easy for professors to sexually harass us and aggressively bully or penalize student workers who come from marginalized groups.... In recent years, an instructor was sexually assaulted by a professor and the University failed to hold him accountable. Sadly, these events are not uncommon. That is why ... one of our priorities ... is "neutral third-party arbitration."

Such concerns have not been specific to Columbia (e.g., see Flaherty, 2018, "Brown Agrees," on the graduate employee union at Brown).

Another social justice area that graduate employees have foregrounded in organizing surrounds international students. Here, management discourse, particularly after the 2016 election, was telling. There were stark differences between university messaging about recruitment versus unionization, though both reflected academic capitalism in how student employees and prospective students are exploited for their cheap labor or monetized for their tuition revenue. But the messaging intersected differently with the heightened xenophobia of post-2016 times.[18]

Amid the Trump administration's discourse and actions regarding immigration and travel bans, university messaging to international graduate students was, in some cases, that unionization could lead to them losing their visas and being deported. As an article in *The Nation* framed it, "This University Suggested International Students Could Be Reported to ICE if They Unionized: And it's not the first to do so" (Bittle, 2017). One source for the claim was an FAQ site Washington University, St. Louis, posted in response to a graduate employee unionization campaign, with, as the article said, the not-so-veiled threat that "Washington University . . . would be legally bound to call ICE if international students went on strike" (para. 2). But that was not true. "While the university appeared to present a neutral account of the law, the response to the question is misleading. It's true that F-1 visa holders who cease to be students are no longer permitted to be in the country, but it's the university, not ICE, who decides when an international student is no longer a student. And for the university to revoke student status because of a strike or other action relating to unionization would be a clear violation of federal labor law" (para. 3).[19] The article then identified several other graduate student union campaigns in which similar misinformation was provided by universities. In recent years, that included Columbia, Northwestern, and Princeton.[20]

Such managerial misinformation/intimidation tactics have been used at public universities, too (Bittle, 2017). For example, in November 2014, at the University of Oregon, the Graduate Teaching Fellows Federation (2014) wrote to the law firm Harrang, Long, Gary, and Rudnick P.C. regarding the "University of Oregon Administration's Strike FAQ," demanding the university print a public retraction.[21] :The list of FAQs includes the following: 'Q 11. How does a strike affect international GTFs? International GTFs should be aware that their work visa status may be impacted depending on the duration of a strike.' International students . . . feel the University is threatening deportation should they engage in organizing, striking, and/or other union activities." (para. 2) Some public universities have used these tactics to fight organizing campaigns. At Penn State University, management invoked the same ICE quote as had been used at Wash U: "If the student has stopped taking courses or stopped performing research and that is what is required for their program, the student's record should be terminated immediately and they will have to leave the U.S." Management then indicated that "the union cannot protect their 'international graduate employees' immigration status" (Quilantan, 2018, para. 2). Neither statement was true.[22]

In some universities, such chilling messages about possible deportation have been utilized, apparently without any cognitive dissonance, alongside university recruiting messages to prospective international students that "#YouAreWelcome Here." The hashtag mantra was part of a national, post-2016 election campaign initiated at Temple University (2018) to encourage and support international student numbers, which are a major source of revenue.

For example, Penn State had a video as part of its recruiting campaign, in which the president, Eric J. Barron, spoke to the sense of "inclusivity" and "community," which extended to international students. An international student was featured saying, "We are all one big family." The video closed with the president stating, "We are Penn State, and #YouAreWelcomeHere." Apparently, that sentiment did not apply to international graduate students who might vote for a union (and might be on strike).

Similarly, the University of Oregon (2016) had a #YouAreWelcomeHere "Dear Ducks" video for international students in which President Michael Schill (really) stated, "Each one of you out there belongs in this university, and we care about you." Again, apparently, this did not apply to international students going on strike.

Finally, on international issues, in relation to the spring 2024 protests regarding the Middle East, some locals have denounced universities' (mis)handling of protestors. In late May 2024, UC student workers (with the postdoc union) staged a walkout at UC Santa Cruz to support protestors who had been arrested/disciplined (Quinn, 2024, "UC Academic Workers").

Now I turn to the contracts to see how graduate employees bargained these issues.

Graduate Employee Contracts

In examining the terms and conditions of graduate employee CBAs, I turn to two of the book's research questions about the (im)balance between managerial discretion and professional rights and the negotiation of broader social justice issues. The former is addressed by looking at "bread and butter" issues such as benefits (salaries have been straightforward and yielded impressive gains), workload, and health and safety, as well as "professional" issues such as professional development and academic freedom. The latter is addressed by looking at provisions on sexual harassment and other forms of discrimination against international students.

The national, searchable database HECAS that I have utilized for studying faculty contracts has few contracts for stand-alone graduate employee units. So, I have accessed twenty-five CBAs online, of which fifteen are in public and ten in private universities, reflecting the greater number of units with contracts in the former and the surge of organizing in the latter.[23]

Although disproportionately affiliated with UAW and UE, unions with "workers" in their names, and although a prevailing mantra of the graduate employee campaigns has been "the university works because we do," that terminology of "worker" is largely absent from the CBAs. The main exceptions are references to workers' compensation and to hourly student workers.[24]

Nevertheless, as shall be seen, workplace safety and workload provisions are omnipresent in the CBAs.

Benefits

Many of the benefits demands of graduate employee campaigns—for example, around mental health, parental/family leave, and childcare—reflect the changing workforce and changing expectations about respecting and addressing workers' full humanity and quality of life. They also reflect larger sociopolitical debates about societal and employer responsibilities to people as well as equity— for example, given the disproportionate share of caretaking responsibilities borne by women. Thus, they intersect traditional bread-and-butter demands for basic benefits with the progressive push to intersect workplace justice and social justice.

Mental health was explicitly addressed in roughly one-third of the CBAs, sometimes in establishing a working group or as an issue in labor and management meetings. Harvard's contract makes the connection to social justice with this phrasing: "The parties agree that workplace health and safety include concerns regarding mental health and may implicate racial justice issues."

More common were childcare provisions, found in sixteen contracts, often in a separate article. It typically took the form of subsidies or stipends, ranging in amount. Sometimes, it was complemented by a "Parental Relief Fund." Perhaps the strongest provision was in Massachusetts' CBA, which established a "Family Issues Committee" with equal labor and management representation and a specific amount to be allocated to the university's "Health and Welfare Fund" for employees' childcare support.

Most common were parental/family leave provisions, found in twenty of the contracts—in Oregon's case, it was a pilot program, reflecting the recency of the demand. The range of paid leave was wide (unpaid leave was for longer periods), with a low of one week. In most CBAs, the length was three or six weeks.

Safe Working Conditions

All but two of the graduate employee contracts had workplace health and safety language. The detail, and therefore management responsibilities and employees' rights, varied considerably. But all established that graduate employees had the right to a safe and healthy workplace.

In some cases, language consisted of but a sentence or two. For example, the University of California contract indicated that "the University shall make reasonable attempts to maintain in safe working condition the assigned workplace and equipment." Some others also made reference to "reasonable effort" but then added that at the request of an employee (Florida) or shop steward (New Mexico State), either the employer should respond or that (in the case of NYU) two representatives of the University and of the Union would meet to discuss health and safety matters. Still others, as with Temple University's contract, called for labor and management to "meet and discuss regularly" such matters. And some (e.g., Washington) established either that there would be such meetings twice a year, or (as at UIC and UIUC) ongoing labor and management committee discussions. The most detailed provisions of multiple sections and pages were in relatively recent contracts at three Ivies (Columbia, Harvard, and Yale). Finally, arguably the most powerful provision in affording graduate employees a voice in the safety of their workplace was in the University of Massachusetts' contract, which established a Joint Health and Safety Committee with two union and two administration representatives (the chairmanship alternating) to meet quarterly or more frequently.

Workloads

Given they are also students, graduate employees have campaigned to define their workloads and delimit departments/supervisors' discretion to demand work beyond that, so as to facilitate assistants' educational progress. All but three of the CBAs had such defined/delimited workloads. Almost all defined averages per week, explicitly referring to fluctuations in workweeks such that, as stated in the Michigan State contract, "over the course of the semester . . . the average number of hours worked per week . . . shall not unreasonably exceed the above." Many included phrasing about the assigned work not being more than could be "reasonably expected" to be done in the allotted time or for hours to be "reasonable."

A few contracts were more specific and, significantly, provided recourse beyond the student speaking to the department head or graduate college dean. Washington's contract specified that notwithstanding fluctuations in hours per workweek, they "shall not exceed thirty hours in a given week except by the [employee's] consent." Wayne State's provision, which was quite detailed on how workload is defined, went further, affording graduate employees the right to grieve excessive workload. The UIC contract did as well (notably, UIUC's did not)—noteworthy as well was this sentence in the grievance article, "An assistant who participates in the grievance procedure shall not be subject to discipline or reprisal because of such participation." That matters as the subject of the complaint or grievance can be a professor or supervisor. Graduate employees are negotiating their rights relative to management and to their faculty.[25]

Professional Development

Almost half (twelve) of the contracts had PD provisions. Almost none spoke to mentoring, though Clark's had an article on "professional feedback" with some detail on what that entailed). Several simply afforded access to graduate employees of existing campus PD services (e.g., that had been available only for faculty). A few spoke to PD/training for teaching. And a few spoke to support for professional travel (or, as at American, supporting PD expenses) with Massachusetts' contract creatively specifying that 2 percent of the total payroll for graduate employees would go to a professional growth fund (and much detail about its allocation).

More expansively and giving voice to employees, Brandeis's contract established a Professional Development Planning Committee, with five members each from the Union and management. Oregon's contract also established a committee but with less union representation.

Most powerfully, by way of giving employees a collective voice, Michigan State's contract allocated monies to the union "to operate a professional learning community which addresses issues concerning cultural sensitivity, race, privilege, and/or power imbalances that may arise in undergraduate instruction." Importantly, this provision placed control of PD (curriculum) with the employees collectively. Moreover, graduate employees rightly intersected "professional" issues with social justice considerations in relation to better serving students.

Academic Freedom

Although it is a core "professional" value in academe, only five of the twenty-five graduate employee contracts had language supporting teaching and research assistants' academic freedom. By contrast, seven (three in private universities) invoked "academic freedom" only in the contract's management rights clauses. UIC's contract reflected the extent of academic discretion that entailed, "The University and the Union agree that academic freedom is one of the values essential to higher education. It is further agreed ... that the University retains sole and exclusive control: (1) To make all academic judgments concerning ...; (2) To determine all academic policies." It is academic freedom in service of managerial discretion, not of employees' rights. An additional contract (Temple) stated that "TUGSA/AFT understands and agrees that academic matters are outside the scope of collective bargaining." Such language reflected management's position in its amicus briefs and (dis)information that graduate employee unions threaten universities' academic autonomy/freedom.

Of the five contracts supporting graduate employees' academic freedom, four (Florida, Michigan State, Rhode Island, and Massachusetts) spoke in language such as the "reasonable latitude" that graduate assistants have in "exercising their professional judgment." The strongest provision was in Brandeis's contract, which invoked academic freedom as being "essential to the public good and the mission of the University." It then detailed graduate assistants' "full freedom of scholarly and intellectual inquiry and expression" and to write/speak in public, just not as representing the university.

Sexual Misconduct and Discrimination

Social justice language and issues are present in almost all the contracts, from terminology to physical facilities to due process rights such as independent arbitration (the latter have been at the center of organizing and contract campaigns). In reference to LGBTQ+ identities, "gender expression" was part of the nondiscrimination clauses in eighteen of the contracts (disability is in virtually all of them). In seven of the contracts, there was a reference to or provision for gender-neutral bathrooms, and in six there were provisions about lactation facilities.

Over half the CBAs (fifteen) had independent arbitration for sexual harassment and for racial and other forms of discrimination. In some of those cases, previous contracts lacked such provision, speaking to the recent increased pressure for such recourse. A number of CBAs with provisions for internal due processes had extensive detail in those procedures, which in the negotiations have been management's offer.

A defining feature, then, of the surging graduate employee organizing and negotiating has been, as longtime labor activist/scholar Joe Berry has said to me, to push the academic labor movement to the left, to advance these more progressive demands to intersect workplace justice with broader social justice movements and demands.

International/Immigrant Students

Of the twenty-five graduate employee contracts, nineteen had language on international and/or immigrant students' issues. One indicator of these matters' increased prominence post-2016 and of graduate employee activism in these matters was more recent contracts adding relevant language. For example, whereas NYU's previous contract lacked language, the 2020–2026 contract established an "Accounting and Legal Assistance Fund" (for tax-related and legal expenses) from which international graduate employees can get reimbursed for tax-related and legal expenses. It also committed the university to three meetings a year with union representatives (and others) "to address improving the quality of the experience of international graduate employees" (other contracts also indicated the union would be part of a committee addressing international student issues).

Similarly, California's most recent contract had a provision about supporting DACA student employees if the policy was rescinded (USC's contract also had this language). Another eight contracts had provisions about DACA, with another three including "immigrant status" in their nondiscrimination clauses. Yale's contract had a provision for "Safety in the workplace for immigrant and international workers," which spoke to the university not providing "voluntary consent" to Immigration and Customs Enforcement (ICE), language found in a handful of other contracts. Georgetown's contract not only defined several ways in which it would act to protect immigrant students; it also referred to ongoing legal aid for undocumented students.

The most common language about international students concerned waiving/reimbursing fees, advising support, resources, and accommodating any difficulties that might emerge in the visa process (perhaps particularly in a hostile environment) by holding the appointment open (or deferring it), making exceptions to deadlines, or by providing leave for appointments. Some contracts set up funds for supporting international graduate employees: Brown's established a "Nonimmigrant Graduate Student Assistance Fund" of at least $30,000 for each fiscal year of the agreement (Harvard had a similar fund with the same amounts). Washington's contract established an "International Graduate Employee Accounting and Legal Assistance Fund," which had somewhat smaller annual allocations.

Finally, the Graduate Teaching Fellows Federation negotiated a provision in the University of Oregon's contract, a side letter on "Communication to international graduate employees," which read: "In the event of a legal strike by any employee group on campus, all communications to international graduate employees concerning the effect of participation in said legal strike on the GE's visa and/or residency status may only originate from the Office of International Affairs or Human Resources." That provision spoke directly to management's tactics toward international graduate employees discussed earlier in the chapter.

Now I turn to the background and chronology of postdoc unionizing, public discourse about postdocs, and postdocs' CBAs.

Chronology and Background of Postdoc Employee Unionizing in the 2000s: Academic Restructuring and Career Pressures

As with graduate assistants, postdoc employees' situation has also become increasingly precarious. At one time (as when I did my postdoc in the early 1980s), postdocs were an added step on an extended but predictable academic career ladder although even then postdocs faced a far tougher job market than previous generations (Zumeta, 1985). Now, as I said to the *Marketplace* staff member/reporter, "These would-be apprentices face even less promising prospects." They may end up doing one postdoc after another, in a "postdoc purgatory" of "perpetual postdocs" (Jaffe & Park, 2003; Woolston, 2002). The postdoc has become a holding position with diminishing prospects for tenure-track jobs.

Most postdocs are in STEM fields and are central players in universities' research production, being the principal predictors of grant productivity (Cantwell & Taylor, 2015). Having been encouraged to go into high-demand fields, they believed their academic prospects were high. But, as their numbers increased by 25 percent in the first decade of the 2000s, many ended up in "secondary labor market employment" with low wages, limited benefits, and no job security (Rhoades & Torres-Olave, 2015). Indeed, the opening line in a *Nature* article entitled "Give Postdocs a Career, Not Empty Promises" was, "The career structure for scientific research in universities is broken, particularly in the life sciences" (Rohn, 2011, para. 1) Similarly, tracing the growing gaps between annual PhDs and tenure-track positions, reveals that 70 percent of Life Sciences PhDs pursue postdocs, and only one-quarter are in tenure-stream positions within five years (Schillebeeckx, Maricque, & Lewis, 2013, p. 939).

Small wonder, then, that in the 2000s, postdocs started organizing. In 2002, the National Postdoctoral Association (n.d.) was established "with the goal of fostering necessary improvements to the postdoctoral situation in the United States" (History section, para. 1). Born from an April 2002 DC meeting of *Science*'s Next Wave Postdoc Network, it was an advocacy group focused on academic science and national science policy.

Several postdoc union campaigns also emerged. The first stand-alone union of postdocs was certified at the University of California in 2008 (the first contract was in 2010). That unit accounted for roughly 10 percent of all academic postdocs nationally. By early 2021, there were six stand-alone postdoc units, all but one of which were affiliated with the United Autoworkers (UAW), and five of which were in public universities—University of California (2008), Rutgers (2009), University of Massachusetts, Amherst (2010), University of Washington (2018), and University of Connecticut (2018) (Herbert et al., 2020, p. 20).[26] In 2023, postdocs at Mount Sinai signed their first contract.[27] In a little over a decade, the growth has been remarkable.

Public Discourse about Postdocs and Unionizing

Identity issues have been at the core of public discourse about and organizing by postdoc employees. Are they advanced trainees, apprenticing as "professors-in-training," or are they precarious and exploited employees (Bauer, 2017; Rhoades, 2024)? Also central are what issues are framed and how. And discourse centers on ideologies of processes by which issues should be resolved, which turns on how higher education institutions and society are characterized. In the ensuing pages, I briefly explore public discourse on these matters by key national entities, a national postdoc advocacy group (the National Postdoctoral Association), and local postdoc unions on their websites and in the collective bargaining agreements (CBAs) they have negotiated.

Let me start, though, with some framing quotes from postdoc employee leaders, which center disrespect of their professional status. "The [University of California's] chief negotiator didn't even know who postdocs were. She thought we were graduate students and . . . would refer to us as postdoctoral students" (Camacho & Rhoads, 2015, p. 313). As in the chapter's second epigram, about a postdoc referring to making less than a high school teacher, the status sensitivity is evident, speaking to postdocs' core identity as highly educated professionals.

Two additional quotes also center on status sensitivity and issues of vulnerability and dependence despite their advanced, professional standing.

> Compared to grad school, I felt like things were always much less clear, in terms of what rights we had." (Camacho & Rhoads, 2015, p. 308)
> I could not talk to my PI openly about what I thought. I tried to do experiments and tell him it's not going to work. I learned . . . that I have to do what he said. He told me, . . . "It's my money, I tell you what you should do[;] . . . if you do it on your own you should be a P.I. not a postdoc." (Camacho & Rhoads, 2015, p. 309–310)

Postdocs' professional expectations are not matched by their workplace experiences.

The two quotes again center postdocs' sense of the injustice about their power dependence, which clarifies a critique of the illegitimacy of established professional structures. As in the chapter's last epigram, postdocs perceive "an extreme imbalance of power between postdocs and their supervisors" (Flaherty, 2022, "Seeking Protections," para. 9). As one postdoc leader framed it, the relations are like in a business: "The PI told [the postdoc], 'I am the CEO of the lab, I am the boss, and everybody in the lab, from the technicians to the postdocs have to listen to me.' He viewed it like a business, a type of total control" (Camacho & Rhoads, 2015, p. 308).

For these postdocs, the path to changing the injustice came to be grounded not in working through traditional "professional" mechanisms, but through unionization.

National Entities' Reports

How are the identities, issues, and ideologies surrounding postdocs and improving their working conditions addressed in the reports of key national entities and agencies that shape public policy? I analyzed five reports from 1998 to 2014 from impactful national entities in national science policy.[28] Such public pronouncements offer insight into the public context and perception of these employees' working conditions, to be distinguished from supporting unionization.

Over two decades ago, an Association of American Universities (1998) report expressed concern that while postdocs were intended to be a period of further training for future academic scientists, they were becoming "an employment holding pattern" (p. 2). As the association of leading public and private research universities, it linked the health of academe's scientific enterprise to postdocs' working conditions and path into tenure-track positions in research universities. The AAU report attributed the problematic situation of postdocs serving in multiple, sequenced temporary positions to a "lack of central oversight" by universities in managing postdoc positions (p. 4). It recommended that universities establish policies and procedures to ensure that postdocs got proper mentoring, career development, and publication rights. It called for delimiting their appointment periods to two to three years in any one institution and for six years overall.

Similar concerns and recommendations were offered by the Committee on Science, Engineering, and Public Policy's (COSEPUP) 2000 report, *Enhancing the Postdoctoral Experience*. It spoke to the "perennial postdoc" problem (p. 91), suggesting a five-year limit for such positions in one or more institutions. Although it called for improved university policies, it also suggested, unironically, that postdocs should take "primary responsibility for the success of their experience" (p. 100).

A 2005 report by the National Research Council, *Bridges to Independence: Fostering the Independence of New Investigators*, also spoke to the time spent in such appointments. It called on the National Institutes of Health, as the major funder of academic postdocs to "enforce" a five-year limit in its funding.

In 2012, the National Institutes of Health (NIH) issued a report echoing the previous reports' concerns. It called for universities to require Individual Development Plans and for increased stipends for NIH postdoc awards (Kirschstein National Research Service Award). It also criticized the lack of professional development for postdocs in grant writing, lab management, and more.

The consensus in the policy discourse was reflected in the National Academies of Science report, *The Postdoctoral Experience Revisited* (National Academies of Sciences, Engineering, and Medicine, 2014). It recommended a five-year maximum for postdoc employment (to be succeeded by more permanent employment), echoed the call for increased minimum salaries, and specified the need for comprehensive benefits to include health, family and parental leave, and retirement.[29] And it called for more mentoring from PIs and from postdoc offices that universities should establish.

For all the concerns and the critique of established practices, none of the reports addressed social justice issues nor mentioned unionization.[30]

National Postdoctoral Association (NPA)

Not surprisingly, given its origins in a *Science*-sponsored DC meeting, the National Postdoctoral Association's (NPA) public discourse in many ways matched that of the national reports. The scholarly identity of postdocs was preeminent. Similarly, the NPA website and report addressed key bread-and-butter and professional issues featured in the national reports.

Yet, in contrast to the national reports, the NPA addressed social justice issues. And it was hostilely "neutral" regarding unionization.

The NPA's website made no reference to postdocs as employees (and it characterized their wages as "stipends, not salaries"). Rather, repeated references were to postdoctoral "scholars," defined as "an individual holding a doctoral degree who is engaged in a temporary period of mentored research and/or scholarly training" (para. 1).[31] That scholarly identity is grounded in an ideology of special, highly qualified, individual professionals.

That scholarly, science-centered, professional identity reflects the NPA Board of Directors, Committee Leaders, Officers, Advisory Council, and professional staff. None (as of May 2024) had past union experience or were affiliated with any union. Moreover, the short bios provided read like short bios for federal grant proposals, expressing a professional ideology of individuals' scientific/academic merit. So, it makes sense that the NPA adopted an advocacy approach to improving postdocs' working conditions, seeking to persuade federal policymakers and campus administrators with data and policy proposals they would adopt. From its founding, "The NPA sought to crystallize the diffuse postdoc debate and provide a focal point for achieving administrative and policy changes." Indeed, many of the NPA board and advisory council members have been/are campus directors of postdoctoral affairs.[32] The underlying ideology is that change comes through persuading campus managers.

The one NPA website reference to unions was buried, requiring multiple clicks. Clicking the "unionization" link led to a one-line sentence: "The NPA takes a neutral stance on the unionization of postdocs." But that is not so. The reader is led to a one-page document, "Overview of Postdoc Unionization" (2019), which reads like a management FAQ. One source was the National Right to Work Legal Defense Foundation, Inc., an anti-union group. Other bulleted points were generally often, or always, untrue: "Unions engage principally in collective bargaining and negotiated grievance procedures"; "Unions do not usually provide career development services or networking opportunities across a spectrum of organizations"; and "A significant portion of membership dues go to a union's strike fund."[33]

There was much overlap in the bread and butter and the professional working conditions issues identified by NPA as problematic and those identified in the national reports. But the NPA addressed social justice issues such as sexual harassment. The website's "advocacy" tab had resources on sexual harassment. It also provided links to NSF reports on sexual harassment and to criticism of the Trump administration's various Executive Orders about international travel and people.

Postdoc Union Websites (and Contracts)

Postdoc union campaigns and units have mostly not (with one exception) framed these employees on websites or in campaigns (or contracts) as "workers." For example, the first stand-alone local to be established was UAW Local 5810 (University of California), represented on its homepage as "the union of more than 6,500 postdoctoral scholars," a term that also appeared in its CBA. Rutgers' postdoc local's website referred to "Postdoctoral Associates" a term, along with "fellows" used in the CBA's "Recognition" clause. UAW Local 6950 (University of Connecticut) referred to "postdoctoral research associates."

The one exception proved the rule. The Columbia Postdoctoral Workers Union's name foregrounded the worker identity. Still, the subheading on the website was "a union for postdoctoral researchers," who in the CBA were defined as "research scientists."

However, postdocs' union campaigns/negotiations spoke to their workplace exploitation, vulnerability, and precarious employment. Those conditions were made worse and framed as particularly unjust given postdocs' professional qualifications.

Postdocs' professional identity played an important role in the issues foregrounded in their organizing and contract campaigns. Virtually all addressed professional issues of mentoring and career development. Thus, one set of bargaining demands for University of Washington postdocs was improved professional supports, rights, and opportunities: "We demand the right to be Principal Investigators on research grants, control over the dissemination of research products produced through our labor, provision of funds to cover the costs of work-related travel, access to free career services, and paid time off for job interviews.

Another set of demands focused on workload, such as affording postdocs time to advance their own work. So, too, the Columbia Postdoctoral Workers negotiated such issues in a "professional development" article that included provision for "Individual Development Plans" with the postdocs' supervisor, involving providing development opportunities and ongoing professional/career discussions.

Further, postdocs at Columbia, Washington, and virtually all the campaigns combined such professional demands with bread and butter demands around benefits and social justice matters, speaking to their full humanity. Here, as with graduate employees, postdoc unions are in the vanguard of the academic labor movement, intersecting workplace justice with social justice considerations that are amplified for members with marginalized identities.

As in the second epigram of the chapter, about some postdocs having caregiving responsibilities, a consistent demand of postdoc unions has been for family leave and child care. For example, the University of California postdocs negotiated for (and won) expanded or doubled (to eight weeks) of fully paid parental and family leave and an annual childcare subsidy (Campbell & Jacobson, 2023). Beyond that, postdocs at Mount Sinai negotiated the first-ever housing article, guaranteeing three years of subsidized housing for new postdocs.

On social justice issues, postdoc unions have consistently negotiated for redressing the visa burdens experienced by international postdocs (who, as the UC postdocs pointed out, constitute 65 percent of their members—Campbell & Jacobson, 2023), to address bullying and harassment, and for independent external arbitration in sexual harassment and racial discrimination cases.[34] In the words of the University of California postdocs, "We won historic protections from bullying and harassment, protections that for the first time address all forms of bullying and abusive conduct, a critical victory in a hierarchical workplace where workers' future prospects depend on supervisors' approval" (Campbell & Jacobson, 2023, para. 11). So, too, the Columbia postdocs engaged in advocacy on social justice issues. Thus, they posted an open letter to management with their bargaining demands and this preface:

> Even though at our first meeting we expressed that harassment and discrimination are real issues, and that current policies are insufficient, the administration disregarded our report and proposed that Postdocs . . . should be required to address sexual harassment, discrimination, and bullying through the university's existing procedures, without any option of taking such grievances to neutral arbitration. . . . We know that issues like bullying, sexual harassment, and various other forms of discrimination and harassment are widespread problems that we have experienced, or witness our colleagues experiencing, on a regular basis.

The letter invoked #MeToo and #MeTooSTEM lawsuits, outings of faculty predators, and other examples of how "existing processes have failed us."

Postdoc organizing has entailed a systemic critique of established professional and organizational structures, advancing an ideology that the path to change was through union organizing and negotiation. That was clear on the "About" page of the University of Washington postdoc union website, listing reasons provided by postdocs for why they had joined the local. As one said, "Only through legally-binding representation will we as postdocs be able to effect the necessary changes to improve the working conditions for ourselves, and future generations of postdocs." Similarly, in testimony on the homepage of the Sinai Postdoc Organizing Committee, one postdoc stated, "I believe unionizing is the best way to gain leverage in negotiations over our working conditions."

The Postdoc Contracts

In discussing the terms and conditions of employment negotiated in the country's seven CBAs for stand-alone postdoc units (which I have accessed online), I return to two of the book's research questions about the (im)balance between managerial discretion and employee rights and about the negotiation of broader social justice issues. The former is addressed by looking at "bread and butter" issues such as salaries and benefits, appointment, workload, and due process surrounding discipline and/or dismissal, as well as at "professional" issues such as mentoring and professional development, intellectual property, and academic freedom. The latter is addressed by looking at provisions on sexual harassment and other forms of discrimination and those addressing international students.

Salary

Postdoc locals have negotiated both salary floors and general raises. On the former, the NIH has established minimum stipend levels for Ruth L. Kirschstein awards. Two of the postdoc CBAs referred to that floor. Two established comparable floors without mentioning NIH. And three went far above that floor, setting minimums at $60,000, $66,737, and $72,500, respectively, the day before a strike at Columbia and after four- and two-week strikes at the University of California and Mount Sinai.

All the CBAs provided for general salary raises (and bonuses). In six of the contracts, that ran in the range of 2 to 3 percent guaranteed increases beyond substantially raised floors. The Columbia contract also provided lump sum bonuses. At the University of California, the combination of cost-of-living and experience increases was 7.5 percent.

Leaves/Benefits

All seven stand-alone postdoc units' CBAs had strengthened family and/or parental leave provisions, though there was variation in the details. All but one (Rutgers) provided for paid leave. Several provided not only for childbirth but also for adoption, though one (Columbia) included a condition of adoption of children six years or under. Most substantially increased leave times (e.g., they were doubled in the University of California's contract to eight weeks).

Years of Appointment and Workload

All seven of the postdoc units had provisions specifying one-year minimum appointments although the particulars varied slightly (Columbia's provision accorded management discretion with the clause "unless the University determines that circumstances require otherwise"). Emphasizing postdoc appointments' temporary nature, the CBAs also all identified maximum periods of appointment, again with some variation in the particulars. At Columbia and Mount Sinai, the maximum was three years versus five in others. In three cases, the maximum included previous postdoc appointments at other universities, though the University of California contract indicated that "under unusual circumstances the University may grant an exception to this limit, not to exceed a sixth year" (University of California).

Two other contracts gave more room for managerial (and PI) discretion with the wording "shall generally not exceed." Some CBAs provided for flexibility to the maximum if the postdoc desired it.

On workload, five of the seven CBAs explicitly referred to hours of work, with important particularities related both to the professional status of postdocs and to concerns about their exploitation. Thus, although the University of Connecticut's CBA identified forty hours as the "typical workload," it also indicated that postdocs were "exempt" employees who shall not receive overtime. By contrast, the other contracts that spoke to workload used the language of "at least 40 hours" per week, also indicating that as exempt employees, postdocs were not eligible for overtime pay. For example, "The workweek for full-time exempt appointees is normally at least 40 hours, with the emphasis placed on meeting the responsibilities assigned to the position, on making progress toward their professional goals, and on demonstrating their research and creative capabilities, rather than on working a specified number of hours" (University of California). Columbia University's CBA indicated that "required work schedules must be reasonable, and related to the research needs"—a sentence identical to that found in the CBAs of Mount Sinai, the University of California, and the University of Washington.

The contract language on workload holds two issues in tension. On the one hand, given their status (and identity) as professionals, according to the Department of Labor under the Fair Labor Standards Act, postdocs are exempt employees who are not eligible for overtime. At the same time, the specification in most CBAs of forty hours and that postdocs' workload be "reasonable and related to research needs" was consistent with concerns that they were being exploited to the detriment of their own careers.

Discipline/Dismissal

A key motivating issue in organizing postdocs has been their vulnerability, born of total dependence on principal investigators and lack of due process rights. The language about discipline and/or dismissal varied slightly across the CBAs, but all had provisions for postdocs to grieve the decision with arbitration, thereby delimiting managerial and PI discretion. Columbia's CBA had a special provision for international postdocs: "In cases of discharge where an international employee's current visa status may be affected, the Union and the University will use best efforts to expedite the grievance and arbitration process."

All but one CBA had "just cause" language in such matters (research misconduct followed a separate university process).[35] The importance of such language was evident in how postdoc locals featured these contractual gains. For example, the University of Massachusetts, Amherst, postdoc union website indicated that discipline and dismissal could only be for "just cause" and elaborated the due process procedures that surrounded that (so, too, with the postdoc union websites at Columbia and the University of Connecticut). The postdoc union's "contract improvement" webpage at the University of California indicated that prior to unionization, "Postdocs could be disciplined or dismissed arbitrarily, or 'at will.' UC could lay off Postdocs at any time and for no reason without notice or compensation." By contrast, the CBA stated, "UC must prove 'just cause' in order to discipline or dismiss Postdocs. Layoffs require very specific conditions and Postdocs must receive at least 30 days notice and pay before being laid off."

Mentoring and Professional Development

All but one of the CBAs embedded such language in contractual provisions, establishing this as a right of postdocs and a responsibility of the employing university, and PI provisions were similar and strong, giving postdocs' rights to regular mentoring and programs of professional development and career services. The University of California provision is instructive: "A Postdoctoral Scholar . . . is engaged in a temporary and defined period of mentored advanced training to enhance the professional skills and research independence needed to pursue his or her chosen career path." In other words, postdocs had the right to receive advanced training for their own careers, not simply be employees serving their employers' interests.

Most commonly, provisions called for postdocs to have the right to "Individual Development Plans" (IDPs). Terminology was consistent, but the process and level of mentoring varied. For example, the University of Massachusetts, Amherst, CBA held that all postdocs have IDPs, with details about meetings the first month and regular meetings, with Research Progress Reports at least annually. By contrast, under the University of Washington's CBA, the postdoc needed to initiate an IDP although the provision also indicated that there should be regular meetings and an annual review (the University of California CBA had similar language). Beyond that, contract language spoke to "basic mentorship obligations" in regard to postdocs.

Another common provision in five CBAs was for professional development. Sometimes (as at the University of Massachusetts, Amherst), that was largely for career services. In other contracts (University of Washington), contract language also indicated that "A reasonable portion of paid work time shall be allocated to professional development activities" (versus as before when it was at the discretion of the PI).[36]

Intellectual Property and Academic Freedom

On intellectual property, five postdoc CBAs had provisions on postdocs' claims to the property they created. In all but one case, it was a reference to university policy preceding unionization, with the caveat that management could revise the policy outside collective bargaining. The language in the University of Connecticut's article read, "The Union acknowledges that the University may revise, issue, and/or develop bylaws and policies respecting intellectual property at any time. Such policies and any changes shall apply to Postdocs, as employees." Much the same was true of the provisions in three other contracts. The strongest language was in the newest contract at Mount Sinai, which established postdocs' intellectual property rights and grievable protections against retaliation for pursuing or participating in complaints.

None of the CBAs referred to postdocs' academic freedom. That is remarkable, given postdocs' central involvement in producing important and sometimes highly contested knowledge.

Sexual Harassment/Misconduct, and Racial Discrimination

Postdoc locals have linked stronger systemic oppression protections against harassment and racial discrimination (and bullying generally) to established processes of grievance, calling for neutral, independent arbitration. That was one focal point of negotiations (and strikes), given the postdocs' sense that internal processes had failed and that such matters should be subject to independent external arbitration in a grievance process. After coming within a day of striking, Columbia's postdocs won with a contract that had stronger language on sexual harassment and discrimination, including the right to appeal a university decision to a neutral arbitrator.[37] The website of the University of Washington postdocs featured as a contract gain stronger language around discrimination and harassment, including grievance processes to facilitate such complaints. It also provided protections against retaliation for those who file complaints.[38] The University of Connecticut's contract also provided additional due process and protections for those filing discrimination and/or harassment complaints, including beyond existing university procedures, through grievance and arbitration. And the University of Massachusetts, Amherst contract also provided a grievance avenue to postdocs in cases of alleged discrimination or sexual harassment and elaborated institutional responsibilities, including training.

International Students and Visas

Each of the postdoc CBAs had language about international employees, and the websites of several featured this and other actions regarding international students and employees. Rutgers' CBA included greater assistance to help in navigating the nonimmigrant visa process and the immigration process for international postdocs. Columbia's CBA provided visa support and accommodation for working remotely if returning to the U.S. was delayed, as did the University of Connecticut, which had an "International Postdoc Rights" article to address the situation of postdocs whose return to the U.S. was delayed: "A Postdoc whose return to the U.S. is delayed by a U.S. government initiated background check or by the legal requirement that they return to their home country prior to readmission to the U.S. will at the discretion of the PI be placed on unpaid leave status for a period determined by the PI. . . . If the PI approves it, and if it is otherwise authorized by law, the Postdoc may be permitted to work remotely during some or all of this period." The University of Massachusetts, Amherst, CBA set up a visa reimbursement fund from which postdocs could receive up to $1,000, and it waived International Postdoc Office fees for processing paperwork. And the University of California and the University of Washington postdoc union CBAs established labor-management committees that would, in part, address international employee issues.

Key Takeaways

To summarize, graduate and postdoc employee locals have organized and struck at unprecedented levels. Their organizing and contract campaigns have been game-changing economically, professionally, and socially. As the PBS staff person asked me in the fall of 2016, "Why are they organizing?" The answer, in part, is for respect. More than that, these would-be apprentices have been negotiating new forms of contingency in an aging, changing academy. Again, as she asked, "What are they gaining?" The answer is quite a lot, in traditional bread and butter issues, in professional supports and rights, and in social justice matters. In the process, they re-energized an academic labor movement in which these employees have taken the lead.

Beyond extraordinary gains in salaries and benefits, graduate and postdoc locals have negotiated important gains that have shifted the (im)balance of power in the workplace by establishing terms (and periods) of employment and workload as well as due process rights that delimit managerial (and PI) discretion. They have negotiated substantial rights in professional (development) issues, advancing their jurisdictional claims and reducing professional stratification. And they have systematically successfully negotiated remarkable gains on a range of social justice issues.

The old academy's designation of graduate and postdoc employees as temporary trainees/apprentices who are supportively supervised in their (further) education belies the new contingent realities they experience in the academic workplace and marketplace. Graduate and postdoc employees are renegotiating hybrid identities. The former are rejecting universities' claim that their student status preempts/overrides their employee status. The latter are rejecting their status as indentured trainees/apprentices beholden to the principal investigators who hired them, claiming their status as independent employees to whom PIs and universities have obligations.

Reflecting their hybrid identities, graduate and postdoc employees have organized and negotiated around rights and jurisdictional claims that reflect traditional and professional unionism. Contract provisions spoke to wages and benefits and terms of employment. Yet, they also spoke to mentoring/training and career development.

Reflecting the times, graduate and postdoc employees have also centered social justice issues that play out in the workplace. Thus, they have successfully negotiated strengthened provisions surrounding discrimination, sexual harassment, and xenophobia. In the process, they have redefined bread-and-butter issues to include the intersection of workplace and social justice.

Further, as evidenced by the explosion of organizing and of strikes, graduate and postdoc employees have challenged the managerial ideology that academia is functioning well and can be improved through "professional" structures and practices. They have increasingly and expansively embraced a collective bargaining identity and an ideology that the path to systemic change requires collectively organizing, mobilizing, and re-negotiating a new academy.

The sustained resilience and ongoing mobilization of graduate and postdoc employees in their organizing and contract campaigns, which sometimes span not just years but decades, has been remarkable. Even more impressive is that these contingent academic employees have, like contingent faculty, moved to the center of the academic labor movement, reinvigorating it in articulating broader critiques of the academy, academic capitalism, and social injustices and in establishing unionization as the path to a better, more progressive academy.

Part 2

Faculty Negotiating Retrenchment and Technology amid Management's Austerity Agenda

●●●●●●●●●●●●●●●●●●●●●●

As a newly minted PhD in 1981 from a flagship public research university, I applied to over one hundred tenure-track faculty positions and ended up with a postdoc. It was a tough academic labor market in allegedly tight financial times. Denoted the decade of "reduction, reallocation, and retrenchment" (Mortimer & Tierney, 1979), the 1980s were filled with managerial claims of budget short-falls, the "imperative" to reallocate resources, and "required" faculty retrench-ment (layoffs). More faculty were being hired off the tenure track as managers pushed for greater faculty productivity, including through distance education.

Higher education has been characterized by these managerial discourses and practices in each subsequent decade of my academic career. Each has seen pro-gram reorganization and elimination. In each, academics have been retrenched even as growing numbers and proportions of precarious academic positions—part- and full-time faculty and postdocs—have been hired. And in each decade, managers have sung what two labor leaders/scholars called the "Austerity Blues" of fiscal stress (Fabricant & Brier, 2016). In this context, new technologies for delivering education have been promoted to reduce faculty labor costs and increase productivity.

It makes one wonder, particularly in that notwithstanding the ongoing refrains of managers and policymakers, most colleges and universities have not experienced financial exigency in any meaningful sense. That has held true even through a recession and a pandemic: most higher education institutions remain financially solid (except small private institutions—see Jaquette, 2013, and Lederman, 2018—and some regional public universities and community colleges). Indeed, Brint (2018) has detailed how American universities are "stronger than ever."

It is no wonder, then, that faculty have questioned the need for reduction, reallocation, and retrenchment in core academic programs and personnel (Newfield, 2008, 2016). It is no wonder that academic labor has questioned management's practices, priorities, and commitment to institutions' public purposes. And it is no wonder that faculty (and other academic employees) have been organizing after the 2008–2009 economic collapse and during and after the COVID-19 pandemic at unprecedented levels, around financial issues and institutional priorities.

Alongside an ongoing questioning by academic labor of management's austerity claims and priorities, there has been another pattern. Faculty's voice in institutional decision-making through shared governance structures at the institutional level has declined. As was evident in the research university faculty campaigns discussed in chapter 2, organizing faculty see unions as a mechanism for enhancing their voice and giving legal force to shared governance in the face of management running higher education more like a business than a not-for-profit entity.

The shared governance idea of faculty voice is articulated in the AAUP's 1966 "Statement on Government of Colleges and Universities" (though the term was absent in the statement). Two decades later, the AAUP issued a "Statement on Academic Government for Institutions Engaged in Collective Bargaining," which spoke to collective bargaining's role in strengthening shared governance (AAUP, 2015). On March 10, 2020, AAUP's then-president, Rudy Fichtenbaum, issued a "Statement on COVID-19 and the Faculty Role in Decision-Making" that reiterated those earlier statements (AAUP, 2020), emphasizing the importance of faculty having access to key financial information and defining their right to speak out about institutional matters as part of academic freedom.

So, too, in 1999, with increased technology-enhanced education, the AAUP issued a "Statement on Distance Education" (AAUP, 2006, pp. 211–213). It emphasized the significance of foregrounding educational purposes in utilizing new technologies, so they are not simply a means for increasing productivity and revenue. The statement also emphasized the primacy of faculty voice in distance education decision-making: "As with all other curricular matters, the faculty should have primary responsibility for determining the policies and practices of the institution in regard to distance education" (p. 212). The phrasing, as shall be seen in the analysis of collective bargaining agreements (CBAs), is that conventional academic processes apply to decision-making (e.g., course approval) regarding the new technologies.

The chapters in this section of the book then center on faculty and particularly on tenure-track faculty, although the stratification between them and contingent faculty is also considered. Two of the three chapters examine how faculty have organized amid, challenged, and negotiated three managerial practices surrounding claims of financial stress. The first concentrates on furloughs, in organizing and in the contracts. The second addresses financial exigency-based layoffs, and retrenchment for reasons other than financial exigency in collective bargaining agreements (CBAs). The third chapter examines the contractual negotiation of instructional technologies amid an austerity agenda.

Turning to these chapters, I note that four decades into my career, now as a full professor, still at a flagship university, I hear the ongoing austerity blues and experience the ongoing austerity measures from management. I have found myself being subjected to and organizing against such managerial practices—furloughs—as contingent faculty, staff, and graduate assistants were laid off or nonrenewed. And I have also been part of a faculty activist group (later to become a union) organizing against the university's acquisition of an online, for-profit "university," with no meaningful shared governance input, to generate new revenue.

6

Challenging Management's Austerity Practices

• •

Organizing amid and Negotiating Furloughs

This is a gift. This is perfect. (My comment to Howard Bunsis after the University of Illinois Senates Conference Executive issued a defense in 2010 of the system administration's furlough proposal)

#FirstandWorst, #WhyJustUA, #FirstandStillWorst (three hashtags used in twitter posts by members of the Coalition for Academic Justice UA [CAJUA], responding to the University of Arizona's imposition of furloughs in April 2020)

We all will share in this as a team and we all will sacrifice as a team, but in a manner that respects your work, your contributions and your compensation

> and benefits, to the highest extent possible. (University of Arizona President in email to UA employees about furlough/financial mitigation plan, April 17, 2020)

Management's arbitrary imposition of austerity practices can be a compelling catalyst for organizing campaigns and contract negotiation. That is particularly true when there are intersecting concerns about faculty voice and institutional trajectory. That was the case at UIC in 2010 and the University of Arizona (UA) in 2020.

Here, I bookend an analysis of collective bargaining agreements with explorations of organizing around furloughs at the University of Illinois, Chicago, in 2010 and the University of Arizona in 2020. The University of Illinois system's imposition of furloughs helped catalyze the successful unionizing campaign of tenure-stream and full-time, nontenure-stream faculty at UIC, as in the chapter's first epigram. A decade later, the imposition of extreme furloughs at the University of Arizona catalyzed the emergence of an activist coalition of faculty, staff, and graduate employees, whose messaging framed the furloughs as out of touch with the data and out of line with what peer institutions were doing (as in the second epigram). Four months to the day after the furlough announcement, United Campus Workers Arizona, Local 7065, of the Communications Workers of America (CWA) was chartered.

In both cases, voice and public purpose were front and center in the organizing, emblematic of patterns nationally in faculty mobilizing and negotiating. For example, a labor leader at Rutgers wrote of the 2023 strike there: "Why are academic workers striking? Simply put, they are fed up with the priorities of the corporate university that put profit ahead of the academic mission of research, teaching and service" (Kumar, 2023, para. 5) The union's website read, "Let's turn Rutgers' priorities right side up."

The two organizing campaigns I address here sought to counter growing privatization and to rebalance their universities' priorities. So, too, during my time at the AAUP, and subsequently in other organizing campaigns, organizing was catalyzed by and against managers' privatization discourses and practices. Similarly, at the center of contract campaigns and mobilizing existing bargaining units have been critiques of higher education's disinvestment in its academic employees and public purposes.

Also, faculty's organizing and negotiating has sought to counter corporatization, and to rebalance the centralization of power and resources in senior administration. In implementing austerity measures, the penchant of managers and their defenders is to invoke team and family metaphors. Yet, claims of "shared sacrifice" can ring hollow given such corporatization and the accompanying vast disparities between the salaries of senior administrators and those of most (academic) employees. For example, in response to the University of Arizona president's language (see the third epigram), a Latin American doctoral student said to me, "I don't think they understand that though we may be on the same stormy seas, they are in yachts and we are in rafts" (that they cut adrift).

In between considering the two organizing campaigns, I analyze the incidence and terms of furlough provisions in CBAs nationally. I concentrate on faculty voice in the decision-making (respect for employees) and consider whether and how provisions call for rebalancing the priorities and investments or cuts between academic and nonacademic units (respect for institutions' educational and public purposes).

First, though, I set the stage by exploring changing patterns in higher education of management, shared governance, and the role of unions.

Strategic Management, Shared Governance, and Unions

The emergence of an austerity agenda in the 1970s and 1980s corresponded with the ascension of "academic capitalism" (Slaughter & Rhoades, 2004), and of more centralized strategic management to steer institutions through allegedly tight financial times. That involved restructuring academic employment and eroding faculty voice in governance, with increased numbers/proportions of nontenure-track (part- and full-time) faculty being hired relative to tenure-stream faculty. It also involved growing numbers/proportions of nonacademic support professionals and administrators, expanding managerial capacity and control of increasingly "managed professionals" (Rhoades, 1998a, 1998b). To trace these patterns, I review the empirical literature on centralized strategic management, national organizations' policy statements on shared governance, and academic literature on unions and governance.

Centralized Strategic Management

Each decade since Mortimer and Tierney's (1979) volume has seen defining studies speaking to a shift to the managerial center in institutional strategic decision making. In the 1980s, Keller's (1983) *Academic Strategy: The Management Revolution in American Higher Education* noted declining enrollments, increasing costs, greater competition, and rapid change, and chided higher education for resisting "modern management." Keller called for active strategic decision-making, providing guiding principles and cases. For him, the problem was faculty and old forms of academic governance that were an obstacle and in decline—here, he quoted two scholars: "Faculty senates, for the most part, are gradually withering away, leaving only an empty forum for the speeches of academic politicians. The real effectiveness of faculty senates seems to be at an all-time low" (Rourke & Brooks, 1966, p. 128). The solution was active, "enlightened academic management."

A decade later, Schuster, Smith, Corak, and Yamada (1994) offered an amended take on "strategic governance." Having searched for examples of Keller's "Joint Big Decisions Committees" (JBDC) to study, they found none. So, they did case studies of "Strategic Planning Councils" (SPC). Whereas Keller's JBDCs were small groups of central managers and senior faculty selected by the president, operating outside established governance structures, Schuster et al.'s SPCs were part of those structures. Still, they were small groups of central managers and senior faculty (who were disproportionately White men).

Relatedly, Clark (1998) wrote about "entrepreneurial universities" in a European context. Detailing "organizational pathways of transformation" that emerged from his case studies, one key was a "strategic steering core" of central administrators and senior faculty that operated through "collegial entrepreneurialism" (Clark, 2000).

Although Slaughter and Leslie (1997) also wrote of "entrepreneurial universities," they problematized "academic capitalism's" shifting funding streams and priorities that moved universities away from supporting educational functions. Later, Slaughter and Rhoades (2004) retheorized academic capitalism's ascendant market logics that entail increasingly centralized strategic management and corporatization within. Justified by an austerity discourse, power was being concentrated in central administration's "extended managerial capacity" (Slaughter and Rhoades, 2004, p. 25) as in the private economy's "revenge of the managers" (Goldstein, 2014), with "mean" (p. 269) practices (e.g., layoffs, reduced job security, and de-unionization) toward production workers to reduce their labor costs.

Throughout the 2000s, scholars have traced the increased intersection of colleges and universities with private markets in ways that reduce faculty voice (Brint, 2018; Geiger, 2004; Newfield, 2003).[1] That has been especially evident in elite public and private universities (Barringer, Taylor, & Slaughter, 2019). And that has been one of the drivers of and themes in the organizing and contract campaigns of academic employees.

University managers have spoken of the need for strategic management, for moving beyond entrenched structures of shared governance. Thus, Michael Crow and William B. Debars of Arizona State University wrote of "designing" the "new American University" (2015). And a former University of Michigan president has several post-presidential books on the imperative of change—most tellingly, *A View from the Helm* (Duderstadt, 2007), discussing how presidents can steer the university in the new century. As Gumport (2002) has written of this managerial model, "The major responsibility for managers is to read the market . . . and attempt to reposition accordingly" (p. 55).

Much empirical work also speaks to challenges that "require" changes in shared governance. For instance, Tierney and Lechuga (2004) started with the assumption that the challenges confronting colleges and universities required changes in shared governance. Reporting the results of a national survey of provosts and faculty senate leaders in four-year institutions, Tierney and Minor (2003) noted the ongoing importance and yet growing critique of shared governance structures as ill-adapted to responding to pressing fiscal and strategic demands. Especially valuable for my analysis was the finding that respondents did not report that faculty had a formal say in strategic planning.

The most authoritative piece of empirical research on shared governance (Gerber, 2014) traced the power and fate of shared governance over time. The title conveys the message—*The Rise and Decline of Faculty Governance*. Some of that erosion is traceable to the academic workforce's reconfiguration, with the rise of nontenure-track faculty who have little to no job security, protections of academic freedom in speaking out about institutional matters, and little role in shared governance. Much of the erosion was also attributed to the rising utilization of business managerial practices and the growing embeddedness of corporate logic in strategic decision-making.

Whatever the causes of the erosion of tenure-stream faculty's voice in and through shared governance, that sense of lost respect for faculty's voice is at the heart of tenure-track faculty organizing campaigns and of many contract negotiations.

Policy Statements on Shared Governance

Discussions of higher education governance are generally framed by some version of "shared governance," a concept historically defined/advanced by the AAUP. Thus, I partially frame this chapter with the 1966 AAUP "Statement on Government of Colleges and Universities," which set forth the concept—though without actually using the term (AAUP, 2015). Notably, the Association of Governing Boards of Universities and Colleges (AGB), a management association that had "commended" (Association of Governing Boards of Universities and Colleges, 1998, p. 2) the AAUP's 1966 statement, has also issued subsequent statements/publications that I review, which point to changing times as a rationale for increased central, strategic management (AGB, 1998, 2014, 2017a). If AGB continues to invoke shared governance's value (AGB, 2017b), it also emphasizes boards and presidents' primary strategic, financial, and fiduciary roles.

Although there are varied interpretations of what it means, and although it has eroded, shared governance carries ongoing currency. It is a common touchstone and leverage point for faculty/management negotiations over participation in decision-making. It has carried an outsized discursive weight in the ongoing negotiation of the balance of power between management and academic labor, much the way the AAUP's classic 1940 statement on academic freedom and tenure has done. Indeed, academic freedom, tenure, and shared governance are a tripartite foundation of tenure-track faculty's working conditions. If AAUP's statements lack legal weight, they have been important in negotiating CBA language (which does carry legal weight) on retrenchment.

The AAUP's classic statement on college government accorded different roles for different parties. In academic matters, "The faculty has primary responsibility for such fundamental areas as curriculum, subject matter and methods of instruction, research, faculty status, and those aspects of student life which relate to the educational process. On these matters the power of review or final decision lodged in the governing board or delegated by it to the president should be exercised adversely only in exceptional circumstances" (AAUP, 2015, p. 120). The statement also identified special roles for boards and presidents regarding strategic decisions, but it emphasized the importance of faculty involvement here too. Notably, it neither questioned whether final authority rested with management nor separated out decision-making realms in which faculty were not involved. It called for meaningful faculty involvement in all realms.

Over the years, AGB has issued several statements and papers on (shared) governance, continuing to express the enduring significance of the concept even as it takes a different stance on the particulars. AGB (1998) has distinguished between academic and institutional governance. As with the academic literature, AGB invoked changes that require more active and timely decision-making in downsizing, program reorganization, and reallocation of resources to respond to student and market changes than "cumbersome" (p. 3) internal processes allow. Moreover, while invoking the value of shared governance, a 2017 statement restricted a meaningful faculty role to matters of educational design and delivery (2017b, p. 1).

Further, AGB statements spoke to the importance of constituencies other than tenure-track faculty. For example, its 2010 "Statement on Board Responsibility for Institutional Governance" indicated that, "The meaningful involvement of faculty and other campus constituencies in deliberations contributes to effective institutional governance," even as it called for more active and greater presidential and board strategic leadership (p. 4). AAUP policy staff saw this as quite problematic, for it decentered the special role of "the faculty," by which was meant tenured faculty.

My sense then (like now) was that the voice and governance role of academics is more important than ever. But, I also felt shared governance needed to be "invigorated." A similar such view/call can be found in the AGB's work, including that of its 2014 National Commission, of which I was a member.[2] Too often a site of "shared pain" and "shared frustration," academic senates and shared governance needed "reinvigoration."

I agree(d). That is what I have heard as general secretary and subsequently, from faculty groups nationwide. It's what I have heard from other academic employees. It's what I hear now as a member of United Campus Workers, Arizona. It is at the center of organizing campaigns—academic employees demanding respect (and legal standing) for their collective voices.[3]

Part of the challenge and opportunity is to leverage that shared governance concept, a term of art for tenure-track faculty, into one that advances the collective voice of all employees in shaping their workplaces and their institutions' trajectory. A first step, as the AGB's National Commission articulated, was including contingent faculty. "At most institutions, the right to participate in faculty shared governance is confined to those on the tenure track, who now make up less than 25 percent of the American faculty" (AGB, 2014, p. 12). Also excluded are other academic employees as well as support staff. Moreover, more than representation by employment status, it is fundamentally important, by way of reinvigorating and extending shared governance's franchise, to address the demographic diversity of who is included in shared governance. Currently, enfranchisement in shared governance is disproportionately of White, male, tenured faculty (see the last epigram of the next chapter) to the exclusion of marginalized populations.

Unions and Shared Governance

From the inception of faculty unionization, scholars, observers, and managers have claimed that it threatened collegial shared governance. Management has continued to articulate and expand that claim amid campaigns, that unionization threatens collegial shared governance, and more broadly, collegial relations. Although there is not enough study of unionization and shared governance (Cain, 2020; Wickens, 2008), the empirical literature contradicts the claim. Indeed, it is employees' concerns about the lack of shared governance that have "fostered organizing efforts" (Cain, 2020, p. 75).

The classic work on this issue found there was an "unexpected peaceful coexistence" of faculty senates (a traditional form of collegial decision-making) and unions (Kemerer & Baldridge, 1981).[4] These same scholars' national survey of presidents and union leaders in all 240 unionized institutions at the time, and of presidents and faculty senate leaders in a sample of nonunionized institutions found that unions do not adversely affect faculty involvement in decision-making, and that unionized faculties are better off (Kemerer & Baldridge, 1975). Indeed, "Presidents on unionized campuses sense that they have lost power to faculty as a direct consequence of faculty unions" (p. 51). That is partly why management so consistently resists unionization—it reduces their discretion. And that is why faculty were and are unionizing: "One of the primary causes of faculty unionization as revealed in our 1974 research is the desire of faculty members to secure greater influence over governance" (Kemerer & Baldridge (1981, p. 262). Further, whereas faculty have organized partly because of the ineffectiveness of senates alone to ensure faculty voice, unions have enhanced senates' influence: "Despite prophecies to the contrary . . . senate influence over academic issues and union influence over economic matters are greater now than five years ago on campuses where the two have co-existed through the negotiation of several contracts" (Kemerer & Baldridge, 1981, p. 263).

Notably, given my focus on who shares in governance, the authors suggested that unions will "realign" the balance of power on campus, including within the professoriate: "Traditionally, senior professors and administrators have dominated the decision-making practices of most colleges and universities. Faculty collective bargaining will seriously challenge that pattern of governance, because junior faculty and part-time faculty choose unions to make their voices heard" (Kemerer & Baldridge, 1975, p. 62). Organizing, then, is about shifting (and democratizing) balances of power not just between faculty and management, but also within the professoriate.

More recent work further suggests that with faculty unions can come cooperative decision-making. A historical case study of a large, urban community college found that despite varying types and levels of conflict between faculty unions and management, the differences were "reconcilable," and several factors "tend to mitigate conflict and allow for collegial decision-making" (Hartley, 2010, p. 318). Among those were personal ties between the central administration and union members, open sharing of data, establishing common facts, and focusing on solutions.

Contrary to the claims of many academic managers about the "special" and "collegial" culture and practices of the academy being threatened by unionization, it is the lack of input into decision-making that has long driven unionization. Early faculty unionization was particularly prominent in less prestigious institutional sectors where faculty had little say in governance matters. Thus, the growth of new bargaining units was far greater in community colleges than in four-year institutions (Herbert et al., 2020). So, unionization has established structures and mechanisms for a more effectual tenure-stream faculty voice where it was limited before (Garbarino, 1975).

Surveys of faculty in the 1970s about governance also underscore the point. Responses emphasizing the need for faculty voice were associated with support for faculty unionization and were more prevalent in less prestigious sectors of higher education (Ladd & Lipset, 1973). So, too, with another national study of "faculty discontent" with their limited role in governance finding that it contributed to unionization (Garbarino, Feller, & Finkin, 1977).

Governance was similarly a driving issue found in case studies of unionizing faculty in four-year institutions in the 1990s (Arnold, 2000), and of a faculty union in a community college (Hartley, 2010). So, too, research in the 2000s revealed the importance of faculty unions in strengthening shared governance. Drawing on Kaplan's (2004) national survey of presidents and faculty senate leaders in four-year institutions, Stephen R. Porter (2013) measured the existence of shared governance and estimated the causal effect of unionization on faculty's role in decision-making in fifteen areas. He concluded that "unionization greatly increases faculty influence over institutional decision-making" (p. 1192). That included decision-making in strategic and financial areas where, though faculty voice was relatively weak, "unionized faculty have significantly more influence than non-unionized faculty" (p. 1202).

Far less explored in the literature has been what segments of the academic workforce are included in governance. Some research has addressed contingent faculty involvement. Kezar and Sam (2013) analyzed contingent faculty's role in "institutionalizing equitable policies." Other scholars have spoken to contingent faculty working through collective bargaining to gain some governance role at the department level, but only minimally in senates (Klainot-Hess, 2022; Tolley, 2018). Still, other work by union activists has considered contingent faculty's role in internal union governance, which can translate into proposals at the bargaining table. Thus, Geron and Reevy (2018) explored the rising role of lecturers in governance in the California Faculty Association, as did Hoffman & Hess (2014; see also Berry & Worthen, 2021). So, too, Negri (2018; see also Berry & Worthen, 2021) traced governance issues within the Professional Staff Congress at CUNY, between tenure-stream, full-time, nontenure-track, and part-time/adjunct faculty (as well as "higher education professionals" and graduate assistants). In both cases, ongoing internal union negotiations have contributed to those respective unions being at the forefront of advancing adjunct and contingent faculty rights in contract language.

Even less consideration has been given in the literature to embodied patterns of faculty involvement in governance, whether by field of work, generational status, or faculty's gender and ethnic identity. Kezar and Sam (2013) spoke to departmental variation in working conditions of contingent faculty, including in the implementation of contractual provisions regarding their involvement in governance, Though he does not explore the issue, Hartley (2010) noted generational differences between the "old guard" and newcomers in their views about the union, administration, and governance. Davenport (2018) has discussed shared governance (and organizing) in HBCUs, thus attending to race. Yet, we largely lack an empirical understanding of how governance and representation are raced and gendered. An important exception is Rhoades, Canton, and Toombs's case analysis (2023) of race and internal union governance over time.

The empirical findings of unions' positive effects on faculty's governance role are consistent with the AAUP's position (and that of other academic unions), articulated in two key statements, a "Statement on Collective Bargaining" in 1973 (revised in 1984 and 1993), and a 1988 statement that indicates, "As the Association's *Statement on Collective Bargaining* asserts, 'collective bargaining can be used to increase the effectiveness of [institutions of faculty governance] by extending their areas of competence, defining their authority, and strengthening their voice in areas of shared authority and responsibility'" (AAUP, 2015, p. 325). Relatedly, a former AAUP Director of organizing has written of "Protecting Shared Governance through Collective Bargaining" (Mauer, 2016).

Nevertheless, although there can be synergies between collective bargaining and shared governance, there can also be tensions between the strategies operationalized in collective bargaining as they relate to shared governance in retrenchment. Cain (2020) reviewed some of these cases. One of them played out in a retrenchment of sixty-two tenure stream and 104 nontenure-eligible faculty. The action led to a "censure" of SUNY by the AAUP, which criticized it for neither properly consulting the faculty senate nor providing appropriate hearings and notice, as called for in the Board's policies (and in the AAUP's Recommended Institutional Regulations). In response, the administration said it had followed Article 35 of the CBA, which did not call for such consultation with the senate.[5] As shall be seen in the subsequent chapter, most CBAs have far more contract language on due process regarding impact and implementation than on involvement in decisions about whether to retrench faculty.

Summary

Over time, higher education has experienced more centralized managerial power. Faculty voice has eroded. That is connected to the surge of faculty unionization in the 2000s, particularly in universities.

As reviewed in chapter 2, part of the resurgence, centering faculty voice, was the establishment of new bargaining units in major public research universities. At the University of Illinois, Chicago (UIC), a key catalyst was the university system's implementation of furloughs, a case I now detail.

The Case of Furloughs: Organizing UIC

Imposition of Furloughs—Action and Response

"This is a gift. This is perfect." I emailed this February 11, 2010, to Howard Bunsis, then Chair of the AAUP's Collective Bargaining Congress (CBC). It was the early days of a joint AAUP/AFT/IFT union campaign at the University of Illinois, Chicago (UIC), to organize tenure-stream and full-time nontenure-track faculty. Bunsis (2010) had done an analysis of the University of Illinois system's finances. An Eastern Michigan University accounting professor, he had done many such reports. Bunsis's analysis disputed the system president's claims that the state's "escalating financial crisis . . . require[d]" the UI to "furlough" faculty and staff at the system's three universities (UIC, University of Illinois, Springfield, and the University of Illinois, Urbana-Champaign) for four days (Smile Politely, 2010).[6] It was not a reduction in positions (retrenchment), but a "temporary leave of absence without pay" of roughly 2 percent.[7]

Although the subject line of management's memo and news release was, "U of I to furlough 11,000 employees, freeze hiring to stem cash crisis," the memo's verbiage was about a more general "financial crisis." By contrast, Bunsis' analysis demonstrated that the university was in solid financial health. The immediate cash flow challenge resulting from (in the words of management's memo) "unpaid state appropriations" (committed monies that were being held back) was temporary and could be remedied in less dramatic ways than furloughs.[8]

Around that time, amid the recession, the management strategy of furloughing staff was sweeping the country. The previous year, the AAUP president and I had sent out a member newsletter (March 24, 2009) entitled, "Furloughs—NOT the Simple Solution." It opened with the paragraph: "It is still early days for fully evaluating higher education's response to the worldwide recession, but a number of institutions are exploring unpaid furloughs as a short-term solution. In some cases, administrations seem to be using the external economic crisis to justify extraordinary internal measures without sufficiently consulting with faculty, providing them with adequate information about the financial condition of the institution, or taking into account alternative measures for addressing whatever financial challenges the institution faces."

The newsletter urged AAUP advocacy chapters and bargaining units to negotiate with administrations in examining institutional budgets to explore alternative sources of revenue reduction, including, as a last resort, deferred compensation. Two key points were that such decisions should not be unilateral (faculty voice) and that decisions should prioritize protecting academic programs and personnel (institutional priorities). Shared governance was being violated under cover of a financial crisis. And the longstanding disinvestment in educational personnel and mission was being amplified.

Five months later, I worked with the CBC Executive Committee to issue a resolution (August 18, 2009) that was circulated to AAUP bargaining units and state conference members entitled, "Turn It Around, Don't Give It Away." The framing was about reordering institutional priorities.

Recent decades have witnessed: (a) a systematic shift of institutional monies from educational to administrative expenditures; (b) a disjuncture between rapidly rising tuition versus overused and underpaid contingent faculty and graduate student employees; (c) a growing gap between rising numbers of Full Time Equivalent students and the numbers of tenure-track faculty; and (d) a growing gap between faculty/academic professional and senior administrative salaries. Each of these patterns work to the detriment of educational quality, institutional effectiveness, student access and success, and broad social benefit.

The resolution stated faculty "should not give their pay away in temporary measures that do not structurally readjust higher education's direction." Rather, they should gain access to institutional financial data, exercise a fuller academic voice, and propose measures to reverse long-standing trends by reinvesting in core academic missions and personnel.

Just two months into the UIC campaign, on January 19, 2010, two weeks after management issued its furlough memo, I sent out an email to UIC faculty entitled, "The Failure of Furloughs: Better Alternatives."[9] I gave examples of bargaining units that had successfully fought against and/or provided alternatives to furloughs. One was the University of Toledo, where the AAUP faculty union produced an analysis of administrative costs entitled "Pigs at the Public Trough," which got picked up in the local media and led to the university backing off its proposals. Therein lay one of collective bargaining's benefits, I asserted: It "can give effective force to the collective voice and will of the faculty to define the future, not only for themselves, but for the students and communities they serve." Furloughs failed to reverse either a "structural imbalance" in institutional expenditures or the academy's movement from its public promise. In urging faculty to reject "top-down" proposals, I closed with one word: "Organize."

The University Senates Conference Executive's Response, and the Need for an Independent Faculty Voice

The January 2010 "Bunsis Report" analyzing UIC's finances had been distributed to faculty at the UI system's universities. In response, on February 10, 2010, the executive of the UI system's University Senates Conference issued a rebuttal to all faculty: "Because Mr. Bunsis is already on record opposing faculty furloughs it is no surprise that he was chosen to conduct this audit, nor what his analysis concludes. We believe that this report and the blog summary make a number of claims that are factually incorrect, incomplete, and/or misleading" (UI University Senates Conference, 2010, p. 1). It invoked management's austerity language of "difficult decisions": "That is why we need to make some difficult decisions now to prepare for the prospects of even more dire shortfalls in the future. Given the wider state crisis, unfounded optimism seems foolish" (pp. 2–3).

The dismissive, even condescending tone of the University Senates Conference Executive's (USCE) response was part of what represented such a "gift" to the UIC campaign. These system senators did more than offer full-throated support of the administration's actions. They matched management's often disrespectful tone and tropes that faculty just don't understand the complicated issues at hand, are inaccurate in their analyses, and are imprudent in their proposals. The phrasing about Bunsis's analysis's "unfounded optimism" being "foolish" was pitch perfect in disrespecting faculty voice. That provided an opportunity for us to gain credibility with the faculty in a high-profile, high-stakes public empirical dispute about the actual state of university finances and to further clarify the need for a union as an independent faculty voice.[10]

From Furloughs to Misplaced Managerial Priorities

The USCE's response was an opportunity to challenge management's crisis/austerity discourses and to pivot to foregrounding management's misplaced priorities, shifting the debate's focus to patterns of expenditures over time. Indeed, the USCE's memo supported Bunsis's analysis on the question of institutional priorities, validating two key points of the campaign: "We do agree [with the Bunsis report] that administrative cuts should be made to minimize the extent of cuts necessary to our academic activities. We also agree that if the UI should receive its entire state appropriation, then a way to refund the furloughs and pay cuts should be found" (p. 4).

Within a week of the USCE's memo, Bunsis and I sent a response to UIC faculty, foregrounding themes about the decreasing support for instruction even as administrative costs were increasing (Bunsis & Rhoades, 2010). One closing bullet was, "Any reduction in spending should not come from the employees, but from administrative costs and administrative spending. We will indicate below how administrative costs have outpaced educational costs at UI, and how the administration continues to forecast increases in administrative costs even as they propose non-refundable furloughs and further reduced shares of institutional monies spent on the core educational mission" (p. 10). We underscored the need to strengthen an independent faculty voice to redress the imbalanced past expenditure patterns that managers were perpetuating into the future. In detailing the UI's financial health, we called managers to account for allegedly tough choices in tight times, which apparently were neither tough nor tight.

Furloughs and the ensuing exchange with USCE catalyzed further growth of the campaign's organizing committee. It also connected the union campaign more clearly to larger issues of support for public education's public purposes. Bread (and roses) issues mattered, but so did issues of the university's public purposes.

Underlying and animating UIC faculty leaders' organizing efforts was their questioning of the university's direction—its leaders and its trajectory. In their view, management was leading their urban university down a corporatization path, taking it away from its academic missions and its public role in providing access to and serving the community's underserved populations. The faculty on the organizing committee were proud of and committed to their institution's urban place and mission.

One example of such larger concerns was a faculty-organized campus forum on March 8, "UIC Joint Furlough Day: A Day of Action in Support of Public Education" (UIC Joint Furlough March 8, 2010). The idea was for faculty to use a furlough day to educate the public about the issues at hand. The messaging foregrounded management's misplaced priorities and spoke to examples of this, from reductions in student services and course offerings to increases in minimum class size and tuition. A consistent theme I heard (and articulated as a participant) was the disproportionate, adverse impact of cuts that targeted programs serving lower-income students and students of color who were the historical focus of UIC and many faculty.

Furloughs and finances, then, were vehicles for talking about the university's priorities, educational purposes, and public commitments. For expenditures are statements about priorities and values, as are collective bargaining agreements.

Furloughs in the Contracts

Given the furloughing of faculty since the 2008 recession, two questions arise about CBAs: (1) To what extent was there mention of furloughs?; and (2) What conditions were said to justify furloughing faculty, and what was the role, if any, of faculty in deliberations about those conditions and how furloughs would be implemented?

Incidence of Furlough Provisions

Interestingly, provisions about furloughs were almost entirely lacking in the CBAs. Only fifteen contracts in the HECAS database had any mention or provision about furloughs for faculty. Of those, nine were in two-year institutions.

Prior to the 2020 pandemic, this managerial strategy had largely fallen from favor, although not entirely. In 2017, dysfunctional Illinois politics again contributed to some of the state's regional universities (but not the University of Illinois) instituting furloughs for faculty (Lobosco, 2017; Rhodes, 2017; Tate, 2017). Perhaps not surprisingly, then, Southern Illinois University, Carbondale (SIUC), was one of only six four-year institutions in the HECAS database to have a provision about faculty furloughs. Such limited numbers may be due to administrations moving to measures such as retrenchment for financial exigency or other reasons, discussed in the next chapter.

Conditions of the Furlough Provisions

What was in CBAs' furlough provisions? All but two of the fifteen left the decision about whether to implement furloughs entirely to administration (Shawnee State University's contract provided for consultation with a "Joint Review Committee" about a reduction in force, but not about furloughs). The strongest exception was the contract of Western Illinois University: "The University will not activate involuntary furloughs in the 2010–2011 and 2011–2012 academic years." The other exception was the Sierra Joint Community College District contract that laid out various measures that may be required to address a "fiscal emergency." One of those measures was "temporary furloughs," which required "unit approval" (what that meant was not specified).

In all other cases, the decision was management's.

Yet, three contracts adopted a defensive strategy and established limiting conditions that must be met before an institution could implement furloughs. The first spoke to alternative cost-cutting measures that involved prioritizing academic personnel for protection. Southern Illinois Carbondale University's contract indicated that furloughs "will only be implemented if other workable cost saving measures (including but not limited to reductions in non-essential services, hiring freezes, suspension of new initiatives, etc.) are not sufficient to mitigate the crisis." The limiting conditions in the other two contracts were mostly about alternatives focused on the academic side of the house. Fort Hays State

University's provision read, "Prior to the furlough or pay reduction action, the University must attempt to cut costs by first seeking voluntary employee attrition, such as retirement, phased retirement, sabbaticals and/or various leaves, and by considering other cost cutting measures, including but not limited to requiring administrators with faculty rank to teach at least one course for no additional compensation." The Community College of Allegheny County contract provided that there be some consultation with the union: "The College shall consult with the Federation on the manner of rescheduling work . . . so as to complete the academic calendar or other activities which may have been interrupted. Following such consultation, the College may either reschedule the work or may furlough Employees as necessary. The manner of furloughing shall be accomplished in consultation with the Federation."

In all but a few cases, then, the decision of whether to furlough was effectively a management right. Broward Community College's contract specified this under "Board Rights": "To retain, discharge, lay off, recall, relieve from duty, furlough, promote, demote, suspend, transfer, or assign employees and to establish and apply the criteria and conditions for the same." And Rogue Community College's CBA read, under Article 12 on the "work year," "Non-contract days may also include unpaid furlough days scheduled during a particular contract year for budgetary reasons." None suggested management try to rebalance academic and nonacademic expenditures.

Even in the contracts that identified some actions that should be taken before furloughs, the final decision remained in management's hands. For example, the SIUC contract read, "In the event of a temporary financial crisis, the Board of Trustees may determine that unpaid furlough days or unpaid administrative closure days are necessary to address the financial crisis."

What faculty mostly have succeeded in negotiating is a defensive strategy of minimizing the scope of furloughs, thereby reducing management's discretion. Thus, several contracts delimited and capped a specific number of furlough days. Along these lines, Treasure Valley Community College's provision read, "Furlough Day: The Association, as part of this Article, agrees that it shall grant one furlough day during the fall quarter of either the second or third year of this Agreement. The College shall determine the specific date of the furlough day, but it must be exercised during the Fall quarter of one of those years."

Southern Oregon University's contract had a memorandum of understanding specifying a limit of three instructional days. Sonoma County Community College's contract specified that half of the furloughed time must be instructional days. By contrast, SIUC's contract stated that "the Chair/Director and Faculty member shall schedule furlough/administrative closure days in a manner that does not disrupt the Faculty member's teaching schedule." Los Angeles Community College District's contract held that the faculty would have health benefits and the district would pay its share of the premiums during furlough days.

Arguably the most significant furlough provision was that of Ohlone Community College. Its distinctive memorandum of understanding provided for the return of monies generated by furloughs if the state's projected budget shortfall was less than anticipated.

> During this time of uncertainty and without an actual commitment from the State, the district and UFO agree that the economic situation may change in the future. However, the District and UFO enters into this MOU with the understanding that the District expects to receive the revenue promised by the State. It is under these terms that the district and UFO agree to concessions to close the projected (revised) budget gap of $680,000. . . . The savings from these reductions will be used to meet the agreed upon $329,000 of UFO concessions. Any amount of money that comes back to the district/ college under the projected budget shortfall of $680,000 is proportionally set aside for return to UFO members.

The memorandum implemented one of the suggestions offered by Bunsis and me in our response to the University Senates Executive of the University of Illinois: "The last option, after the above three have been exhausted, would be to ask the UI system's employees to accept a temporary reduction in pay [*that would later be refunded to them*]. When the university gets the appropriation due from the State, as is almost certain to happen, then the pay reduction should be paid back to the employees, with interest" (Bunsis & Rhoades, 2010, p. 3). In short, if furloughs are a temporary solution to a short-term financial challenge, the foregone salary monies should be refunded at a later point. The solution to the longer-term financial challenge lies in reversing a decades-long pattern of disinvestment in instruction.

If a major managerial strategy in Illinois and many states from 2009 to 2010 was furloughs, between then and the winter/spring of 2020, the dominant management strategy and issue was program elimination and retrenchment. COVID changed that.

COVID-19 and Organizing against Furloughs

As with the 2008 to 2010 recession, the COVID-19 public health and economic crisis of 2020 saw many institutions invoking furloughs. The earliest and most dramatic announcement was made on April 17, 2020, by UA, of furloughs for most staff of four to seven weeks (versus the four days of furlough UIC announced a decade earlier).

The announcement brought immediate, vociferous criticism from faculty and staff about the extreme furloughs. The "Senior Leadership Team" defended their "plan" (which lacked operational detail) by saying that it was a way to avoid layoffs. When pressed to explain why the university was pursuing this path when almost no peer universities were doing so, the response was that other universities would eventually enact furloughs and that UA was leading the way in enacting prudent planning.

Within weeks, a Coalition for Academic Justice, UA (CAJUA), was formed of faculty, staff, and graduate employees. Early on, activists were posting the hashtag critique/question on social media, #FirstandWorst and #WhyJustUA, as well as working in action groups to focus on university finances and gather data nationally on other institutions' furlough plans. The organizing began with a Facebook chat group, the core members of which were in the Colleges of Education and of Social and Behavioral Sciences. The organizing that grew out of that network was almost all virtual, through email lists and Zoom meetings. Many of the early participants were social justice activists involved in many initiatives and groups on and off campus, including previously protesting the university police's criminalization of three Latina students protesting the presence of ICE (Immigration and Customs Enforcement) on campus. Virtual organizing leveraged preexisting, real, face-to-face networks to create broader online communities. The numbers rapidly grew to over 200 (and later 600).

By mid-May, a few other public research universities also announced furloughs—for example, University of Wisconsin, Madison, and University of Georgia—but for four to nine days, not four to seven weeks (Cole, 2020; Kim, 2020). Neither of Arizona's other two public universities (Arizona State University and Northern Arizona University) had announced furloughs. NAU later would, but at one-third the level of the UA, and the monies were subsequently reimbursed. Furloughs, then, were not a system-level decision.

Pressure from CAJUA, along with that of other groups on campus, led to a revision of the furlough plan. Management agreed to introduce a "floor" to the furloughs—employees making less than $44,500 would be exempt.

A month later, CAJUA generated an alternative furlough plan that called for more of the financial burden to be borne by central administrators, a more progressive scale that didn't stop at $200,000, and a higher furlough floor. Providing data on executive compensation increases of 20 to 30 percent, CAJUA framed its proposal much like others around the country that featured "Chop from the top" themes. It also provided data on the disparate impact of furloughs on lower-paid employees. And it centered the need to protect the public university's core missions.

Then, on the morning of June 25, 2020, CAJUA hosted an open forum presentation from Howard Bunsis, whose financial analysis was instrumental in catalyzing the UIC campaign. More than 500 people attended on Zoom. Bunsis's analysis revealed that the UA was in solid financial health. As of the fall of 2019, it had over $805 million in unrestricted reserves. In closing his presentation, Bunsis indicated that the UA should be leveraging its reserves, refinancing debt, and borrowing monies to address its projected deficits (which he detailed as being significantly inflated). There was no need to furlough faculty/staff.

That afternoon, the Faculty Senate hosted a meeting of the university's General Assembly (of faculty). Out of that meeting came a vote on whether to delay furlough implementation to mid-September (instead of July 1) to provide time for management and faculty to develop a financial mitigation plan with no or significantly reduced furloughs. In a record turnout of 41.2 percent of eligible voters, 89 percent voted for delay. On July 1, the president indicated furloughs would be delayed until August 10.

CAJUA operated outside formal shared governance and the university (with the local press and meeting internally with folks, including a group of deans) but also worked through the senate to get the general assembly vote on the university's furlough plan and criticized the administration for bypassing shared governance in its furlough decision. It worked with the chair of the faculty to establish a General Faculty Financial Advisory Committee (GFFAC) on furloughs, with over one-third of its members from CAJUA.[11]

GFFAC's charge was to develop a comprehensive financial mitigation plan that relied less on furloughs. It met daily throughout the last half of July, including regularly with the Provost and the Chief Financial Officer (who refused to provide critical data). At a faculty senate meeting on August 3, GFFAC presented its report in a Zoom meeting again attended by over 500 people. The meeting also included presentations about two other university decision-making processes that CAJUA and faculty generally opposed due partly to the lack of shared governance. The GFFAC report provided multiple alternatives to management's extreme furlough plan and documented that, contrary to the president's claim, relatively few peer universities had furloughed employees and had done so at a much lower level. Nevertheless, on August 7, the president communicated to faculty and staff that he was proceeding with the original plan, though he would consider GFFAC's ideas in moving forward (that fall, he reduced the furloughs by 50 percent, but they remained #FirstandStillWorst).

Employees' activism was about more than furloughs. In its name, discourse, and advocacy, CAJUA (the name intentionally centered justice) critiqued the university's corporatization and decision-making, layoffs and nonrenewal of "career track" (contingent) faculty, graduate employees, and staff, and of COVID reentry plans that put essential employees at risk. It critiqued misplaced priorities that failed to serve marginalized populations of students, staff, and community members who were disparately impacted by the pandemic and recession.

Overall, what animated the organizing was a deep sense of being disrespected and of disgust regarding the discourse and actions of central administration in its announcements about furloughs, about reentry plans amid COVID, and about the acquisition of a predatory, online, for-profit "university," Ashford, announced early the morning of August 3.

As in the final epigram of this chapter, the president's April announcement about furloughs closed with, "We all will share in this as a team and we all will sacrifice as a team." Such claims of shared sacrifice infuriated employees as it further clarified how detached from their lived realities central administrators were. Many viewed these statements as being entirely inconsistent with the reality of management's practices. And that carried over to other policy realms and managerial announcements. For example, at the August 3 Faculty Senate meeting, the president claimed the acquisition of Ashford University would help the university better fulfill its land grant mission and serve students of color. This claim was made despite Ashford's extremely low graduation rate and extremely high student debt and default rates with a population disproportionately of lower-income students of color and veterans. In response, Sandy Soto, a faculty member, a leader in CAJUA and the unionization drive, and eventually the first President of the United Campus Workers of Arizona (UCWAZ) responded, "Do you think we're idiots?!"

On August 18, 2020, the UCWAZ, Local 7065 was chartered by the Communications Workers of America, just four months after the first furloughs announcement. It was the newest United Campus Workers (UCW) local, in a national CWA initiative dating back years, focused on southern states with laws hostile to collective bargaining (e.g., Georgia, Louisiana, Tennessee—see Rhoades, 2021).[12]

Another UCW local, 3265 of Georgia, also confronted university actions in 2020 around furloughs (and reentry). There, employees successfully made their voices heard. Although furloughs were announced in May 2020, by July, the university pulled back from its proposal (Shearer, 2020), after a UCW Georgia campaign that spoke to the system's large reserves and strong finances (and Moody's rating), criticized the inequitable furloughs, and creating an interactive "Chop from the top calculator."

The university that came the closest to UA in furloughs was one featured in chapter 2, the University of Oregon (UO). The UO president announced furloughs for central administrators (Brown, 2020), layoffs of staff in auxiliary units, and a proposed plan for progressive furloughs based on five budget scenarios (United Academics University of Oregon, 2020; UO Matters, 2020). However, these proposals had to be negotiated with the faculty union, which rejected a management threat to lay off all nontenure-track faculty (or reduce them to .1 FTE) if the furlough proposal was not accepted. The "Memorandum of Understanding" that was agreed to in August backed off significantly from the original proposal (Warner, 2020). It restored FTE to contingent faculty who had received reduced assignments, and the institution capped pay cuts at one-fifth of the original proposal's worst scenario, less than one-fourth of the amount for UA.

The moral here is that unions matter. And they can matter in ways that do not always appear in specific contract language. The United Academics University of Oregon's (UAUO) CBA does not have furlough language. But when management was considering temporary "pay reduction," they were obliged to negotiate with the union over these changes in working conditions.

Key Takeaways

Implementation of furloughs was a widespread management strategy in the 2008–2009 recession and re-emerged at a lesser level amid the pandemic when layoffs and restructuring were more widespread. Despite their widespread use in that former time period, only fifteen contracts (six in four-year and nine in two-year institutions) in HECAS addressed temporary furloughs. Only three of those embedded limiting conditions. Most adopted a defensive strategy of minimizing the scope of furloughs. An outlier was Ohlone Community College's contract, which held that "any amount of money that comes back to the district/college under the projected budget shortfall . . . is proportionally set aside for return to United Faculty of Ohlone members." However, as noted at the end of the previous section, bargaining units still have the power to negotiate temporary pay reductions even when there is no specific contract language.

Significantly, furloughs' imposition can catalyze organizing (and contract) campaigns, as detailed in each of the two time periods, in the cases of UIC and UA. That is particularly true when the campaigns connect the larger patterns of corporatization, privatization, and misplaced institutional priorities. The reason is that whatever management's particular austerity practice, they tend to be about a "'disaster academic capitalism'" (Flaherty, 2020, "Not the Same University," Disaster Academic Capitalism section, para. 3) that does not "waste" a crisis, but uses it to justify amplifying preexisting patterns of disinvestment in core educational functions and public purposes. The term combines Naomi Klein's (2007) phrasing with that of Sheila Slaughter and I (2004) from three years earlier (Flaherty, 2020, "Not the Same University"). The concept suggests that institutions capitalize on crises "'to restructure and retrench, with management trying to bypass deliberative, strategic, shared governance'" (Disaster Academic Capitalism section, para. 3), amplifying ongoing patterns of corporatization and privatization. An independent faculty voice is all the more important in this context to recalibrate and reverse past patterns of misplaced priorities and eroded public purposes. Otherwise, the academic core of the institution is "hollowed out" as the institution becomes a site primarily to leverage institutions' positioning as firms, and their private market opportunities (Letizia, 2016).

Furloughs are neither a short-term fix nor a long-term solution to what ails the academy. As I wrote while AAUP general secretary, the "failure of furloughs" is threefold. They fail to reverse the longstanding disinvestment in academic personnel and programs versus administrative ones because furloughs are across the board and not differentiated by employees' functions. Second, they fail to reverse the erosion of faculty voice in campus decision-making. And third, they fail to reverse patterns of academic capitalism that are taking higher education away from its public purposes and from underserved communities, even most recently in the midst of the havoc wrought by the pandemic and recession to a disproportionate effect on marginalized students and communities. Furloughs are a problematic and arguably disastrous perpetuation of old patterns that fail to recalibrate the academy's course in a new, more progressive direction.

Transitioning to the next chapter, most institutions, though, in the most recent economic crisis, did not implement furloughs. They turned instead to lay-offs and retrenchment for financial exigency and other rationales.

7

Negotiating Management's Austerity Practices

• •

Retrenchment for Financial Exigency and Other Reasons in the Contracts

Can we just agree that at least half of institutional expenditures should go to instruction? (Howard Bunsis, presenting financial analyses of university expenditures, criticizing misplaced priorities and calling for increased investment in education)

The faculty or an appropriate faculty body will have access to at least five years of audited financial statements, current and following-year budgets, and detailed cash-flow estimates for future years. (Recommended Institutional Regulation, 4.c.2.i. on "Termination of appointments by the institution in the case of Financial Exigency"—AAUP, 2013)

Thank you for speaking to the inclusion of non-tenure-track faculty and faculty of

> color in decision-making. If 'shared
> governance' is just about the tenured,
> largely White faculty, you see what
> happens—I count only three faculty of
> color in this room [of 60 or so]. (Faculty
> member at the forum of PROFS—Public
> Representation Organization of the
> Faculty Senate—on shared governance in
> Wisconsin, May 3, 2018)

In the 2020 recession, some higher education institutions experienced financial stress, more invoked stress than experienced it, and a relative few declared financial exigencies.[1] Many retrenched faculty for financial and other reasons, in a demonstration of "disaster academic capitalism" under cover of COVID-19 (Flaherty, 2020, "Not the Same University"). Faculty layoffs have made national news at Vermont State Colleges (St. Amour, 2020), Western Missouri State University (Flaherty, 2020, "Not the Same University"), the University of Akron (Flaherty, 2020, "Budget 'Bloodbath'"), and the Pennsylvania State System of Higher Education (Burke, 2020), among others. Indeed, by mid-May 2020, the *Chronicle of Higher Education* had documented layoffs at over 200 colleges or universities (Chronicle Staff, 2020). By late fall, they were at historic levels (Bauman, 2020), falling disproportionately on employees from marginalized populations (Douglas-Gabriel & Fowers, 2021; Long, Van Dam, Fowers, & Shapiro, 2021; Rhoades, 2021). Among faculty, cuts fell most heavily on contingent faculty, who are more likely to be women and/or faculty of color.

During my time at the AAUP (2009–2011), two of its national leaders were instrumental in challenging management's austerity measures. They called out the decades-long pattern of disproportionate growth in administrative costs amid proportional declines in full-time, tenure-stream faculty and in education's share of institutional expenditures. One of them, Rudy Fichtenbaum, a Wright State University economics professor, was AAUP president from 2012 to 2020. The other, Howard Bunsis, an Eastern Michigan University accounting professor, was on the Executive Committee while I was there. Both did reports for faculty groups across the country, analyzing institutional finances. Both called for rebalancing institutional priorities to refocus on core academic functions, as in the chapter's first epigram.

That message was at the center of AAUP's union drives. It mobilized faculty in existing AAUP bargaining units (and advocacy chapters) to negotiate to rebalance institutional priorities to better serve educational and public purposes (a mantra of virtually all faculty units nationally). Along those lines, as president, Fichtenbaum spearheaded revision of AAUP's Recommended Institutional Regulation (RIR) #4 on the "Termination of appointments by the institution" for

146 • Faculty Negotiating Retrenchment

financial exigency or other reasons, such as program discontinuance.[2] The revised regulation was developed by the AAUP's Committee A on academic freedom and tenure (AAUP, 2013, 2015).[3] The revision reflected Fichtenbaum's presence, financial expertise, and focus on institutions' externally audited financial records (see the second epigram).

The revised RIR #4, detailed below, helps frame this chapter's analysis of retrenchment provisions in CBAs, for financial exigency and other rationales. The findings are also framed by my 1998 analysis (Rhoades, 1998a). Both center the (im)balance between managerial discretion and faculty's voice and due process rights. They also center whether/how provisions perpetuate professorial stratification. Who shares in shared governance? Which segments of faculty are enfranchised, by status of employment and demographics, and which are not? (See the third epigram). Finally, the analysis centers on whether/how conceptions of public goods/benefits are invoked in provisions.

The Contracts: Financial Exigency

Between the 2008–2009 and 2020–2021 recessions, the AAUP made substantial changes to its RIR #4 on faculty retrenchment. The most dramatic changes/additions in the section on financial exigency lay in its specificity in defining financial crises and alternative measures for addressing fiscal challenges. An opening clause defining exigency was revised: rather than "an imminent financial crisis that threatens the survival of the institution as a whole," (AAUP, 2006, p. 24) it was defined as, "a severe financial crisis that fundamentally compromises the academic integrity of the institution as a whole" (2015, p. 81). Inserting "academic integrity" speaks to prioritizing core educational purposes.

The new regulation also specified that "there should be an elected faculty governance body or a body designated by a collective bargaining agreement" (AAUP, 2015, p. 81) that addresses these financial issues, attending to institutional priorities. As with the University of Illinois' University Systems Executive discussed in chapter 6, such elected bodies can sometimes align with management, Nevertheless, the specification is important because a common managerial strategy is to appoint an ad-hoc task force, and/or meet with hand-picked faculty/senators, bypassing the elected, representative body acting as a whole.

On the matter of alternatives to retrenching faculty, a new clause supplemented the old RIR's sentence about the first step being to pursue "feasible alternatives to termination of appointments": "including expenditures of one-time money or reserves as bridge funding, furloughs, pay cuts, deferred compensation plans, early retirement packages, deferral of nonessential capital expenditures, and cuts to non-educational programs and services, including expenses for administration" (AAUP, 2015, p. 81).[4] The new RIR also included a bulleted section that began, "Before any proposals for program discontinuance on grounds of financial exigency are made, the faculty or an appropriate faculty body will have opportunity to render an assessment in writing of the institution's financial condition" (AAUP, 2015, p. 81). That operationalizes prioritizing academic/educational missions/programs, which is important given that academic capitalism expands support and auxiliary units' personnel/offices to enhance managerial capacity/power (Slaughter & Rhoades, 2004).

The new section then identified data that should be made available, including "at least five years of audited financial statements, current and following year budgets, and detailed cash-flow estimates for future years"[5] (AAUP, 2015, p. 81). Further, as program discontinuance could be involved, it indicated that the faculty body "will have access to detailed program, department, and administrative-unit budgets" (p. 81). Committee A's subcommittee report also offered guidance on analyzing institutions' finances, whereas the old regulation only indicated that the crisis needed to be "a demonstrably bona fide financial exigency" without defining it.

In analyzing financial exigency provisions, I first considered their incidence overall and in four- versus two-year institution contracts.[6] I then examined the definition, if any, of financial exigency. Was it the old AAUP language of "demonstrably bona fide"? Was it defined as exigency for the institution or for an academic unit, reflecting the shifting managerial strategy of defining exigency as applying to units, a much lower bar (Rhoades, 1993; Slaughter, 1993b)? Further, I explored whether or how contracts spoke to a faculty role in determining/declaring a financial exigency and whether that followed the spirit and/or letter of revised RIR #4. Finally, I addressed whether, per the new RIR, nonacademic alternatives to retrenchment were identified that protected/prioritized academic functions and personnel.

Incidence

About one-quarter (26 percent) of the 506 contracts had financial exigency language, greater than one-fifth (19 percent) in the 1990s (Rhoades, 1998a). The incidence was far greater in four-year than two-year institution contracts (as in 1998). Of 131 provisions, almost twice as many (eighty-six) were in four- as in two-year institutions' (forty-five) contracts, though HECAS had far more contracts of two- (354) versus four-year institutions (152).[7]

Exigency Simply Mentioned

In thirty-eight provisions that spoke to financial exigency, the term was only mentioned, often as a passing reference with no detail, or as a rationale for retrenching faculty. There was no definition or faculty involvement.

Financial Exigency Defined

Defining financial exigency can delimit managerial discretion. Just nine (five in four-year and four in two-year institutions) CBAs utilized the term "demonstrably bona fide," roughly the same proportion of CBAs (2 percent) found in the

1990s (Rhoades, 1998a, Table 3.1). For example, Lincoln University Pennsylvania's contract read, "Termination of a continuous appointment because of financial exigency should be demonstrably bona fide." Negotiated by an AAUP local, it also invoked the 1940 AAUP statement on academic freedom, as did Monroe Community College's contract (not an AAUP unit).

Some contracts utilized some of the demonstrably bona fide terms or related language. Nine (seven in four-year institutions) referred to "bona fide." Four used "demonstrable" or "in good faith," as in Owens Community College, "As a result of financial exigency determined in good faith by the Board of Trustees of the College."

Less than one-third (thirty in four-year and seven in two-year institutions) of the 131 contracts defined financial exigency in relation to the institution as a whole. That 28 percent was nearly twice the 15 percent found in the 1990s (Rhoades, 1998a, Table 3.1). Some contracts did that in relation to "demonstrably bona fide" language, as with Pratt Institute: "Financial exigency must be demonstrably bona fide and fully explained and documented to the faculty to the effect that unless the Institute effectuates the inherent economies, the viability of Pratt Institute is endangered." Others did not: "financial exigency which is defined as an imminent financial crisis which threatens the survival of the Institution as a whole" (Kalamazoo Valley Community College).

By contrast, consider the definition in Western Washington University's contract, "'Financial exigency' is defined as a condition of projected deficit in the University's operating budget of such magnitude that reduction in faculty is necessary." Relying on "projected deficits" gives free rein to management.

One contract (Saint John's University) defined exigency as departmental: "Department financial exigency exists when a thorough evaluation of the financial status of the department, including consideration of total income generated, ordinary direct operating expenses and projected savings through faculty attrition and other economies, nevertheless indicates its lack of fiscal viability." That makes it far easier for management. Many departments within a financially viable institution might be experiencing financial stress. Such a definition also means the institution's financial assets (e.g., reserves, endowments, or property), which might counterbalance revenue shortfalls, are not considered.

It was significant, then, that Lincoln University Missouri changed its policy definition of "financial exigency" in 2017 (Flaherty, 2017, "Lincoln U Changes"; Lincoln University Office of the President, 2017) to specify that it "may be declared by the president . . . either for the entire University, or for specific colleges, schools, departments, or programs." A few years later, the university claimed exigency to justify laying off forty-one faculty and staff, even as its president indicated that "the university is not in any immediate danger of going under: 'Lincoln is not about to close its doors'" (Sitter, 2020, "Lincoln Faculty Union Offers Plan," para. 7). The faculty union contested the need for such cuts, proposing alternatives to ensure "high quality education" and address students' graduation needs (para. 12). Yet, the university proceeded with layoffs (of five faculty) and a 2.5 percent pay cut for all employees (Sitter, 2020, "Lincoln Cuts Employee Pay"). Three months later, the university retracted the pay cuts, indicating that the anticipated budget losses did not materialize (Sitter, 2020, "Lincoln Retracts Pay Cuts"). That speaks to why relying on comprehensive externally audited financial reports, as found in Lincoln University Pennsylvania's contract, is preferable to budget projections.[8]

Only a few contracts (three in four-year and three in two-year institutions) utilized terminology approximating the AAUP's RIR #4 about the institution's academic integrity. As one of its longtime union leaders was AAUP President Fichtenbaum, it's not surprising that Wright State University's contract, negotiated just after the AAUP adopted the revised RIR #4, incorporated aspects of the recommended language. Exigency meant "that severe financial problems exist which threaten the University's ability to maintain its academic operations at an acceptable level of quality." So, too, another Ohio AAUP unit's contract (Bowling Green State University) embedded such language: "Financial exigency, defined as financial problems so severe that they threaten the University's ability to maintain its operations at an acceptable level of quality." Several contracts of AAUP bargaining units in Ohio (Cleveland State University, University of Akron, University of Cincinnati, Cuyahoga Community College, and Southern State Community College) defined exigency as applying to the whole institution, exemplifying how networks within a state can impact contract negotiations.[9]

Contract language matters, even if provisions are limited.

Consider Quinnipiac University (a private university). Prior to 2006, when management filed a successful challenge to and decertification of the tenure-stream faculty bargaining unit, its contract detailed enrollment and financial conditions that had to be met before tenured faculty could be laid off for financial exigency: "An actual decline of full-time equivalent day students of at least 6.5% in one academic year. . . . An actual decline of full-time equivalent day students of at least 8.5% over a two-year period. . . . An actual decline of full-time equivalent day students in one academic year plus a projected decline for the subsequent academic year, totaling at least 9%. . . . A deficit balance in the unrestricted current fund of the College of at least $430,000." Yet, the term, "financial exigency" did not appear in the 2007 Faculty Handbook, which replaced the CBA. The handbook referred instead to "compelling financial reasons," defined as, "an actual or impending circumstance that poses a serious risk to the financial health of the university." That gave management extraordinary discretion.[10]

Contracts also matter in establishing due process rights in implementing retrenchment, and faculty's involvement in that process, as discussed below. Although Quinnipiac's Handbook defined a faculty role in developing plans, it did not define due process guiding retrenchment (e.g., notice, order of layoff, reappointment rights, recall rights for two years), unlike the CBA.

Alternatives and Faculty Involvement

Language defining alternatives to retrenching faculty that must be pursued first (especially if they protect academic personnel and programs), and defining a faculty role in that process are important, as is language specifying access to financial information. An example of a strong provision was again in Wright State University's contract. It called for data/information to be made available to the union: "Should the University President anticipate the need for retrenchment of Bargaining Unit Faculty Members, the data and information upon which this decision is based shall be provided to the AAUP-WSU."[11] It also specified establishing a "Joint Committee on Retrenchment," "with three members appointed by the University and three members appointed by the AAUP-WSU." That committee could recommend alternatives to retrenching faculty, as in, "Such recommendations may include ways to relieve the exigency by raising additional funds, by reallocating funds, or by cutting or eliminating specified activities." BGSU's contract language was much the same.[12]

Another strong article was in Rider University's CBA, which spoke to information that must be provided the union: "The University shall also be required to provide the AAUP ... with documenting evidence supporting the conclusion that one or both of the above reasons for lay-off exists." It also pointed to the need to pursue alternative forms of savings: "Contemporaneously with the lay-off of bargaining unit members, other reasonable and prudent savings effected by the University through means other than by the lay-off of members of the bargaining unit." That language dated back to the 2007 contract.[13]

Rider's contract was also unusually strong in its "meet and confer" (versus what is known as "meet and defer") language, in that decisions could be grieved by an independent arbitrator.

> Within a 21-day period following the University's notice to the AAUP, representatives of the University and the AAUP shall meet to discuss and confer concerning the University's proposed lay-off plan. . . . The AAUP may refer the matter to arbitration, . . . In the event of such an arbitration, the University and the AAUP shall each submit to the designated arbitrator their respective proposals and the arbitrator shall be absolutely required to adopt and accept either the proposal of the University or that of the AAUP as to the appropriate number of lay-offs, if any, the departments, disciplines or professional staffs to be eliminated or curtailed, and the bargaining unit members to be laid off, if any. The parties' final proposals shall be the subject of a hearing before the arbitrator.[14]

Another contract negotiated by an AAUP affiliate (with a former Executive Committee member—Estelle Gellman) was Hofstra University's. It specified alternatives to layoffs that included reducing expenditures on non-academic personnel and programs: "Prior to the reduction of faculty because of bona fide financial exigency, the Administration shall consult with the appropriate academic constituencies, including the AAUP, and take steps to attempt to curtail costs in other areas, such as the indirect costs of sustaining non-academic and academic programs. Also, consideration shall be given to the reduction in the number of administrative and support lines and the filling of academic and administrative vacancies with qualified members of the Hofstra faculty."

More typically, contracts defined alternatives that consisted of measures focused on academic personnel, such as faculty attrition, as in Shawnee State University's contract: "If it is determined that reductions in academic units and/or faculty members are imminent due to financial exigency as described in Section 1D above, the President will schedule a joint meeting with the Provost, Shawnee Education Association President, and Ohio Education Association representative regarding this matter. This meeting may consider such actions as voluntary early retirements, voluntary, and/or mandatory furloughs, etc."

Of the thirty-two contracts (twenty in four-year and twelve in two-year institutions) that indicated faculty can offer alternatives to layoffs, twelve (nine in four- and three in two-year institutions) spoke to prioritizing academic personnel and/or programs. Portland State University's FT contract indicated that the President should consider, "the balance between academic personnel and other elements of the budget." More explicitly, the University of Cincinnati's contract referred to "reallocating current general funds," and indicated that, "Before retrenchment of Faculty, budgets shall be cut or activities eliminated or reduced that . . . (b) are not in direct support of academic programs, or (c) are not essential for continued operation of the academic program of the University." Similarly, Central Oregon Community College's contract referred to "a reasonable effort to reduce non-salary expenditures" and to "delayed capital expenditures." And Monroe Community College's contract stated that "the College shall first determine which non-personnel expenditures shall be curtailed before laying off faculty."

One of the strongest provisions was that of Northern Illinois University (COMB): "In the event of a declared university-wide financial exigency resulting in a layoff of a bargaining unit member(s), the Union shall have the right to form a Layoffs Review Committee. [It] shall have the right to make written recommendations to the Provost and Board of Trustees. Upon request by the Layoffs Review Committee, the Employer shall provide: at least five years of audited financial statements, approved current-year budget, and the following-year budget." That is the sort of detail that RIR #4 called for. The provision went on to address the need to prioritize academic programs in making recommendations: "In making its written recommendation, the Layoffs Review Committee may consider factors that include, but are not limited to, the following: a. That all feasible alternatives have been pursued, including expenditure of one- time money or reserves as bridge funding, furloughs, pay cuts,

Faculty Consultation

The faculty consultation sections of provisions mostly focused on defensively negotiating the retrenchment plan and impact. Moreover, they mostly spoke not just to exigency, but also to other rationales for retrenchment. The fifty-five contracts providing for some faculty consultation (most of which—thirty-eight—were in four-year institutions) varied by who was to be consulted, the form, and the extent of involvement in decision-making.

The strongest consultation language accorded a role to institution-wide faculty bodies that were elected by the bargaining unit, part of the established governance structure, or to which the union could appoint people: "CSU-AAUP shall have an opportunity to present alternative plans for alleviating the fiscal problem. If there is no agreement between CSU-AAUP and management on alternative(s) for alleviating the fiscal exigency, a CSU-AAUP representative(s) shall have the opportunity to appear before the designated subcommittee of the Board." (Connecticut State University). The joint committee model was also evident in Delaware State University's contract: "Following a declaration of financial exigency, a joint Financial Exigency Committee shall be formed and shall consist of five members appointed by the Administration and five members appointed by the Association.... The purpose of the Committee shall be to develop recommendations to provide sufficient savings for relieving the exigency."[15]

By contrast, Temple University had "meet and defer" language. Still, it provided for some sort of consultation at the department or college level: "Before sending notices of termination because of retrenchment, consultation on the proposed retrenchment shall take place with the Chairperson of any department or program affected and the Dean and College or School curriculum committee of any College or School affected. Also, the Educational Program and Policies Committee of the Faculty Senate shall be advised of the proposed retrenchments." The phrase, "shall be advised" is telling.

Management Right

In some contracts (ten, three in four- and seven in two-year institutions), the declaration of financial exigency was explicitly identified as a "management right." For example, the University of Alaska's contract included, to "declare and respond to financial exigency" under Article 16 on Management Rights. Such explicit identification was even found in some cases in which the contract ensured some faculty consultation. Thus, the University of Nebraska, Kearney's contract provided for faculty consultation and consideration of alternatives to layoff, yet clarified, "The Faculty Advisory Committee recommendation shall be advisory only and the final decisions regarding the necessity of reduction in force shall be reserved to the Administration of the Board."

Countering Managerial Discretion

A simple and strong counter to managerial discretion was language that just said "no." For example, one sentence in the University of Oregon's contract read, "The employment of a bargaining unit faculty member will not be terminated due to financial exigency during the term of this Agreement." However, there is another condition justifying layoff, "academic reasons," which leads us to the next section.[16]

The Contracts: Other Rationales for Retrenchment

Retrenchment of faculty without just cause can be undertaken for rationales other than financial exigency. A common one is program discontinuance and/ or program reorganization, which may accompany managerial invocations of financial stress (Slaughter, 1993a, 1993b).

Beyond that, management may try to capitalize on a real or claimed emergency to exercise managerial discretion in retrenchment—so-called "disaster academic capitalism" (Flaherty, 2020, "Not the Same University"). A dramatic example was the University of Akron's management, which proposed laying off ninety-six faculty, invoking a "force majeure" clause in the CBA (Bowling Green State University's contract also has this clause—the only two cases in HECAS): "The parties recognize that catastrophic circumstances, such as force majeure, could develop which are beyond the control of the University and would render impossible or unfeasible the implementation of procedures set forth in this Article." When the faculty union challenged the action, the case went to independent arbitration. The arbitrator ruled for the university, reasoning that the pandemic was, a "catastrophic event" that "could not have been anticipated" and was beyond the university's control. They accepted the university's claims regarding financial stress despite considerable evidence to the contrary, and its claims that spending reserves or borrowing, as many universities were doing, would not be prudent, compromising the institution's future (Buettner, 2020).

Nevertheless, the faculty voted against a new contract which included the layoffs.[17] Ultimately, the negotiated contract did not include layoffs. Instead, it provided for a small pay cut, linked future bonuses to enrollment growth, and included a $3,000 payment to faculty for having converted their courses to online formats (Geist, 2021).[18] Everything is negotiable.

One strategy for delimiting managerial discretion in effecting faculty retrenchment through program reorganization or elimination is, as with exigency, to specify conditions constraining such decision-making. The AAUP's RIR #4 has a section on "discontinuation of program or department," which was revised (as with the one on exigency) in 2013, changing the title "Not Mandated by

Financial Exigency" to "For Educational Reasons" and prioritizing educational considerations in decision-making (AAUP, 2015, p. 82). New language was also added about notice, so faculty "will promptly be informed of this activity in writing and provided at least thirty days in which to respond to it" (p. 82). And the revised RIR called for a role for contingent faculty in governance matters: "Tenured, tenure-track, and contingent faculty members will be invited to participate in these deliberations" (p. 82).

Another particularly significant addition to RIR #4 was in defining a "program": "Academic programs cannot be defined ad hoc, at any size; programs must be recognized academic units that existed prior to the decision to discontinue them. [They] should designate a related cluster of credit-bearing courses that constitute a coherent body of study within a discipline or set of related disciplines" (AAUP, 2015, pp. 82–3). That language sought to prevent management from targeting particular sub-programmatic areas and/or faculty members for layoff.[19] Such an issue emerged in 2012–2013, at the University of Northern Iowa (UNI). In March 2012, management proposed a program discontinuance with layoffs. Amid deliberations with the faculty union (an AAUP affiliate), AAUP's Committee A became involved, appointing an investigating committee, which at the end of 2012 issued a report setting the stage for a possible vote of censure.[20] Among the "issues of concern" were whether the university's fiscal situation warranted such drastic action, the lack of meaningful faculty participation in decision-making, and the identification of programs for termination. On the latter, the committee noted the university's governing board had developed a definition of "program" after negotiations of this matter with the faculty union had reached impasse. Faculty were assigned to programs by the administration without clear educational criteria. Ultimately, ongoing negotiations by the union and faculty senate with the new UNI president resulted in no faculty layoffs.[21] The case exemplified how collective bargaining can operate in concert with shared governance structures to strengthen faculty voice.

UNI was not an isolated case then (or now) of significant program reorganization and faculty layoffs. The Committee A subcommittee's report on financial exigency discussed retrenchment in the pre-2013 years. Program reorganization and layoffs were becoming more common (that pattern has continued). What is often at stake in such reorganization, and what is so important, is not just faculty voice but also academe's educational and public purposes, and prioritizing higher education's core functions. In the report's words (AAUP, 2013):

> Program closures on the scale we have recently witnessed represent a massive transfer of power from the faculty to the administration *over curricular matters that affect the educational missions of institutions*, [emphasis in original] for which the faculty should always bear the primary responsibility. In most cases, the decision to close programs are made unilaterally and are driven by criteria that are not essentially educational in nature. . . . [They] appear to reflect . . .

Negotiating Austerity Practices • 155

> a widespread belief that faculty positions and instructional costs are the first
> expenditures an institution should seek to trim, as opposed to expenditures
> on administration or capital projects. (p. 20)

The findings in this section are organized around the categories and analysis from Rhoades (1998a), and in relation to the revised RIR #4. A major focus, then, was on managerial discretion versus professorial voice and due process rights. That involved tracking the incidence of provisions, and the range and specificity of rationales provided for retrenchment, as well as the nature and strength of faculty involvement in decision-making about program discontinuance and retrenchment. It also involved tracking language about impact, delimiting arbitrary managerial actions through stipulations regarding order of layoff, notice, reassignment, and recall rights. Another major focus was on whether provisions countered or perpetuated stratification among segments of faculty. And, as a gauge of adjunct faculty's role in deliberations, I considered the incidence of these provisions in PTO contracts. Also, I contrasted language in FT contracts with language on contingent faculty in COMB or PTO units at the same university. Finally, I considered whether language (a) foregrounded educational considerations, prioritizing cutting administrative costs first; (b) was clear on defining "program"; and (c) included language ensuring contingent faculty participation in the process.

Incidence of Provisions

Almost all of the COMB and FT contracts (95 percent) had retrenchment provisions, higher than the 86 percent of the 1990s (Rhoades, 1998a, p. 98).[22] By contrast, only 14.5 percent (ten of sixty-nine CBAs) of PTO contracts had such provisions.[23]

Language in PTO Contracts

Some contracts had related language about part-time faculty members' right to be reappointed. More common were provisions affording them the possibility after a certain period of service to one-year or multi-year appointments. That could be a leverage point for a provision indicating that adjunct faculty had a right to the institution's "good faith consideration" in reappointment, except amid program reduction. Thus, George Washington University's PTO contract accorded adjunct faculty "good faith consideration" for reappointment except in circumstances including "elimination or downsizing of a department or program, or a reduction in the number of courses or sections (hereinafter, 'courses') offered in the applicable semester, but the impact shall be limited to the relevant course(s) taught by the Faculty member." Within the same metro local (SEIU 500), American, Georgetown, and Howard universities had the same language, as did Montgomery Community College. Two PTO units (Tufts and Northeastern universities) in another SEIU Local (509 in the Boston metro area) also had the "elimination" language.[24]

Such acknowledgment of program curtailment as a cause for nonrenewal raises the possibility of a provision specifying alternatives to nonrenewal (such as reassignment), or recall, as in some CBAs covering full-time faculty. Language could also provide health care for a period of time and/or a version of severance pay found in some CBAs covering full-time faculty (not unlike course cancellation fees provisions in many PTO contracts—Rhoades, 2017a).

Overwhelmingly, PTO contracts lacked language ensuring adjunct faculty involvement in shared governance generally and particularly in program reorganization or elimination. Yet, exceptions are instructive. GW's contract indicated that regular part-time faculty compensation included an expectation of performing service at the department level. Relatedly, Emerson University's PTO contract had provision for part-time faculty to select a "liaison" (paid $300 per semester) to represent them in department-level meetings and committees. More extensively, Lesley University's contract had an "Inclusion" article that ensured part-time faculty representation on the University Council and Faculty Assembly, as nonvoting members. And Columbia College's contract provided for (unpaid) departmental representation for adjunct faculty. Finally, a few PTO contracts, like the University of Alaska's and University of Maine's identified labor/management committees in which adjunct faculty had some collective voice.

One contract (of the Vermont State Colleges) explicitly afforded adjunct faculty some role in curricular deliberations. Its "Faculty governance" article spoke to the value of a Faculty Assembly (FA) including all faculty, and indicated that, "Any proposal to abolish course offerings must be considered under the terms of this paragraph."

The University of Vermont's contract, which also afforded adjunct faculty a role in shared governance, underscores professorial stratification and full-time faculty's possible reluctance to include part-time colleagues in shared governance. Its Faculty Governance article indicated that part-time faculty involvement was subject to rules and by-laws of departments, and was only possible at the institutional level if the full-time faculty in the senate approved it.

> The parties recognize that the participation of all faculty in the institutional life of the University strengthens the institution, and therefore Departments, Schools and Colleges shall be encouraged to incorporate part-time faculty colleagues into governance. However, bargaining unit members shall be eligible to be members of and participate, by voting or otherwise, in College, School or Department meetings and governance only if, and so far as, authorized by the By-laws and other applicable guidelines of those colleges, schools or departments. Bargaining unit members shall be eligible to be members of and participate in (by voting or otherwise) the Faculty Senate and its Committees only if, and insofar as, authorized by the Faculty Senate in its Constitution and By-laws.

Range and Specificity of Rationales for Retrenchment

Rationales for retrenchment were referenced in 38 percent of CBAs with retrenchment provisions. That was much less than the 58 percent Rhoades (1998a, p. 98) found, likely because of the far larger size of the current database, the larger proportion of CBAs with retrenchment provisions, and the number of PTO contracts.

The nature of the rationales varied considerably and could be quite broad. Language like that found in the University of California's contract for non-tenure track faculty was fairly typical: "which occurs because of a lack of instructional need due to a lack of work, budgetary considerations, or programmatic change." That provides extensive discretion to management. So, too, with the Vermont State Colleges (FT) CBA, which, in addition to "program or discipline curtailment," identified "Declining enrollment in a department or program," or "faculty staffing needs at the College." Two-thirds (66 percent) of CBAs with rationales had such broad language.

In a few cases, retrenchment was identified as a management right, as in this CBA: "If the Employer determines that the number of employees is in excess of its current requirements, it shall have the right to reduce the number of employees in a given subject area, field or program" (Kalamazoo Valley Community College, COMB).

Nevertheless, a significant number of contracts specified rationales. Most common were those that specified what enrollment declines justified retrenchment, as in this case: "E. Insufficient enrollment for full-time faculty load is defined as one of the following: 1. In the second consecutive semester in which every member of a given discipline did not have a basic load. . . . 2. In case any member of a given discipline cannot be assigned any part of a load" (Schoolcraft Community College, COMB). Two Ohio universities (Bowling Green State and Akron) also had specific language: "Significant reduction in enrollment of a college, department/school, or program continuing over five or more consecutive academic semesters (not including summer) and which is expected to persist."

The University of San Francisco's contract provided another strategy— binding arbitration—that ensured the enrollment decline needed to be specific to the unit of layoff.

(B) *Layoff of a Tenured Association Member Due to Decline in Enrollment.* Any layoff in this category shall not be subject to arbitration provided, however, that (1) the issue of whether or not the decline in enrollment as stated in the reasons given for layoff has occurred and, (2) the issue of whether or not the scope of the layoff is commensurate with the decline in enrollment in the department or program in which layoff is made shall be subject to arbitration. . . . With regard to the latter . . . the arbitrator shall have the authority to reinstate the Association member.

158 • Faculty Negotiating Retrenchment

Some contracts also specified that the rationale for retrenchment must be embedded in a regular review of programs, through established governance structures.

Educational Reasons (AAUP)

A small number of CBAs (8 percent) had language that referenced and/or prioritized "educational reasons" in retrenchment decision-making. Several, like that of Eastern Michigan University (FT), delimited program reduction to normal governance processes, "owing to programmatic changes resulting from a Program Review conducted with appropriate faculty input." Similarly, the University of Oregon's (COMB) CBA foregrounded academic needs and required consultation with faculty: "A bargaining unit faculty member's employment may be terminated upon the determination by the President that a legitimate academic need for a discontinuance or reduction of a program or department exists. The above determinations must be made pursuant to university procedures providing for faculty and other appropriate input and be based on financial or academic considerations that reflect long-range judgments about the academic mission of the university. Legitimate considerations allowing termination do not include cyclical or temporary variations in enrollment." The last sentence identified conditions that did not qualify as educational reasons.

Along those lines, the University of Connecticut (COMB) contract held that program discontinuation and faculty retrenchment should be, "for reasons consonant with the long-range educational mission of the University." Also, see Delaware State University's CBA language: "The parties agree that any formal decision to reduce or discontinue a program or Department shall reflect long-range judgments that the educational mission of the University will be enhanced by the changes and shall not be based upon cyclical or temporary variations in enrollment."

Even stronger wording was found in the University of Cincinnati's CBA: "The [rationales] of the Administration . . . and the Board . . . shall be based entirely on the consideration that the long-range educational mission of the University as a whole will be enhanced by the discontinuation. These reasons shall not include cyclical or temporary variations in enrollment, nor shall they be primarily based on possible financial advantages which might accrue should the discontinuation occur."

Professorial stratification was evident in such provisions. For example, Portland State University's FT contract specified educational rationales in some detail: "In reaching a decision [about program reduction] . . . the President will consider, among other matters, institutional guidelines concerning the mission and educational development of the institution; departmental effectiveness and productivity; enrollment historical, current and projected; the state of development of departments." Yet, Portland State's PTO contract merely mentioned "program reduction" as a condition for retrenching faculty, and did not specify educational considerations.

Some provisions invoked educational concerns that included addressing the broader interests of students and the community.

> In the process of discontinuing programs, three basic considerations must prevail: 1) maintenance of a strong and vigorous university, 2) fulfillment of commitments to students in the process of completing discontinued programs, and 3) the fulfillment of established faculty rights and due process. (Pittsburgh State University, COMB)
>
> In the development of the recommendations, the parties agree to keep foremost in mind the needs of the students, the community, and the College's mission and goals. (Imperial Valley College, COMB)

In Ohio, five universities' contracts had related language, with the phrasing, "arrangements which can be made to allow students enrolled in the program to satisfy degree or certificate requirements," delimiting managerial discretion with an obligation to meet students' needs.

Montana State University, Billing's CBA spoke to meeting the state's needs: "In selecting the areas where the terminations will occur, primary consideration will be given to the University's responsibility to offer an appropriate range of courses and program, and to maintain a balanced institutional effort that is responsive to the needs of the students and the state."

Finally, a particularly distinctive clause spoke to accreditation in identifying reasons for program discontinuation. Shawnee State University's CBA read, "Lack of quality as identified in internal academic program reviews or external accreditation reviews." That centered on educational reasons and delimits managerial discretion in applying criteria, invoking the judgment of an external entity.

Faculty Involvement

Faculty involvement in decision-making about retrenchment can come into play at different points in time, about different aspects of the process. It can address whether retrenchment is called for and/or focused on bargaining impact. On the former, I have coded CBAs as having specific and strong, modest "meet and confer," or weak and perfunctory "meet and defer" mechanisms for faculty involvement. Were faculty involved in developing plans (strong), offering alternatives to plans (modest), or being informed about what had already been developed/decided (weak)?

Of CBAs with retrenchment clauses, 42 percent addressed faculty involvement (slightly less than the 46 percent found in 1998). Of those, nearly a third (30 percent) had weak language. Nearly half (46 percent) had relatively strong provisions. Another quarter (24 percent) had modest provisions.

Faculty involvement in regards to impact was more common than in shaping decisions about whether to retrench, as one contract clarified: "The decision to reduce/reassign bargaining unit members is within the inherent management authority of the College and is not subject to bargaining other than the impact of the action on members of the bargaining unit" (Seminole State College, FT).

Yet, strong faculty involvement could involve working through established program review processes (e.g., of the Faculty Senate) to make the "whether to retrench" decision: "Any program discontinuation which results in the layoff of a bargaining unit member must be approved through established university curricular procedures prior to any layoff recommendation or decision" (Central Michigan University, COMB, tenure-track). The declarative language of "must be approved through" is fundamental, prioritizing faculty voice and academic rationales (the nontenure-track faculty contract lacked such language).

One of the strongest examples of ensuring faculty involvement was in the Pennsylvania State System of Higher Education's (COMB) contract. It required that the local chapter president and faculty union at the system level be notified one year in advance of retrenchment plans. It detailed a "meet and discuss" process with the union (APSCUF) that involved the administration providing "accurate information, statistics, or financial data related to any such proposed [curricular] change." And the union could grieve the meet and discuss process with binding arbitration.[25]

Similarly, the University of New Hampshire's CBA centered established governance structures very early in the process: "The President shall notify the Association and the Faculty Senate Agenda Committee of the initiation of a program review in which programmatic displacement of bargaining unit faculty is possible or contemplated, at least one academic year prior to the approval of said long-range program changes by the Board of Trustees." This defensive, due-process strategy established long timelines that delimit arbitrary managerial discretion. The provision also established a joint committee composed almost solely of faculty: "The President will establish a Joint Review Committee, composed of the President's representative, three (3) bargaining unit faculty elected from the college or school involved, and three (3) other bargaining unit faculty members chosen by the Faculty Senate Agenda Committee. The . . . chair will be chosen by its members." The CBA also built in a role for the Faculty Senate, union, and faculty in the affected unit. The University of Cincinnati's contract did the same.

> After receiving the Administration's recommendations and reasons and the response, if any, from the AAUP, Faculty Senate, and/or the Faculty Members in the program, Academic Unit, or college which it is proposed to discontinue, the Board may either decide to drop the matter, or it may decide that probable cause for discontinuation exists. In the latter case, the Faculty Senate shall . . . select a committee with full authority to consider the Administration's

recommendation. This Committee shall consist of five Faculty Members, at least two of whom shall be members of the Faculty Senate. In addition, the AAUP shall have the right to appoint one non-voting member to the Committee. In addition, the Faculty Members in the program, Academic Unit, or college proposed for discontinuation shall have the right to select one non-voting member to the Committee who shall be outside of such program, Academic Unit, or college. Before final recommendations are made . . . the Committee shall consult with the Faculty Members in the program, Academic Unit, or college proposed for elimination.

That contrasts dramatically with Rogue Community College's (COMB) contract, which afforded management discretion to "establish a process for consultation and discussion with faculty members selected by the College President prior to the development of any RIF plan."

Although four-year institutions were more likely to have faculty involvement language (and stronger language) in their CBAs than were two-year institutions, there were exceptions. Many community college contracts in Washington had provisions for "Dismissal Review Committees," consisting of faculty, to which retrenched faculty could appeal. Extensive detail (often more than three pages) surrounded the processes these committees followed (despite such a strong faculty voice, management retained authority over the final decision).

Contingent Faculty Involvement?

There was no explicit provision for contingent faculty involvement in retrenchment decisions in the contracts of COMB units. Also, examples of universities with tenure-track and nontenure-track units revealed no provision for contingent faculty's voice in these matters. Thus, Eastern Michigan University's contract for tenure-track faculty had a strong meet and confer provision on these matters, whereas the full-time nontenure track faculty CBA had nothing.

Alternatives to Retrenchment

A number of contracts had provisions calling for consideration of alternatives to retrenchment before faculty layoffs. However, they only spoke to reducing costs for academic personnel through measures such as attrition and early retirement.

A handful of contracts had provisions that constituted a defensive strategy of preserving academic personnel and costs in relation to non-academic ones. For instance, "Non-bargaining unit personnel at the University shall not perform bargaining unit work if qualified faculty members who are on layoff accept the work offered" (Lake Superior State University, COMB).[26] Relatedly, Portland State University's (FT) contract spoke to maintaining "the balance between academic personnel and other elements of the budget." In Wayne County Community College's contract, that protection explicitly applied only to full-time faculty employment: "Administrators employed by the College who are absorbed or merged into a department shall not be permitted to assume teaching assignments which result in the layoff or reduction in hours of FULL-TIME employment of any member of the Bargaining Unit."

One important example spoke to maintaining instructional personnel's share of institutional expenditures: "Recognizing its commitment to the teaching faculty, the College will endeavor to reduce the non-teaching force proportionately" (Jackson Community College). Ideally, from a social justice orientation, such language would be declarative and would specify senior segments of the nonteaching force. Otherwise, cuts would likely come primarily from lower-wage support staff who were disproportionately people of color. Such specifications are important by way of social justice-oriented unionism.

Unit of Layoff—Program?

It is important to ensure in retrenchment processes that the unit of layoff be determined prior to layoff plans, preventing managers from acting arbitrarily and targeting particular faculty. Nearly one-third of retrenchment provisions (30 percent) addressed unit of layoff.

Some provisions gave managers total discretion in determining the layoff unit. "The layoff may be at an organizational level of the University such as a division, college, school, department, area, program, or other level of organization of unit as the University deems appropriate" (Michigan State University, COMB non-tenure track). Florida International University's (COMB) contract used the same "at any organizational level" and "as the University deems appropriate" language, with an additional sentence: "The sole instance in which only one (1) employee will constitute a layoff unit is when the functions that the employee performs constitute an area, program, or other level of organization at FIU." The same language was found in seven of the eight contracts in four-year institutions in Florida.

Other contracts specified the unit of program for layoff: "In this Article, 'program' shall refer to a specified curriculum that meets undergraduate or graduate degree requirements such as general education program, minor, certificate, major or other degree concentration" (Southern Oregon University, COMB). The contracts of four-year institutions that identified layoff units tended to make reference to departments, programs, or other such units and to connect program elimination to established processes of academic program review.

Notably, seven of the sixteen community college CBAs in Oregon had delimiting language predefining the unit of layoff in another way. Rogue Community College's (COMB) contract read: "A layoff unit is a recognized group of courses and/or activities by which members are grouped for purpose of this Article and which are set forth in Appendix D." Lane Community College's (COMB) contract defined eight different units, as well as multiple subunits within them.

Although the terminology was different (and more standardized) in Washington community college contracts, they similarly delimited managerial discretion. Of the twenty-eight CBAs for community colleges, twenty-three defined pre-established "Reduction in Force" units for layoff that were detailed in the CBA.

Beyond the CBAs, California's state education code delimited management's discretion regarding layoff units, defining "Faculty Service Areas" that almost all community college CBAs invoked. As in the Chabot-Las Positas CBA (COMB), all faculty were assigned an FSA, and FSAs were the appropriate unit of layoff: "Faculty Service Areas (FSAs) are established according to the Disciplines List, as adopted by the State Board of Governors of California Community Colleges, including any subsequent modifications thereof. The Faculty Association and the District shall utilize the 'Minimum Qualifications for Faculty and administrators in California Community Colleges' document" (Education Code Section 87743.3). The Grossmont Cuyamaca Community College District's (COMB) CBA prohibited after-the-fact reconfiguration of layoff units: "Change in the meaning and interpretation of the word 'Discipline' Sections of this Article that address reassignment, layoff, transfer, and reductions in force shall not be changed by virtue of regulations adopted by the Board of Governors...without AFT having first had the opportunity to negotiate such changes."

Order of Layoff

Order of layoff was addressed in 75 percent of retrenchment provisions, a smaller proportion than the 84 percent in the 1990s (Rhoades, 1998a, Table 3.4), though now, as in the 1990s, 71 percent of all the contracts in the database defined layoff order. Such provisions establish a due process right for at least some faculty. However, it was common for provisions to accord management discretion in implementing the prescribed order due to faculty members' qualifications or not compromising programs' educational needs. For example, managers could violate the prescribed order "where less senior members of the unit are essential to the program."

Typically, order referenced faculty members' status of employment and/or seniority of service (the latter was generally a tiebreaker in deciding among faculty with the same status of employment). Far fewer contracts prioritized qualifications and/or performance. Status of employment almost always took priority, including over time-based seniority of employment. Thus, recently hired tenured faculty had priority over longstanding nontenure-track faculty.

Professorial stratification was perpetuated by the vast majority of provisions. Sometimes that translated into explicitly defined "bumping rights": "Faculty members subject to reduction of staff in Subsection A. 1 above, shall have the right to bump another faculty member of least seniority in another discipline in which they are qualified, providing that they have greater seniority than the faculty member being bumped" (Oakland Community College, FT).

Another source of the prescribed order of layoff was in state statutes. Most two-year college contracts in Illinois and California referred to a state law/statute regarding community colleges and tenure. An example in California read: "Pursuant to Education Code Section 87743, the services of no regular employee shall be terminated while any probationary employee, or any other employee with less seniority, is retained to render a service in an FSA for which that regular employee is both qualified and competent as defined in Section 15.6" (Foothills/DeAnza Community College). The statutes encoded professorial stratification.[27] Some contracts went further in delimiting managerial discretion. Lewis and Clark Community College's contract added the sentence: "In implementing Section 3B-5 [of the Illinois Community College Tenure Act], the Board's determination of the skill and ability of faculty members to perform the remaining work available shall not be done in an arbitrary or capricious manner." Prairie State College's contract set an absolute limit on exceptions to the set order: "In case of layoff, within each Departmental Seniority List by range, the Board may exercise one exemption from seniority layoff, and choose to select the next senior employee indicated on the Departmental Seniority List by range."

Some CBAs of four-year institutions also set limits on management diverging from the prescribed order of layoff. Temple University's contract (COMB) required management to provide written justification for deviating from the order established in the contract. Wright State University's (COMB) contract established a faculty committee to review and make recommendations regarding variations from the defined order: "To deviate from the order of retrenchment specified in Sections 17.6.3–17.6.4.3, the University must first obtain and consider in good faith independent recommendations regarding that deviation (specifically, whether the deviation is necessary in order to meet programmatic, curricular, or other academic needs) from the impacted members' Department Chair(s) and from a committee appointed by AAUP-WSU."

Some contracts (twenty-two) mentioned diversity in relation to the order of layoffs. Typically, language foregrounded diversity and/or affirmative action in order of layoff. "The order of layoff within a department . . . shall be modified to ensure . . . compliance with the University's Affirmative Action Goals" (Portland State University, FT). Western Washington University's (COMB) contract was more specific: "In instances where application of the Retention Priority Criteria (above) shall have an adverse impact on the University's affirmative action goals and obligations and the University's commitment to a diverse and high quality faculty, the University shall make a good faith effort to prevent that impact by awarding retention priority to one or more tenured female and/or minority faculty members or other protected groups." In yet more specificity, the University of Massachusetts, Dartmouth's (COMB) contract set benchmarks for maintaining diversity: "the persons laid off shall be . . . in such a way as to preserve the same percentage of minorities and women within the bargaining unit as existed prior to retrenchment." And in Delaware State University's (FT) contract, there was a provision that if there was a conflict between the priorities of "academic program integrity, affirmative action, and seniority," then "the Association shall select two (2) representatives to meet with the appropriate Academic Dean, Provost/Vice President and the Department Head(s) involved in the case of Departments."

Notice of Layoff

Many CBAs (43 percent of those with retrenchment clauses) specified that retrenched faculty had the right to written notice for a period of time prior to layoff, somewhat lower than found in the 1990s (54 percent—Rhoades, 1998a, Table 3.4).[28]

Generalizations are difficult because many contracts accorded different periods of notice for different categories of faculty and different levels of seniority. Differentials were often identified for faculty of different employment statuses and with different levels of seniority.[29] Still, as RIR #4 calls for a minimum of thirty days, it is important to know that the modal period of notice found in the 1990s was two to six months (Rhoades, 1998a, pp. 111–112), whereas, in the current database, it was between three months and a year.

Notice can be a defensive strategy to delimit managerial flexibility, as in Owens Community College's contract. It provided a "notice" period of two years to laid-off faculty. It also accorded faculty recall rights for two years. Along similar lines, the University of Cincinnati and Wright State University contracts had a graduated schedule of notice based on years of full-time service, and if that notice was not met, the faculty member(s) received salary and benefits. Similarly, Oakton Community College's (COMB) CBA read, "Should only one year's notice be given, of program termination, the College will provide up to a maximum of one full year of base pay and full tuition/fee reimbursement." Significantly, the language did not stratify full-time and "regular" part-time faculty. Finally, the contracts of Illinois community colleges invoked a state statute requiring sixty days' notice of layoff. If such notice was not met, tenured faculty members "shall be deemed reemployed for the ensuing school year."

Generally, notice provisions embedded professorial stratification in the CBAs. There were often dramatic differences in periods of notice based on employment status. For example, in the University of Alaska contract, nontenure-track faculty in their first two years got seven days' notice, whereas tenure-track faculty in their first and second years got three and six months' notice, respectively. Notably, in an earlier 2016 CBA, nontenure-track faculty got the same period of notice as did tenure-track faculty.

Reassignment in Lieu of Retrenchment

A substantial minority of retrenchment clauses (42 percent) had language regarding "reassignment," the same incidence as in the 1990s (Rhoades, 1998a, Table 3.4). Such clauses represent another defensive strategy of bargaining impact.

166 • Faculty Negotiating Retrenchment

Although they were relatively common, overwhelmingly, these provisions included phrasing according considerable discretion to management. Typical phrasing included "shall try to," "reasonable effort," "good faith effort," "will endeavor to," and "make every effort." In most CBAs, faculty members had to seek an alternative position. And getting one was not guaranteed.

Some contracts had a related benefit that involved retraining for other positions, as in the Community College of Beaver County (FT) contract (though it left managers much discretion): "If the College deems that it would be beneficial to retrain a retrenched faculty member and if there are sufficient budgeted funds, a retraining sabbatical leave will be granted to such retrenched faculty member for educational retraining purposes." Other CBAs were far stronger in affording faculty the right to retraining: "Tenured faculty may not be laid off as a result of a program discontinuance or reduction unless the tenured faculty member has first been given an opportunity to retrain for another faculty position for which he/she is qualified" (Central Washington University, COMB). Reassignment/retraining clauses generally embedded professorial stratification in what faculty were eligible, as in this case, only tenured faculty.

Recall after Layoff

Establishing recall rights for laid-off faculty is a major defensive strategy to delimit managerial discretion in program reduction. Two-thirds of CBAs (67 percent) with retrenchment clauses established the right of retrenched faculty to be on a re-employment list. The typical period of such recall rights fell between one and three years (the longest was six years—see Evergreen State College's COMB contract—and it applied to all "regular faculty").

Most contracts stratified recall rights by faculty's employment status. For example, Eastern Michigan University's (FT, tenure-stream) CBA provided nontenured faculty with one year and tenured faculty with four years. Cuyahoga Community College's (FT) contract accorded tenured faculty five years and nontenured faculty no recall rights.

Recall provisions afforded laid-off faculty the right to reclaim positions in their units. They typically restricted managerial discretion in making new hires in retrenched units if it was in a position for which the laid-off faculty member was qualified.[30] "No department in which a layoff is in effect shall hire new faculty until all tenured faculty eligible for recall in that department have been offered recall, unless failure to hire new faculty would seriously impair the ability of the department to meet its needs as determined in Section 5(a)1 above" (Portland State University, FT). In contrast to the above language, which provided wiggle room to managers, consider the University of Oregon's (COMB) contract language: "If a bargaining unit faculty member's appointment is terminated under this Article, the work of the affected faculty member will not be performed by replacements within a period of three years, unless the affected faculty member has been offered reinstatement and at least 30 days in which to accept or decline it."

Key Takeaways

Managerial discourse and public policy in higher education have, for many decades, been about "reduction, reallocation, and retrenchment." Over time, there has been important, incremental establishment and expansion of contract language on retrenchment.

The proportion of contracts with provisions about financial exigency was almost twice that in the 1990s. But only a very small number (twelve) identified alternatives to retrenchment to prioritize core academic missions by calling for reductions in nonacademic expenditures, initiatives, and personnel.

Almost all CBAs (95 percent) had retrenchment for other rationales provisions, more than in the 1990s (86 percent). However, the proportions that provided specific rationales for retrenchment (38 percent) and for faculty voice in decision-making (42 percent) were less than in the 1990s (59 percent and 46 percent, respectively). A minority had provisions that identified the priority of educational reasons in retrenchment decision-making (8 percent), and that identified a unit of layoff (30 percent), as suggested in the AAUP's RIR #4. Some referred to students' needs and broader societal interests. But much work remains to be done.

As to whose voices were represented, there was little to no provision for the inclusion of contingent faculty voices. Only a very few PTO contracts provided the pathway or possibility of building in these faculty's voices. Moreover, order of layoff, notice, reassignment, and recall provisions, to differing degrees, often perpetuated existing professorial stratification, by status of employment and thus by faculty demographics. The path to a new progressive normal requires more than incrementally increasing due process and voice for the already "propertied" (i.e., tenured and disproportionately White male) faculty. It requires negotiating dramatically amplified due process and voice in the decision-making of disenfranchised academic employees.

8

Protections and Possibilities in Negotiating a Progressive Academy amid New Circuits of Production

· ·

I remember when people said that TV was going to fundamentally change education. Never happened. (comment from a close colleague at a professional conference, Rhoades, 1998a, p. 173)

The examples I've provided below of contract language on technology-mediated instruction are structured around the principal areas you identified in our . . . phone conversation—course assignment, development, and pay; observation and evaluation; ownership; and retrenchment and outsourcing. (May 2014 note about contract analysis I did that leaders of a bargaining unit had requested)

The use of new technologies in teaching . . . should be for the purpose of advancing the basic [knowledge] functions of colleges and universities. . . . As with all other curricular matters, the faculty should have primary responsibility for determining the policies and practices of the institution in regard to distance education. (AAUP 1999 statement on distance education)

Consider the needs and limitations of students who may lack access to the internet or face other obstacles to completing their coursework remotely, and . . . provide accommodations for those who are not currently able and/or equipped to participate effectively in an online scholastic environment. (March 11, 2020, response of University of Illinois Chicago United Faculty to the pandemic)

If, at one time, over a quarter century ago, it could be said that most faculty were skeptical about and reluctant to use new instructional technologies (first epigram), that is no longer true.[1] As I said to a labor leader in 2021, amid the pandemic, "It's pretty strange isn't it—for decades, management has complained that not enough faculty are willing to teach online, and now that so many faculty want to teach remotely, managers are insisting we have to be teaching in-person." As shall be seen later in the contract analysis, management has sought to cap faculty involvement in technology-mediated education and require their physical presence on campus, including for office hours.

The pandemic has offered academic labor the opportunity to strengthen, flip, and broaden the script in negotiating contractual provisions about instructional technology. That has included bargaining fuller defensive protections against involuntary assignment, surveillance, reducing faculty positions, and appropriating faculty's intellectual property. It also has included flipping an old script of faculty resistance to new technology in bargaining a more proactive role for faculty in shaping the adoption of, training and support for, and the use and evaluation of technology-mediated education, which more faculty are utilizing. It has further included broadening the script by bargaining social justice- and public purpose-oriented provisions. Negotiating a progressive academy amid new circuits of production in instruction entails imagining and bargaining possibilities, not just protections.

Strengthening the Defensive Script

For all their possibilities, new technologies in higher education, as in the larger economy, present threats to working conditions, jobs, and workforce configuration. In that larger economy, they can adversely impact, degrade, and replace skilled work (Braverman, 1974; Noble, 1977; Zuboff, 1988) and be a strategy for increasing productivity by cutting labor costs (Goldstein, 2014), as well as for reducing worker power (Brady, Baker, & Finnigan, 2013; Goldstein, 2014; Kalleberg, 2009). Such patterns and strategies have also been operating in higher education. Faculty's working conditions have degraded, with rising numbers and proportions of adjunct and full-time contingent faculty working in a "gig academy" (Kezar, DePaola, & Scott, 2019). The growth of distance and technology-mediated education has been central to that, with managerial extension of power over technology-mediated curriculum/programs and by often hiring more adjunct faculty to teach those courses (Rhoades, 1998a, 2007; Smith & Rhoades, 2006), over whom management has more control.

Not surprisingly, faculty bargaining units have negotiated protections regarding this "new circuit of production" in "academic capitalism" (Slaughter & Rhoades, 2004). In management's eyes, technologically-mediated distance education offers the promise of increased productivity and revenues (by tapping into broader student markets and having larger class sizes) while reducing labor costs (through standardized courses taught by adjunct faculty). So, faculty's defensive posture (second epigram) makes sense. (Smith, Rhoades, & Dougherty, 2011; Rhoades, 1998a).[2]

A central feature of that defensive posture is to either ensure that participation in distance education is voluntary or to provide extra compensation as an incentive to do that work, or both. The Association of Pennsylvania State College and University Faculties (APSCUF) had strong language along these lines. And as a sign of more faculty choosing to teach online, management sought to renegotiate that language. About a decade ago, the APSCUF president related that "They want to eliminate the compensation. They want to do more [distance education] without paying for it" (personal email, November 2013). Management wanted technology use to increase productivity at reduced cost rather than paying faculty for their expertise (and time) and "enskilling" the work (Rhoades, 1998a). The union succeeded in maintaining per-capita compensation but at a reduced rate over time. Management's desire for faculty to do more distance education gave the union leverage (see Slaughter & Rhoades, 2004, p. 160).

New instructional/learning technologies have been promoted by managers, policymakers, and foundations (e.g., Gates and Lumina—see Haddad, 2021), as innovations that enhance educational quality and opportunity. Any faculty opposition to this incomplete "completion agenda" (Rhoades, 2012a) that fails to address faculty working conditions is framed as resistance to change, students' needs, and "new realities."

Yet, that framing overlooks old, on-the-ground realities about technological "innovations." They can be more about enhancing power and revenue generation than being responsive to students' needs. As a community college colleague, a former lecturer and new department head overseeing distance education said to me in 2021, "I'm realizing from my new vantage point that these "innovations" that are being pitched to us [faculty] as helping to serve more students, really entail management exercising greater control, standardization, and surveillance of the curriculum." Working in a metro area in which most students were first-generation and Latinx, she noted research demonstrates that optimally serving students depends on contextualizing curriculum and evaluation practices to their (communities') lived experiences. However, the hyper-standardized, "innovative" online courses did not allow the adjunct faculty who taught them to adapt the curriculum and grading processes to their students. As the mantra goes, faculty's working conditions are students' learning conditions.

Flipping the Script

Beyond establishing due process protections against the adverse effects of new technologies, for some time faculty have also adopted a more proactive stance in negotiating voice and control in distance education. In a pattern accelerated by the pandemic, there has been a flipping of the script regarding voluntary assignments to distance education, and, by extension (pun intended), to remote courses. Certainly, academic labor's position on technology-mediated education continues to be that assignment to distance education be voluntary (Rhoades, 1998a; Smith, Rhoades, & Dougherty, 2011), as articulated in a union report on community colleges in New York: "While all faculty should be given the opportunity to develop and teach Distance Education (DE) courses, no faculty member should be required to teach a DE course" (NYSUT, 2013, p. 22). Just as certainly, though, amid the pandemic, faculty have consistently opposed management's rush to go "back to normal" with face-to-face instruction. They have tried to negotiate the option of continuing teaching remotely.

As early as 1999, the AAUP issued a statement on distance education that emphasized the primary role of faculty in all curricular matters. The statement also foregrounded educational versus financial matters in decision-making about distance education, as in the third epigram. Often, in CBAs, that translates into decision-making about distance education following the regular academic governance processes that attach to other curricula. The aim is to proactively ensure professorial control of technology-mediated education.

More and more faculty are engaged in remote education. More are articulating a preference for such modalities in a pattern that one analyst suggests is gendered, for it accommodates various caretaking responsibilities. Along these lines, United Academics University of Oregon tried (unsuccessfully) in the early fall of 2021 to negotiate a policy enabling faculty who are caregivers with (unvaccinated) children twelve and under to teach remotely. The union's effort was in support of such a request by the university's Center for the Study of Women in Society (UAUO, 2021). As in the broader economy, remote work is being normalized, and more workers are negotiating for that option.

Broadening the Script

Whether or not a faculty member has taught a distance education course, they have almost all utilized course management systems. Moreover, after a pandemic in which almost all colleges/universities went to remote course delivery for some time, virtually (pun intended) all faculty now have experience in technology-mediated instruction (and advising). That calls for broadening the script in negotiations to address new forms of technology-mediated education, such as hybrid and flipped classes, and meeting students during virtual office hours. It also calls for addressing broader social justice and public-purpose considerations in technology use amplified in the pandemic.

Pre-pandemic, there had already been a generational shift in using instructional technology and a gendered dimension making remote work attractive to caregivers (Eaton, 2020). Coming out of the pandemic more classes are being taught in hybrid forms that combine face-to-face with online learning. It is time to broaden the scope of bargaining beyond traditional distance education.

Moreover, there are good reasons to ask, "Why not the 'New Flexible'?" instead of the managerial push of "returning to 'normal' after COVID-19" (Saia, Nerlich, & Johnston, 2021). We have learned we can operate in ways reflecting "universal design," more accessible for people with disabilities (and other marginalized populations). "The reality of the COVID-19 pandemic is that it magnified systemic inequities for marginalized communities, including BIPOC, the elderly, those living in poverty . . . and people with disabilities" (Saia et al., 2021).

"Normal" consisted of historic, ongoing systemic inequities (see also, Mohr, 2021).

The pandemic has made clearer than ever and resurfaced concerns about a digital divide in students' access to high speed Internet. Thus, the University of Illinois Chicago United Faculty bargaining unit in March 2020 called on the university to meet students' access needs amid the pandemic (fourth epigram). This included not simply access to computer labs and libraries, "but should also involve creative and proactive solutions such as making available mobile hotspots and laptops so students can work remotely." UICUF also called on the university to provide "grants to students with financial limitations to attain equipment and internet needed to participate in online courses."

Such negotiating beyond the direct interests of the two parties at the bargaining table represents academic labor broadening the script in negotiating technology-mediated education. It affords an opportunity to emphasize that negotiations go beyond management and labor, implicating students and the academy's public purposes. That can be seen, for example, in negotiating intellectual property provisions that benefit students and communities, the essence of "public interest bargaining" (Rhoades, 2015c, 2017b). Academic labor's best future is in negotiating for workplace justice connected to social justice in the academy and the broader public interest (Rhoades, 2021).

Chapter Organization and Questions

The themes of strengthening, flipping, and broadening the script speak to faculty negotiating protections and possibilities in a progressive academy amid new circuits of production. With the near-universal adoption of course management systems and an accelerated pandemic shift to hybrid and remote teaching/advising and curriculum, instruction has all become technology-mediated beyond conventional distance education. Thus, I start with three analyses of contractual provisions that reach beyond fully online and fully face-to-face education, addressing hybrid classes, virtual office hours, and course management systems.

Subsequently, findings are presented in relation to considerations that have defined most language about technology-mediated education in past analyses (e.g., Rhoades, 1998a) and presently. I examine contractual provisions about assignment, workload, office hours, compensation, class size, training and support, evaluation and surveillance, academic governance, displacement/retrenchment, and intellectual property.

At the analytical core are questions of how contractual provisions affect the (im)balance of power between managerial discretion and faculty rights, as well as the voice and stratification among segments of faculty. So, too, I explore whether and how public purposes/benefits and educational quality are addressed/invoked.

The Contracts: Beyond Distance Education

Hybrid Education

To what extent do contracts address technology-mediated "hybrid" education, and has that incidence changed over time? As a marker of how "institutionalized" it has become, what definitions of hybrid are embedded within contracts?

Hybrid Education–Incidence in the Contracts. A decade-old analysis of four-year institution CBAs found only six contracts that mentioned hybrid education (Rhoades, 2017b). In the current HECAS database, twenty-one contracts did so—that is 14 percent of such CBAs in the database.

Such language was far more present in two-year institutions' CBAs, of which 107 had language about hybrid education (30 percent of 354 such contracts). Although no comparable national baseline comparison is available, a decade-old analysis of such contracts in New York revealed some limited contractual language on the topic: "Faculty . . . are now embracing it [online learning] in the form of blended/hybrid courses. The trend is reflected in an expansion of contract and policy language in our locals to address blended/hybrid courses" (NYSUT, 2013, p. 6). Further, analysis of archived CBAs in HECAS revealed that some current CBAs with language about hybrid education lacked such language fifteen to twenty years ago (e.g., Grand Rapids Community College, Schoolcraft College, and West Shore Community College). So, as technology advances, language is slowly being negotiated into CBAs.

Definition of Hybrid Education. The definition of hybrid varied widely in CBAs in the percentage of time face-to-face versus online. In some cases, it was vague (or nonexistent), as with Bend Community College's contract, which read, "Hybrid Course—A course that displaces some, but not all face-to-face class time with web-based tools." Similarly, Central State University's contract defined as hybrid, "Any course offered by the University in which some portion of traditional face-to-face "seat time" has been replaced by online or interactive video course activities." Other contracts defined hybrid in terms of "significant" portions of the course being online, or specified particular percentages of time, which varied: "Blended Learning Course (also known as Hybrid or mixed mode): any course offered by the University in which 30–79%) of class meetings and/or instructional activities are replaced with online instruction" (Shawnee State University), and "HYBRID: There is a mix of distance and face-to-face instruction, with at least 51% of the instruction online" (Western Michigan University). Over time, that percentage even varied sometimes in the same institution. Erie Community College's pre-2008 contract left the proportion up to the faculty member, whereas later contracts specify at least 40 percent of hybrid courses must be online.

That latter point speaks to faculty desire to teach remotely, evident as well in Saginaw State University's contract, which gave faculty discretion in this regard: "Faculty may substitute up to 5 contact hours of instruction in any 3 or 4 credit face-to-face course with online instruction at their discretion." Any more than five contact hours required approval through the normal academic governance process.

In almost all cases, language about hybrid education was embedded within larger provisions about distance education (Western Michigan University's article on "eLearning" was an exception). In some cases, though, different language for hybrid courses was identified. For example, Hofstra University's CBA indicated that in contrast to a full distance learning course, faculty could request but were not "entitled to" a stipend for developing a hybrid class. Pierce College District's CBA dealt with training—in "hybrid pedagogy"—specific to blended courses.

Office Hours

Beyond teaching courses remotely, can some proportion of advising in required office hours be held remotely? Management may seek control of faculty time and of their campus presence, a hotly contested issue amid but also prior to the pandemic, especially in two-year institutions. Some contracts defined the number of hours and/or days faculty must be on campus even if they are teaching solely at a distance.

The pandemic has strengthened an emergent faculty push to work remotely, as generational and gendered differences play out regarding scripts about work(place): "Faculty who have resisted web-based teaching and learning now are embracing it in the form of blended/hybrid courses. This trend is reflected in an expansion of contract and policy language in our locals to address blended/hybrid courses" (NYSUT, 2013. p. 6). In a conversation preceding a 2020 virtual webinar panel on bargaining amid the pandemic, Cynthia Eaton, the author of that analysis, observed that she was seeing even more new language specifying conditions surrounding virtual office hours. She said this language spoke to the preferences of younger faculty, especially those who are women and/or caretakers for more flexible work arrangements. Control over their time was preferable to being, in Eaton's characterization, "chained to the desk." Such issues reflect a larger societal dynamic as it plays out in collective bargaining of how women's participation in the workforce is compromised by the lack of affordable child and elder care, again clarified and heightened in the pandemic.[3]

If current negotiations of technology-mediated education reflect the emergence of new circuits of production, they also are simply a new variation on an old theme about controlling faculty's time and place of work. Dating back to older modalities of teaching physically at remote sites, some CBAs, particularly of four-year institutions, had built-in protections of faculty time. For example, Central Michigan University's contract spoke to teaching at sites distant from the main campus—such faculty "shall be compensated for travel time at a rate of not less than 30¢ per mile for travel either from their residence or from Mt. Pleasant, Michigan, to the location where the course is being taught." It had a special provision ensuring that faculty would not be required to teach on-campus at "non-traditional times." Relatedly, the University of Minnesota, Duluth CBA read, "1.2 If travel to a remote site is required on a regular basis . . . additional compensation of $15/hour of travel shall be provided. 1.3 If total teaching, preparation (on-site), and travel time is greater than 8 hours, or if travel distance is greater than 50 miles and course starting time is before 9 A.M. or course ending time is later than 8 P.M., the member will be reimbursed for an overnight stay." In contrast to such provisions, there is virtually (pun intended) no protection of faculty personal time with distance and hybrid education. This can be read as new technology bringing greater managerial control of faculty time/work. But it can also be read as faculty seeking greater control over their time and work, by working remotely.

The negotiation of "virtual" office hours also represents an ongoing labor-management negotiation over how and where faculty best serve students. Particularly in two-year institution contracts, there is sometimes great specificity in provisions defining faculty time spent on tasks (e.g., office hours) and where that work should be done.

Here faculty unions could broaden the script of their negotiations. Who benefits from requiring on-campus office hours in commuter institutions in which most students attend part-time, live off campus, and work up to forty hours a week? Who benefits from such requirements in institutions where over two-thirds of the faculty are part-time, with many teaching at more than one campus? Neither students nor employees are served by such requirements. Virtual office hours can be an optimal adaptation to part-time students' lives, filled with paid work and caretaking responsibilities. And they afford a private space for discussing sensitive educational (and other) matters, as most community college faculty who are adjuncts lack private space in which to meet students. That rationale is explicit in some units' contract language about adjunct faculty's access to private office space (Rhoades, 2020).

The implications of the above are profound for negotiating access to quality working conditions, which, as seen in chapter 4, in materials/facilities focus considerably on adjunct faculty access to office space. What if negotiations shifted to include supporting such faculty's home use of infrastructure (Internet) and hardware (laptop) to meet students' needs?

The prevailing script now, in two-year college settings, is a longstanding one of management seeking control over professorial autonomy in required time on campus. The CBAs of many two-year colleges detailed management's expectations about faculty's required time on campus (partly concerning office hours). The contract of the County of Lake Community College District gives a sense of the level of detail: "Faculty members shall be required to keep ten office hours per week. Office hour periods are to be no shorter than thirty minutes. Faculty members shall keep at least one office hour each day at a facility, extension site, or clinical setting, Monday through Friday, except when the College shall not be in session, and except one of such days in the week may be omitted if the faculty member is not regularly scheduled to teach on such day."

Many provisions allowed faculty who teach classes online to fulfill some portion (in some cases, all) of their required office hours virtually: "Office hours for distance education courses may be conducted in the virtual classroom environment. The faculty member shall not be required to be in their assigned campus office during the period of the online office hours" (Clatsop Community College). The substitution of virtual office hours was often proportional to the assignment of distance education courses, as with Mt. Hood Community College's contract: "The number of virtual office hours will be proportional to the distance-learning component of the faculty member's basic contract workload" (which was capped at 70 percent distance education courses). Sometimes, such office hours were capped, as at St. Louis Community College: "For those that teach online or hybrid format or in a clinical setting: A faculty member may schedule up to 2 of their 10 campus hours in a virtual format. If the faculty member teaches

2 or more online or hybrid courses within their load, they may schedule up to 4 of their 10 campus hours in a virtual format."

The negotiating script is getting flipped, with faculty negotiating for more flexibility. That is explicit in the history cited in Elgin Community College's CBA.

> Whereas, the 2014–2016 CBA between the Board of Trustees ... and the Elgin Community College Faculty Association ("ECCFA") in Article 4.5 provides, in limited circumstances, the ability of a faculty member to use virtual office hours through the College's course management system; Whereas, ECCFA proposed for the expanded use of virtual office hours during the 2016 negotiations for a successor CBA; Whereas, the Board was inclined to reject the proposal, but after reviewing the matter, it has entered into this letter of agreement with ECCFA allowing the expanded use of virtual office hours through a pilot program format, to be evaluated upon completion.

The administration's resistance to the idea was evident in the next section of the clause.

> The pilot program ... will be administered by ECC's Instructional Improvement and Distance Learning department. ... Virtual office hours shall be provided exclusively through the College's course management system. ... No more than ten full-time faculty members and five unit adjunct faculty members may participate in the program with pre-approval of the divisional dean and the vice president of teaching, learning, and student development. ... A maximum of three (3) office hours per week for full-time faculty members and one (1) office hour per week for unit adjunct faculty members may be delivered in the pilot format. Selected faculty shall successfully complete training on virtual office hours provided by ECC's Instructional Improvement and Distance Learning department. ... At the conclusion of the ... semester, the pilot program shall sunset and be evaluated by the administration for a recommendation to the board.

The level of managerial monitoring, resistance, and control was striking.

Management's focus here was to require faculty's "campus presence" to control their "time on task," partly through controlling where the tasks are done.[4] For example, at Wayne County Community College, virtual office hours had to be conducted at the college's Distance Learning Support Center. At Spoon River College, "Faculty who are permitted to teach their entire load online must maintain at least four of their eight on-campus hours in person."

By contrast, Montgomery Community College's CBA enabled faculty who teach fully online to hold all office hours virtually. So, too, stated the Minnesota State College and University Faculty's contract (faculty in two-year settings):

"If a faculty member's entire assignment is online, the office hours can be held entirely online."

Course Management Systems

As specified in the Elgin Community College contract above, there was some reference in CBAs to course management systems (CMS). My interest in CMSs was partly related to monitoring, control, and surveillance of faculty time and work. I was also interested in whether and in what ways faculty had individual and/or collective rights as to using course management systems and in whether these were linked to students' educational and privacy interests.

A few contracts (as with Elgin's) required faculty to utilize course management systems or platforms as the vehicle for conducting virtual office hours. Such systems facilitate managerial oversight and surveillance of faculty work. More broadly, such systems also render faculty (and students in their classrooms) susceptible to off- and on-campus political and student groups' surveillance, which can compromise academic freedom and students' privacy (Dougherty, Rhoades, & Smith, 2018). Consider Florida International University's contract language on class recordings: "No one who is not enrolled . . . will be granted access to recorded lectures and discussions in that class except as approved by the employee."

As for faculty's individual and/or collective voice in decision-making about technology-mediated education, only eight contracts in HECAS had language providing even some level of faculty consultation in the choice and use of a CMS. One of the strongest examples was in McHenry County Community College's contract: "The responsibilities of this [Distance Education] committee include but are not limited to the following: a. Review and recommend Distance Education/Learning Management System (LMS) policies and procedures; b. Review and recommend procedures for the adoption of new technology to enhance or promote curriculum and student success; c. Review requests for the adoption of new technologies to enhance or promote curriculum and student success." The referenced Distance Education committee included three faculty members appointed by their academic divisions. Wright State University's contract provided for several layers of academic governance: "21.4 Any major changes to the technology or course management system that supports distance learning will be reviewed and recommended through the IT governance infrastructure. Before making any such major changes, however, the University will solicit recommendations from the Academic Services Committee, from the college committees assigned to consider distance learning pursuant to Section 21.3, and from a seven person University Distance Learning Committee consisting of one Bargaining Unit Faculty Member selected by and from each of the College Committees identified in Section 21.3." Another mechanism for ensuring an academic voice in decision-making was provided in Shasta College's (COMB) contract: "4.6 The selection of the college Course Management System shall be by a committee of active online instructors with recognized online teaching experience. . . . The committee will recommend the selected CMS to the District for final evaluation."

The remaining contracts that provided for faculty voice in decision-making about CMSs did so in less specified ways. Three community college contracts in Oregon had language about College "collaboration" with a faculty committee to "designate a common learning management system that it will provide and support" (Lane Community College—Clackamas Community College's FT and PTO contracts had the very same language). Also, Lansing Community College's contract read, "Decisions for adoption of new course management systems will continue to be made collaboratively between faculty and administrators." And Robert Morris University's contract read, "Consultation on significant changes to the Learning Management System will occur between faculty and the University."

The above exceptions prove the rule of managerial discretion, which was explicit in Imperial Valley College's CBA: "If the District changes to a new course management system . . . the District will provide training to faculty members. . . . The Association will have the right to consult with the District on the training to be provided and the transition time needed for implementation of any new course management system." Management can change the course management system at will; the faculty union can only consult with the District on implementation and training. Nassau Community College's contract established that managerial discretion even more completely: "The College shall determine the course management system to be used."

In sum, there were some examples of provisions that afforded faculty voice and rights in regard to new circuits of production "beyond distance education," suggesting that faculty unions are beginning to flip the script. Overwhelmingly, though, bargaining units are behind the technology curve in negotiating technology-mediated education, ceding rather than strengthening the script of managerial authority in these realms.

The Contracts: Distance Education

Three decades ago, a defining study of CBAs nationally (Rhoades, 1998a, Table 5.1) found that 63 percent lacked provisions about distance education. That has changed dramatically (as has the introduction of provisions, as noted above, regarding technology-mediated teaching and advising). Now, 75 percent of CBAs have such provisions, which are fairly evenly distributed among contracts of four-year (74 percent) and two-year (76 percent) institutions.[5]

In presenting the findings, I focus on provisions that speak to the (im)balance of power between management and labor, "professional" issues, and public interest matters. The first address whether use of technology is voluntary, workload, pay, evaluation, and job security (displacement by technology). The second speak to a labor-based conception of quality focused on workplace conditions (class size, training/support), voice in decision-making about distance education (academic governance), and ownership/control over their intellectual property. The latter is any language invoking public benefits.

Voluntary Assignment and Workload

Historically, faculty unions have foregrounded protections to ensure that using instructional technology is voluntary and not a required workload. As NYSUT's (2013) "Negotiating the Distance and Beyond" analysis of two-year college contracts in New York advised, "No faculty member should be required to teach a DE course" (p. 22). Yet, as more faculty have taught and demonstrated interest in technology-mediated instruction, management, especially in two-year colleges, has sought to delimit such assignments in their workload. Both patterns are evident in the CBAs.

Among four-year contracts, twenty-five (of the 112 addressing distance education) ensured that assignment was voluntary. Another fourteen delimited faculty's time off/on campus—all dealing with whether and what proportion of office hours could be held virtually if faculty were teaching remotely. Thus, Youngstown State's contract indicated that faculty who are teaching fully online can also hold virtual office hours exclusively.

Among two-year colleges, 114 (of 288) ensured that assignment was voluntary. As well, ninety-seven addressed faculty's time on campus versus working remotely. Contracts in two-year colleges far more often and more aggressively delimited or controlled faculty's time and place of work during office hours but also in campus presence.

A succinct example of voluntary assignment language was Henry Ford Community College's full-time faculty contract: "A teacher shall not be required to teach a course by means of Distance Education" (the PTO unit contract had no such clause). Another, from Clackamas Community College, very unusually, was for a part-time-only unit contract: "The use of instructional technologies to support classes is an educational choice that should be left to the judgment of each individual faculty member." A counter-example was East Central College's contract, which stated, "Full-time faculty may be required to teach evening courses, online courses, or at any campus location in order to meet their contractual load." A small number of CBAs' made voluntary assignment conditional, as in Terra State Community College's contract: "If there are insufficient volunteers to develop and/or teach distance learning courses, the College may require faculty to develop and/or teach a distance learning course."

Yet, many provisions set caps on the proportion of workload that could be performed online. For example, Mott Community College had a provision entitled, "Ceiling on On-Line Classes for Full-Time Faculty." It was no more than 50 percent online (no such ceiling existed for part-time faculty). Big Bend Community College set the bar lower, providing a rationale: "To ensure a sufficient presence on campus, unless authorized by the Vice President of Instruction, full-time Academic Employees shall teach a minimum of 1/3 of their teaching load as traditional face-to-face classes."

Other two-year college CBAs stipulated that faculty must spend a certain amount of time on campus as part of their workload. For example: "Faculty members teaching exclusively online and/or at a location off campus will be on campus where their department office is located at least one day per week" (Lansing Community College). Big Bend Community College's contract provided a rationale: "Full-time Academic Employees teaching e-learning courses are expected to maintain a substantial level of contribution to the campus community."

An exception to that pattern was in Bergen Community College's contract: "BCC faculty members may fulfill their in-load teaching contractual obligation through on-campus, online, hybrid, or media courses, or through any combination of these teaching modalities. Faculty members may teach any number of their in-load courses in any of these modalities." So, faculty are negotiating both defensively and to flip the script.

Compensation

I found (Rhoades, 1998a) that extra compensation was provided in 36 percent of distance education provisions. Most were one-time payments for developing a class. Two were for prorated pay. The others were piece rate or flat payments. One exception was in the contract of the Pennsylvania State System of Higher Education, which defined a prorated cap (no more than one-fourth of the academic year salary per credit hour), and which was later renegotiated down.

Now, 38 percent of the contracts that addressed distance education had compensation provisions (overwhelmingly in the contracts of two-year colleges, 139, versus in four-year institutions' contracts). Many provided one-time payments for developing a course, but many others provided additional compensation. And a number provided prorated pay. Notably, Ocean County Community College's PTO contract had pay prorated to class size, and Spoon River College also had extra pay for class size over the cap. Finally, Green River College had stipends for additional distance education classes, plus pay proportionate to class size.

In all of the above cases, faculty have negotiated remuneration for the additional work involved in distance education (and sometimes for class size), as a disincentive to management to overload faculty with larger classes.

Class Size

Class size provisions were in twenty of the 112 contracts in four-year institutions addressing distance education, and 112 of the 268 in two-year institutions.[6] Most were either hard caps/limits or language that distance education classes must be equivalent in size to comparable face-to-face classes. At issue were workload (i.e., preventing speedup) and quality.

In four-year institution contracts, roughly half indicated equivalent class sizes for distance and face-to-face classes, and half set hard caps. A few indicated that class size would be set by departments or by pedagogical considerations.

In two-year institution contracts, a little less than half established class sizes for distance education equivalent to those for face-to-face classes. The rest set hard caps, a small number of which were below caps for face-to-face classes.

One noteworthy strategy in a handful of two-year institution contracts regarding quality was a provision that the class size of a technology-mediated class be smaller the first time it was taught: "The first time a faculty member teaches a particular distance learning course, it shall have a maximum enrollment of twenty (20) students. Subsequent offerings of the same course by the same instructor shall have the same class size limit as its non-distance learning counterpart course" (Oakland Community College). Muskegon Community College's contract capped distance classes at 70 percent of on-campus class sizes, addressing the extra workload they can bring. Wayne County Community College's contract went further: "Enrollment in any class shall be capped at 75 students for non-distance learning courses and 33 for distance learning courses."

Evaluation and Surveillance

One contract provision pointed to part of what faculty were negotiating against. Tallahassee Community College's contract indicated that "the Dean may enter an online course at any time to assess instructional quality." The concern was/is about not only arbitrary managerial actions but also student and external public surveillance and intervention compromising academic freedom and quality. On the latter point, see Dodge City Community College's contract: "Broadcast and rebroadcast telecommunications may be used only for two-way student/instructor communication, not for viewing by the general public unless otherwise agreed to by the instructor and the College."

In four-year institution CBAs, there were twenty-six provisions about evaluation and/or surveillance. Overwhelmingly, the provisions focus on protections. About a third required notice before visiting the class remotely, and another third addressed restrictions on taping. For example, the University of Maine (FT) contract indicated that taped classes could not be used for evaluation (the University of Massachusetts, Amherst, said there could only be taping for evaluation if there had been a complaint). A few contracts (Chicago State and Oakland University, for example) spoke to evaluation of the modality and distance education curriculum, beyond the individual faculty member.

In two-year institution CBAs, there were 107 such provisions. Over one-third (thirty-seven) provided for either notice before a classroom observation or prohibited taping. Some specified that taping was only for educational purposes, and a few invoked a condition of monitoring being allowed if there was a concern about a problem. For example, under an online instruction clause, Richland Community College's contract read, "Direct email interchange between students and faculty shall not be monitored by the College without prior notice and reasonable suspicion of improper conduct." Finally, some exemplars provided for a collective faculty role in evaluation, as at Mt. Hood Community College and Lane Community College, discussed below in the academic governance section.

Contract language about surveillance focused on ensuring faculty protections against unannounced surveillance of technology-mediated classrooms, mostly by managers, but also by students and the public, who might target faculty (Dougherty, Rhoades, & Smith, 2018). To that end, many provisions proscribed the taping and/or distribution of recorded classes, or specified they could only be used for educational purposes. One contract, of Lane Community College, distinctively focused also on protecting students' privacy, broadening the negotiating script: "Faculty and student privacy shall be protected and respected. No observation or monitoring of student-student or faculty-student interaction shall take place without prior agreement with the faculty member(s) responsible for the class, and prior notification of the students involved."

Displacement

The classic labor/management struggles over (new) technology revolve around whether it will replace or reduce employees, weaken the bargaining unit, and/or shift investment to other categories of employees. That contest defines faculty negotiations with management over technology-mediated education. It has played out in defensive and proactive faculty strategies. As shall be seen, language matters in these negotiations.

In the 1990s, only eleven contracts (5 percent of all CBAs then) had language protecting faculty from being displaced by the use of instructional technology. And five invoked technological change as a rationale justifying retrenching faculty (Rhoades, 1998a, pp. 187, 194–195).

In the current database, fifty-five CBAs (11 percent of all CBAs) had displacement provisions. That is an improvement, but still a very small percentage of CBAs.

Overwhelmingly, contract language addresses either displacement of faculty from the institution using distance education or contracting it out. In either case, the phrasing matters. Some contracts, as with Youngstown State's used "it is not the intent" language: "It is not the intent of the University to use distance education technology to permanently reduce, eliminate, or consolidate full-time bargaining unit positions at the University." Similarly, Wenatchee Valley College's contract on subcontracting read, "The administration agrees that it is not the intent of the District to replace full-time positions by subcontracting credit courses with outside contractors."

Some other contracts used imperative phrasing that left little discretion to management. For example, the Community Colleges of Spokane's CBA read, "No academic employee will be displaced because of distance learning or computer-aided courses, unless such courses are a condition of employment."

The Community Colleges of Philadelphia contract went beyond that: "No distance education sections shall be instructed or conducted unless the College instructor of record is a member of one of the two faculty bargaining units of the Federation."

Keeping technology-mediated instruction within the bargaining unit has taken various forms. It can mean keeping faculty who teach remotely in the bargaining unit—an important negotiation, in that, for example, eight contracts in four-year institution contracts indicated that faculty whose load is entirely remote were not included in the bargaining unit. It can mean ensuring faculty in the unit are not displaced by staff outside the unit, a contingency that Lane Community College's contract addressed: "Staff hired specifically for the development and delivery of distance learning courses cannot displace current faculty who refuse distance learning assignments." Another particularly forward-looking provision was in St. Mary College's contract: "Also included in the bargaining unit will be any Bargaining Unit Faculty positions at the College's locations in California and in its LEAP and online programs created during the term of this contract where the Bargaining Unit Faculty member is the instructor of record for matriculating students for credit-bearing courses at the College." The optimal game is not simply to protect existing positions, but also to proactively negotiate to ensure that as management invests in expanding technology-mediated instruction, the bargaining unit grows proportionately (see Rhoades, 1998a, pp. 195–196).

In response to managerial privatizing initiatives, like contracting out, protecting and ensuring the bargaining unit's growth involves ensuring that all technology-mediated education is done by bargaining unit members. Thus, some faculty bargaining units have negotiated against larger academic capitalist ventures that involve outsourcing segments of the curriculum, as in this case: "Courses traditionally taught by full-time faculty members, or courses they are capable of teaching which lie within the curricular purviews of BCCC course offerings, will not be awarded to other institutions for transmission into the campus by electronic means" (Bucks County Community College). That has included historically, mobilizing against public universities' online "deals" with for-profit entities such as eCollege, a division of Pearson (Straumsheim, 2013). One of my favorite protest signs from such organizing was held by adjunct faculty in a Campus Equity Week march in Texas—"Hire teachers, Fire Pearson, Fund Public Education" (Tamayo, 2013). That is broadening the script in negotiating the new circuits of production, for higher education's publicness.

Training/Support

By way of professional issues, in the 1990s (Rhoades, 1998a), only nine contracts had training provisions (11 percent of CBAs addressing distance education). One required training before faculty could teach a distance education class. Only two allocated monies (minimal) for such training/support. That offered little evidence that management was investing in enskilling faculty and ensuring quality instruction with the new modalities.

Now, thirty-nine four-year institution contracts (35 percent of CBAs addressing distance education) had training/support provisions. In six cases, it was required, and in just two, monies were specified for that training. Notably, one was for part-time faculty. "During each of the three (3) years of this Agreement, the College shall provide $18,000 to be used for educating part-time faculty members in the use of new technologies in their disciplines" (Rhode Island School of Design). Also importantly, APSCUF's contract provided for "faculty members' input into the design of the training."

In two-year institutions, 121 contracts (46 percent of CBAs addressing distance education) had training/support provisions. About one-third (forty-four) required training before teaching, a big shift from the past. Only a couple designated monies for that work, and most language was unspecified.

Yet, there were a number of exceptions and exemplars. Bergen Community College's contract provided a full program of training, as well as mentors. Centralia Community College's contract provided $5,000 annually to be disbursed by the Learning Management Training System committee to train adjunct faculty. Wayne County Community College's contract established a Pilot Mentoring program giving release time to two full-time faculty with distance learning expertise to mentor others.

As a transition to the ensuing section on academic governance, some CBAs established various forms and levels of collective faculty control over the training. Mt. Hood Community College's (COMB) contract situated that control in a Distance Learning Advisory Committee, reporting to a vice president and the faculty senate (with faculty members appointed by the senate and an equal number of administrators), responsible for coordinating and reviewing a Faculty Academy (the PTO contract at that institution provided for representation of a part-time faculty member on the committee). Antelope Valley College's contract indicated that the training be overseen by the faculty senate. The Los Rios Community College District's contract indicated that the training would be developed with the faculty union. And although it was not specific to technology-mediated education, Lane Community College's contract established that professional development would be coordinated by a Faculty Professional Development Committee consisting of eight union members appointed by the Faculty Association and one ex-officio administrator. The chair was a bargaining unit member who served as the Faculty Professional Development Coordinator.

Academic Governance

In the 1990s, eleven CBAs (14 percent of contracts addressing distance education) had provisions for collective academic control of distance education (Rhoades, 1998a, p. 200). Three indicated distance education course approval or assignment processes would follow standard procedures used for other curricula, and eight specified substantial collective faculty input into such decision-making.

Now, a considerably larger number of CBAs had such provisions—thirty-five in four-year institution CBAs (31 percent of contracts addressing distance education), and eighty-five in two-year institution CBAs (32 percent of contracts). Moreover, a far larger number (twenty-five in four-year and thirty-nine in two-year institutions) ran decision-making about technology-mediated education through standard academic governance processes. The rationale underlying these provisions was made explicit in some CBAs, like that of Clackamas Community College: "Quality Control 1. It is a shared goal that distance education courses will meet Clackamas Community College's standards of academic quality and effectiveness. Therefore, distance-education courses ... shall follow the usual processes adopted in the ... curriculum approval process." The faculty's curricular control was to ensure quality control.

CBAs that established specific committees for managing technology-mediated education often afforded faculty specific control over key realms of curricular decision-making (in one other case, vested in the academic department). Some of the provisions, as at South Suburban College provided a full page of detail about the role of (in that case) the Distance Learning Committee. Reflecting the broadening of technology-mediated activities, the University of Massachusetts, Dartmouth's contract shifted terminology in the early 2000s from the Distance Learning Committee to the e-learning committee. In another marker of the times, Wayne State's contract established a labor/management committee amid the pandemic, "In recognition of the unprecedented changes to online teaching brought on by the COVID-19 global pandemic."

Shasta Tehama Trinity Joint Community College District's contract indicated that distance education courses and programs would be treated like any other. Yet, it also very unusually provided for a central faculty role in choosing a course management system. "The selection of the college Course Management System shall be by a committee of active online instructors with recognized online teaching experience. . . . The committee will recommend the selected CMS to the District for final evaluation." In McHenry County College's contract, the Distance Learning Team was responsible for reviewing and making recommendations about distance education/learning management systems policies, and requests for adopting new technologies. And Bellevue Community College's contract indicated that all technology decisions needed to be taken in an "inclusive process" involving faculty, staff, and students.

Intellectual Property

Double the proportion of CBAs addressing distance education now (44 percent) spoke to intellectual property compared to the 22 percent of the 1990s (Rhoades, 1998a, p. 187). Yet, the basic features of these provisions remained much the same.

Overwhelmingly, provisions focused on ownership, share of the proceeds, and reuse. Overwhelmingly as well, ownership depended on whether the property was created on the faculty member's own time, with "substantial use of institutional resources" (or comparable phrasing), or as a "work for hire."[7]

What most faculty negotiators have successfully sought to protect against is defining distance education as a work for hire, with the institution thereby owning the property. West Shore Community College provided an interesting example of how such a provision in an earlier contract had been dropped in more recent CBAs. Thus, the 2004 contract had the following language: "All distance learning development shall be executed on a work-for-hire basis. Copyrights for all distance learning course materials shall be held by the College. If a distance learning course is sold by the College to another institution or sold on a license basis, the faculty developer shall receive 50% of the gross sale amount." The 2022 contract had no such first line. Although there was a "work for hire" section of the article, it was not specified for all distance education. And there was a provision for joint ownership even when substantial college resources were used.

As in the 1990s, the provisions were heavily weighted toward faculty sole ownership or joint ownership (if there was substantial use of institutional resources), with some examples of faculty owning the intellectual property even if substantial resources were utilized. The vast majority also accorded faculty creators first right of refusal or some sort of control over the reuse of intellectual property.

One irony of the "substantial use of college resources" condition is that adjunct faculty create property, tend to have limited access to institutional resources, and yet few Part-Time Only contracts had intellectual property provisions. Almost a decade ago, I made this observation to a very savvy labor organizer, who then emailed me in reply: "I am always interested in expanding what we are doing in bargaining, and intellectual property rights have come up a lot. . . . Many of our members are interested in owning . . . intellectual property 'objects'—such as video of them made for online classes" (personal email, April 2015).

My response to her underscored that part-time faculty are exploited not only in terms of their low-wage labor relative to what they are generating by way of credit hours, but they have also been reduced to deliverers of classes rather than creative producers of the curriculum.

Adjunct faculty create intellectual property, literally on their own time in their own space. It is far easier said than done, but they could negotiate a claim to that property in their CBAs, for themselves as creators, and perhaps in part collectively for their locals (Rhoades, 2013c).[8]

There were exceptions to the pattern. For example, Henry Ford Community College's adjunct faculty unit CBA accorded ownership to faculty—the materials for their class are theirs "regardless of the degree of support from the college." Similarly, Union County Community College's adjunct faculty contract accorded intellectual property rights for the course materials to the employee.

And, among other examples, Desert Community College's adjunct faculty CBA held that "all distance learning and other educational materials developed by an Adjunct Faculty Member will be owned by that employee (even when a stipend is paid)."

Turning now to the next section on public interest, it is worth pausing to imagine negotiating intellectual property provisions that broaden the script and go beyond the two parties of labor/management capitalistic negotiation at the table to consider public claims on some of the benefits by students and the communities we serve, and that support and help finance the institution (see Rhoades, 2015c, 2017b).

Public Interest/Benefit

The incidence of CBAs addressing public interest/benefit matters in technology-mediated education (nine CBAs in four-year and twenty-nine in two-year institution contracts) was quite limited. Yet, the exceptions are instructive exemplars pointing to important ways of broadening the script in negotiating a more progressive academy.

As institutions continue to emphasize the expansion of online and e-learning options, some provisions spoke quite clearly to the intersection of access and enrollments, quality, and infrastructure support. The Community Colleges of Spokane contract read: "AHE and CCS recognize that classes delivered online can offer educational opportunities to people who would otherwise be unable to attend college. At the same time, both AHE and CCS recognize that eLearning poses special challenges to students, AEs [academic employees], and CCS infrastructure and support personnel. AHE supports using technology to further student access and student success. However, AHE is mindful of the limitations of CCS's technological infrastructure and the technology provided by CCS for instruction." The provision went on to indicate: "Therefore, neither CCS nor AHE will expand online offerings without due concern for student success and AEs' welfare. It is the intention of CCS and AHE to increase online offerings at a measured and a managed pace." So, the faculty negotiated institutional commitment to not scaling up e-learning beyond its capacity to provide quality support and working/learning conditions.

Two other examples of contract language even more explicitly stated that distance education's purposes and offerings should be based on educational, not financial, goals: "The parties agree that meeting students' needs and expanding access, not cost efficiencies are the primary drivers of distance education" (Pennsylvania State System of Higher Education). Similarly, San Diego Community College's contract indicated that "expanding access, not increasing productivity, shall be the primary determining factor."

The explicitly invoked but generally vaguely defined benefits to students and the public of increased access, and the expressed concern with ensuring quality and effectiveness were the most common of the public interest considerations in the contracts. In a few cases, that translated into more specific support for students studying at a distance.[9] For example, the Pennsylvania State System of Higher Education contract had provision for supporting students at remote sites with the technological means and materials for interacting with faculty. Chicago State University's contract stated that "the Office of Distance Learning shall (3) provide technical support and customer service . . . to students taking a distance education course [and] . . . (5) assist in the assessment of student capability to use education technology."

Beyond the important, but general need to serve students' support needs, the following contract spoke specifically to addressing the needs of "diverse" populations: "The District and AFT share a mutual interest in providing the highest quality learning opportunities to the widest possible range of students. The District and AFT seek to provide leadership and innovation in meeting the distance education needs of students from diverse populations consistent with the mission of the District" (Seattle Community College). That language framed access in ways that went well beyond matters of time and space (and convenience) to address the particular needs of the (diverse) population/place that so many community colleges disproportionately serve. It framed access in a more social justice-informed sense of the term.

Key Takeaways

New circuits of production in instruction bring problems, requiring protections for academic employees and students, and promise, providing opportunities for faculty to negotiate the new technologies' possibilities for realizing a more progressive academy. The protections involve strengthening defensive strategies in negotiating technology-mediated education as well as flipping to more proactive strategies for negotiating labor-based conceptions of quality in faculty's working conditions. The possibilities entail broadening the strategies beyond labor and management to address public interests.

At the core of most contract language about distance education is a defensive framing of employees' rights and professional autonomy relative to managerial discretion in utilizing technology-mediated education. A far larger proportion of CBAs now have distance education provisions than before 2000 (see Rhoades, 1998a). And the largest proportion of those embeds important protections for employees amid distance education's expansion in this time period, with management's austerity agenda aspiration that technology will increase "productivity" and reduce faculty labor costs. Yet, there remains much room for expanding and strengthening employee protections, particularly for adjunct faculty, as ongoing professorial stratification persists. For management's expansion of adjunct faculty affords it more discretion in controlling distance education.

Part of protecting not just faculty but also students is flipping the script from a purely defensive to a more proactive stance of gaining more academic control over and support for an expanding curricular realm. Increasing proportions of faculty, coming out of the pandemic and in a generational and gendered pattern, are embracing technology-mediated education and wanting more flexibility in their instructional assignments and more control over their time. They are now negotiating the opportunity to teach and have office hours remotely, whereas management is seeking, especially in two-year settings, to control faculty time by capping full-time faculty's distance course assignments and virtual office hours and requiring them to be on campus for particular periods of time. As noted earlier in the chapter, that has implications for negotiating access to instructional resources and support, particularly for adjunct faculty, investing in what is required to do remote work (e.g., laptops, Internet access) rather than simply offloading those costs to individual faculty.

More than that, faculty have been negotiating a labor-based conception of quality control and quality working conditions to better serve students' learning conditions. Thus, a substantial proportion of the expanded incidence of distance education provisions cap class size, ensure faculty control of course and program approval, provide training and support for faculty, and, in a few cases, even control the evaluation of distance education programs.

Given the wider infusion of technology into on-campus curriculum through hybrid courses, virtual office hours even for face-to-face classes, and course management systems, it is important to broaden the script in negotiating technology-mediated education. Although a larger proportion of CBAs now address technology-medicated education beyond distance education than before 2000, bargaining units and contracts are behind the curve.[10] The vast majority fail to address the new circuits of production.[11]

Part of broadening the script is negotiating for and connecting to larger constituencies beyond the two parties at the table, labor and management (Rhoades, 2015c). Some contract provisions/language connected to students (e.g., to their training and support) and to the public interest. But these exceptions and exemplars prove the rule that overwhelmingly CBAs did not address such constituencies or considerations.

The possibilities of a more progressive academy and of technology-mediated education in enhancing those possibilities will be optimally advanced by contracts that embed defensive provisions addressing past or ongoing labor/management negotiations, by more proactive provisions assuring faculty control of their time and the curriculum, and by provisions that broaden the negotiations by addressing students and the public interest.

9

Organizing and Negotiating for Respect and Public Purpose

• • • • • • • • • • • • • • • • • • • •

Toward a New Progressive Normal

> The Winds of Change Shift: An Analysis of Recent Growth in Bargaining Units and Representation Efforts in Higher Education. (Herbert 2016b)
>
> The organizing never stops. (Alphonso Mayfield, February 2018)
>
> Overwhelmingly, the activism is driven by intersecting economic, workplace, social justice issues, foregrounding institutions' most vulnerable workers and students. (Rhoades, 2021)

Respect

Aretha Franklin had it right in 1967, and her message is just as relevant today. It's about R-E-S-P-E-C-T. Underlying the organizing and contract campaigns analyzed in this book have been academic employees' demands for respect for workers, their work, and for higher education's public purposes.

In part I of the book, respect was addressed for systemically marginalized academic employees who have moved to the center of the academic labor movement in negotiating a new, more progressive academy. As explored in chapter 5, that played out in organizing campaigns and contracts of graduate and postdoc employees, whose employers often claim they are primarily students and/or trainees. Graduate assistants' mantra of "the university works because we do" and postdocs' centrality to research productivity centers them as exploited employees with constrained opportunities for tenure-stream faculty positions. They are organizing and negotiating in ways that demand respect and due process protections for their full humanity in workplaces in which they are often subjected to excessive work demands, bullying, harassment, and discrimination.

As explored in chapters 3 and 4, the demand for respect also animates organizing and negotiating for adjunct and full-time contingent faculty. This new faculty majority faces systemic invisibility and structural underinvestment in their working conditions. They are demanding recognition of their existence and contributions to their institutions, as well as substantially better working conditions. Yet, employers claim fiscal constraints make contingent faculty's demands unrealistic, as in a September 26, 2022, exchange at Rutgers University. Two part-time lecturers' union representatives asked whether the President would meet their demands of "equal pay for equal work." He replied:

> [That] is a powerful phrase that is compelling on the surface and ignores the layers of complexity underneath it. . . . I do believe in respecting all of our workforce. I do believe that there is a problem with higher education that we did not invent. I've talked about this openly, the adjunctification of higher education is a significant problem. I do believe that our full-time faculty, tenure-track faculty need to carry more of their full teaching load and have less special deals, and I do believe that PTLs, in a perfect world, which I cannot finance right now should be making considerably more money, [but] I can't fix all the problems in higher education." (Rutgers AAUP-AFT Academic Worker Union, 2022)

As I tweeted: "In a revealing sleight of speech the President: dismissed part-time lecturers with the tired, 'it's more complex than you understand' trope; demonized tenure-stream faculty for their 'special deals' and not working harder; and acted as if the university's finances were his ('I cannot finance [that] right now')."

As evidenced in that exchange, managerial disrespect also manifests toward tenure-stream faculty, as explored in part II of the book. Chapters 6, 7, and 8 dealt with tenure-stream (and contingent) faculty organizing and negotiating around managerial austerity practices and new circuits of producing instruction. Their campaigns were animated by a sense of faculty voice being lost and of institutions' academic and public purposes being compromised.

Across the board, academic employees are seeking a greater voice in shaping their working conditions and the priorities and trajectory of institutions that have become increasingly corporatized in governance and privatized in ways that compromise their educational and public missions. Increasingly, academic employees see unions as the means for enhancing their working conditions and voice. Conventional "professional" structures such as academic senates, from which contingent faculty and graduate/postdoc employees have largely been excluded, have been bypassed, co-opted, or ignored.

Shifting Winds of Change

The 2000s, this book's empirical focus, have been a time of union organizing in numbers not seen since the 1960s and 1970s. That has been particularly true of the most vulnerable segments of academe—adjunct and full-time contingent faculty as well as graduate and postdoc employees (Herbert, 2016b).[1] Part of the shifting "winds of change" (Herbert, 2016b) in the academic labor movement is that the most disrespected segments of the workforce have become the vanguard of organizing (Rhoades, 2021, 2024).[2] These are the academic employee equivalent of Zweig's (2012) "working class majority." The path to a more progressive academy, as I discuss in the last section of this chapter, lies in a broad alliance between them and the more established tenure-track professorial (upper) middle class, along with other employees and groups on campus and beyond.[3]

The organizing has been taking place in unprecedented realms (i.e., private institutions) and levels not seen in decades (i.e., in public research universities), as discussed in chapter 2. Much of it has been undertaken in locals affiliated with unions not historically involved with academic employees, as detailed in chapters 3, 4, and 5.

The Organizing Never Stops

The increased organizing has been about not just new bargaining units but also more expansive, aggressive organizing and contract negotiation by existing bargaining units, as detailed in chapters 6, 7, and 8. The energetic spirit is captured succinctly and defiantly in the face of ongoing assaults on employees' right to bargain (briefly mapped in chapter 2), in a phrase articulated by Alphonso Mayfield (President of Florida Public Services Union) and by adjunct faculty leaders at a February 2018 metro launch event in Miami. It was just months before the *Janus* Supreme Court case that would eliminate "agency fee" (or "fair share") union dues for nonmembers. The phrase was, "The organizing never stops." It underscored that even as many attendees were organizing to seek recognition for new bargaining units, others were negotiating first contracts, and still others (like Mayfield himself) were leaders and members of longer established unions, organizing to expand membership, build strength, and negotiate ever stronger contracts.

Intersecting Workplace Justice with Social Justice

The increased organizing has entailed campaigns that intersect workplace justice with broader social justice issues and with higher education's public responsibilities and missions. It is intentional that above, I invoked a quote from a leader of color in a union (SEIU) whose historical roots and current dynamism are in immigrant communities and communities of color (Aguiar & McCartin, 2023; Fink & Greenberg, 1989; Stillman, 2010). In contrast to the tenure-stream professoriate, which is disproportionately White and male (Kline, 2018; McChesney & Bichsel, 2020), contingent (growing) segments of the academic workforce are those with the largest proportion of women and people of color (Finkelstein, Conley, & Schuster, 2016) and international members. Their organizing and contract campaigns are often grounded in coalition building that cuts across workforce and demographic groups. Therein lies the path to building a new progressive normal.

In this chapter, I first summarize key findings about why academic employees are organizing and what they are gaining. Then, I address literature that has informed and, I hope, will be informed by my work. Finally, in seeking to shape the future, not just better understand the past, I close with principles for organizing and negotiating, with "activist funds of knowledge."

Key Findings: #WhyWeOrganize and #HowUnionsMatter

In summarizing the findings for each of the book's parts and chapters, the discussion is partly organized around two hashtags that have driven my academic work and my praxis in the labor movement: #WhyWeOrganize and #HowUnionsMatter. Relatedly, I return to the three research questions that drove my analysis: (1) What identities, issues, and ideologies about effecting change are expressed in the organizing and contracts of academic employees?; (2) How do the organizing and contracts affect the (im)balance of power between managers' discretion and employees' jurisdictional rights, due process rights, and voice in the collectively negotiated formal terms and conditions of labor that may define the latter and thereby delimit the former?; and (3) What are the ways that professional stratification is being (re)negotiated and reduced as well as sometimes re-inscribed in organizing campaigns and in contract provisions? For all three, I was also interested in whether and how conceptions of justice and public benefit were invoked.

Part I: From the Margins to the Center; Contingent Academic Employees Organizing and Negotiating a New Academy

In not just numbers and proportion of the academic workforce, but also in union organizing, the 2000s represented a reversal of historical patterns. The new faculty majority of faculty are part-time (adjunct) and full-time contingent faculty (Maisto, 2012, 2024). The academy has seen an expansion of graduate and even more so of postdoc employees who are doing more of universities' central academic work. Moreover, union organizing has by far been the greatest among adjunct and full-time contingent faculty and graduate employees in private universities and among postdoc employees in public universities (Herbert, 2016b). Contingent academic employees, the focus of this section, have moved from the margins to the center of academic organizing (largely through (inter) national union affiliates other than the three academic unions).

Chapter 3: Bread and Roses, and a Labor-Based Conception of Quality; A New Faculty Majority Organizing a New Academy

How and why have contingent faculty been organizing in the 2000s in unparalleled numbers, revealing a rapidly growing collective bargaining identity within this workforce? Remarkably, many of these campaigns of low-wage, precarious employees were in well-resourced private universities that are powerful employers in a David versus Goliath contest. Also, remarkably, contingent faculty have successfully reframed the conversation about quality education, countering prevailing managerial (and foundation) narratives that frame faculty as the problem.

The adjunct faculty campaign at GW was analogized to the "Bread and Roses" strike of (largely immigrant and female) textile workers in Lawrence, Massachusetts. Creative strategies and tactics in both cases enabled employees to overcome vehement resistance from the authorities. For GW adjunct faculty, those included leveraging big-picture research and public campaigns to win student and public support.

Subsequent "metro campaign" (another creative strategy), organizing at multiple campuses within a metro region, built on the approach and resounding success of SEIU, Local 500's academic organizing. In one metro area after another, SEIU came to dominate new contingent faculty organizing, disproportionately in private universities and colleges, with high rates of success. Other unions have adopted variations of the metro strategy, to considerable success.

Other markers and catalysts of contingent faculty organizing were the transformation of two leading locals (CFA and PSC) of higher education systems on either coast, which centered adjunct faculty issues, and the emergence of a national advocacy group, the New Faculty Majority, which effectively utilized an "inside/outside" strategy to change national affiliates and locals.

Consistent campaign messaging has centered on issues of bread (wages and benefits), roses (respect), and quality education. It has successfully framed contingent and especially adjunct faculty as working in an unjust system of structured disrespect as exploited, invisible instructors. It has also characterized that system as compromising educational quality. Re-centering the significance of faculty to the public interest, contingent faculty have articulated a labor-based conception of educational quality, with the mantra that faculty's working conditions are students' learning conditions.

Chapter 4: Negotiating Bread and Roses and Labor-Based Quality into Part-Time-Only and Combined Bargaining Unit Contracts

What have adjunct and contingent faculty gained through unionization, relative to managerial discretion and to professorial stratification? To what extent and how have the contracts they have negotiated addressed educational quality and/or public benefits?

Unionizing adjunct faculty have realized substantial gains in compensation, in raising salary minimums, in multi-year across-the-board raises, and in increased benefits. Some bargaining units have negotiated pay parity in the per-course remuneration for courses for part- and full-time faculty or pro rata pay indexed against a proportion of that paid to full-time faculty, thereby reducing professorial stratification.

Adjunct faculty have also gained contractually by negotiating class cancellation fees, which establish some jurisdictional claim, vis-a-vis management for their scheduled classes. The gains were important but small—most CBAs (except in SEIU, metro campaign contracts) do not have class cancellation fee provisions, especially in COMB bargaining units. And a rationale in many CBAs for canceling an adjunct faculty member's class continues to be that they are being "bumped" by full-time faculty filling out their course load.

Adjunct faculty's gains have been even greater in advancing a labor-based conception of quality, grounded in quality working conditions, such as access to instructional resources and professional development. A little less than half the CBAs covering adjunct faculty had access to instructional resources provisions, and three-quarters had access to professional development language. And although that access remained stratified relative to full-time faculty, there were important patterns of parity built into some CBAs (almost two-thirds of PTO units had such access to instructional resources provisions, and almost one-quarter had pro-rated parity for access to PD, all in COMB unit contracts). Finally, slightly more than one-fifth of instructional resources and PD provisions explicitly referred to quality and public interest, though in narrow terms.

Chapter 5: More than Would-Be Apprentices; Graduate Student and Postdoc Employees Organizing and Negotiating amid New Forms of Contingency in an Aging, Changing Academy

As remarkable as the extraordinary levels of organizing among graduate and postdoc employees have been, the scope of what has been negotiated and gained has been equally remarkable. Following a long history of organizing in public universities, graduate employee organizing has proliferated in private universities.

By contrast, the far more recent phenomenon of postdoc organizing has been concentrated in public universities. Both sets of employees, though, have organized primarily with nonacademic unions such as UAW, UE, and SEIU. And both have been engaged quite recently in unprecedented levels of strike activity (Herbert, Apkarian, & Van der Naald, 2023).

There also has been extensive overlap in what has been negotiated and gained, and in the range of workplace and social justice issues addressed. Certainly, wages have been front and center, with graduate and postdoc employees organizing and negotiating around wage levels that left them unable to afford living near the universities that employ them. Benefits, too, have been central campaign issues, with greater emphasis on childcare and caregiving. That reflected employees' life/career situations and their unwillingness to forego such benefits as part of what was once a temporary apprenticeship on the way to a tenure-track faculty position. Finally, these employees have successfully negotiated issues of sexual harassment, racial discrimination, and the need for independent external arbitration of such matters. Their gains have been game changers for these employees economically, professionally, and socially, and have catapulted them into the vanguard of the academic labor movement, defining these social justice matters as the new "bread and butter" issues of unions.

Part II: Faculty Negotiating Retrenchment and Technology amid Management's Austerity Agenda

Much organizing has also taken place among tenure-track faculty, including in combined units with contingent faculty. Much organizing and negotiating has centered on managerial practices that are part of a longstanding, labor-cost-cutting austerity agenda. What tenure-track faculty have fought for in these campaigns is a meaningful voice in shaping their working conditions and their institutions' trajectory. In the case of direct attacks on their employment, through furloughs and retrenchment, that has been more of a proactive stance in decision-making, which was found in some contracts, though overwhelmingly the negotiations were about limiting managerial discretion through bargaining impact. In the case of indirect attacks on job security and control over work and the workforce with new technologies, that negotiation was again both defensive and more proactive, although overwhelmingly the negotiations were about delimiting managerial discretion and bargaining impact.

Chapter 6: Challenging Management's Austerity Practices; Organizing amid and Negotiating Furloughs

Amid two key moments in the 2000s, the crash of 2008–2009 and the pandemic, management implemented the "temporary" disaster academic capitalism strategy of across-the-board furloughs of employees. That strategy catalyzed organizing campaigns that intersected with other (e.g., social justice) issues animating the mobilizing. The furlough strategy is a quintessential example of "the revenge of the managers" (Goldstein, 2014), of labor cost cutting in service of increased managerialism. That is, on a baseline, decades-long trend of disproportionate increases in senior administrative costs and corresponding decreases in expenditures on faculty and instructional costs, across-the-board furloughs effectively further hollow out the academic core of higher education. They do so not simply in numbers but in the further disenfranchisement of meaningful faculty voice and in furtherance of an academic capitalist logic that fails to distinguish between (and protect) the academic core and the managerial periphery.

As detailed in the chapter, implementing furloughs directly gave rise to distinctive organizing campaigns. They were distinctive partly in the common cause that was formed across categories of employees, one marker of how far academic employees have come in building coalitions and forming cross-category configurations of locals. They were a step as well in connecting the organizing of academic employees around broader critiques of corporatization and misplaced priorities in higher education.

For all that, there was very little evidence of that organizing translating into negotiated contract language. There were very few contractual provisions for furloughs. And only a few provided limiting conditions on furloughs. Nevertheless, they, along with the examples of mobilizing beyond the contracts, point to how faculty and employees more broadly can effectively fight against furloughs, including demanding that the "temporary" take-backs be restored.

Chapter 7: Negotiating Management's Austerity Practices; Retrenchment for Financial Exigency and Other Reasons in the Contracts

The last two decades have seen a continuation of ongoing managerial austerity practices bringing retrenchment of faculty, reorganization and discontinuation of academic programs, and reduction of faculty voice in shaping higher education's trajectory. As compared to the 1990s, there were far more CBAs with financial exigency provisions, and almost all had program reorganization and retrenchment provisions.

During this time period, AAUP leaders sought to provide guidance in strengthened recommended institutional regulations for how faculty can realize a more meaningful voice and impact in these deliberations by demanding access to specific sorts of financial data. In many regards, there were exemplary defensive strategies such as defining the unit of layoff and long notice requirements, as well as proactive strategies for ensuring faculty collective voice in deliberations about program discontinuance and retrenchment. But there were far from enough of such provisions.

Equally importantly, there is an opportunity to reverse management's misplaced priorities by embedding language requiring reductions in nonacademic personnel and expenditures before discontinuing academic programs and retrenching faculty. A small number of provisions built such language about alternatives into their retrenchment articles. What has not yet been realized, though, is the consistent articulation of a compelling mantra about re-centering the academic core that is comparable to adjunct faculty's mantra about faculty's working conditions being students' learning conditions, which is prevalent, even dominant now in the public discourse. Contract negotiations will be strengthened to the extent that academic employees can organize and mobilize public support regarding what faculty are negotiating for.

Regarding professorial stratification, I found little to no evidence of contracts ensuring that contingent faculty were meaningfully involved in deliberations about retrenchment. Quite the contrary. In various ways, whether in order of layoff or notice of layoff, the CBAs largely perpetuated a multitiered system of academic employment. The path to realizing a greater voice for faculty in shaping higher education's trajectory lies in negotiating a more inclusive conception of shared governance that enfranchises and draws on the energy, insights, and lived experiences of what has for some time been the New Faculty Majority, a majority in which faculty of marginalized communities are more represented than in the ranks of tenure-track and especially tenured faculty.

Finally, here, the advancing of faculty voice will be strengthened by connecting that voice to purposes that serve students and the larger public good, modeled again on the success of the contingent faculty labor movement.

Chapter 8: Protections and Possibilities in Negotiating a Progressive Academy amid New Circuits of Production

Whereas negotiations once reflected largely a defensive script about faculty utilizing new circuits of production, this chapter found substantial evidence in contractual provisions of the dominant narrative about technology-mediated education being flipped and broadened. The latter included a small but important number of provisions going beyond distance education to address hybrid classes, online office hours, and course management systems. They are important exemplars for faculty negotiating greater voice and rights relative to forms of technology-mediated education that almost all faculty utilize. That is particularly true given a generational and gendered pattern of faculty wanting greater control over and flexible use of their time by working remotely. The notion and location of educational space for teaching, learning, and advising are changing, moving beyond the physical classroom (and office) in ways that could ideally reflect the core ideas of disability rights activists regarding universal design. The contracts are only barely beginning to embed that growing reality.

As compared to the 1990s, there were double the number of contractual provisions addressing technology-mediated education. That included considerably more provisions protecting individual faculty and the collective workforce from management requiring faculty to do distance education and replacing/displacing/reducing current and future full-time and bargaining unit members by expanding or outsourcing distance education. Also, there were far more proactive provisions affording faculty greater control of, rights to, and voice in and control of matters surrounding technology-mediated education. Ensuring academic governance of courses, training and professional development for faculty utilizing these modalities, and in some cases, faculty control of that training entailed faculty negotiating labor-based conceptions of quality, prioritizing quality working conditions.

Throughout, there were few, but important examples of contracts reducing professorial stratification and addressing students' needs and the public interest. Coming out of the pandemic, there is much need for expanding provisions that designate support for students. For there continues to be a digital divide in access to such technology.

Summary of What the Findings Mean

Beyond the specific findings of particular chapters, it is worth coming back to an overriding and ongoing theme throughout as to why academic employees are organizing and what they are getting. Part of what they gain is what they would lose in the absence of collective bargaining.

Consider the twenty-day strike at Wright State University in February 2019. The faculty bargaining team's chief negotiator was Rudy Fichtenbaum, then President of the national AAUP and longtime faculty leader at WSU who had been part of organizing to get the 2010 anti-union law in Ohio rescinded (McNay, 2013). After protracted negotiations, WSU's management "imposed" a contract that took away the right to bargain health care, nullified full-time, contingent faculty's due process rights and security, expanded possible furlough days, made merit pay a process controlled by department heads and deans, and had no raises. In Fichtenbaum's words, it "was about trying to silence the union . . . and the faculty. It was about power and control" (Democracy Now!, 2019). As the *InsideHigherEd* journalist covering the story, wrote, "Perhaps more than anything, the strike was about respect" (Flaherty, 2019, "Standing Up," para. 8).

What did the strike gain? WSU faculty (re)gained the right to bargain health care, continuing status security and due process rights for FTNTTF, the existing, peer-driven merit pay system, a one-day per semester cap on furlough days, and a 2.5 percent raise for each of two years, plus a 3 percent increase in the minimum salary. Collective organizing and negotiation matters. Because academic employees together can bring management to the table and to a resolution that respects workers and their work. That is why, as Fichtenbaum said at the 2011 going away party that AAUP collective bargaining leaders organized for me, "We never do anything alone."[4]

Contributions to the Literature; Implications for Future Research

The book's analytical focus is on the dynamism of collective union organizing and contract negotiations over time and place in relation to the (im)balance of power between labor and management, the jurisdictional struggle surrounding professional stratification, higher education's educational mission and public purposes, and social structures and movements beyond the academy. In each regard, it makes a contribution to and is suggestive of future paths for the academic literature. For the academic literature has come a distance in addressing unions, but it has a long way to go. Unions see higher education as a fertile site for organizing far more than scholars do for researching.

Much has been written about the management and direction of colleges and universities. Much too little work addresses negotiations between management and organized academic labor of higher education's working conditions and trajectory. Although much has been written about different segments of faculty and contingent academic employees, far too little work addresses the intraprofessional collective negotiations among unionized academic employees. Finally, although much has been written about how members of marginalized communities experience, navigate, and work to transform higher education, there is far too little work on the intersection between workplace justice and social justice in academic employees' collective negotiations.

In each of the above regards, the book makes a contribution to and charts a path for studying "the higher education we choose, collectively" (Rhoades, 2014a), through union organizing and contract negotiations. It takes us beyond the individualistic, professional ideology that frames so much of our research design and scholarship, which addresses groups of individuals more than organized collectives in colleges, universities, and nationally. It brings employees back in as organized labor.

There is an irony here in the higher education literature, in which "academic capitalism" (Slaughter & Rhoades, 2004) is a highly cited concept/theory/phenomenon. The vast majority of those who cite it "get" the market orientation and practices part of the concept. What is far less common for higher education colleagues (and students) to "get" is the social relations of production part of the theory. Capitalism is about intersecting sets of social relations, including between management and (organized) labor, played out at times in collective negotiations, as well as in organized management and political attacks on (organized) labor (Goldstein, 2014).

Yet, academic capitalism is about more than relations between disembodied "labor" and "management," absent consideration of people's identities. It is inextricably intertwined with settler colonialism (and accumulation of land—see Nash, 2019), racism, and White supremacy (and slavery). Given Salazar's (2022;

see also Salazar, Jaquette, & Han, 2021) work, I cannot do academic capitalism the (disembodied) same.

In recent decades, much higher education scholarship has focused on persons and populations of people with marginalized and minoritized identities. Most commonly, the focus is on individuals experiencing oppressive systems. However, increasingly, there is literature on activism and collective navigation of and challenges to systems of oppression as they operate in higher education. With important exceptions, that work does not intersect issues of capitalism (for an exception, see Dache-Gerbino, Kiyama, and Sapp, 2018) or of organized labor (for an exception, see Harper, 2023). Outside the field of higher education, Dénommé and Savage (2021) have intersected workplace justice and social justice in negotiating a collective bargaining agreement in a Canadian university that "indigenizes" what knowledge and voices count. Thus, analogous to how it is common to speak about the "intersectionality" of various identities, I am suggesting layering another dimension of intersectionality on top of those considerations. How do those identities intersect with and play out in employees' lives, such that they may collectively seek to negotiate workplaces (and unions) that more fully intersect their full humanity in conceptualizing a just workplace?

Throughout the book, I have also foregrounded matters of time in organizing and contract campaigns. Generally, social science is not particularly strong at addressing such matters. However, there are some superb examples in the literature of scholars adopting different disciplinary perspectives and methodological strategies for speaking to the time dimension. For example, Tim Cain has compiled an impressive body of work providing a historical perspective on various aspects of and current issues in collective bargaining (e.g., see Cain, 2020). Kezar and Sam (2013) provide a superb example of multiple case studies of thirty institutions, most of which had faculty unions, of how contingent faculty develop equitable policies. Finally, Berry and Worthen (2021) have provided a creative historical case study of a faculty union (the CFA). From key events and points in time, they have traced the iterative progression of how particular issues have been handled and negotiated within and by the union. My contribution has been to provide both national and local perspectives on the iterative unfolding of organizing and negotiations, pointing to possibilities for further explorations of organizing and contract campaigns.

Finally, what I have tried to do is to model how academic writing can combine scholarly and practitioner/activist stances (see Camacho & Rhoades, 2015). Given the prevalence of participant observation in social science research historically, as well as of participant action research and auto-ethnography, I would hope to see more academic scholarship adopt these methods in studies of organized labor in higher education. It makes sense for us to write in ways that reflect our lives of collectively working to shape the places in which we work, including in unions (Rhoades, 2014a). I hope this book will stimulate scholarship along these lines.

Principles of Action and in Action for Negotiating a New Academy: Activist Funds of Knowledge

In opening and throughout this book, I have offered the theme, "Now is the time," invoking a phrase on the cover of a "Thank You" card sent from Washington State University faculty. That underlies the book's focus on "organizing professionals." In this closing section of the book, I invoke a phrase offered by a WSU faculty member during my visit, "I want to be FOR something" (also quoted in chapter 1). That underlies the book's focus on "academic employees negotiating a new academy." Academic employees are often on the defensive, defining themselves by what they are against. That is important. Yet, it is also important to articulate and proactively negotiate what they working for. As United Faculty Florida member Sean Trainor (2022) said, "You need to make management fight your fight, to address issues you define as important."

Here, I offer three sets of principles of action and in action for developing, organizing around, and negotiating a broader vision for a new academy. They are neither recipes nor "best practices." Their use depends on the particular community of academic employees. It is contingent on their context and the purposes employees define.

The principles emerge from the unionizing and contract campaigns analyzed in this book. They also express my experience in the academic labor movement. The first set calls for a collective identity that embraces coalitions and embodies respect for all workers. The second calls for a focus on issues that intersect workplace justice and social justice, and address educational quality and higher education's public purposes. The third set calls for an ideology and praxis that entail time, affect, and resource mobilization.

Taken together, they constitute "activist funds of knowledge," my adaptation of and homage to the "Funds of Knowledge" (FoK) concept coined and embodied by dear colleagues (Gonzalez, Moll, & Amanti, 2005; Kiyama & Rios-Aguilar, 2018; Moll, Amanti, Neff, & Gonzalez, 1992). Defined as "historically accumulated and culturally developed bodies of knowledge and skills essential for household or individual functioning and well-being" (Moll et al., 1992, p. 133), the FoK concept is grounded in the lived realities of borderland, working-class Latinx communities. It speaks to the value, efficacy, and resilience of shared ways of knowing and being in minoritized communities that face dominant, dehumanizing systems of oppression that disrespect them. Although the dominant system does not recognize their value, FoK are effective and powerful in members of these communities negotiating these systems.

Similarly, historically accumulated and culturally developed ways of being, skills, and bodies of knowledge are at play in and effectively employed by communities of academic labor activists negotiating the dominant academic capitalist higher education system that dehumanizes and disrespects them, their work, and higher education's public purposes. They are evident in how activists learn from, build on, and utilize knowledge and lessons of previous and other organizing and/or contract campaigns (e.g., in metro campaigns, inside/outside strategies, national coordination against a hostile NLRB, in sharing contract language within and across states/unions, and in national coalitions).

Over decades of studying and participating in communities of academic labor activism, I have seen, experienced, and tried to enact such historically accumulated, and ways of knowing and being, pieces of collective wisdom. They are principles and processes of action, and embodied in action. Here, I offer a distillation of such principles to contribute to these "activist funds of knowledge."[5] Like the wandering storyteller in Mario Vargos Llosa's book (1989), I hope to contribute to fertilization across space and time, of the living culture of labor communities.[6] To paraphrase that book's repeatedly invoked phrase, my offering is, "[This], anyway, is what I have learned."

Coalitions and Collective Identity

Coalitions are essential to enhancing academic employees' union activity. That has been evident in the organizing and contract campaigns analyzed here and in employees' successful strikes, most recently and dramatically in 2022 and 2023. Ideally, employees' collective identity goes beyond themselves, expressing and enacting respect for other workers and groups on and off campus. That means (a) getting beyond a sense of "specialness," (b) working through differences within coalitions by focusing on the shared goal, and (c) leveraging support and strength beyond the employees.

In getting over "specialness," the academic labor movement has come a long way. A challenge has been for tenure-track faculty to get beyond that identity as a professional, as "special," linked to seeing themselves as acting independently and "apolitically" above the fray, using their expertise to inform policymakers, but not directly and collectively negotiating policy and practice.[7] As I wrote of tenure-track faculty twenty-five years ago, "The challenge faculty and faculty unions now face is whether they can manage to work in concert as a collectivity to more proactively direct the academy and whether they can reorganize themselves with other production workers who are currently at the margins of the organization, before faculty themselves are increasingly reorganized to the margins of the academic enterprise" (Rhoades, 1998a, p. 279).

I have encountered attitudes about specialness in organizing campaigns at research universities, as discussed in chapter 2. They were evident in discussions about whether to have a card campaign or a secret ballot election at UIC (where AAUP staff and leaders argued that although adjunct faculty and graduate employees had used card check, tenure-track faculty were different). They were evident in questions from tenure-track faculty at UCHC, UIC, and UO about whether faculty "like them" and at institutions "like theirs" (which at UO they meant universities that were Association of American Universities members) were unionized. And they have been evident in the anti-union campaigns in some major research universities of some tenured faculty who framed unions as a threat to the institution's quality and standing.

Nevertheless, tenure-track faculty at several public research universities have unionized in the 2010s and 2020s. Moreover, the configuration of several new bargaining units has included multiple categories of academic employees. At UO and Oregon State University, the units include tenure-track, nontenure-track, and adjunct faculty, as well as postdocs. At UIC, there are separate bargaining units for tenure-track and full-time, nontenure-track faculty, but the two are very cooperative. The UICUF's (United Faculty) executive board includes nontenure system members. Its president in 2023 was a lecturer. And when UICUF struck in January 2023, one of the demands was greater job security for nontenure-track faculty. The University of New Mexico's bargaining unit includes all full- and part-time faculty. And there has been growth in combined units of tenure-track and contingent faculty (Herbert, 2016a; Herbert, Apkarian, & Van der Naald, 2020). Further, during the COVID pandemic, there was solidarity between tenure-track and contingent faculty, with the former prioritizing the latter in negotiations (Rhoades, 2021).

Finally, over the last decade, national academic labor coalitions inclusive of various campus workers on campuses have emerged. In 2011, a Campaign for the Future of Higher Education was launched, a national coalition of academic labor groups led by tenure-track faculty but inclusive of contingent faculty. A decade later, Higher Education Labor United emerged, a national coalition that is even more inclusive in categories of employees and affiliates. Consider its "vision platform": "In collaborative shared governance, in which all categories of faculty and staff, student groups, and unions participate at all levels and have decision making power and key leadership roles, and surrounding communities have avenues to participate in balanced collaborations and partnerships" (Higher Ed Labor United, n.d.). That is a far cry from the AAUP's tenure-track faculty-centric framing of shared governance. The national campaigns have adopted an "inside/outside" strategy seeking to effect change within (inter)national affiliates in which members participate even as they form a separate "outside" organization to shape national policy discourse and practice.

Working Through the Challenges of Coalitional Work. For all their benefits, coalitions have challenges. As Ben Jealous, a Maryland gubernatorial candidate in 2018, put it, "If you are comfortable in your coalition, your coalition is too small" (Murphy, 2018, p. 37).[8] The key is to keep a larger endgame in sight to work through challenges as a necessary path to building strength.

One example of managing longstanding challenges lies in intra-union coalitions among segments of employees. For example, the Professional Staff Congress at CUNY originated in 1972 by merging the Legislative Conference (full-time faculty and professionals, mostly in four-year colleges) and the United Federation of College Teachers (part-time faculty, full-time lecturers, and staff, mostly in two-year colleges). Tensions between these different categories of employees persist. Yet, after the election of a reform caucus, PSC became more engaged with local labor and community groups in progressive campaigns.

Another progressive local, the California Faculty Association, has also navigated tensions among internal groups. Some of that is between tenure-track and lecturer (contingent) faculty (Berry & Worthen, 2021; Hoffman and Hess, 2014). That continued with the election of a reform coalition that prioritized enhancing working conditions for contingent faculty (Rhoades, Berry, & Worthen, 2023). Some of the tension is among identity groups. CFA leaders have increasingly centered anti-racist and social justice work, navigating the resulting resistance (Rhoades, Canton, & Toombs, 2023).

At the national level, I experienced the challenges of navigating cross-union coalitions, as discussed in chapter 2, in the AAUP/AFT joint campaigns. They involved intense inter- and intra-union negotiations, heightened by the fact that prior to their joint organizing agreement, the AFT had been "raiding" AAUP-affiliated locals.[9] Yet, working through the tensions resulted in major organizing victories.

So, too, New Faculty Majority founders and leaders were members and activists in different (inter)national unions (e.g., the AAUP, AFT, NEA, SEIU, and USW) and locals (some were unaffiliated with any union). They included adjunct faculty, full-time nontenure-track faculty, and tenured faculty. NFM worked through caucuses/groups within national unions and locals, navigating inter- and intra-union politics. There were also sensitivities around employment status, gender, and ethnic identity in who speaks for contingent faculty and what issues/strategies are prioritized. Yet, NFM leaders' commitment and ability to work in and through multiple coalitions paid off.

The importance of coalitions has been nowhere plainer than in the case of two of the most noteworthy strikes of 2022 and 2023 (strike activity in those years was at unprecedented levels—see Herbert, Apkarian, & Van der Naald, 2023). It was also plain in two other strikes in recent years that received far less attention.

UAW 2865's student worker strike, discussed in chapter 5, was the largest in U.S. history, covering 48,000 University of California researchers, student employees, and student researchers and lasting a then-unprecedented forty days (Herbert et al., 2023). Support from other employees (e.g., faculty, postdocs) was important in sustaining it. And pressure from Democratic politicians contributed to resolving it through mediation.

Political pressure was also key in bringing management to the table and resolving the weeklong strike of three Rutgers AAUP/AFT bargaining units. The solidarity among those units (part-time lecturers, tenure-track faculty, and health care faculty) was remarkable, and a powerful example of the value of coordinated action among coalitions of workers and external groups (Herbert et al., 2023). Nevertheless, Rutgers' president, despite considerable private pressure and public shaming surrounding the first strike in Rutgers' history (the faculty union was established in 1970), threatened to take strikers to court, claiming that their action was illegal. Governor Phil Murphy, a Democrat, intervened and initiated management/labor talks (Roberts-Grmela, 2023).

At Clark College in Washington, after about two years without a contract, the faculty went on strike for two days (Gillespie, 2020). The student newspaper was supportive, and students walked the picket lines, which contributed to a positive public perception of the strike. Faculty from Portland Community College across the state line also walked the picket line. And local Teamsters showed up to picket the emergency board meeting. Such support made a public statement and also emboldened the faculty.

At American University, after nearly eighteen months of bargaining, a staff union (of first-year advisors) affiliated with SEIU Local 500 went on a weeklong strike during move-in week for students in the fall of 2022 (Knox, 2022). There was support from local unions, as well as from local and statewide politicians in the DC Council, the Maryland House of Delegates, and the Democratic candidate for governor. Union members leafletted students and parents. Some students joined the picket line. Others shared content on social media. Then, students walked out, en masse, from an opening convocation while the president was speaking. Management settled (Rodrigues, 2022).[10]

In negotiations and strikes, the internal strength and external leverage gained from coalitions can be instrumental. The principle here is pressures that can be brought to bear on management by labor are substantially enhanced by employees going beyond themselves and building strong coalitions. This, anyway, is what I have learned.

Intersecting Workplace Justice, Social Justice, and the Public Interest

Led by the contingent academic employees, organizing and contract campaigns have embedded issues that intersect workplace and social justice, and that address educational quality and higher education's public purposes. Arguably, a full understanding of academic capitalism and academic labor and successful negotiation of the former by the latter calls for such issues to be centered in what is being negotiated. Negotiating a more progressive academy entails academic employees challenging structures in working conditions that express historical and ongoing racialized, hetero-normed gendered (and ableist) systems of exploitation and domination. And it entails calling out prevailing systems for compromising educational quality and the public interest, connecting academic employees' situation to public interests.

Intersecting Workplace Justice and Social Justice. Matters of employment (class) are intertwined with matters of identity.[11] That intersection becomes all the more important as the academic workforce becomes more diversified, as it has particularly with graduate and postdoc employees and contingent faculty. It also becomes more important as units with tenure-track faculty focus more on social justice issues and serving their diverse students. It is clearly part of the identity of the new unions now organizing academic employees.

In the 2000s, the issues negotiated by graduate employees shifted. Whereas in the early 2000s, some locals articulated critiques of corporatization and addressed social justice issues (see Rhoades & Rhoads, 2003; Rhoads & Rhoades, 2005), now virtually every graduate employee organizing and contract campaign centers sexual harassment and racial discrimination, calling for independent external arbitration of these matters. As for the more recent phenomenon of postdoc employees, their campaigns also center such issues as well as childcare and international employees and the protests about Palestine.

In some bargaining units with tenure-track faculty, social justice issues have also increasingly been centered in their governance, negotiations, and advocacy. Partly, that is connected to the students they are serving (and to broader social movements and communities). For example, CFA leaders throughout the 2000s have sought to build "a more perfect union" (Rhoades, Canton, & Toombs, 2023). That project has been not just about enfranchising contingent faculty but also about centering social justice and anti-racist work in the union's internal governance, in bargaining proposals, and in better serving their diverse students and surrounding communities. Relatedly, among the animating issues in the union drive leading to UICUF were not only enhancing contingent faculty's working conditions but also better fulfilling the urban mission of the university in serving lower-income, minoritized students and communities.

Finally, part of the strength of SEIU's entry into academic organizing is its invocation of core themes that link academic employees' causes to those of the larger labor movement, particularly of low-wage employees. SEIU's origins lay with immigrant and minoritized workers (and it remains diverse in membership). Moreover, it has been a central player in the women's movement (Bhargava, 2010), including with Local/District 925 (aka, 9 to 5) in Washington.

Speaking to the Public Interest. Given that academic employees bargain essentially in public and with the public, they must speak to the academy's public purposes and to the public interest in ways that resonate externally. As I have observed, "The route to success as a union (and as a profession that is under fire) is to tap into the key public interest issues that define state and community politics" (Rhoades, 1998a, p. 277).

One of higher education's public purposes is educating undergraduates. And one of the most successful mantras of academic employees in recent years has been invoked by the New Faculty Majority and in virtually all contingent faculty campaigns: "Faculty working conditions are students' learning conditions" (Maisto, 2012, 2024). Its genius is in linking faculty's interests with those of students (and higher education's core purposes). And it undermines managerial discourse that pits students against faculty, claiming that enhancing faculty working conditions will require higher tuition.

Public interest campaigns can also go to broader issues. For example, the United Faculty of Florida has worked in coalition with various groups, in support of campus safety, to defeat legislative efforts to allow open carry on Florida's public campuses (Nissen & Churchill, 2020). The local's leaders wrote that part of building a more proactive, progressive union was, "Taking cues from the bargaining for the common good approach with the recent teacher uprisings," to ask, what is UFF's plan to win "the schools our students deserve?" (p. 389).

Appeals to public interest that go beyond employees (and the campus) can be built into contract negotiations, even when they are settled outside the contract. For example, although much of the focus of a January 2023 strike at UIC was on increased minimum salaries for nontenure-track and tenure-track faculty, and increased job security for the former, one of the key demands was for expanded student mental health resources (Boyle, 2023). In the words of Aaron Krall, the union (UICUF) president, "'We want to support our students. We want to support the staff. We want to support the mission of our university especially the mission for undergraduate education'" (para. 13). Similarly, in AFT President Randi Weingarten's words, "'that is what bargaining for the common good means'" (Quinn, 2023, "University of Illinois," para. 17). Although management insisted that the issue was outside the scope of the CBA, they did agree to make a commitment to invest in increased mental health support for students. Along similar lines, as part of their "bargaining for the common good," the Lane Community College Education Association faculty union successfully defeated an administrative effort to close the college's student health clinic (personal communication, September 21, 2023).

"Bargaining for the common good" refers to a labor movement coalition and initiative that goes beyond the scope of traditional collective bargaining (McCartin, 2016; McCartin, Sneiderman, & BP-Weeks, 2020). It involves identifying issues that resonate with allies and communities.[12] Another relatively recent example is United Academics, University of Oregon negotiating for the university to invest funds for childcare facilities in the community, with a share of the slots going to UO employees (University of Oregon, 2023). Again, collective bargaining provided a framework for structuring commitments made outside the CBA.

Such broad mobilization strategies can also be linked to a particular college's public mission. City College of San Francisco's accreditation has been threatened because of its democratic governance (seen as too strong), structure of administration (seen as too weak), and finances and faculty wages (seen as too high). Moreover, it is a college serving its community with lifelong learning opportunities that don't fit the neoliberal model of "productivity." The faculty local worked with students and community groups to advance a broader struggle about the college's role in serving the city and countering gentrification (Rein, Ellinger, & Legion, 2020).

The public interest issues discussed above facilitate the coalitions of groups discussed in a previous section coalescing around shared interests. The principle here is framing organizing and contract campaigns around the intersection of workplace and social justice issues, a labor-based conception of educational quality, and the broader public purposes of the academy, which leverages public and political support. This, anyway, is what I have learned.

Time, Affect, and Resource Mapping

In their organizing and contract campaigns, unions are about commitment to an ideology and praxis regarding change that is premised on the essential significance of collective action. In my studies and work, and from labor activists, I have learned three relatively overlooked strategic considerations about collective action: (a) time/timing matters—change takes both time and timely action; (b) affect matters—collective action is catalyzed and sustained by the link between employers' disrespect and employees' emotions; and (c) resources matter—collectively imagining and acting on possibilities are contingent on employees recognizing and respecting their range of resources.

Time and Timing. As evidenced in this book, organizing and negotiating campaigns take time and patience, and depend on timing. Whether in the organizing campaigns of tenure-track faculty discussed in chapter 2, the GW adjunct faculty campaign in chapter 3, or graduate employee campaigns in private universities in chapter 5, the successes were years in the making, preceded by failures and/or false starts. And then after gaining recognition, first contract negotiations generally take a year and a half or two.

As frustrating as managerial resistance can be, protracted negotiations can build union strength and willingness to take action (e.g., a strike) as well as public support for such actions. For example, one of the Clark College leaders said that if there had been a strike vote in the first year of negotiations she would not have been ready (Southerland & Kamara, 2023). Similarly, the extended negotiations and strikes at Rutgers and the University of California increased public support and political pressure on management. Public strategies used by unions and allies can take time to play out and gain momentum.

Picking the right moment is key as well. Perhaps the most dramatic example of that was the unionized staff's decision at AU to strike during move-in week when new students and their families were coming to campus.

Managerial Disrespect and Employee Affect. Managerial actions and discourse can be among the best catalysts of organizing. On so many occasions they trigger visceral reactions from academic employees. Beyond that, successful mobilizing is contingent on overcoming the challenge of engaging employees over extended periods of time, whether that be in an organizing, contract, or strike campaign. Capitalizing on being disrespected and managing emotions to maintain a sense of possibility even after setbacks are key.

One example of managerial disrespect's triggering effect was Clark College's strike. After two years of bargaining, management came to the table with a "last, best offer" of a 0.3 percent raise. As two faculty union leaders said, "that absolutely energized the faculty," who voted to strike (Southerland & Kamara, 2023).

Yet, if managerial disrespect can energize countermobilization, it can equally have an enervating effect. Rather than indignation, it can lead to resignation amid successive, disheartening managerial actions. The disrespect becomes normalized, even internalized, and employees may "awfulize" but have no sense of there being options or may fear challenging the situation. So, a core part of organizing is to cultivate, in small and large ways, privately and publicly, a sense of injustice, and of possible alternatives.

Even when significant numbers of employees have translated their indignation into collective action, another challenge is to sustain engagement and energy over time, and in the face of risks (as in strikes) and setbacks. Students' support can be key, as noted in chapter 3 in the case of the protracted negotiations at GW. More recently, at AU, one of the strike captains spoke to the powerful, visceral effect striking staff felt at the sight of students streaming out of the opening fall semester convocation in support of them, "we expected maybe 10–20 students would walk out, but there were hundreds, and as I filmed it, folks on the picket line were in tears" (personal communication, fall 2023).

In less dramatic situations as well, in Studs Terkel's words (2003), "keeping the faith in troubled times" is an important challenge. The raised expectations that are part of organizing are sometimes dashed, and those who are "raising hell" (McAlevey, 2012) often catch hell on the way. As has been evident throughout this book, many successful organizing and contract campaigns were built on and came after previous defeats, and were marked by setbacks as well as victories. That is part of the choices and emotions of collective action, to cultivate a collective sense of critical hope (Duncan-Andrade, 2009) that recognizes oppression, and grounds its faith in developing the material resources and audacious aspirations that define the best collective efforts.

Collectively Imagining and Resource Mapping. A key to organizing is connecting workers' sense of injustice to a sense of possibility. Partly, that involves collectively imagining alternatives to what management calls the current or "new" "realities." Partly, it also involves employees recognizing and mapping their range of resources.

As McAlevey (2012) has written, "Organizing, at its core, is about raising expectations: . . . About what they [workers] have a right to expect from their employer . . . Expectations about what they themselves are capable of, about the power they could exercise if they worked together, and what they might use that collective power to accomplish (p. 12). More than a defensive reaction to what managers and others frame as the "new normal," employees' expectations are encompassed by envisioning possibilities of what could be. They entail imagining and working toward "life as it should be" (see Wasserman's 1966 lines in *Man of La Mancha*).[13] Much of collective negotiations are about iterative asks and wins. Yet, the best organizing and contract campaigns articulate a larger vision of what employees are working for, toward a more progressive academy.

Yet, collective organizing has a more practical side, too, in mapping and mobilizing resources toward the envisioned ends. A standard strategy in unionizing campaigns is to map and rate member support for a union by academic unit, putting the office visits and evaluations in a spreadsheet. Such workplace mapping could benefit from also mapping support by employees' identities (e.g., race/ethnicity and gender orientation), as well as by tapping into pre-existing networks of other activism.

Collective action can also benefit from a more expansive mapping within and beyond the bargaining unit, on and off campus, of material and nonmaterial resources. That has been clear in mobilizing supportive coalitions, whether of students, of other campus employees, or of off-campus groups and politicians. It is also clear in how academic employees have framed issues and mantras in relation to educational quality and broader social movements, with themes, social networks, and images that can all constitute nonmaterial as well as material resources that can be leveraged. Davis (2019) has discussed such "culture jamming," which is a process of utilizing "images, sounds, and text are appropriated from popular culture . . . for points of social and cultural critique" and detailed it in relation to a student activist group (pp. 118–119).

It is important in these mapping and mobilization processes for employees to realize and respect the resources they have rather than adopting a deficit perspective emphasizing what they lack. Indeed, as has been seen with adjunct faculty, material poverty can be leveraged as a strength in negotiating with well-resourced universities. So, too, graduate employees' campaigns have benefitted from the moral resource of graduate assistants being both employees and students whom the university should support. As with funds of knowledge, all employees have resources they can mobilize. Labor should not underestimate its own strength, thinking creatively about its resources and powers.

Likewise, labor should not overestimate management's media and political savvy, strength, or unity. As in Leonard Cohen's *Anthem* lyric, "There is a crack in everything. That's how the light gets in." Labor needs to leverage those fissures.

Summary. Much in mobilizing collective action hinges on beliefs and practices/praxis about effecting change. The principle here is that collective action is optimized by strategies that play out over time and are timely, that are sensitive to the visceral dimensions of action, and that are attuned to the range of resources available to those who are organizing. This, anyway, is what I have learned.

Closing Thought

Now, in closing this book, I recognize that the situation is fluid. That is the nature of academic employees organizing and negotiating their terms of employment and their institutions' and the higher education systems' future trajectory. When I am asked what I think will happen in the future, I respond, "It depends." The situation and outcomes are contingent. They are contingent upon local bargaining with management and upon larger state and (inter)national contexts, such as the 2024 election of Donald Trump, and the contest surrounding employees' collective bargaining rights, as well as on those employees' actions, which are also fluid.

A major aspect of the contest being contingent is employees' willingness to organize and negotiate. Will they move "from awfulizing to organizing?" Will they act on the premise that, as I have articulated in many settings over the years, "everything is negotiable" (and that such negotiation is iterative), as in the labor movement hashtag, #WhenYouFightYouWin? Do they see and feel that, at the very least, they gain self-respect and a sense of efficacy in the process, whatever the immediate outcome?

The future will be shaped by academic employees' past and ongoing efforts to organize, including by past failures. It will also be shaped by their vigilant enforcement of the formal terms and conditions of work embedded in the CBAs they have negotiated. The extent to which each wave of academic employees moves the academy toward a new progressive normal will be a function of their and their predecessors' organizing and negotiation for respect and higher education's public purposes.

Acknowledgments

My debts and the depth of my understanding of unions, organizing and contract campaigns, and collective bargaining have accumulated and been enhanced over many decades. Whatever the shortcomings of my understandings, they are entirely mine.

This book has been percolating in my mind and gradually emerging onto the written page for over a decade. Happily, the review of the book proposal, first chapters, and then the full manuscript has moved far more expeditiously. Thank you to Peggy Solic, senior editor of Rutgers University Press, for her encouragement from the very start, and for her unflagging, upbeat energy. Thanks as well to the reviewers for their very positive readings and thoughtful suggestions that were almost uniformly spot on, in my view substantially enhancing the book.

Before becoming an academic employee, I had my first formative, visceral encounters with organized labor through my summer work and my wife's work. To fellow members of the United Paperworkers International Union in the early 1970s, you taught me in so many ways at the workplace level (beyond the wages and benefits) what a union and solidarity mean about rights, power, respect, and safety, vis-à-vis the employer and foremen. To my wife, Janet, and her fellow schoolteachers of the United Teachers of Los Angeles, you demonstrated in the late 1970s what a successful job action requires—ongoing communication, trusted shop stewards, solidarity, and resolve in participating in a walkout after long negotiations to exercise power, demand appropriate compensation for your expertise, and leverage management for a just contract you knew the district could afford (one of many lessons from you, Janet).

As with, *Managed Professionals*, this book's contract analysis drew on the National Education Association's extraordinary Higher Education Contract Analysis System (HECAS). In my three-decade involvement with NEA, I have learned so much from staff and leaders, from coauthoring chapters with NEA

216 • Acknowledgments

staff analyzing contracts for the *NEA Almanac of Higher Education* to presenting to and interacting with annual Higher Education conference attendees. In addition to those who shepherded me into that work, I am grateful to Valerie Wilk (sadly, now deceased) and others who, more recently, have facilitated my involvement and ongoing tutelage in all matters union.

Without my time as the last AAUP General Secretary, this book would not have been possible. My first year there, I made fifty-nine airline trips to connect with folks in the field, so there are far too many leaders, members, and staff (local, state, and national) that I've learned from to name here. The learning curve was steep, the admiration for peoples' capacity and commitment to the work was deep, and the experience of the organizing campaigns, of ongoing interactions with locals, and of the Committee A work was invaluable.

Although the people with the AAUP are too many to acknowledge, I must name two leaders and one staff member. Howard Bunsis's tutelage, support, financial expertise, and energy in support of workers are such that I am privileged to be your friend. Rudy Fichtenbaum's leadership and advocacy locally and nationally, wonderful letters to university presidents calling them out, financial expertise, and your wisdom about never doing anything alone leave me forever grateful for having learned from and alongside you. And Sara Kilpatrick, your calm, savvy, and skills as a new Executive Director of the Ohio Conference in mobilizing against the assault on faculty's collective bargaining rights were (and are) remarkable, emblematic of so many staff behind the scenes who make it all work.

On the ground, schooling about unions has come at the hands of colleagues at other (inter)national unions and locals as well. Again, they are far too numerous to name, but the joint AAUP/AFT campaigns in which I participated were advanced seminars, providing insight into union governance and operations, organizing, high-level strategizing, and the nuts and bolts of forming a union, negotiating a first contract, and building on that foundation in future organizing and contract campaigns. From so many locals, I have similarly been schooled in supportive ways, including from leaders and staff in the Association of Pennsylvania State College and University Faculties (APSCUF), the California Faculty Association, the Professional Staff Congress, Rutgers AAUP/AFT, the United University Professions, and so many more.

After leaving the AAUP, I came to serve on the Foundation of the New Faculty Majority. The patience and grace of contingent faculty colleagues—with their media and organizational savvy, commitment, expertise, and heart—inspire me. To name a few, you have afforded me advanced study and continuing education in labor history (Joe Berry), in creative and forward-looking organizing (Anne McLeer of SEIU Local 500 and Robin Sowards of USW), in navigating competing union and complex policy realms (Maria Maisto), and in understanding the deeply embodied, lived experience of contingency in academe (all NFM colleagues).

In subsequent years, I was fortunate, thanks to the support of Malini Cadambi Daniel, then of SEIU, now of the PSC, to participate in six metro campaign launches across the country. Interaction with local faculty, SEIU staff, and fellow speakers at these events was an enriching learning experience in the balancing of national campaigns with local workers' realities.

Over nearly two decades, I have benefitted enormously from participating in the annual conferences and, for the past many years, from serving on the board of the National Center for the Study of Collective Bargaining in Higher Education and the Professions, as well as co-editing with superlative colleagues the *Journal of Collective Bargaining and the Academy*. From the time that Richard Boris drew me into the national center's work, I experienced another course of learning from labor and management colleagues, not least of all Richard himself, about all things collective bargaining. Subsequently, Bill Herbert has been a supportive and extraordinary tutor in collective bargaining matters, complemented by profoundly important empirical work in tracking and publishing about developments in collective bargaining.

Intellectually, as the old dog in the group, which made for quite a shift from my pre-*Managed Professionals* days, I have been profoundly influenced by my colleagues in the Center for the Study of Higher Education, as well as by my students. It is from them that I have most deeply learned and internalized the significance and essential need of intersecting workplace justice with social justice. As I have communicated to Karina Salazar, I can never do academic capitalism and labor analysis in the same way thanks to her scholarship and insight. Much the same is true of the work, insight, and generous collegiality and friendship of other colleagues in the Center, in order of them becoming colleagues here, Jenny Lee, Regina Deil-Amen, Nolan Cabrera, Amanda Kraus, Whitney Mohr, JD Lopez, Z Nicolazzo, Judy Marquez Kiyama, Moira Ozias, Heather Haeger, and Leslie Gonzales. My work and life are profoundly enriched by you all, as well as by the extraordinary students we serve, teach, and are taught by.

To colleagues who formed the Coalition for Academic Justice, UA, and then within months formed United Campus Workers, Arizona, being part of a collective brings another level of understanding of this work. It also brings friendships and a sense of solidarity that cuts across and bridges the all too many silos that separate us. And the ongoing collective struggle to shape the trajectory of our university is profoundly meaningful and fulfilling work alongside you.

Finally, to Janet, and to my daughters, Elizabeth and Olivia: as you have moved into workplaces beyond and within academe on your amazing journeys lighting up the world, I have learned through you so much and so deeply the problems and possibilities of workplaces. In so many ways, your experiences clarify that respect for workers, for their work, and for their public purposes calls for unions to intersect workplace and social justice in negotiating a better world.

Notes

Chapter 1   Now Is the Time

1   Yet, as is discussed in chapter 5, for postdoc employees, professional status is a recent and hard-earned one and can be connected to a sense of being an exploited employee whose working conditions belie the promise of "professional" status. That can translate into a belief that the path to enhancing their working conditions is through unionization and collective bargaining.

2   Another emergent category is "researchers"—the first such unit was formed in November 2018 at the University of California (see Flaherty, 2018, "U California Researchers"). Moreover, some graduate assistant bargaining units have emerged that include undergraduate employees, and the latter are now also forming their own bargaining units.

3   UCWs are "minority" unions in states without enabling legislation for public sector unionization and lacking collective bargaining rights. As this book addresses CBAs, I have not focused on UCWs until the end of chapter 6 and the concluding chapter. A "wall-to-wall" union includes all employees, from student workers to various categories of staff and faculty.

4   That identity is a stubborn one, to the point of denial—for nineteen years, I was Director of the Center for the Study of Higher Education (and for eight of those, a department head as well), a low-level academic administrator. Yet, I always maintained teaching/advising and research activities as a professor, identified simply as the first among equals, and never referred in department head meetings to my departmental colleagues as "my faculty."

5   "Chapters" are campus groups of faculty members organized around advancing the association's basic principles (faculty file with the national office for chapter status). "General Secretary" was the title of what is now called the "Executive Director." When I began in January 2009, the AAUP was in dire financial straits. In talking with leaders and staff about restoring the AAUP's financial stability and expanding its organizing, I half-joked that I had not taken the job to be the AAUP's last general secretary. By the end of my two-and-a-half years, with the help of Secretary/Treasurer Howard Bunsis and Chief Financial Officer Tess Esposito, the association went from large operating deficits to equally large surpluses. A small and growing

219

220 • Notes to Pages 6–8

reserve was built. Several large bargaining units that were either not paying (full) dues to the national association or were threatening to disaffiliate (or asking to pay reduced dues) were retained and/or restored to paying full dues. Moreover, membership grew due to a new dues structure and membership campaign, particularly with four successful union campaigns of large bargaining units that I helped foster, authorize, and/or oversee. Still, I *was* the AAUP's last general secretary. After I departed, the AAUP's Council voted to rename the position "Executive Director," partly to clarify role expectations relative to the president.

6 Some faculty units—such as Portland State University's full-time faculty unit and two of the largest faculty units in the country, the State University of New York's United University Professions (UUP), and the City University of New York's Professional Staff Congress (PSC)—include various academic and non-academic professionals, in student affairs, academic affairs, and medical center positions (what I call "managerial professionals"—see Rhoades, 1998b). Also, in many faculty units, librarians and counselors are included (with faculty status), sometimes not. The all-too-common tendency to overlook and ignore these professionals can cause resentment and division, as in the troubled relations between the UUP and the AAUP, with which it was once affiliated. A general secretary in the 1990s had mistakenly referred publicly to the UUP as United University *Professors* (not Professions), and the AAUP's policies and practices (in its "Redbook") accorded little to no recognition of academic professionals. During my time as general secretary, I presented to the UUP's Delegate Assembly, apologizing for the earlier general secretary's statement and speaking to the value of the professionals, many of whom I noted were like the graduate students in my academic program at the University of Arizona. I also worked to build recognition for academic professionals into the AAUP's policies and procedures. That work was rewarded with a vote by the UUP delegate assembly to stay affiliated. However, after I departed the AAUP, the UUP disaffiliated.

7 Berry and Worthen (2021) provide a valuable iterative analysis of this for one system-wide faculty union, focusing on contingent faculty.

8 On the latter point of reinscribing stratification, I thank Ben Baez for this insight.

9 In specifying a labor-based conception of quality working conditions, I reject and provide an alternative to managerial/policy discourses of "excellence" and "efficiency" that so often are used to leverage/control academic employees and/or are deployed in anti-union arguments.

10 CBAs vary greatly in length (from twenty-nine to several hundred pages) and in the language and detail covering the topics addressed in this book. On some matters (e.g., intellectual property), for some categories of academic employees, many or most contracts do not have language. On other matters (e.g., layoffs), most contracts have language, but that may mean a few sentences, a paragraph, or several pages. Almost all contracts have language/articles on recognition (what employees are included in/excluded from the bargaining unit), management rights, nondiscrimination (against union members for their activities or by demographic category), salary, benefits, appointment, workload, and grievance, among other matters.

11 The National Center for the Study of Collective Bargaining in Higher Education and the Professions has a comprehensive directory of contracts and is currently working on making that a searchable database, probably available in 2025.

12 Complicating that long game, not uncommonly, there are transitions in faculty union leadership (and in bargaining team membership). For example, the community college faculty leader (and her colleague) in question was subsequently replaced

Notes to Pages 9–15 • 221

in a union election by leaders seeking more "amicable" relations with the administration. In the next round of "interest-based bargaining" contract negotiations, the college president began with an ultimatum about a contract provision (counter to all protocol for the interest-based bargaining, or IBB, process), and the new faculty union president admonished a faculty negotiator for "scowling" too much in the bargaining sessions. Yet, former faculty leaders can return to advance their cause another day. In this case, the accommodationist leader was replaced in the next election, and the activist faculty leader worked with colleagues to advance the rights of adjunct faculty by establishing class cancellation fees and by embedding for them peer-based faculty evaluation, much like the strong language already in place in the contract for tenure-track faculty.

13 Part of the reason for these requests was that it had been some time since some units or chapters, even larger ones, had received a visit from someone from "naaational," the derogatory way that some members would refer to the national AAUP office (Rhoades, 2009b). Part of the reason is also that no matter the particular union in question, there is generally tension between the national office and locals who feel they are not being sufficiently served for the dues monies they send to the national office.

Chapter 2   A Critical Juncture and a Distinctive Dynamism

1 Ufot, with previous union experience and a law degree, and an activist who would later head the New Georgia Project, was the national staff's one Black (and Person of Color) professional at the time.

2 Academic employees in private, independent higher education are subject to federal law, whereas those working in public colleges/universities are subject to state law and public employment relations boards.

3 The law also prohibited employers from collecting dues (on behalf of unions) and prevented unions from collecting agency fees from nonmembers. And the recertification vote was determined by a majority of members, not by a majority of voters.

4 Membership of one of the state's strongest locals of schoolteachers declined by 30 percent (Umhoefer, 2016). For details on three other public sector unions in Wisconsin, see Nack et al. (2020).

5 In the statewide coalition that developed to repeal SB 5, an AAUP faculty leader was asked by other labor leaders why the state had targeted faculty with a special provision that was based on the U.S. Supreme Court's 1980 *Yeshiva* decision, which held that tenure-stream faculty at Yeshiva University (a private institution) were managers, and thus not statutory employees under the National Labor Relations Act (many private institutions nevertheless voluntarily chose to continue to recognize the union and not seek decertification). It emerged subsequently that Ohio's Inter-University Council of public university presidents was behind the *Yeshiva*-like language in SB 5. One cannot overestimate the importance of the legislation including police and firefighters in contributing to its repeal. Ads against SB 5 featured citizens speaking to the importance of the rights of firefighters who had saved family members.

6 By the end of 2017, "all seven faculty and graduate student bargaining units passed the new threshold [two-thirds majority] for [annual] recertification—most by wide margins" (Flaherty, 2017, "Under New Law," para. 1).

7 The local also posted this: "Because the *Janus* decision was a key goal of a right-wing campaign of attack on public employee unions, we expect those attacks to heighten in the aftermath of the decision. This summer, you may be contacted by a group

222 • Notes to Pages 16–18

calling themselves the Freedom Foundation or Concerned Citizens for Responsible Unions or some other obfuscating name. These well-funded groups contact union members and try to talk them out of union membership. . . . [We] will be working with our fellow unionists . . . across the country to coordinate our pushback against these attacks" (Hammond, 2018, para. 8).

8 This is calculated from a 1998 baseline of 496 bargaining agreements nationally for faculty and staff; by January 2006 there were 575 agreements—see Moriarty & Savarese (2006) for the directory of faculty contracts and bargaining agents.

9 The AAUP General Secretary formally authorized collective bargaining campaigns in consultation with national office staff, the elected President and Executive Committee, and the Collective Bargaining Congress.

10 There were faculty at medical schools who were part of larger faculty bargaining units. At the time. there was also a stand-alone medical school, the University of Medicine and Dentistry of New Jersey, with unionized faculty. However, it had unionized as part of a larger Rutgers system.

11 For some Health Center faculty, that history left a residue of concern. Would the AAUP abandon them again? As the AAUP organizing staff explained to me, they had felt clinical faculty had little interest in the campaign and that the state labor board might be "hostile" to medical school faculty's right to bargain because they might be seen as managers. But in the AFSCME campaign, the state labor board ruled favorably.

12 During the election campaign that was quite short (less than six months), there was one national office staff member (other than me) to visit UCHC, despite faculty requests. There were limited phone contacts during the campaign by this and a senior staff member. However, Howard Bunsis, of AAUP's CBC, was very involved.

13 Non-compete clauses prevent employees for a specific time period from leaving to work for a competitor company.

14 Most bargaining units have at least one paid staff member, in addition to elected faculty leaders and members who take on various roles/tasks (e.g., grievances, bargaining team). In some, as with Ed Marth, that staff person essentially manages elected faculty leaders. That runs counter to the preferred AAUP model of locals being run by faculty, not staff (it also runs counter to the larger labor movement ideal of democratically member-run unions; see Berry, 2005, pp. 43, 83). Yet, there are benefits of having an executive director with institutional memory and networks with local players on and off campus. UCHC faculty came to Marth, not main campus faculty. And in writing the national office about UCHC, Marth indicated that the "UConn AAUP Executive Committee has not met since May and will not meet until the semester begins."

15 Marth's (unrealized) plan was that the UCHC unit would eventually merge with (and expand) the main campus faculty unit.

16 The players can be key in campaigns, and assessment is partly to do with their capacities and how they are viewed by other employees. Within a few days, the head of organizing at AAUP had called Marth to offer support and ask whether the clinical faculty's "practice plans" were negotiable subjects of bargaining, which vary by state. The counsel Marth was utilizing from the Storrs unit indicated they would be. The head also asked about the possible merger and whether that would affect the bargaining unit (the merger was eventually taken off the table by the state legislature). As he wrote to Marth, "I know that I'm a worrier," followed by, "we would love to do what we can to contribute to a successful organizing effort" (personal communication, July 20, 2009).

17 The state's public employment relations board defines who is included in the prospective bargaining unit (and can vote).

18 The office visits/conversations organizers believe are central involve talking with employees about their working conditions and willingness to organize collectively. They feel, and are, political. That can be uncomfortable. As a union organizer colleague once said to three adjunct faculty organizing committee members at a café where he was discussing their campaign, "There's a reason Jehovah's Witnesses travel in pairs." The faculty members had spent months holding symposia, lectures, and open meetings, and posting leaflets. Such activities are normal parts of academic life. But organizing conversations are different. As one of the activists asked, "How can we make such conversations less awkward?" I interjected, "In virtually every campaign that I've been involved in, every group of core activists, like you, hit a sort of emotional wall, an obstacle to the further progress/success of the campaign." That wall was moving beyond their comfort zone to doing one-on-one organizing conversations with colleagues. Most successful campaigns involve this work. An organizing drive is not just about organizing forums and seminars. It is hard and awkward. But to get beyond the 20 percent or so of employees who immediately support a union, organizing conversations are essential.

19 A UCHC faculty member had created an online forum with open-source software, requiring no registration and allowing for discussion of issues and concerns. It was an effective mechanism for surfacing, building, and mobilizing faculty support.

20 A basic strategy is to map/rate member support for a union by academic unit through office visits. But that leaves unconsidered pre-existing networks of activism along political and identity lines.

21 As discussed in chapter 3, adjunct faculty's win at George Washington University also violated that convention. That was partly what underlay faculty leaders' choice of Service Employees International Union (SEIU) as an affiliate over AFT—the former's willingness to go to an election with less than 60 percent.

22 That was true, not just at UCHC. The AAUP's campaign at Bowling Green State University, where a decade before one had failed, had stalled in 2008 but was revitalized by new local leaders, national AAUP staff, and AAUP faculty/staff from Ohio and Michigan locals. In October 2010, BGSU faculty voted 391 to 293 for a union.

23 Thanks to Ben Baez for suggesting putting "professionals" in quotation marks. Thanks, too, to Steve London, a former PSC leader, for underscoring this point. Finally, thanks to Joe Berry and Robin Sowards, adjunct activists (and the latter a United Steelworkers staff member organizing academic employees), who articulate and live a commitment to the idea that (contingent) faculty are workers who should align with all workers.

24 In fall 2008, before I became AAUP General Secretary, the association and AFT were negotiating a "no raid" joint organizing agreement. Some AAUP units were being approached by or were themselves approaching AFT staff to explore affiliation with the larger (one of the biggest in the country), more politically powerful union (as part of the AFL-CIO). The "no raid" agreement was a commitment to not court bargaining units of the other union. This was key to AAUP's financial survival—some of its largest units were considering disaffiliating in favor of the AFT (or to reduce AAUP dues and pay the difference to the AFT). To me, the agreement was so important that I only agreed to become General Secretary when I got confirmation from a colleague at AFT that it was signing. The joint organizing part of the agreement identified eight public research universities (including UIC) as joint campaign targets.

224 • Notes to Pages 21–23

25 AAUP is higher education only and has a brand of being a "professional" association focused on academic freedom, shared governance, and tenure. By contrast, AFT is seen as a schoolteacher's union (85 percent of its members are in public schools, though many are support staff). As an indicator of this distinction, at the beginning of the UCHC campaign, some faculty, having heard of the AAUP/AFT agreement, expressed strong reservations regarding affiliation with AFT. We made it clear that UCHC was not part of the agreement. Relatedly, many AFT and NEA higher education members and staff believe the identities and issues of higher education members are insufficiently centered and advanced by the national affiliates in their campaigns/agendas. Higher education employees represent only roughly 15 and 5 percent respectively of AFT and NEA members. That plays out in mantras that center public schools. A major NEA one is "Great Public Schools for Every Student." Similarly, a major AFT mantra amid the pandemic was "Safe and Welcoming Public Schools for all."

26 For instance, in the AAUP's failed 1996–1997 University of Minnesota campaign, there was overwhelming opposition among engineering faculty (Rhoades, 1998a, p. 3).

27 Similarly, the Bowling Green State University campaign was delayed by a university effort to split the bargaining unit between tenure-track and FTNTT faculty. But unlike in Illinois, the university's claim was withdrawn before the State Employment Relations Board of Ohio addressed it.

28 The AAUP's founders were from elite private and public research universities. The vast majority of members now are outside that sector but still in four-year institutions.

29 After extensive involvement in the UIC and other campaigns and decades of working with higher education unions, I do see differences among unions' organizing models, but they can be overstated, as within each organization, there are variations in how campaigns and units operate. Each has ongoing tensions among staff, local faculty, and national leaders. In each, organizing staff seek to advise/guide local faculty and identify/support local faculty who they believe are best suited for leadership. And in each case, local faculty depend on but also have some level of reservations about and occasionally disdain for national staff. Given their competition for members (and their dues), national staff can overstate differences in trying to persuade local faculty to affiliate with them.

30 The most hotly contested disagreement was over the process by which faculty would elect (or not) to have a union. The IFT and AFT had worked to get "card check" into Illinois law, which meant the state public employment board's certification decision was based on whether 50 percent of the bargaining unit plus one had signed union authorization cards within a certain period of time. AAUP staff and leaders (who mostly came from states without card check laws) believed tenure-stream faculty would oppose this process and wanted a secret ballot election (in which a decision was carried by 50 percent plus one of those voting). AFT staff pointed out that card check had been used successfully in other campaigns. AAUP staff and leaders' response was that those campaigns were of adjunct faculty and graduate employees, who were different. Tenure-stream faculty, they insisted, would see card check as undemocratic. I suggested we ask the UICUF organizing committee—it was their campaign. They wanted card check.

31 In this case, the resistance was partly about organizing research university faculty. But there was also skepticism about organizing adjunct faculty, graduate employees, and postdocs. The preceding general secretary, Ernst Benjamin, an otherwise astute student of and leader in academic labor and a longtime, respected AAUP leader

who had ongoing contact with staff, said to me when I started that there was little opportunity for new organizing, particularly with tenure-stream research university faculty, whose sense of professional status would undermine any campaign (sometimes it did). Unionization, he said, had reached its saturation point. Benjamin was also skeptical about the payoff of organizing adjunct faculty. The general secretary before him (Mary Burgan), who also maintained contact with the staff, opposed graduate employees unionizing. Many of the seventeen professional staff were skeptical about the value of union work, which they felt took away from the AAUP's core policy work. Even organizing staff saw policy work as primary, spending much time with "advocacy" (non-collective bargaining) chapters. Some felt I was making the AAUP too like the AFT in emphasizing organizing. Ironically, a decade later, in 2022, AAUP became affiliated with the AFT as a "national regional council" with independence and autonomy in its work.

32 The risk aversion was not shared by the elected leadership. Quite the contrary. The president, executive committee, most of the governing council, and all of the Collective Bargaining Congress (CBC) strongly supported the organizing campaigns, which they saw as key to increased membership and the AAUP's financial health. CBC's Executive Committee allocated significant resources to hiring short-term organizing staff, who it explicitly emphasized should be working on the road in organizing campaigns.

33 The AAU is a group of (now) seventy-one top public and private research universities in the U.S. and Canada.

34 In May 2024, tenure- and nontenure-track faculty at the University of Pittsburgh, another AAU institution and the largest faculty unit in a decade to unionize (Flaherty, 2021, "A Union Victory"), voted to ratify their first collective bargaining agreement (United Steelworkers, 2024). In April 2024, tenure and nontenure-track faculty at the University of Kansas voted for a union, affiliated with AAUP/AFT (Lawhorn, 2024).

35 As at UCHC and UIC, it seemed inconsequential to many tenure-stream faculty that other academic employees were unionized at their university (the UO had one of the country's oldest graduate employee unions), or that tenure-stream faculty were unionized at Portland State University. For many, those other academic employees (and institutions) were seen as qualitatively different.

36 For Rutgers, it was nineteen years (admitted in 1989 to the AAU). Stony Brook was unionized twenty-eight years before it was admitted to the AAU, in 2001. Buffalo and Florida were unionized sixteen and nine years before being admitted (in 1989 and 1985).

37 The AAUP's Collective Bargaining Congress designated a member (Gerald Turkel) to regularly connect with and support the staff on the campaign. And Howard Bunsis did an analysis of university finances.

38 See note 30.

39 On June 37, 2018, a joint AAUP/AFT bargaining unit at OSU of 2,400 members that included tenure-stream, full- and part-time contingent faculty, and postdocs was certified.

40 See *Preserving Excellence at Illinois* (https://preservingexcellence.blogspot.com/). One of the three coauthors (Burbules) was a member of the Executive Committee of the University Senates Conference, which provided a pro-administration response to an AAUP analysis of the system's finances in the early days of the UIC campaign (see chapter 6). Although he had written critically about globalization,

226 • Notes to Pages 27–40

neoliberalism, and education (e.g., Burbules & Torres, 2000), apparently, he did not recognize neoliberalism in his university.

41 Notably, a later joint AAUP/AFT drive at the University of New Mexico succeeded in separate full- and part-time faculty units (due to state law) (Flaherty, 2019, "University of New Mexico").

42 Susan Schurman, labor scholar and former Dean of Rutgers' School of Management and Labor Relations school said of a presentation I did on SEIU's metro campaigns to organize contingent faculty (Rhoades, 2015a), "I've been a critic of competition between unions. But the case of SEIU persuades me that such competition can be a good thing." As Schurman further suggested, SEIU's success likely encourages locals of other national affiliates to bargain stronger provisions.

43 A decade later, only 6 percent of full-time faculty in private colleges/universities were covered by collective bargaining agreements, compared to 38 percent in publics (Ehrenberg, Klaff, Kezsbom, & Nagowski, 2004, p. 211). Still, dozens of faculty bargaining units in these settings continue, and a few fought off decertification efforts by the administration (see Metchick & Singh, 2004).

44 That is true despite slight declines in the last two decades. In the 2000s, the percentage of public sector employees represented by a union has declined slightly— from 41.9 percent in 2000 to 37.9 percent in 2017 (Bureau of Labor Statistics, 2018a). That is still far higher than 6.5 percent union density among private sector workers (Bureau of Labor Statistics, 2018b).

45 The National Education Association (NEA) is now almost forty times larger than the UMW. Also, for perspective on the significance of higher education workers, even in traditional trade unions, roughly one-fourth of all UAW members are higher education employees (Herbert et al., 2023).

46 The substantive focus of much scholarship in the early years and in a few cases in later years was on correlates of support for unionization (e.g., Ladd & Lipset, 1973, 1975), the effects of unions on wages (e.g., Ashraf, 1992, 1999; Leslie & Hu, 1977, and later, Henson, Krieg, Wassell, & Hedrick, 2012), faculty governance (e.g., Baldridge & Kemerer, 1976; Kemerer & Baldridge, 1981; and later, S. Porter, 2013), and the climate of collegiality (e.g., Birnbaum & Inman, 1984; Lee, 1979, and later, Hartley, 2010).

Chapter 3 Bread and Roses, and a Labor-Based Conception of Quality

1 In a history of the strike that included interviews with participants, Watson (2005) suggested the story was apocryphal. "Local legend has it that a photograph from the strike showed a woman holding a picket sign reading, WE WANT BREAD, BUT WE WANT ROSES, TOO! No such photograph has ever been found" (p. 256). The phrase first appeared in a James Oppenheim poem (1911) a year before the strike. Yet the slogan and strike's significance in the labor movement, which took up the rallying cry, starting with Upton Sinclair's 1915 labor anthology, up through custodial workers in the 2000s are real (Milkman, Bloom, & Narro, 2010; O'Brien, 2000). The phrase's significant political truth is enduring, whatever the historical "truth" of its origins.

2 The term "adjunct" has problematic connotations and is descriptively inaccurate when applied to faculty in part-time positions (part-time is a misnomer, too, because faculty often work in several such positions at once), who are nearly half of the instructional workforce. But it is the term of use in the academic literature, policy discourse, and for many activist faculty. On the issue of respect, a contingent

Notes to Pages 40–45 • 227

faculty activist/author framed their introduction to an edited book's section on the making of the new contingent majority, "R-E-S-P-E-C-T" (Hohl, 2024).

3 The Coalition on the Academic Workforce's (CAW) 2010 survey, organized by disciplinary associations and supported by the AAUP and AFT, is the largest national survey of nontenure-track faculty to date. It included 10,331 responses from faculty in part-time positions (and 9,519 from full-time non-tenure-track faculty), of whom 22.6 percent had health benefits and 41.4 percent retirement benefits through their academic employer.

4 See Alker (2024), Angell (2024), Juarez (2024), and Loiselle (2024) on how contingent faculty labor is gendered, raced, and classed.

5 That political stance and claim are supported by academic research (Chingos, 2016; Eagan & Jaeger, 2008, 2009; Ehrenberg & Zhang, 2005; Jaeger & Eagan, 2011a, 2011b; Ran & Xu, 2018; Umbach, 2007; Schudde, 2019; Xu, 2019).

6 Context matters, including party politics and organized labor's prominence in them. The Senate, controlled by Republicans, had tabled a proposal for hearings, after which Socialist Congressman Victor Berger, "had taken his case to both President Taft and the House Committee on Rules." The latter, which approved hearings in a Democrat-controlled House of Representatives, consisted of three Republicans and eight Democrats, one of whom, William Wilson, was a founder of the United Mine Workers (Watson, 2005, p. 185)

7 The strike's trigger was a pay reduction, the owners' response to a new state law that reduced women and children's working hours from fifty-six to fifty-four per week (in the past, mill owners had maintained wages after such changes).

8 The strike led to President Taft sponsoring legislation establishing a national commission (the "Walsh Commission") on industrial relations, chaired by a noted progressive era reformer who advocated for better working conditions and pay, and equal opportunities for women. Promoted by President Taft, it was created by Congress on August 23, 1912 (when in November, Taft lost the election to Wilson, the latter appointed the commissioners). The commission heard testimony from a Who's Who of the day, including Clarence Darrow, Louis Brandeis, "Mother" Jones, "Big Bill" Haywood, Henry Ford, and Andrew Carnegie. It published its report in 1916, promoting collective bargaining and focusing on the workplace, not broader politics. Thirty years later, the older son of former President Taft cosponsored a major revision of the Wagner Act, the Taft-Hartley Act, that restricted organized labor's activities and power.

9 As discussed in chapter 2, the AAUP and AFT did not like to file for an election unless they had cards from 60 percent of the proposed bargaining unit. The same had been true of UAW.

10 To file for an election, national labor law requires that at least 30 percent of the proposed unit have signed cards.

11 The election was open to all part-time faculty who had taught at GW within the last two academic years, excluding summer sessions.

12 See McLeer (2024) on the managerial "playbook" of such campaigns, including "third partying" the union as an "external entity," claiming unionization will lead to fewer courses for adjuncts and higher tuition, saying unionization will compromise collegial practices and academic relationships, and appealing to academic snobbery, saying unions are not for professional employees (e.g., casting SEIU as a union of janitors).

13 A similar difference was discussed in chapter 2 between the AAUP and AFT approaches to campaigns at UIC.

Notes to Pages 45–48

14 The event also focused on nine GW and two Georgetown students who had been arrested protesting GW's employment policies.

15 At high-tuition institutions, the fact that students are taught by low-wage adjunct faculty who have advanced degrees, undermines that promise of return on tuition investment. Years ago, an adjunct faculty activist, Susan Michalczyk at Boston College sent me a Dan Wasserman political cartoon published in the *Boston Globe* (April 16, 2014). The cartoon's four frames portray an adjunct faculty member saying to his class, "This college wants you to get a degree . . . so you don't end up doing temp work . . . with low pay, no security, and lousy benefits. . . . Like my job as an adjunct professor" (www.bostonglobe.com/wasserman).

16 As will be discussed in chapter 4, adjunct and full-time contingent have negotiated contract language around educational quality issues such as access to instructional resources and professional development. Another quality issue related to evaluations. As a faculty leader at GW said (personal communication, September 25, 2014), when faculty proposed evaluation language for the contract, management's bargaining team "fell out of their chairs"—they had not expected that. For faculty, such language stemmed from a desire to enhance professional development through an approach to evaluation that emphasized classroom observation by peers. Faculty sought to ensure that student evaluations or complaints would not be the sole basis of their review or nonrenewal.

17 The first contract raised the minimum salary by up to 32 percent (SEIU, 2012); subsequent contracts provided across-the-board 3 percent increases, and further increases for adjunct faculty with PhDs (Karim, 2012). The first contract also provided increased job security, including greater rights to reappointment as well as "just cause" and binding arbitration language for discipline and dismissal. It further included evaluation language (requiring more than student evaluations) to ensure that faculty are not non-renewed for capricious reasons.

18 Competition among institutions (with their own budgets and niches) works against such cooperation. Cross-institution management/labor organizational structures exist in statewide systems, but those have a central, system-wide boss.

19 Duquesne University adjuncts had voted to affiliate with USW but a September 2020 ruling by the NLRB on religious exemptions to coverage to the NLRA undermined that possibility.

20 In August 2017, the full-time faculty union at Point Park University ratified its first CBA, thirteen years after it was certified. The full- and part-time faculty union at the University of Pittsburgh was certified in 2021 (after an earlier failure—see Schackner, 2019), with the first contract ratified in 2024 (Schackner, 2023a). And graduate employees at Pitt re-initiated a card drive in the fall of 2023 after losing an earlier election by 39 votes (Schackner, 2023b). SEIU Local 500 has also expanded in the employees it is organizing, including graduate employees and some staff at American University, for example.

21 The number was "intended to recall the original, directly democratic university in Bologna," which was communicated to new members.

22 Pennsylvania, state labor law (see Herbert, 2016b) and rulings that framed part- and full-time faculty as having a shared community of interest allowed for the accretion of part-time faculty into an existing bargaining unit of full-time academic employees. The 2015 election of 1,400 adjunct faculty (and professionals) at Temple University to join the Temple Association of University Professionals was the largest single election of adjunct faculty in two years and involved them joining a union (AFT) representing the most adjunct faculty (80,000) in the country (AFT, 2015).

Notes to Pages 49–56 • 229

23 The next closest union was AFT, with 22 percent of newly represented NTT faculty (in AFT, AAUP/AFT, and AFT/NEA affiliated units). By contrast, the big three academic unions totally monopolized organizing of tenure-track and combined tenure-track, nontenure-track faculty in public institutions.

24 Some controversy surrounded these campaigns' "branding." Although they took place under the auspices of SEIU locals, the promotional literature and messaging was under the banner of "Faculty Forward."

25 Having spoken at six of these campaign "launch" events (Boston, Chicago, Los Angeles, Miami, Oakland, and Seattle), I can also attest to variations in local faculty's strength (relative to staff) and in tactics. At one, there were nearly as many SEIU staff as there were local faculty. As for tactics, Local 925's approach was much like the USW model in Pittsburgh—indeed, local leaders there drew on the USW organizer's expertise (personal communication, October 10, 2015), a marker of the national nature of the contingent faculty labor movement.

26 There is some debate about the value of such nationally driven (what some call "corporate") campaigns, with some activists critiquing "Fight for 15" for being staff (or consultant) driven, not worker driven, and for emphasizing short-term mobilization around a narrow policy goal rather than organizing workplace strength. But social networks can be fostered by such campaigns, within and across low-wage sectors of employment and between workers on and off campus, a connection/effect overlooked in academic studies of "Fight for 15" (e.g., Rhomberg, 2018). Union presence in a region can contribute to this. Thus, some adjunct faculty activists in Miami had been in graduate employee unions in local universities, a potential incubator for subsequent union activism.

27 Susan Meisenhelder, the first reform coalition president, was a former lecturer.

28 The competing slate in the election was led by the heir apparent to Irving Polishook, the PSC president of 25 years.

29 CFA leaders have sat on the AAUP's Committee on Contingent Faculty, its National Council, Executive Committee, and Committee A.

30 As AAUP General Secretary during the first few years after NFM's foundation (later serving on its Foundation Board), being regularly in touch with leaders and staff in various academic unions, there clearly was major concern and consternation within the academic unions about how NFM would comment on their work and initiatives.

31 Subsequently, the General Accounting Office also did a report on contingent faculty (Flaherty, 2017, "Under New Law").

32 That connector role is much like what the GW organizer said of students.

33 In closing this section, it should be acknowledged that other advocacy groups have also been key in the contingent faculty labor movement, most notably COCAL, the Coalition of Contingent Academic Labor, which has held conferences since 1996 (Berry, 2005; Berry & Worthen, 2018). An important network for contingent activists, it has helped spawn ideas and actions that have garnered national attention.

34 That student activism and the progressive history of the institution also contributed to Georgetown's administration not claiming "religious exemption" from the National Labor Relations Act. Moreover, the Just Employment Policy, grounded in Catholic social teaching, was a factor in some places, like Pittsburgh, for larger community involvement, supporting adjunct faculty's right to collectively bargain (Aleva, 2013).

35 Such tensions can also sometimes be found between tenure-track and contingent faculty bargaining units at the same institution, especially when they have different union affiliates.

230 • Notes to Pages 56–66

36 Another 15 percent were tenure-track faculty, leaving 65 percent of newly represented faculty being in contingent-only units. Because of the 1981 *Yeshiva* ruling of the Supreme Court, no such combined units are found in private institutions, where tenure-track faculty do not have statutory rights under the NLRA.

37 It also was clear in the disparate health impacts among faculty from marginalized populations, who are disproportionately contingent faculty.

38 Solidarity among workers in the pandemic has also emerged beyond faculty to include other campus workers. For example, at UICUF, the faculty union supported and called for greater access to personal protective equipment and disinfectant for custodial workers.

39 Many thanks to Anne McLeer (2020) for this observation and suggestion.

Chapter 4   Negotiating Bread and Roses and Labor-Based Quality into Part-Time-Only and Combined Bargaining Unit Contracts

This chapter includes material from Rhoades' (2017a, 2020) contract analyses, varying and updating the text and analysis and adding analyses of adjunct organizing, salaries, and pay equity.

1 By contrast, in the 1990s, analyses of unionization reflected an issue that had long driven tenure-track faculty negotiating, protecting tenure-stream faculty's rights amid management employing growing numbers of part-time faculty (DeCew, 2003). Thus, I focused on "collective workforce" protections such as defined ratios of full- to part-time faculty to limit the latter's growth and restrictions on part-time faculty hiring during layoffs (Rhoades, 1998a).

2 Adjunct faculty are typically defined as less than .51 full-time equivalent (sometimes as less than .66 FTE), although for unit definition, "adjunct" and "part-time" can be different. Thus, in Florida, faculty are categorized by job code, not FTE. Nevertheless, given common usage, I denote adjunct faculty units as part-time only (PTO).

3 The gains have come at different levels, in different ways, and for different categories of part- and full-time nontenure-track faculty, making any overall assessment misleading. Plus, pay-per-course generally varies among academic units, so gains are often characterized as "increases of up to x percent" because the level of the increase depends on the (varied) base.

4 The bargaining unit includes full- and part-time faculty (and professional staff), but there are separate contracts.

5 The union successfully fought against centralizing student "evaluations" in an Office of Academic Affairs, which could be a tool used to discipline (adjunct) faculty. It negotiated retaining faculty evaluation in the hands of peers (with a committee including part-time faculty assessing the use of the student survey instrument). It designated student feedback as "surveys," not "evaluations," specifying that they could not be used to initiate disciplinary procedures in order to protect adjunct faculty's academic freedom and to protect faculty from marginalized communities from patterns of gender and racial/ethnic bias by students.

6 Similarly, in 2022, adjunct faculty at NYU signed a contract providing for pay parity for those who teach studio classes in art and performance, plus a 34 percent increase in the minimum salary.

Notes to Pages 67–76 • 231

7 See Moser's note 22 for other contracts he identified.

8 Generally, such provisions accord longer term contracts to adjunct faculty who have consistently taught classes over a particular period of time. For example, CUNY's CBA provided three-year contracts for faculty who have taught two classes a semester in the same department for ten consecutive previous semesters (Flaherty, 2017, "Some 1,500 Adjuncts"). And faculty on multi-year appointments can only be terminated for "just cause" (though that incentivizes departments to ensure a break in adjunct faculty's semesters of employment). One of the major wins in the Tufts PTO contract was that most adjunct faculty got one-year contracts, those with more than four years of service got two-year contracts, and those with more than eight years got three-year contracts. News coverage called these rights "'unheard of at most institutions'" (Benderly, 2014, para. 1).

9 As USW staff member Robin Sowards has indicated, "First contracts are . . . the foundation of the house, not the house itself. It's the job of the local union to keep building" (personal email, January 14, 2016).

10 Relatively few studies analyze union contracts covering part-time faculty (e.g., Leslie & Ikenberry, 1979; Levin, Kater, & Wagoner, 2011; Rhoades, 1998a), and they tend not to address these academics' agency. Some exceptions include Sam's (2012) historical case study of collective bargaining at a community college, Kezar and Sam's (2013) case study, Kezar's (2012) edited volume, including contributions by adjunct faculty activists, and Berry and Worthen's (2021) historical overview of adjunct faculty activism and case study of the CFA contract.

11 The Local 500 contracts are for American, Georgetown, George Washington, Howard, and Trinity Washington. The Local 509 contracts are for Brandeis, Boston University, Northeastern, and Tufts.

12 The statewide pattern speaks to an important aspect of circulating ideas about contract language through various mechanisms, statewide as well as national (in meetings/conferences and databases/reports). For example, in speaking at a 2017 statewide Oregon Education Association summer conference for community college locals, I witnessed such collective work in building a cross-institutional contract language database. The New York State United Teachers' report about negotiating "beyond the distance" (NYSUT, 2013) is a more developed example of such a database. And the NEA's HECAS is a national example.

13 That constitutes intra-professional stratification, in contrast to the inter-professional jurisdiction disputes (and bump chains) that Abbott (1988) and other sociologists address.

14 Similarly, Kezar and Maxey's (2016) "learner centered model" of faculty employment calls for adjunct faculty's access to office space, course materials and resources, and PD.

15 That has been evident in a decades-long national "completion agenda" (Humphreys, 2012) advanced by and embedded in foundations (e.g., Lumina), the Department of Education, and accrediting bodies (Gaston, 2014). Similarly, performance-based budgeting processes have been widely adopted at the state and system level (Dougherty & Natow, 2015; Hillman, Fryar, & Crespin-Trujillo, 2018; Perna & Finney, 2014), although the empirical evidence is clear that they have consistently failed to substantially increase graduation rates and other student outcomes (Hillman, Tandberg, & Gross, 2014; Hillman et al., 2018; Shin, 2010). They have, though, "worked" in establishing a policy regime dominated by heightened accountability, manufactured scarcity, and continued disinvestment in the academic workforce, which perhaps is the point.

Notes to Pages 86–91

16 Some other non-academic unions have played a significant role as well (e.g., UAW and USW).

17 In the words I have heard from Joe Berry, a leading adjunct activist, "The best contracts for part-time faculty are in joint units of full- and part-time faculty, and the worst contracts for part-time faculty are also in joint units." Another prominent adjunct activist and organizer, Rich Moser (2014), has written, "The positive potential of combined units is not, however, automatic, and was often realized only after sustained political efforts by contingent faculty," (p. 89) as documented by Berry and Worthen (2021) with the CFA.

Chapter 5   More than Would-Be Apprentices

1 Graduate employee unions often represent less and more than graduate teaching and research assistants. Most include teaching assistants, but many do not include research assistants. Moreover, many include graduate student employees working in administrative/professional positions. Others include undergraduate employees.

2 A process that is delayed/deferred by there being no mandatory retirement age.

3 That is true even in science, technology, engineering, and math, where, by one estimate, only one in four doctoral students will attain a tenure-track faculty job (Stephan, 2012, p. 170).

4 See Cantwell, 2011, on "academic insourcing." As in the opening epigram, many graduate employees are future contingent faculty competing for those jobs. For example, while at the AAUP, I met with leaders of the Lecturers' Employee Organization (LEO), representing nontenure-track faculty, at the University of Michigan. They related how lecturers were being displaced by graduating doctoral students who were being given teaching postdocs when they did not find tenure-track positions. As one said, "Ten years ago, we were them" (as UM graduates). As for postdocs, employers' lesser obligations to them versus graduate students/ employees provide an incentive to hire the former, who have more training, especially if graduate employees are unionized, as I found in a study for UAW, where postdocs were negotiating their first contract at the University of Massachusetts, Amherst (Rhoades, 2012b). The Graduate Employee Organization included research assistants who had negotiated substantial salary and benefits increases in the 1990s. In the early 2000s, postdocs, who had not yet unionized, increased by 47 percent, nearly double the national rate (Cantwell & Taylor, 2015, Table I), and graduate research assistantships shrank by 12 percent.

5 I focus on stand-alone units, not those in which graduate employees are included with faculty, as at the City University of New York in the mid-1960s (Cain, 2018).

6 In the early 1970s, graduate assistants at Adelphi University sought to join a bargaining unit of full- and part-time faculty, but the NLRB ruled there was not a sufficient community of interest and that they were primarily students (Rinschler, 2010). Two years later, the NLRB ruled that eighty-three graduate research assistants in Stanford's physics department seeking recognition as a union were primarily students, not employees, invoking the Adelphi case.

7 In public universities, graduate employees' rights are governed by state employment relations boards and state law.

8 GSOC was supported by 98.4 percent of prospective bargaining unit members.

9 NLRB members are presidential appointments confirmed by the Senate in staggered five-year terms. The membership majority has been from the President's party.

Notes to Pages 91–99 • 233

10   Two undergraduate unionizing groups, at Grinnell College and Reed College, also decided to withdraw their petition to the NLRB "because they fear a federal board appointed by President Donald Trump would reject their request and set back unions at colleges across the country" (McFetridge, 2018, para. 1). Notably, three private universities (Brandeis, Tufts, and the New School) in "blue" states recognized and eventually settled contracts with their graduate employee unions, signing first contracts during this time—Brandeis in April, Tufts in October, and New School in November of 2018.

11   Already in January 2024, another new graduate employee unit at Washington State University (which also included some undergraduate workers) signed its first contract (Quinn, 2024, "Washington State U"). The WashU Undergraduate and Graduate Workers Union has generated an interactive chart, adapting Herbert et al.'s (2023) chart, naming new units by the year they were formed and providing links to them (https://wugwu.org/resources/graduate-and-undergraduate-student -unions). The growth of undergraduate units has been extraordinary as well (Herbert et al., 2023). Although some graduate student unions include undergraduate workers, my focus is on graduate employees, who account for 93 percent of newly organized student employees (Herbert et al., 2023).

12   SEIU organized five units, as did UAW, but the latter organized bigger units, accounting for 70 percent of new unionized student employees (Herbert et al., 2023).

13   Relatedly, electoral margins in favor of unionization were extraordinarily high (91 percent) in the new organizing (Herbert et al., 2023).

14   The contest reflected enduring tensions within the AAUP over graduate assistants and collective bargaining more broadly (see Cain, 2020; Hutcheson, 2000), which I observed in my time there among staff and leaders. For example, while then-AAUP President Cary Nelson (and I) pushed the new RIR language, there was much resistance to the terminology among the task force and Committee A members.

15   Ambash had also represented Brown University in the 2004 NLRB case. Ironically, although NYU was much mentioned in the brief, it was not a signatory—it had recognized its graduate employee union and signed a contract. Also, two signatories (Brown and Harvard) four years later had signed contracts with graduate employee unions, as did Columbia two years after that. Although many private universities experiencing union drives did not sign, the American Council on Education filed an amicus brief that largely mirrored the brief of Columbia and the Ivy League universities.

16   The brief rejected the view that graduate assistants are apprentices in a legal or figurative sense. Yet, it also asserted that doctoral education is designed to prepare the next generation of academics, which sounds like an apprenticeship.

17   The union organizing started in January 2014, originally representing only graduate workers, but expanding later to include undergraduate workers and renamed Student Workers of Columbia. By fall, cards supporting unionization had been gathered from 1700 workers, and GWC-UAW asked for voluntary recognition from the university. The administration hired a union-avoidance firm. The students then filed their petition with the NLRB on December 12, 2014. After the August 23, 2016, NLRB ruling, management filed a brief objecting to it and then challenged the successful December election of GWC-UAW as the bargaining agent, which the NLRB rejected. Yet management still refused to meet or negotiate.

18   International students pay high tuition and get no aid, which yields high net tuition revenue. A rich scholarly literature documents the colonialist, capitalist framing

234 • Notes to Pages 99–109

and recruitment of international students (e.g., see Rhoades, Castiello-Gutierrez, Lee, Marei, & O'Toole, 2019, and Stein & Oliveira de Andreotti, 2016). For two international graduate students' perspectives, see Castiello-Gutierrez and Li (2020).

19 Subsequently, the university updated the post: "'The University would not report a student's change in status to the government unless it determined that . . . it must do so in order to be legally compliant'" (Bittle, 2017, para. 5).

20 At Columbia, see the accurate FAQ of UAW Local 2710: "Administration's anti-strike campaigns often target international students because their visa status makes them more vulnerable. You should know that international students have the same rights as US citizens to participate in union activity. It is illegal for Columbia to retaliate for protected activity" (https://columbiagradunion.org/faq/).

21 After eight days, the strike was concluded through mediation, and the union won 5 percent raises to minimum pay as well as funds for medical and parental leave (http://gtff3544.net/home-page/history/).

22 Also see Schackner's (2018) article, "Is Fear over Visa Status Being Used to Derail Penn State Unionization Effort?"

23 The privates were American, Brandeis, Brown, Clark, Columbia, Georgetown, Harvard, NYU, USC, and Yale; the publics were California, Florida, Illinois-Chicago, Massachusetts, Michigan, Michigan State, New Mexico, New Mexico State, Oregon, Oregon State, Rhode Island, Temple, Urbana-Champaign, Washington, and Wayne State.

24 Other exceptions included the locals' name for the Columbia Student Workers and the University of Massachusetts Amherst contract, which had one reference to "graduate student worker."

25 Along those lines, a handful of contracts defined inappropriate duties for graduate employees (American's contract had a section, "Duties that are not appropriate," which included a sentence, "TAs and RAs are not expected to provide personal services to the supervisor"). Similarly, New Mexico's contract had this, "Bargaining unit members shall not be required to perform personal errands for the supervisor."

26 The one private is Columbia University (2018). In subsequent years, postdocs have been included in four faculty units—Fordham University (SEIU), Goucher College (SEIU), Oregon State University (AAUP/AFT), and University of Oregon (AAUP/AFT) (Herbert et al., 2020, p. 20). Also, postdocs were added in 2020 to a preexisting United Faculty Florida (NEA/AFT) faculty bargaining unit at New College, Florida.

27 At Cal Tech, a Graduate and Postdoc union was formed in late 2023.

28 See also Rhoades (2023) for a fuller analysis of these reports.

29 Most postdocs are approaching forty, increasingly are parents, and lack access to paid maternity leave (Flaherty, 2017, "Survey of Parent Postdocs").

30 That is remarkable in that the NAS report cited an article (Cantwell & Lee, 2010) in which "neo-racist" treatment of postdocs was featured.

31 Also, the NPA's logo is a light bulb, with the explanation, "Introduced in January 2018, this new logo seeks to highlight the potential of our members, both as scholars on the brink of discovery" (https://www.nationalpostdoc.org/page/About#NPALogo).

32 Thus, in its 2017 report, NPA called for establishing such offices as a "best practice" (Flaherty, 2018, "Best Practices"), asserting that, "At the heart of every strong set of institutional postdoc policies and programs, sits a vital and vibrant postdoc office and postdoc association" (Ferguson, McTighe, Amlani, & Costello, 2017, p. 4).

Notes to Pages 109-128 • 235

33 As of May 2024, the website link on unionization, under "Advocacy" requires membership info to log in (which is not the case for other advocacy topics).

34 The UC postdocs also negotiated provisions beyond the American Disabilities Act for temporary accommodations for postdocs with disabilities to kick in immediately to cut through the bureaucracy that can reduce such access.

35 The exception was Rutgers's contract, which had different language: "No unit member shall be discharged, suspended or otherwise disciplined except for a legitimate, non-arbitrary reason that, given the facts and circumstances known to the employer, exists at the time." The CBA then delineated the due process attached to that action.

36 The University of California CBA also established a labor-management committee to explore issues, including "professional development issues." Rutgers University's CBA had a side letter regarding coordinating support services for postdocs.

37 The CBA also had a side letter providing for a labor/management task force addressing issues including abusive and intimidating behavior.

38 The contract also included a "bathroom equity" clause to ensure access to gender-neutral bathrooms.

Chapter 6 Challenging Management's Austerity Practices

1 Although Brint (2018) indicated that "Academic values, traditions of shared governance, and deference to professional expertise are the braking mechanisms that slow the advance of market logic" (p. 258), his 2000 and 2012 survey data on provosts revealed increased managerial influence, particularly in decision-making realms that are the focus of this chapter. Thus, 56 percent of respondents in 2000 said decisions about "program consolidations and closings" were "administrator only/primary ones; that increased to 62 percent in 2012 (p. 273).

2 I was the lone faculty member on the twenty-six-person commission, selected because of relations dating from being the general secretary. After my departure, AGB reached out to the AAUP's new executive director but got no reply. AAUP's national staff and leadership were largely isolated from the DuPont Circle policy world of AGB and management associations (see Rhoades, 2009a), which had been one source of AAUP's policy influence in matters such as shared governance. Shortly after I started at the AAUP, a senior staff member organized a reception, inviting folks from various associations and unions. For almost all, it was their first time in the offices. As general secretary, I worked to intersect the AAUP with other Washington entities, reinserting a faculty voice in the policy world. That included connecting with AGB, whose offices were the same address as AAUP but one block west.

3 The AAUP has connected the renewed vigor of shared governance to a renewed definition of academic freedom that protects speech about institutional matters. In response to a 2006 Supreme Court case, *Garcetti v. Ceballos* (which, though not about higher education, was being applied to university settings), the association's Committee A on Academic Freedom and Tenure issued a report, the executive summary of which stated that these court rulings "pose a serious threat to academic freedom and the ability of faculty in public institutions to participate freely in academic governance" (AAUP, 2009, p. 64). The rulings allowed employers to discipline employees for speech about their employer's practices made in the course of their duties, as with faculty speaking about institutional policies, either in formal shared governance committees or in their individual

236 • Notes to Pages 129–134

speech. The AAUP report (2009) provided examples of suggested wording in institutional policy (and in CBAs) to "clarify" that academic freedom protects not just teaching, research, and extramural speech but also speech about institutional matters, whether or not that is done as a member of an academic governance committee.

4 The findings are particularly compelling given that Kemerer was Assistant to the President at a SUNY campus, and Baldridge was Assistant Vice-President for Academic Affairs at a California State University campus.

5 The AAUP has a process for investigating cases of possible violations of academic freedom and tenure (and sometimes of shared governance). The national office's Committee A appoints an investigating committee, which files a report and makes a recommendation (that is voted on at the association's Annual Meeting) about whether to put the institution in question on the censure list. The SUNY case became a bone of contention between the AAUP and the United University Professions (UUP) of SUNY because AAUP's report was quite critical of the article the union had negotiated for lacking shared governance (AAUP, 1977, p. 258). At least two rationales underlay UUP's stance on Article 35. The first is solidarity—bargaining unit members should not participate in legitimating/enacting program closures and bargaining unit layoffs. The second is a defensive strategy—the aim is to bargain impact and implementation to make retrenchment so procedurally complex that management will be deterred and/or the union will have a strong basis for grieving its actions. Subsequent conversations with UUP about possibly getting SUNY off the censure list were undercut by the Article 35 language. It was not the only factor underlying strained relations between the organizations (see chapter 1, note 6).

6 Graduate assistants, who are unionized, were exempted from the furloughs, as were employees with annual base salaries of $30,000 or less (who were also unionized). Senior administrators were to be furloughed for 10 days (Smile Politely, 2010).

7 In a small number of CBAs, "furlough" refers to a faculty member on layoff status, waiting/hoping to be "recalled." For this chapter, I analyzed provisions that utilize "furlough" in the more conventional sense.

8 Some may also have viewed this as a "political" response to leverage the state legislature to release the monies, but the invocation of a larger, longer-term financial crisis makes it clear that it was part of management's ongoing agenda.

9 Although generally, in the UIC joint campaign, communications were coordinated and approved with the AAUP president and CBC Chair as well as the regional AFT staff member overseeing the campaign (who generally sought approval up the AFT line of command), in this case, that was not done.

10 Beyond the UIC case, it is not unusual for senate executives, leaders, and some faculty senators to align themselves with management and not be an independent faculty voice. Similarly, although the union organizing committees at other AAUP campaigns, such as Bowling Green State University and the University of Oregon, included some members of those institutions' senates, there were also senate members/leaders who were skeptics or opponents of the union campaign (union campaigns often hope that the local faculty senate will remain "neutral," perhaps holding open forums on unionization). So, too, at elite public universities, sometimes groups of "prestigious" faculty form anti-union groups that frame their opposition as defending quality and collegiality (e.g., at the University of Minnesota in the late 1990s and at the University of Washington and the University of Illinois, Urbana-Champaign, in the 2000s).

Notes to Pages 140–147 • 237

11 A few months prior to the furlough announcement and subsequent formation of CAJUA and then UCWAZ, a new chair of the faculty was elected in response to gender and social justice concerns about the previous chair, who was seen by many as more an apologist for administration than an advocate for faculty. The new chair, Jessica Summers, was instrumental in working with CAJUA to leverage faculty senate elections and the formation of senate advisory committees. With the formation of UCWAZ in August 2020, union activists identified a slate of union- and faculty-friendly candidates for the winter of 2022 elections. The top two positions (chair and vice-chair) went to those members of the slate, as did several other positions, which made possible even more aggressive subsequent actions by the senate, including a vote of no confidence. Senate and union leadership can coordinate and work hand-in-hand.

12 See also Quinn (2023, "Lacking Collective Bargaining"). Lacking collective bargaining, UCW locals concentrate on other ways of mobilizing and engaging in political and community action. The Arizona local was distinctive in the prominence of tenure-stream faculty (roughly half of the members) in its origins.

Chapter 7 Negotiating Management's Austerity Practices

1 There has been financial exigency and institutional mortality among small, private colleges/universities. Moreover, community colleges and regional public colleges and universities have been hit by enrollment declines and financial challenges (Orphan, 2018, 2020).

2 RIR's are intended to shape institutional policy and practice. Based on them, AAUP's Committee A negotiates with institutional managers over violations (or the institution's failure to follow its own policies), seeking to persuade them to revise their policies to adhere to the RIR (generally, negotiations do not involve rehiring retrenched faculty). Based on an investigating committee's examination and management's actions, Committee A determines whether to recommend "censure" at AAUP's annual meeting (attendees vote on the recommendation) and put the institution on a public list of "censured" institutions (see Cain, 2020, on related matters).

3 In a break from the past, when law professors and academics from non-collective bargaining, Research 1 universities chaired and dominated the committee, Fichtenbaum's Committee A appointments included a chair (Henry Reichman) who was not a law professor and people (like Reichman) from collective bargaining and non-elite settings.

4 Some such measures (spending reserves, cutting administrative costs) were proposed in Bunsis' 2010 UIC report and in his and my response to the University Senates Executive letter (see chapter 6).

5 As Fichtenbaum and Bunsis hammer home in their presentations, budgets are merely management projections (that is why they start with "B" and end in "S"). They inflate costs and understate revenues to justify actions. Analysis of an institution's financial health requires audited financial statements over several years on actual revenues and expenditures, as well as following-year budgets.

6 Chapters 3 and 4 addressed differences between PTO and COMB units. That makes little sense here. Part-time faculty can be nonrenewed with no explanation (thus, only five of the 131 contracts with language on financial exigency are for PTO units).

238 • Notes to Pages 147–153

7 The pattern was consistent with Tiede's (2020) study of academic freedom and financial exigency policies in four-year, mostly non-unionized institutions.

8 The clause spoke to financial data AAUP's RIR #4 called for: "Section 5.3. The University shall make available to the Union within ten days of the publication of the documents, such information and data (including the annual audited financial report and a copy of the annual budget request approved by the Board of Trustees for submission to the Commonwealth of Pennsylvania) in the sole possession of the University's administration . . . as are necessary for the negotiation and implementation of this Agreement." Both Lincoln universities are HBCUs, largely overlooked in the faculty union literature (an exception is Davenport, 2019).

9 That network can operate through (in)formal structures and across union affiliates. Contracts in Ohio other than those negotiated by an AAUP affiliate had similar language. Thus, Edison State Community College's contract, negotiated by an NEA affiliate, read, "For the purposes of this section, a financial exigency is defined as that condition when revenues are so limited that the College believes it can no longer continue to fulfill current and/or future financial obligations under the contract without disrupting the administration and program integrity of the College." And that language was present in the 1998 contract before RIR #4's revision.

10 Ironically, underlying the Quinnipiac Board's decertification filing was its claim that given the institution's shared governance structures, faculty were managers and, thus, given the 1980 *Yeshiva* Supreme Court decision (affecting private universities), not eligible to bargain collectively. The National Labor Relations Board agreed. Subsequently, in 2014, sixteen faculty were laid off with two days' notice, no consultation, and no declaration of exigency. The institution justified the layoffs by enrollment decline, although twelve new faculty hires were in process in other academic units (Flaherty, 2014, "Jobless in Two Days"). After the faculty senate censured the President, and a letter from the national AAUP, five faculty were reinstated. Such actions would have been contract violations under the CBA (DeCesare, 2014).

11 The provision also specified the form and timing of the data to which bargaining unit leaders will have access: "The AAUP-WSU shall be provided access and the opportunity to inspect and/or copy any information relevant to the anticipated retrenchment within ten calendar days after the delivery of a written request to the Provost."

12 In another example of how contract language gets circulated/adopted among units, WSU leaders were key players in BGSU's union campaign and first contract negotiation.

13 That likely reflected the savvy of Rider's then faculty union president (Jeff Halpern), a national AAUP leader.

14 Typically, grievances center on whether management followed the process defined in the contract, not on the substantive issues at hand.

15 Delaware State had a national AAUP leader (Jane Buck, AAUP President from 2000–2006) in its local leadership for many years; Connecticut State also had a longtime statewide/national leader (Vijay Nair).

16 A caveat is in order. Retrenchment can be justified for other financial reasons: "A bargaining unit faculty member's employment may be terminated upon the determination by the President that a demonstrably legitimate financial need for program elimination or reduction exists." Yet, it delimited that condition: "Legitimate considerations allowing termination do not include cyclical or temporary variations in enrollment, or finances."

17 The vote was 184 to 159 (Geist, 2020).

Notes to Pages 153–177 • 239

18 The force majeure language remained in the contract.
19 For a contrary case of language according management discretion, consider the case of Sonoma State University, where in the 1980s, twenty-four faculty were retrenched. Although the CBA defined "Teaching Service Areas" as the work units for retrenchment, it defined them as being determined by management, including arbitrarily (Slaughter, 1993b, p. 262).
20 See note 2.
21 At the request of UNI faculty groups, the AAUP delayed its censure vote and then, given the new UNI president's actions, closed the case.
22 Three terms were most common in CBAs—retrenchment, layoff, and reduction in force.
23 That is unsurprising. Given the semester-by-semester nature of much part-time faculty employment, management need not justify non-renewal.
24 Within that local, Emerson University and Lesley University's contracts did not have such language despite having multi-semester/year contract provisions. As the Boston metro contracts were negotiated by the same union lawyer, the variation is worth further study.
25 However, the remedy of the arbitrator "shall be limited to ordering additional meet and discuss between the parties."
26 Thus, management could not shift nonacademic personnel to do the work of laid-off bargaining unit members.
27 The codes stemmed from legislative efforts to ensure that community colleges maintain the ranks of tenured/tenure track faculty.
28 The difference is likely partly due to my focusing coding on notice to the faculty member being retrenched, not to the bargaining unit, which more contracts ensured.
29 The reason for retrenchment also mattered. For example, in Rogue Community College's contract, the notice was 180 days for layoff due to technological change and forty-five days for enrollment changes.
30 Sometimes, recall rights for tenured faculty were embedded in state statutes (e.g., in California and Illinois).

Chapter 8   Protections and Possibilities in Negotiating a Progressive Academy amid New Circuits of Production

1 The comment was from a close colleague who was listening to a presentation suggesting that new instructional technologies would dramatically impact instruction.
2 The bargaining unit's leadership team had reached out as they were approaching contract negotiations. They were developing demands to negotiate and to mobilize members. In our call, they had identified a range of concerns about technology-medicated education, centered on defensive matters, and wanted examples of exemplary language.
3 During the pandemic, many women dropped out of the broader workforce to take care of children who were not in school (Bateman & Ross, 2020; Kashen, Glynn, & Novello, 2020; Modestino, 2020). Within the academy, too, COVID impacted faculty in gendered (and raced) ways (Kelliher, 2021), though research on these matters in higher education predates the pandemic (Misra, Kuvaeva, O'Meara, Culpepper, & Jaeger, 2021; Misra, Lundquist, & Templer, 2012).
4 Thanks to Joe McConnell for clearly articulating these points in a virtual webinar (National Center for the Study of Collective Bargaining in Higher Education and

240 • Notes to Pages 179–204

the Professions, 2020). As a management-side lawyer, his framing spoke to the concerns of his firm's clients.

5 Overall, the provisions of four-year tend to be considerably more detailed than those of two-year institutions, although there is much variation within each sector.

6 Rhoades (1998a) did not analyze class size.

7 For a fuller analysis of intellectual property provisions in four-year institutions, see Rhoades (2017b).

8 That local's contract still lacks such a provision. Flathead Valley Community College takes the exploitation to another level. Although the full-time faculty CBA has a generous provision according those faculty full ownership of their intellectual property, for the adjunct faculty bargaining unit, there is a provision that they can take a for-credit class (for which they pay) to develop or convert a face-to-face to a distance education or hybrid course, which the college then owns.

9 A lesser, but still important, example of broadening language to include students was Wright State's contract, which indicated that "any changes to the technology or course (learning) management system will be made by the University with considerations of feedback from both the Faculty Senate and students."

10 Negotiating beyond purely distance education is also important because students are increasingly taking both distance and face-to-face courses versus being in purely distance education courses, where the numbers are declining post-pandemic, though they are still higher than pre-pandemic numbers (Coffey, 2024, "Students Distancing").

11 Generative Artificial Intelligence tools are but one example of new circuitry that could impact various realms of bargaining, from intellectual property to workload and workforce issues, for instructional employees (Coffey, 2024, "Boston University").

Chapter 9   Organizing and Negotiating for Respect and Public Purpose

1 There continued to be some growth in public institutions, on a much bigger baseline, of bargaining units affiliated with the AFT, NEA, and/or AAUP, including in tenure-track units, combined units, and units in two-year institutions. Prior to 2000, most growth in new locals was of tenure-stream faculty, in public community colleges, and in units affiliated with the AAUP, AFT, and NEA.

2 A similar pattern can be found in the broader labor movement, as with Amazon and Starbucks workers, and in the latter 1990s, with custodial workers.

3 That includes largely overlooked professional staff (i.e., "managerial professionals," Rhoades & Sporn, 2001), a growth area of employment.

4 That phrase acknowledged the importance of leaders and groups taking risks, engaging in collective fights. As Fichtenbaum indicated, the willingness of Ohio leaders and members to mobilize against their state's anti-union legislation was fostered by the fight in Wisconsin against such legislation and by my initiative as AAUP General Secretary in calling for and participating in mobilization with Ohio AAUP leaders and members.

5 My aims are partially inspired by Berry and Worthen's lives and work and acknowledgment in their book (2021, p. x), writing that they aimed it to be a "channel of movement knowledge."

6 Unlike Vargas Llosa's wandering storyteller, who is an outsider, I am an ongoing participant in higher education labor communities.

7 Identifying as a professional need not run counter to unionizing. As detailed in chapter 5, unionizing postdocs were very invested in their professional status but also

Notes to Pages 205–212 • 241

identified as precarious, exploited employees. Professional identity can be leveraged, given the chasm between professional expectations and workplace experiences.

8 That quote dates back to the 1960s civil rights movement and has also been attributed to Bernice Johnson Reagon, a Student Nonviolent Coordinating Committee (SNCC) member.

9 Raiding could mean approaching, cultivating relationships with, offering services to, or proposing an arrangement in which the local would pay a share of its dues to the AFT. Notwithstanding the joint agreement, such activities continued in Michigan.

10 Notably, faculty had been disinvited the night before for fear that they, too, would support staff.

11 As Zweig (2012) says, "Working class politics cannot become a substitute for identity politics based on race, gender, or sexual orientation. [It] . . . needs to complement and incorporate these other movements" (p. 133).

12 This is similar to what I have called "public interest bargaining" (Rhoades, 2015b) in higher education.

13 "When life itself seems lunatic, who knows where madness lies? Perhaps to be too practical is madness. To surrender dreams—this may be madness. To seek treasure where there is only trash. Too much sanity may be madness—and maddest of all: to see life as it is, and not as it should be!"

References

Abbott, Andrew. (1988). *The system of professions: An essay on the division of expert labor.* Chicago: University of Chicago Press.

Abbott, Andrew. (1993). The sociology of work and occupations. *Annual Review of Sociology, 19,* 187–209.

Aguiar, Luis LM, & McCartin, Joseph A. (2023). *The history and global impact of SEIU.* Urbana and Champaign: University of Illinois Press. Washington, DC: Service Employees International.

Ahmad, Zach. (2004, May 10). Profs to hold union vote. *The GW Hatchet,* May 10, 2014.

Aleva, David. (2013). Supporting Duquesne University adjuncts. *Pittsburgh Post-Gazette,* Letter to the editor, October 7, 2013. Retrieved from https://www.post-gazette.com/opinion/letters/2013/10/08/Supporting-Duquesne-University-adjuncts/stories/201310080062

Alker, Gwendolyn. (2024). Women's work: A feminist rethinking of contingent labor in the academy. In Eric Fure-Slocum & Claire Goldstene (Eds.), *Contingent faculty and the remaking of higher education: A labor history* (pp. 69–82). Urbana: University of Illinois Press.

American Association of University Professors. (1977). Academic freedom and tenure: The State University of New York. *AAUP Bulletin, 63*(3), 237–260.

American Association of University Professors. (2001). *Policy documents and reports* (9th ed.). Baltimore: Johns Hopkins University Press.

American Association of University Professors. (2006). *Policy documents and reports* (10th ed.). Baltimore: Johns Hopkins University Press.

American Association of University Professors. (2009). Executive Summary: Protecting an independent faculty voice; Academic freedom after Garcetti v. Ceballos. *Academe, 95*(6), 64–66.

American Association of University Professors. (2012). *Academic freedom and tenure: University of Northern Iowa.* Washington, DC: American Association of University Professors. Retrieved from https://www.aaup.org/file/AcademicFreedomAndTenureUNI_0.pdf

244 • References

American Association of University Professors. (2013). *The role of the faculty in conditions of financial exigency.* Report of Committee A of the AAUP, adopted by the Council at the June 2013 meeting. Washington, DC: American Association of University Professors.

American Association of University Professors. (2015). *Policy documents and reports* (11th ed.). Baltimore: Johns Hopkins University Press.

American Association of University Professors. (2020). Statement on COVID-19 and the faculty role in decision making. Retrieved from https://www.aaup.org/news/statement-covid-19-and-faculty-role-decision-making?link_id=4&can_id=57e6b6a766fbd44db31627af81263a9b&source=email-covid-19-and-aaup-principles-2&email_referrer=email_759620&email_subject=covid-19-and-aaup-principles#.XrWbTi3Myu4

American Association of University Professors. (2021). Resolution honoring Phil Kugler of the American Federation of Teachers on his retirement. Retrieved from https://www.aaup.org/resolution-honoring-phil-kugler-american-federation-teachers-his-retirement

American Federation of Teachers. (2015, November 25). Press release: Temple University adjuncts vote to join TAUP, AFT. Retrieved from https://www.aft.org/press-release/temple-university-adjuncts-vote-join-taup-aft

Angell, Diane. (2024). The good, the bad, and the ugly: Being contingent and female in STEM fields. In Eric Fure-Slocum & Claire Goldstene (Eds.), *Contingent faculty and the remaking of higher education: A labor history* (pp. 125–137). Urbana: University of Illinois Press.

Arnold, Gordon B. (2000). *The politics of faculty unionization: The experience of three New England universities.* Westport, CT: Bergin & Garvey.

Ashraf, Javed. (1992). Do unions affect faculty salaries? *Economics of Education Review, 11*, 219–223.

Ashraf, Javed. (1999). Faculty unionism in the 1990s: A comparison of public and private universities. *Journal of Collective Negotiations in the Public Sector, 28*, 303–310.

Association for the Study of Higher Education. (2020). Public comment on the NLRB's proposed rule change regarding graduate assistants' statutory rights to collective bargaining under the National Labor Relations Act. Las Vegas: Association for the Study of Higher Education.

Association of American Universities. (1998). Committee on postdoctoral education. Washington, DC: AAU.

Association of Governing Boards of Universities and Colleges. (1998). *AGB Statement on institutional governance.* Washington, DC: Association of Governing Boards of Universities and Colleges.

Association of Governing Boards of Universities and Colleges. (2010). *Statement on board responsibility for institutional governance.* Washington, DC: Association of Governing Boards of Universities and Colleges.

Association of Governing Boards of Universities and Colleges. (2014). *Consequential governance: Adding value where it matters the most.* Washington, DC: Association of Governing Boards of Universities and Colleges.

Association of Governing Boards of Universities and Colleges. (2017a). *AGB Board of Directors Statement on Shared Governance.* Washington, DC: Association of Governing Boards of Universities and Colleges.

Association of Governing Boards of Universities and Colleges. (2017b, March). *Shared governance: Changing with the times.* White Paper. Washington, DC: Association of Governing Boards of Universities and Colleges.

Austin, Ann E., & Trice, Andrea G. (2016). Core principles for faculty models and the importance of community. In A. Kezar & D. Maxey (Eds.), *Envisioning the faculty for the twenty-first century: Moving to a more mission-oriented and learner-centered model* (pp. 58–80). New Brunswick, NJ: Rutgers University Press.

Baldridge, J. Victor, & Kemerer, Frank R. (1976). Academic senates and faculty collective bargaining. *The Journal of Higher Education, 47*, 391–411.

Baldwin, Roger G., & Chronister, Jay L. (2001). *Teaching without tenure: Policies and practices for the new era.* Baltimore: Johns Hopkins University Press.

Barker, Kathleen. (1998). Toiling for piece rates and accumulating deficits: Contingent work in higher education. In Kathleen Barker & Kathleen Christensen (Eds.), *Contingent work: American employment relations in transition* (pp. 195–220). Ithaca, NY: ILR Press.

Barringer, Sondra N., Taylor, Barrett J., & Slaughter, Sheila. (2019). Trustees in turbulent times: External affiliations and stratification among U.S. research universities, 1975–2015. *The Journal of Higher Education, 90*(6), 884–914.

Bateman, Nicole, & Ross, Martha. (2020, October). *Why has COVID-19 been especially harmful for working women?* Washington, DC: The Brookings Institution. Retrieved from https://www.brookings.edu/essay/why-has-covid-19-been-especially-harmful-for-working-women/

Bauer, Louise Birdsell. (2017). Professors-in-training or precarious workers? Identity, coalition building, and social movement unionism in the 2015 University of Toronto graduate employee strike. *Labor Studies Journal, 42*(4), 273–294.

Bauman, Dan. (2020, October 6). The pandemic has pushed hundreds of thousands of workers out of higher education. *The Chronicle of Higher Education.* Retrieved from https://www.chronicle.com/article/how-the-pandemic-has-shrunk-higher-educations-work-force

Benderly, Beryl Lieff. (2014, October 20). A union contract gives Tufts adjuncts "unheard of" rights. *Science Careers.* Retrieved from http://sciencecareers.sciencemag.org/career_magazine/previous_issues/articles/2014_10_30/caredit.a1400271

Benjamin, Ernst. (2015). How did we get here? The AAUP's evolving emphasis on collective bargaining. *Academe,* January/February, *101*(1). Retrieved from https://www.aaup.org/article/how-did-we-get-here#.Wk4pdiPMyqA

Berry, Joe. (2005). *Reclaiming the ivory tower: Organizing adjuncts to change higher education.* New York: Monthly Review Press.

Berry, Joe, & Saverese, Michelle. (2012). *Directory of U.S. faculty contracts and bargaining agents in institutions of higher education.* New York: National Center for the Study of Collective Bargaining in Higher Education and the Professions.

Berry, Joe, & Worthen, Helena. (2018). The metro strategy: A workforce appropriate, geography-based approach to organizing contingent faculty. In Ishmael I. Munene (Ed.), *Contextualizing and organizing contingent faculty* (pp. 35–60). Lanham, MD: Lexington Books.

Berry, Joe, & Worthen, Helena. (2021). *Power despite precarity: Strategies for the contingent faculty movement in higher education.* London: Pluto Press.

Bettinger, Eric P., & Long, Bridget T. (2010, August). Does cheaper mean better? The impact of using adjunct instructors on student outcomes. *Review of Economics and Statistics, 92*, 598–613.

Bhargava, Nandita. (2010). Seeds of change: How the 9 to 5 women's labor movement rooted a labor revolution (Unpublished senior thesis). Kalamazoo College, Kalamazoo, MI.

Birnbaum, Robert, & Inman, Deborah. (1984). The relationship of academic bargaining to changes in campus climate. *The Journal of Higher Education, 55*(5), 609–620.

246 • References

Bittle, Jake. (2017, October 5). This university suggested international students could be reported to ICE if they unionized: And it's not the first to do so. *The Nation.* Retrieved from https://www.thenation.com/article/archive/this-university -suggested-international-students-could-be-reported-to-ice-if-they-unionized/

Bowen, Howard R., & Schuster, Jack H. (1986). *American professors: A national resource imperiled.* New York: Oxford University Press.

Boyle, Colin. (2023, January 17). UIC professors go on strike, demanding higher pay and more job security. *BlockClubChicago.* Retrieved from https://blockclubchicago.org/2023 /01/17/uic-professors-go-on-strike-demanding-higher-pay-and-more-job-security/

Brady, David, Baker, Regina S., & Finnigan, Ryan. (2013). When unionization disappears: State-level unionization and working poverty in the United States. *American Sociological Review, 78*(5), 872–896.

Braverman, Harry. (1974). *Labor and monopoly capital: The degradation of work in the twentieth century.* New York: Monthly Review Press.

Brint, Steven. (1994). *In an age of experts: The changing role of professionals in politics and public life.* Princeton, NJ: Princeton University Press.

Brint, Steven G. (2018). *Two cheers for higher education: Why American universities are stronger than ever and how to meet the challenges they face.* Princeton, NJ: Princeton University Press.

Bronfenbrenner, Kate, Friedman, Sheldon, Hurd, Richard W., Oswald, Rudolph A., & Seeber, Ronald L. (Eds.). (1998). *Organizing to win: New research on union strategies.* Ithaca, NY: Cornell University Press.

Brown, Jordyn. (2020, April 4). UO president, administrators to take pay cuts in light of COVID-19. *The Register-Guard.* Retrieved from https://www.registerguard.com /news/20200404/uo-president-administrators-to-take-pay-cuts-in-light-of-covid-19

Buettner, Jack. (2020). Arbitration decision and award, grievance #2020–01. Retrieved from https://www.uakron.edu/president/docs/arbitrator-decision-sept2020.pdf.

Bunsis, Howard. (2010, January). Analysis of the financial condition of the University of Illinois system. Washington, DC: American Association of University Professors. Retrieved from https://www.aaup.org/NR/rdonlyres/8FF9B3F8-65F5-41C0-8BA2 -837BEA849E33/0/BunsisanalysisUIC.pdf

Bunsis, Howard, & Rhoades, Gary. (2010, February 15). Response from Howard Bunsis and Gary Rhoades to University Senates Conference memo of 2/10/2010. Retrieved from https://www.aaup.org/NR/rdonlyres/25AE9DF4-3AEF-412B-A69E -1AAC3A88541E/0/UICbunsisresponselinked_2_.pdf

Burbules, Nicholas C., & Torres, Carlos A. (2000). *Globalization and education: Critical perspectives.* New York: Routledge.

Bureau of Labor Statistics. (2018a). Labor force statistics (CPS), Table 3, Unionization of wage and salary workers by occupation and industry. Washington, DC: Bureau of Labor Statistics. Retrieved from https://data.bls.gov/pdq/SurveyOutputServlet

Bureau of Labor Statistics. (2018b). Union members summary. Washington, DC: Bureau of Labor Statistics. Retrieved from https://www.bls.gov/news.release/union2.nr0.htm

Burke, Lilah. (2020, November 2). Pa. state system to lay off more than 100 faculty. *InsideHigherEd.* Retrieved from (https://www.insidehighered.com/quicktakes/2020 /11/02/pa-state-system-lay-more-100-faculty-members

Burton, Miles. (2020, January 15). Over 12,000 comments submitted on NLRB rule as deadline looms. *The Chicago Maroon.* Retrieved from https://www.chicagomaroon .com/article/2020/1/15/12000-comments-submitted-nlrb-rule-deadline-looms/

Cahn, William. (1977). *Lawrence 1912: The bread and roses strike.* New York: The Pilgrim Press.

Cain, Timothy Reese. (2010a). The first attempts to unionize the faculty. *Teachers College Record, 112*, 875–913.

Cain, Timothy Reese. (2010b). "Learning and labor": Faculty unionization at the University of Illinois, 1919–1923. *Labor History, 51*, 543–569.

Cain, Timothy Reese. (2017). Campus unions: Organized faculty and graduate students in U.S. higher education. *ASHE Higher Education Report, 43*(3), 7–163. https://doi .org/10.1002/aehe.20119

Cain, Timothy Reese. (2018). A long history of activism and organizing: Contingent faculty, graduate students, and unionization. In Kim Tolley (Ed.), *Professors in the gig economy: Unionizing adjunct faculty in America* (pp. 46–68). Baltimore: Johns Hopkins University Press.

Cain, Timothy Reese. (2020). Collective bargaining and committee a: Five decades of unionism and academic freedom. *The Review of Higher Education, 44*(1), 57–86.

California Faculty Association. (2019). *Lecturer's handbook, 2019–2020*. Sacramento, CA: California Faculty Association. Retrieved from https://www.calfac.org/sites /main/files/file-attachments/lect_handbook_0719_web.pdf

California Federation of Teachers. (2021). UC lecturers greet new contracts as a "game changer" and "only the beginning." California Federation of Teachers. Retrieved from https://www.cft.org/article/uc-lecturers-greet-new-contract-game-changer-and -only-beginning

Camacho, Sayil, & Rhoads, Robert A. (2015). Breaking the silence: The unionization of postdoctoral workers at the University of California. *The Journal of Higher Education, 86*(2), 295–325.

Campbell, Sydney, & Jacobson, Elsie. (2023). Unionize the postdocs. *Jacobin*. Retrieved from https://jacobin.com/2023/07/postdoc-unionization-uaw-university-of -california-organizing

Cantwell, Brendan. (2011). Academic in-sourcing: International postdoctoral employment and new modes of academic production. *Journal of Higher Education Policy and Management, 33*(2), 101–114.

Cantwell, Brendan, & Lee, Jenny. (2010). Unseen workers in the academic factory: Perceptions of neo-racism among international postdocs in the United States and the United Kingdom. *Harvard Educational Review, 80*(4), 490–517.

Cantwell, Brendan, & Taylor, Barrett J. (2015). Rise of the science and engineering postdoctorate and the restructuring of academic research. *The Journal of Higher Education, 86*(5), 667–696.

Castiello-Gutierrez, Santiago, & Li, Xiaojie. (2020). We are more than your paycheck: The dehumanization of international students in the United States. *Journal of International Students, 10*(3), i–iv.

Center for Community College Student Engagement. (2009). *Making connections: Dimensions of student engagement*. Austin: The Center for Community College Student Engagement. Retrieved from http://www.ccsse.org/publications/national _report_2009/CCSSE09_nationalreport.pdf

Chaduvula, Raju. (2016, October 13). A brief history of the faculty union push at the University of Minnesota. *Minnesota Daily*. Retrieved from www.mndaily.com /article/2016/10/faculty-unions-have-history-on-campus

Chernow, Lizz. (2013, February 13). Union talks divide TA's, adjuncts. *The GW Hatchet*. Retrieved from http://www.gwhatchet.com/2003/02/13/union-talks-divide-tas -adjuncts/

Childress, Herb. (2019). *The adjunct underclass: How America's colleges betrayed their faculty, their students, and their mission*. Chicago: University of Chicago Press.

References

Chingos, Matthew M. (2016). Instructional quality and student learning in higher education: Evidence from developmental algebra courses. *The Journal of Higher Education, 87*(1), 84–114.

Chronicle Staff. (2020, May 13). As covid-19 pummels budgets, colleges are resorting to layoffs and furloughs. Here is the latest. *The Chronicle of Higher Education*. Retrieved from https://www.chronicle.com/article/were-tracking-employees-laid-off-or -furloughed-by-colleges/?cid2=gen_login_refresh&cid=gen_sign_in

Clark, Burton R. (1998). *Creating entrepreneurial universities: Organizational pathways of transformation*. Bingley, UK: Emerald Group Publishing Limited.

Clark, Burton R. (2000). Collegial entrepreneurialism in proactive universities: Lessons from Europe. *Change: The Magazine of Higher Learning, 32*(1), 10–19.

Clark, Gordon L. (1989). *Unions and communities under siege*. Cambridge: Cambridge University Press.

Coalition on the Academic Workforce. (2012). *A portrait of part-time faculty members*. Washington, DC: Coalition on the Academic Workforce.

Coatsworth, John. (2019, April 29). Whether grad students are employees should be decided by law, not politics. *Columbia Daily Spectator*. Retrieved from https://www .columbiaspectator.com/opinion/2018/04/30/whether-grad-students-are-employees -should-be-decided-by-law-not-politics/

Coffey, Lauren. (2024, January 30). Students distancing from distance learning. *Inside-HigherEd*. Retrieved from https://www.insidehighered.com/news/tech-innovation /teaching-learning/2024/01/30/online-college-enrollment-continues-post-pandemic ?utm_source=Inside+Higher+Ed&utm_campaign=a06915327b-DNU_2021_COPY _02&utm_medium=email&utm_term=0_1fcbc04421-a06915327b-197419965&mc _cid=a06915327b&mc_eid=3cf866d28d#

Coffey, Lauren. (2024, April 1). Boston University denies it would use AI to replace striking teaching assistants. *InsideHigherEd*. Retrieved from https://www .insidehighered.com/news/quick-takes/2024/04/01/boston-university-denies-it -would-replace-striking-tas-ai#:~:text=Boston%20University%20Denies%20 It%20Would%20Use%20AI%20to%20Replace%20Striking%20Teaching%20 Assistants

Cole, Andy. (2020, May 11). State of Georgia requires all agencies including the university system, to reduce budgets by 14%. *The George-Anne*. Retrieved from http://www.thegeorgeanne.com/news/article_39dd7216-939f-11ea-bbef -af6582f97e45.html

Cosco, Frank. (2014). The Vancouver model of equality for college faculty employment. In Keith Hoeller, (Ed.), *Equality for contingent faculty: Overcoming the two-tier system* (pp. 200–226). Nashville: Vanderbilt University Press.

Crow, Michael M., & Dabars, William B. (2015). *Designing the new American university*. Baltimore: Johns Hopkins University Press.

Dache-Gerbino, Amalia, Kiyama, Judy Marquez, & Sapp, Vicki T. (2018). The dangling carrot: Proprietary institutions and the mirage of college choice for Latina students. *The Review of Higher Education, 42*(1), 29–60.

D'Ammassa, Algernon. (2024, March 8). NMSU faculty petitions for union recognition. *The Las Cruces Bulletin*. Retrieved from https://www.lascrucesbulletin.com /stories/nmsu-faculty-union-nea-new-mexico,74414

Davenport, Elizabeth K. (2018). Unions, shared governance, and Historically Black Colleges and Universities. In Kim Tolley (Ed.), *Professors in the gig economy: Unionizing adjunct faculty in America* (pp. 123–138). Baltimore: Johns Hopkins University Press.

Davis, Charles H.F. III. (2019). Student activism, resource mobilization, and new tactical repertoires in the "Digital Age." In Demetri L. Morgan & Charles H.F. Davis III (Eds.), *Student activism, politics, and campus climate in higher education* (pp. 122–124). New York: Routledge.

Davis, Lennard, & Benn Michaels, Walter. (2014, February). Faculty on strike. *Jacobin*. Retrieved from https://www.jacobinmag.com/2014/02/faculty-on-strike.

DeCesare, Michael. (2014, June 8). Faculty cuts at Quinnipiac. *Academe Blog*. Retrieved from https://academeblog.org/2014/06/08/faculty-cuts-at-quinnipiac/

DeCew, Judith Wagner. (2003). *Unionization in the academy: Visions and realities*. Lanham, MD: Rowman and Littlefield.

Democracy Now! (2019, February 12). Wright State faculty ends one of the longest strikes at a public university in U.S. history. [Video; interview with Rudy Fichtenbaum]. Retrieved from https://www.democracynow.org/2019/2/12/wright_state _faculty_ends_one_of

Dénommé-Welch, Spy, & Savage, Larry. (2021, January 7). Indigenization through collective bargaining: Lessons and ideas for academic staff associations. *Academic matters: Journal of Higher Education*. Retrieved from https://academicmatters.ca /indigenization-through-collective-bargaining-lessons-and-ideas-for-academic-staff -associations/

DePillis, Lydia. (2015, February 6). Adjunct professors get poverty level wages. Should their pay quintuple? *The Washington Post*. Retrieved from https://www .washingtonpost.com/news/wonk/wp/2015/02/06/adjunct-professors-get-poverty -level-wages-should-their-pay-quintuple/

Dickens, Charles. (1998). *Little Dorrit*. Edited with an introduction and notes by Stephen Wall & Helen Small. London: Penguin Classics. (Original work published 1857)

Dougherty, Kevin J., & Natow, Rebecca S. (2015). *The politics of performance funding for higher education: Origins, discontinuations, and transformations*. Baltimore: Johns Hopkins University Press.

Dougherty, Kristine, Rhoades, Gary, & Smith, Mark F. (2018). Big brother or big Breitbart: Negotiating evaluation in the surveillance age. *The NEA 2018 Almanac of Higher Education*. Washington, DC: National Education Association.

Douglas, Joel. (1990). The impact of *NLRB v Yeshiva University* on faculty unionism at public colleges and universities. *Journal of Collective Negotiations in the Public Sector, 1*, 1–28.

Douglas-Gabriel, Danielle. (2019, February 15). "It keeps you nice and disposable": The plight of adjunct professors. *The Washington Post*. Retrieved from https://beta .washingtonpost.com/local/education/it-keeps-you-nice-and-disposable-the-plight -of-adjunct-professors/2019/02/14/6cd5cbe4-024d-11e9-b5df-5d3874f1ac36_story .html

Douglas-Gabriel, Danielle, & Fowers, Alyssa. (2020, November 17). The lowest-paid workers in higher education are suffering the highest job losses. *The Washington Post*. Retrieved from https://www.washingtonpost.com/education/2020/11/17/higher-ed -job-loss/

Drake, Anna, Struve, Laura, Meghani, Sana Ali, & Bukosk, Beth. (2019). Invisible labor, visible change: Non-tenure-track faculty agency in a research university. *The Review of Higher Education, 42*(4), 1635–1664.

Duderstadt, James. (2007). *The view from the helm: Leading the American university during an era of change*. Ann Arbor: University of Michigan Press.

Duncan-Andrade, Jeffrey M.R. (2009). Note to educators: Hope required when growing roses in concrete. *Harvard Educational Review, 79*(2), 181–194.

250 • References

Eagan, M. Kevin, & Jaeger, Audrey J. (2008). Closing the gate: Part-time faculty instruction in gatekeeper courses and first-year persistence. *New Directions in Teaching and Learning, 115*(Fall), 39–53.

Eagan, M. Kevin, & Jaeger, Audrey J. (2009). Part-time faculty at community colleges: implications for student persistence and transfer. *Research in Higher Education 50*(2), 168–188.

Eggert, David. (2023, November 30). Whitmer signs trio of union-friendly measures. *Crain's Detroit Business*. Retrieved from https://www.crainsdetroit.com/politics -policy/graduate-research-assistants-can-unionize-under-new-michigan-law

Ehrenberg, Ronald G., Klaff, Daniel B., Kezsbom, Adam T., & Nagowski, Matthew P. (2004). Collective bargaining in American higher education. In Ronald G. Ehrenberg (Ed.) *Governing academia: Who is in charge at the modern university?* (pp. 209–233). Ithaca, NY: Cornell University Press.

Ehrenberg, R. G., & Zhang, L. (2005). Do tenured and tenure-track faculty matter? *Journal of Human Resources, 40*(4), 647–659.

Fabricant, Michael, & Brier, Stephen. (2016). *Austerity blues: Fighting for the soul of public higher education*. Baltimore: Johns Hopkins University Press.

Ferguson, Kryste, McTighe, Michael, Amlani, Bhishma, & Costello, Tracy. (2017). *Supporting the needs of postdocs: 2017 National Postdoctoral Association institutional policy report*. Rockville, MD: National Postdoctoral Association.

Fink, Leon, & Greenberg, Brian. (1989). *Upheaval in the quiet zone: A history of hospital workers' union local 1199*. Urbana: University of Illinois Press.

Finkelstein, Martin J. (1984). *The American academic profession: A synthesis of social scientific inquiry since World War II*. Columbus: Ohio State University Press.

Finkelstein, Martin J., Conley, Valerie Martin, & Schuster, Jack H. (2016). *The faculty factor: Reassessing the American academy in a turbulent era*. Baltimore: Johns Hopkins University Press.

Finkelstein, Martin J., Seal, Robert K., & Schuster, Jack H. (1998). *The new academic generation: A profession in transformation*. Baltimore: Johns Hopkins University Press.

Flaherty, Colleen. (2014, January 24). Congress takes note. *InsideHigherEd*. Retrieved from https://www.insidehighered.com/news/2014/01/24/house-committee-report -highlights-plight-adjunct-professors

Flaherty, Colleen. (2014, May 14). Jobless in two days. *InsideHigherEd*. Retrieved from http://www.insidehighered.com/news/2014/05/14/quinnipiac-faculty-reeling-rapid -cuts#sthash.lo2aH5Kz.dpbs

Flaherty, Colleen. (2015, April 23). Anti-faculty union language struck from Ohio bill. *InsideHigherEd*. Retrieved from https://www.insidehighered.com/quicktakes/2015 /04/23/anti-faculty-union-language-struck-ohio-bill

Flaherty, Colleen. (2016, January 14). Big gains for adjuncts. *InsideHigherEd*. Retrieved from https://www.insidehighered.com/news/2016/01/15/does-new-crop-first-adjunct -union-contracts-include-meaningful-gains

Flaherty, Colleen. (2016, January 14). Does the new crop of first adjunct union contracts include meaningful gains? *InsideHigherEd*.

Flaherty, Colleen. (2016, June 1). Notre Dame de Namur recognized tenured faculty union. *InsideHigherEd*. Retrieved from https://www.insidehighered.com/quicktakes /2016/06/01/notre-dame-de-namur-recognizes-tenured-faculty-union

Flaherty, Colleen. (2016, August 24). NLRB: Graduate students at private universities may unionize. *InsideHigherEd*. Retrieved from https://www.insidehighered.com /news/2016/08/24/nlrb-says-graduate-students-private-universities-may-unionize

References • 251

Flaherty, Colleen. (2016, August 30). Crop of 'anti-union' websites sparks criticism from proponents of graduate assistant unions. *InsideHigherEd*. Retrieved from https://www.insidehighered.com/news/2016/08/30/crop-anti-union-university-websites-sparks-criticism-proponents-graduate-assistant

Flaherty, Colleen. (2017, January 10). Adjuncts included in unemployment guidance. *InsideHigherEd*. Retrieved from https://www.insidehighered.com/quicktakes/2017/01/10/adjuncts-included-unemployment-guidance

Flaherty, Colleen. (2017, January 23). Lincoln U changes definition of financial exigency. *InsiderHigherEd*. Retrieved from https://www.insidehighered.com/quicktakes/2017/01/23/lincoln-u-changes-definition-financial-exigency

Flaherty, Colleen. (2017, July 10). Some 1,500 adjuncts at CUNY win three-year contracts. *InsideHigherEd*. Retrieved from https://www.insidehighered.com/news/2017/07/10/some-1500-adjuncts-cuny-win-three-year-contracts

Flaherty, Colleen. (2017, July 13). Union contract includes gains for Duke adjuncts. *InsideHigherEd*. Retrieved from https://www.insidehighered.com/quicktakes/2017/07/13/union-contract-includes-gains-duke-adjuncts

Flaherty, Colleen. (2017, October 12). Tufts adjuncts reach second contract agreement. *InsideHigherEd*. Retrieved from https://www.insidehighered.com/quicktakes/2017/10/12/tufts-adjuncts-reach-second-contract-agreement

Flaherty, Colleen. (2017, November 21). Under new law, Iowa unions vote to recertify. *InsiderHigherEd*. Retrieved from https://www.insidehighered.com/quicktakes/2017/11/21/under-new-law-iowa-unions-vote-recertify

Flaherty, Colleen. (2018, January 5). Best practices for supporting postdocs. *InsideHigherEd*. Retrieved from https://www.insidehighered.com/quicktakes/2018/01/05/best-practices-supporting-postdocs

Flaherty, Colleen. (2018, February 15). Realities of Trump-era NLRB. *InsideHigherEd*. Retrieved from https://www.insidehighered.com/news/2018/02/15/blow-graduate-student-union-movement-private-campuses-three-would-be-unions-withdraw

Flaherty, Colleen. (2018, April 17). U Chicago adjuncts approve first union contract. *InsideHigherEd*. Retrieved from https://www.insidehighered.com/quicktakes/2018/04/17/u-chicago-adjuncts-approve-first-union-contract

Flaherty, Colleen. (2018, June 22). Brown agrees to grad union election terms. *InsideHigherEd*. Retrieved from https://www.insidehighered.com/quicktakes/2018/06/22/brown-agrees-grad-union-election-terms

Flaherty, Colleen. (2018, June 27). Supreme Court rules against public-sector. *InsideHigherEd*. Retrieved from https://www.insidehighered.com/news/2018/06/28/supreme-court-rules-against-public-sector-unions-long-awaited-janus-decision

Flaherty, Colleen. (2018, September 5). A TA union contract, two years later. *InsideHigherEd*. Retrieved from https://www.insidehighered.com/news/2018/09/05/brandeis-grad-students-win-significant-gains-union-contract-even-trump

Flaherty, Colleen. (2018, November 28). U California researchers form union. *InsideHigherEd*. https://www.insidehighered.com/quicktakes/2021/05/25/u-california-graduate-researchers-form-union

Flaherty, Colleen. (2019, February 12). "Standing up for what's right." *InsideHigherEd*. Retrieved from https://www.insidehighered.com/news/2019/02/13/what-lessons-can-be-learned-wright-state-faculty-strike

Flaherty, Colleen. (2019, September 23). Ruling out grad unions. *InsideHigherEd*. Retrieved from https://www.insidehighered.com/news/2019/09/23/trump-labor-board-proposes-new-rule-against-grad-unions

252 • References

Flaherty, Colleen. (2019, October 21). University of New Mexico faculty vote to unionize. *InsideHigherEd*. Retrieved from https://www.insidehighered.com/quicktakes/2019/10/21/university-new-mexico-faculty-vote-unionize

Flaherty, Colleen. (2020, January 17). Clemson English lecturers make $20K less than peers. *InsideHigherEd*. Retrieved from https://www.insidehighered.com/quicktakes/2020/01/17/clemson-english-lecturers-make-20k-less-peers

Flaherty, Colleen. (2020, January 27). The aging faculty. *InsideHigherEd*. Retrieved from https://www.insidehighered.com/quicktakes/2020/01/27/aging-faculty

Flaherty, Colleen. (2020, April 19). Barely getting by: New report on adjuncts says many make less than $3,500 per course and live in poverty. *InsideHigherEd*. Retrieved from https://www.insidehighered.com/news/2020/04/20/new-report-says-many-adjuncts-make-less-3500-course-and-25000-year

Flaherty, Colleen. (2020, May 13). Not the same university. *InsideHigherEd*. Retrieved from https://www.insidehighered.com/news/2020/05/14/missouri-western-cuts-quarter-faculty-along-programs-history-and-more

Flaherty, Colleen. (2020, July 15). Budget 'bloodbath' at University of Akron. *InsideHigherEd*. Retrieved from https://www.insidehighered.com/news/2020/07/16/budget-bloodbath-university-akron

Flaherty, Colleen. (2021, March 15). Green light for student employee unions. *InsideHigherEd*, Retrieved from https://www.insidehighered.com/news/2021/03/15/labor-board-withdraws-planned-rule-against-student-employee-unions?utm_source=Inside+Higher+Ed&utm_campaign=dcd28210d6-DNU_2021_COPY_02&utm_medium=email&utm_term=0_1fcbc04421-dcd28210d6-197419965&mc_cid=dcd28210d6&mc_eid=3cf866d28d

Flaherty, Colleen. (2021, October 20). A union victory at Pitt. *InsideHigherEd*, Retrieved from https://www.insidehighered.com/news/2021/10/21/u-pittsburgh-faculty-votes-form-union

Flaherty, Colleen. (2022, August 10). Seeking protections against bullying. *InsideHigherEd*, Retrieved from https://www.insidehighered.com/news/2022/08/10/postdocs-within-u-california-system-allege-bullying

Fredrickson, Caroline. (2015, September 15). There is no excuse for how universities treat adjuncts. *The Atlantic*. Retrieved from https://www.theatlantic.com/business/archive/2015/09/higher-education-college-adjunct-professor-salary/404461/

Freidson, Eliot. (1984). The changing nature of professional control. *Annual Review of Sociology, 10*, 1–20.

Fuschino, Nicole. (2019, April 25). Life is getting better for part-time faculty after getting contract. *Point Park News Service*. Retrieved from http://www.pointparknewsservice.com/2019/04/25/life-is-getting-better-for-part-time-faculty-after-contract/

Gantert, Tom. (2014, June 20). State agency rules that graduate research assistants are not eligible for unionization. *CapCon*. Retrieved from https://www.michigancapitolconfidential.com/GSRAs-not-public-employees-cant-be-unionized

Gappa, Judith M. (1984). *Part-time faculty: Higher education at a crossroads* (ASHE/ERIC Higher Education Research Report No. 3). Washington, DC: Association for the Study of Higher Education.

Gappa, Judith M., & Leslie, David W. (1993). *The invisible faculty: Improving the status of part-timers in higher education*. San Francisco: Jossey-Bass.

Garbarino, Joseph W. (1975). *Faculty bargaining: Change and conflict*. Berkeley, CA: Carnegie Commission on Higher Education.

Garbarino, Joseph William, Feller, David E., & Finkin, Matthew W. (1977). *Faculty bargaining in public higher education*. San Francisco: Jossey-Bass.

Gaston, Paul L. (2014). *Higher education accreditation: How it's changing, why it must.* Sterling, VA: Stylus.

Geiger, Roger L. (2004). *Knowledge and money: Research universities and the paradox of the marketplace.* Palo Alto, CA: Stanford University Press.

Geist, Robin. (2020, August 5). University of Akron faculty union rejects proposed contract that includes layoffs. *Cleveland.com.* Retrieved from https://www.cleveland.com/education/2020/08/university-of-akron-faculty-union-rejects-proposed-contract-that-included-layoffs.html

Geist, Robin. (2021). University of Akron approves new six-year contract with faculty union. March 1, 2021. *Cleveland.com.* Retrieved from https://www.cleveland.com/education/2021/03/university-of-akron-approves-new-six-year-contract-with-faculty-union.html

Gerber, Larry G. (2014). *The rise and decline of faculty governance: Professionalization and the modern American university.* Baltimore: Johns Hopkins University Press.

Geron, Kim, & Reevy, Gretchen M. (2018). California State University, East Bay: Alignment of contingent and tenure-track faculty interests and goals. In Kim Tolley (Ed.). *Professors in the gig economy: Unionizing adjunct faculty in America* (pp. 172–186). Baltimore: Johns Hopkins University Press.

Getman, Julius G. (2010). *Restoring the power of unions: It takes a movement.* New Haven, CT: Yale University Press.

Gibson, Rebecca. (2015, April). *Tufts University: Lessons from bargaining a first contract for part-time, contingent faculty.* Panel at the annual conference of the National Center for the Study of Collective Bargaining in Higher Education and the Professions, New York.

Gillespie, Katie. (2020, January 14). Clark College, faculty union reach tentative contract deal. *The Columbian.* Retrieved from https://nam11.safelinks.protection.outlook.com/GetUrlReputation

Gilmore, Shawn. (2018). Forming a union: The non-tenure faculty coalition, local 6546 at the University of Illinois, Urbana-Champaign. In Kim Tolley (Ed.), *Professors in the gig economy: Unionizing adjunct faculty in America* (pp. 139–152). Baltimore: Johns Hopkins University Press.

Glaser, James M. (2015, April). *Tufts University: Lessons from bargaining a first contract for part-time, contingent faculty.* Panel at the annual conference of the National Center for the Study of Collective Bargaining in Higher Education and the Professions, New York.

Goldstein, Adam. (2014). Revenge of the managers: Labor cost-cutting and the paradoxical resurgence of managerialism in the shareholder value era, 1984 to 2001. *American Sociological Review, 77*(2), 268–294.

Gomes, Trimmel. (2017, November 29). Report: Adjunct faculty living in poverty. *Public News Service.* Retrieved from https://www.publicnewsservice.org/2017-11-29/education/report-adjunct-faculty-living-in-poverty/a60469-1

Gonzalez, Norma, Moll, Luis C., & Amanti, Cathy. (Ed.). (2005). *Funds of knowledge: Theorizing practices in households, communities, and classrooms.* Mahwah, NJ: Lawrence Erlbaum Associates.

Gorman, Elizabeth H., & Sandefur, Rebecca L. (2011). 'Golden age,' quiescence, and revival: How the sociology of professions became the study of knowledge-based work. *Work and Occupations, 38*(3), 275–302.

Graduate Teaching Fellows Federation AFT/AFL-CIO, Local 3544. (2014, November 11). [Email letter to Jeffery J. Matthews]. Retrieved from http://gtff3544.net/wp-content/uploads/2014/11/International-Grad-CnD-Letter.pdf

Graduate Workers of Columbia. (2016, March 14). Petitioner's reply brief. National Labor Relations Board, case no. 2-RC-143012.

Gravois, John. (2008, January 4). George Washington U. drops opposition to adjunct union and strikes a deal. *The Chronicle of Higher Education*. Retrieved from https://www.chronicle.com/article/George-Washington-U-Drops/40211

Gumport, Patricia J. (2002). Knowledge and the city of intellect. In Steven Brint (Ed.), *The future of the city of intellect: The changing American university*. Stanford, CA: Stanford University Press.

Haddad, Nabih. (2021). Philanthropic foundations and higher education: The politics of intermediary organizations. *The Journal of Higher Education, 92*(6), 897–926.

Hammond, Kristy. (2018, June 27). The Janus decision and United Academics. *The Duck & Cover*. Retrieved from http://newsletter.uauoregon.org/the-janus-decision-and-united-academics/

Harper, Jordan Nicholas. (2023). *On being everything to everyone: Administrative assistants and intimacy in higher education organizations* (Doctoral dissertation). University of Southern California, Los Angeles.

Hartley, Matthew. (2010). Reconcilable differences: Factors influencing conflict and collegiality in a unionized environment. *Community College Journal of Research and Practice, 34*(4), 318–336.

Hendrix, Sheridan. (2024, March 8). A very longtime coming: More than 550 Ohio University faculty announce plans to unionize. *The Columbus Dispatch*. Retrieved from https://www.dispatch.com/story/news/education/2024/03/08/a-very-longtime-coming-ohio-university-faculty-announce-plans-to-unionize/72897275007/

Henson, Steven E., Krieg, John M., Wassell, Charles S. Jr., & Hedrick, David W. (2012). Collective bargaining and community college faculty: What is the wage impact? *Journal of Labor Research, 33*, 104–117.

Herbert, William A. (2016a, January 14). The future of tenure: Implications for university operations and finance. Presented at the Higher Education advanced seminar of the National Federation of Municipal Analysts, Phoenix. Retrieved from https://www.nytimes.com/interactive/2018/04/13/opinion/college-recruitment-rich-white.html

Herbert, William A. (2016b). The winds of change shift: An analysis of recent growth in bargaining units and representation efforts in higher education. *Journal of Collective Bargaining in the Academy, 8*. https://doi.org/10.58188/1941-8043.1647

Herbert, William A., Apkarian, Jacob, & van der Naald, Joseph. (2020). *Supplementary directory of new bargaining agents and contracts in institutions of higher education, 2013–2019*. New York: National Center for the Study of Collective Bargaining in Higher Education and the Professions.

Herbert, William A., Apkarian, Jacob, & van der Naald, Joseph. (2023). Union organizing and strikes in higher education: The 2022–2023 upsurge in historical context. Special section in The state of the unions, 2023: A profile of organized labor in New York City, New York state, and the United States. Ruth Milkman and Joseph van der Vaald. A report of the CUNY School of Labor and Urban Studies.

Hertzler-McCain, Aleja. (2023, January 23). Fordham faculty call off planned strike after agreement over pay increases. *National Catholic Reporter*. Retrieved from https://www.ncronline.org/news/fordham-faculty-call-planned-strike-after-agreement-over-pay-increases

Hewitt, Gordon J. (2000). Graduate student employee collective bargaining and the educational relationship between faculty and graduate students. *Journal of Collective Negotiations in the Public Sector, 22*(2), 153–166.

Higher Ed Labor United. (n.d.). Vision platform. Retrieved from https://highered
laborunited.org/media/2021/09/HELU-Platform.pdf

Hillman, Nicholas W., Hicklin Fryar, Alisa, & Crespin-Trujillo, Valerie. (2018).
Evaluating the impact of performance funding in Ohio and Tennessee. *American
Educational Research Journal, 55*(1), 144–170.

Hillman, Nicholas W., Tandberg, David A., & Gross, Jacob P. K. (2014). Performance
funding in higher education: Do financial incentives impact college completions?
The Journal of Higher Education, 85(6), 826–857.

Hodson, Randy. (2001). *Dignity at work*. New York: Cambridge University Press.

Hoeller, Keith. (Ed.). (2014). *Equality for contingent faculty: Overcoming the two-tier
system*. Nashville: Vanderbilt University Press.

Hoffman, Elizabeth, & Hess, John. (2014). Organizing for equality within the two-tier
system: The experience of the California Faculty Association. In Keith Hoeller (Ed.),
Equality for contingent faculty: Overcoming the two-tier system (pp. 9–27). Nashville:
Vanderbilt University Press.

Hohl, Elizabeth. (2024). Framing part i: r-e-s-p-e-c-t. In Eric Fure-Slocum & Claire
Goldstene (Eds.), *Contingent faculty and the remaking of higher education: A labor
history* (pp. 35–37). Urbana: University of Illinois Press.

Humphreys, Debra. (2012). What's wrong with the completion agenda—And what we
can do about it. *Liberal Education, 98*(1), 8–17.

Hutcheson, Philo. (2000). *A professional professoriate: Unionization, bureaucratization,
and the AAUP*. Nashville: Vanderbilt University Press.

Jacobs, David, & Dixon, Marc. (2010). Political partisanship, race, and union strength
from 1970–2000: A pooled, time series analysis. *Social Science Research, 39*,
1059–1072.

Jaquette, Ozan. (2013). Why do colleges become universities? Mission drift and the
enrollment economy. *Research in Higher Education, 54*(5), 514–543. https://doi.org
/10.1007/s11162-013-9296-5

Jaeger, Audrey J., & Eagan, M. Kevin. (2011a). Examining retention and contingent
faculty use in a state system of public higher education. *Educational Policy, 25*(3),
507–537.

Jaeger, Audrey J., & Eagan, M. Kevin. (2011b). Navigating the transfer process: Analyzing the effects of part-time faculty exposure by academic program. *American
Behavioral Scientist, 55*(11), 1510–1532.

Jaffe, Sam, & Park, Paula. (2003, March 24). Postdocs: Pawing out of purgatory. *The
Scientist, 17*(6). Retrieved from https://go.gale.com/ps/anonymous?id
=GALE%7CA99816530&sid=googleScholar&v=2.1&it=r&linkaccess=abs&issn
=08903670&p=AONE&sw=w)

Jaschik, Scott. (2006, January 13). NLRB orders George Washington U. to negotiate
with adjunct union. *InsideHigherEd*. Retrieved from https://www.insidehighered
.com/news/2006/01/13/nlrb-orders-george-washington-u-negotiate-adjunct-union/

Jaschik, Scott. (2017, February 30). Barnard deal with adjuncts averts strike. *InsideHigherEd*. Retrieved from https://www.insidehighered.com/quicktakes/2017/02/20
/barnard-deal-adjuncts-averts-strike

Johnston, Paul. (1994). *Success while others fail: Social movement unionism and the public
workplace*. Ithaca, NY: ILR Press.

Juarez, Miguel. (2024). Talking back against ableism, ageism, and contingency as a
Latinx instructor and first-generation scholar. In Eric Fure-Slocum & Claire
Goldstene (Eds.), *Contingent faculty and the remaking of higher education: A labor
history* (pp. 138–144). Urbana: University of Illinois Press.

256 • References

Julius, Daniel J., & Gumport, Patricia J. (2003). Graduate student unionization: Catalysts and consequences, *The Review of Higher Education, 26*(2), 187–216.

Kalleberg, Arne L. (2009). Precarious work, insecure workers: Employment relations in transition. *American Sociological Review, 74*(1), 1–22.

Kalleberg, Arne L. (2011). *Good jobs, bad jobs: The rise of polarized and precarious employment systems.* New York: Russell Sage Foundation.

Kalleberg, Arne L. (2018). *Precarious lives: Job insecurity and well-being in rich democracies.* Cambridge, UK: Polity Books.

Kaplan, Gabriel E. (2004). How academic ships actually navigate. In Ronald G. Ehrenberg (Ed.), *Governing academia* (pp. 165–208). Ithaca, NY: Cornell University Press.

Karim, Aliya. (2012, August 15). Adjunct professors take deal for 3 percent pay increase. *The GW Hatchet.* Retrieved from https://www.gwhatchet.com/tag/adjunct -professors-union/

Kashen, Julie, Glynn, Sarah Jane, & Novello, Amanda. (2020, October 30). *How COVID-19 sent women's workforce progress backward.* Washington, DC: Center for American Progress. Retrieved from https://www.americanprogress.org/article/covid -19-sent-womens-workforce-progress-backward/

Keller, George. (1983). *Academic strategy: The management revolution in American higher education.* Baltimore: Johns Hopkins University Press.

Kelliher, Rebecca. (2021, December 30). The pandemic's unequal toll on faculty. *Diverse Issues in Higher Education.* Retrieved from https://www.diverseeducation.com /faculty-staff/article/15286701/as-omicron-rages-on-so-does-the-pandemics-unequal -toll-on-faculty

Kemerer, Frank R. & Baldridge, J. Victor. (1975). The impact of faculty unions on governance. *Change, 7*(10), 50–51, 62.

Kemerer, Frank R., & Baldridge, J. Victor. (1981). Senates and unions: Unexpected peaceful coexistence. *The Journal of Higher Education, 52*, 256–264.

Kerchner, Charles Taylor, Koppich, Julia E., & Weeres, Joseph G. (1997). *United mind workers: Unions and teaching in the knowledge society.* San Francisco: Jossey-Bass.

Kezar, Adrianna. (Ed.) (2012). *Embracing non-tenure track faculty: Changing campuses for the new faculty majority.* New York: Routledge.

Kezar, Adrianna. (2013). Examining non-tenure track faculty perceptions of how departmental policies and practices shape their performance and ability to create student learning at four-year institutions. *Research in Higher Education, 54*(5), 571–598.

Kezar, Adrianna, & DePaola, Tom. (2018). Understanding the need for unions: Contingent faculty working conditions and the relationship to student learning. In Kim Tolley (Ed.), *Professors in the gig economy: Unionizing adjunct faculty in America* (pp. 27–45). Baltimore: Johns Hopkins University Press.

Kezar, Adrianna, DePaola, Tom, & Scott, Daniel T. (2019). *The gig academy: Mapping labor in the neoliberal university.* Baltimore: Johns Hopkins University Press.

Kezar, Adrianna, & Maxey, Daniel. (Eds.). (2016). *Envisioning the faculty for the 21st century: Moving to a mission-oriented and learner centered model.* New Brunswick, NJ: Rutgers University Press.

Kezar, Adrianna, & Sam, Cecile. (2013). Institutionalizing equitable policies and practices for contingent faculty. *The Journal of Higher Education, 84*(1), 56–87.

Kigner, Elise. (2005, October 23). Part-time professor unionization leaders spend Colonials weekend informing parents of their cause. *The GW Hatchet.* Retrieved from https://gwhatchet.com/2005/10/24/part-time-professor-unionization-leaders -spend-colonials-weekend-informing-parents-of-theur-cause/

References • 257

Kim, Yvonne. (2020, April 29). UW furloughs employees, expects to save about $30 million. *The Cap Times*. Retrieved from https://madison.com/ct/news/local /education/uw-furloughs-employees-expects-to-save-about-30-million/article _e7fe35fe-fe8e-5d1b-bc03-32ef31e534e0.html

Kimmeldorf, Howard. (2013). Worker replacement costs and unionization: Origins of the U.S. labor movement. *American Sociological Review*, 78(6), 1033–1062.

Kiyama, Judy Marquez, & Rios-Aguilar, Cecilia. (Eds.). (2018). *Funds of knowledge in higher education: Honoring students' cultural experiences and resources as strengths*. New York: Routledge & Taylor Francis Group.

Klainot-Hess, Elizabeth. (2022). The benefits and limitations of contingent faculty unionization: A comparison of a union and non-union institution. *Labor Studies Journal*, 1–21.

Klein, Naomi. (2007). *The shock doctrine: The rise of disaster capitalism*. New York: Henry Holt.

Kline, Missy. (2018). *The faculty workforce is aging: Is the pipeline more diverse?* [Web log post]. Retrieved from https://www.cupahr.org/blog/the-faculty-workforce-is-aging -is-the-pipeline-more-diverse/

Knox, Liam. (2022, August 28). AU reaches agreement with staff union after weeklong strike. *InsideHigherEd*. Retrieved from https://www.insidehighered.com/quicktakes /2022/08/29/au-reaches-agreement-staff-union-after-weeklong-strike

Krause, Monika, Nolan, Mary, Palm, Michael, & Ross, Andrew. (Eds.). (2008). *The university against itself: The NYU strike and the future of the academic workplace*. Philadelphia: Temple University Press.

Kullgren, Ian, & Kessler, Aaron. (2020, June 26). Unions fend off membership exodus in 2 years since Janus ruling. *Bloomberg Law*. Retrieved from https://news .bloomberglaw.com/daily-labor-report/unions-fend-off-membership-exodus-in-2 -years-since-janus-ruling

Kumar, D. (2023, March 7). One of the US's largest public universities could see first strike in its 257 years. *Truthout*. Retrieved from https://truthout.org/articles/one-of -uss-largest-public-universities-could-see-first-strike-in-its-257-years/

Ladd, Everett C., Jr., & Lipset, Seymour Martin. (1973). *Professors, unions, and American higher education*. Berkeley, CA: Carnegie Foundation for the Advancement of Teaching.

Ladd, Everett C., Jr., & Lipset, Seymour Martin. (1975). *The divided academy: Professors and their politics*. New York, NY: McGraw-Hill.

Langin, Katie. (2019, March 12). In a first, U.S. private sector employs nearly as many PhD's as schools do. *Science*. Retrieved from https://www.sciencemag.org/careers /2019/03/first-us-private-sector-employs-nearly-many-phds-schools-do

Larson, Katherine. (2004, January 26). Column: Adjuncts treated unfairly. *The GW Hatchet*. Retrieved from https://gwhatchet.com/2004/01/26/column-adjuncts -treated-unfairly/

Larson, Magali Sarfatti. (1977). *The rise of professionalism: A sociological analysis*. Berkeley: University of California Press.

Lawhorn, Chad. (2024, April 25). KU faculty members overwhelmingly approve formation of union. *Lawrence-Journal World*. Retrieved from https://www2.ljworld .com/news/ku/2024/apr/25/ku-faculty-overwhelmingly-approve-formation-of -union-will-seek-improvements-in-pay-job-security/

Lederman, Doug. (2018, June 27). A quarter of private colleges ran deficits in 2017. *InsideHigherEd*. Retrieved from https://www.insidehighered.com/quicktakes/2018/06 /27/quarter-private-colleges-ran-deficits-2017?utm_source=Inside+Higher+Ed&utm

_campaign=117abc9646-DNU_COPY_01&utm_medium=email&utm_term=0
_1fcbc04421-117abc9646-197419965&mc_cid=117abc9646&mc_eid=3cf866d28d

Lee, Barbara A. (1979). Governance at unionized four-year colleges: Effect on decision-making structures. *The Journal of Higher Education, 50*, 565–585.

Leslie, D. W., & Ikenberry D. J. (1979). Collective bargaining and part-time faculty: Contract content. *CUPA Journal, 30*(3), 18–26.

Leslie, Larry L., & Hu, Tei-Weh. (1977). The financial implications of collective bargaining. *Journal of Education Finance, 3*, 32–53.

Letizia, Angelo J. (2016). The hollow university: Disaster capitalism befalls American higher education. *Policy Futures in Education, 14*(3), 360–376.

Levin, John S., Kater, Susan T., & Wagoner, Richard L. (2011). *Community college faculty: At work in the new economy.* New York: Palgrave Macmillan.

Levy, Marissa. (2005, September 2). GW, union prepare for court battle. *The GW Hatchet.* Retrieved from https://www.gwhatchet.com/2005/09/02/gw-union-prepare-for-court-battle/

Lincoln University Office of the President (2017, January 18). Board actions. Retrieved from https://bluetigerportal.lincolnu.edu/c/document_library/get_file?uuid=df18c9a6-596e-484d-9e98-311f076acoc1&groupId=6413728

Lobosco, Katie. (2017, June 29). Illinois is starving state colleges and universities. *CNN Money.* Retrieved from http://money.cnn.com/2017/06/29/pf/college/illinois-budget-higher-education/index.html

Loiselle, Aimee. (2024). Framing part ii: Multiple contingencies. In Eric Fure-Slocum & Claire Goldstene (Eds.), *Contingent faculty and the remaking of higher education: A labor history* (pp. 107–109). Urbana: University of Illinois Press.

Long, Heather, Van Dam, Andrew, Fowers, Alyssa, & Shapiro, Leslie. (2020, September 30). The covid-19 recession is the most unequal in U.S. history. *The Washington Post.* Retrieved from https://www.washingtonpost.com/graphics/2020/business/coronavirus-recession-equality/?tid=a_classic-iphone&p9w22b2p=b2p22p9w00098&no_nav=true

Longmate, Jack. (2014). The question of academic unions: Community (or conflict) of interest. In Keith Hoeller, (Ed.) *Equality for contingent faculty: Overcoming the two-tier system* (pp. 156–172). Nashville: Vanderbilt University Press.

Maisto, Maria. (2012). Taking heart, taking part: New Faculty Majority and the praxis of contingent faculty activism. In Adrianna Kezar (Ed.), *Embracing non-tenure track faculty: Changing campuses for the New Faculty Majority* (pp. 190–204). New York: Routledge.

Maisto, Maria. (2024). Common ground for the common good: What we mean when we say, "Faculty working conditions are student learning conditions." In Eric Fure-Slocum & Claire Goldstene (Eds.), *Contingent faculty and the remaking of higher education: A labor history* (pp. 156–178). Urbana: University of Illinois Press.

Marcus, Jon. (2020, July 19). Amid pandemic, graduate student workers are winning long-sought contracts. *The Washington Post.* Retrieved from https://www.washingtonpost.com/education/2020/07/19/grad-student-unions-pandemic/

Mauer, Michael. (2016). Protecting shared governance through collective bargaining: Models used by AAUP chapters. *Journal of Collective Bargaining in the Academy, 8.* Retrieved from http://thekeep.eiu.edu/jcba/vol8/iss1/7

McAlevey, Jane (with Ostertag, Bob). (2012). *Raising expectations (and raising hell): My decade fighting for the labor movement.* New York: Verso Books.

McCartin, Joseph A. (2016). Bargaining for the common good. *Dissent.* Retrieved from https://www.dissentmagazine.org/article/bargaining-common-good-community-union-alignment

McCartin, Joseph A., Sneiderman, Marilyn, & BP-Weeks, Maurice. (2020). Combustible convergence: Bargaining for the common good and the #RedForEd uprisings of 2018. *Labor Studies Journal, 45*(1), 97–113.

McChesney, Jasper, & Bichsel, Jacqueline. (2020). *The aging of tenure track faculty in higher education: Implications for succession and diversity.* Knoxville, TN: College and University Professional Association for Human Resources.

McClure, Bud A. (1999). Tenure at Minnesota: A postmortem. *Thought & Action,* Fall, 97–104.

McFerran, Lauren. [@NLRBMcFerran]. (2021, March 12). In Columbia University, the Board correctly held that student employees are workers deserving the full protection of our labor laws. [Tweet]. Twitter. Retrieved from https://x.com/NLRBMcFerran/status/1370378341409300482

McFetridge, Scott. (2018, December 18). Students drop union organizing effort. *Newton Daily News.* Retrieved from https://www.newtondailynews.com/2018/12/18/students-drop-union-organizing-effort/awuukzu/

McLeer, Anne. (2020, July 24). Presentation at the National Inter-Union Academic Labor webinar, National Center for the Study of Collective Bargaining in Higher Education and the Professions.

McLeer, Anne. (2024). From community of interest to imagined communities: Organizing academic labor in the Washington DC area. In Eric Fure-Slocum & Claire Goldstene (Eds.), *Contingent faculty and the remaking of higher education: A labor history* (pp. 204–215). Urbana: University of Illinois Press.

McNay, John T. (2013). *Collective bargaining and the battle of Ohio; The defeat of Senate Bill 5 and the struggle to defend the middle class.* New York: Palgrave Macmillan.

McPherson, Chad Michael, & Sauder, Michael. (2013). Logics in action: Managing institutional complexity in drug court. *Administrative Science Quarterly, 58*(2), 165–196.

Metchick, Robert H., & Singh, Parbudyal. (2004). Yeshiva and faculty unionization in higher education. *Labor Studies Journal, 28*(4), 45–65.

Milkman, Ruth. (2006). Divided we stand. *New Labor Forum, 15*(1), 38–46.

Milkman, Ruth, Bloom, Joshua, & Narro, Victor. (Eds.). (2010). *Working for justice: The L.A. model of organizing and advocacy.* Ithaca, NY: ILR Press.

Milkman, Ruth, & Ott, Edward. (Eds.). (2014). *New labor, New York: Precarious workers and the future of the labor movement.* Ithaca, NY: Cornell University Press.

Misra, Joya, Lundquist, Jennifer Hickes, & Templer, Abby. (2012). Gender, work time, and care responsibilities among faculty. *Sociological Forum, 27*(2): 300–323.

Misra, Joya, Kuvaeva, Alexandra, O'Meara, Kerry Ann, Culpepper, Dawn Kiyoe, & Jaeger, Audrey. (2021). Gendered and racialized perceptions of faculty workloads. *Gender and Society, 35*(3): 358–394.

Moattar, Daniel. (2018, November 29). How graduate unions are winning—and scaring the hell out of bosses—in the Trump Era. *In These Times.* Retrieved from https://inthesetimes.com/working/entry/21602/graduate_student_unions_trump_nlrb_columbia_brown

Modestino, Alicia Sasser. (2020, July 29). Coronavirus child-care crisis will set women back a generation. *The Washington Post.* Retrieved from https://www.washingtonpost.com/us-policy/2020/07/29/childcare-remote-learning-women-employment/

Mohr, Whitney. (2021). *College, chronic illness, and COVID-19: It's complicated.* (Doctoral dissertation). Center for the Study of Higher Education, University of Arizona, Tucson.

Moll, Luis C., Amanti, Cathy, Neff, Deborah, & Gonzalez, Norma. (1992). Funds of knowledge for teaching: Using a qualitative approach to connect homes and classrooms. *Theory into Practice, XXI*(2), 132–141.

Moriarty, X., & Saverese, Michelle. (2006). *Directory of U.S. Faculty Contracts and Bargaining Agents in Institutions of Higher Education*. New York: National Center for the Study of Collective Bargaining in Higher Education and the Professions.

Mortimer, Kenneth P., & Tierney, Michael L. (1979). *The three "r's" of the eighties: Reduction, reallocation, and retrenchment*. Washington, DC: American Association for Higher Education. (ED284523).

Moser, R. (2014). Organizing the new faculty majority: The struggle to achieve equality for contingent faculty, revive our unions, and democratize higher education. In Keith Hoeller (Ed.), *Equality for contingent faculty: Overcoming the two-tier system* (pp. 77–115). Nashville: Vanderbilt University Press.

Murphy, Laura, & Atkins, Leah M. (2019). Maintaining peer-based faculty evaluation: A case study involving student surveys of teaching. *Journal of Collective Bargaining in the Academy, 11*. https://doi.org/10.58188/1941-8043.1863

Murphy, Marjorie. (1990). *Blackboard unions: The AFT and the NEA, 1900–1980*. Ithaca, NY: Cornell University Press.

Murphy, Tim. (2018). The Jackson advocate: Can Ben Jealous do what generations of Democrats have tried—forge a rainbow coalition that can win? *Mother Jones, 41*(7), 34–41.

Nack, David, Childers, Michael, Kulwiec, Alexia, & Ibarra, Armando. (2020). The recent evolution of Wisconsin public worker unionism since Act 10. *Labor Studies Journal, 45*(2), 145–167.

Nash, Margaret A. (2019). Entangled pasts: Land grant colleges and American Indian dispossession. *History of Education Quarterly, 59*(4), 437–467.

National Association of Graduate-Professional Students. (2016, February 26). Brief *amicus curiae* of National Association of Graduate-Professional Students, in Case 02-RC-143012. Retrieved from https://nagps.org/amicus-brief/

National Academies of Sciences, Engineering, and Medicine. (2014). *The postdoctoral experience revisited*. Washington, DC: National Academies Press.

National Center for the Study of Collective Bargaining in Higher Education and the Professions. (2020, July 24). National inter-union academic labor webinar. NCSCBHEP, New York.

National Labor Relations Board. (2021, March 12). NLRB withdrawing proposed rule regarding student employment. Retrieved from https://www.nlrb.gov/news-outreach/news-story/nlrb-withdrawing-proposed-rule-regarding-student-employment

National Postdoctoral Association. (n.d.). About the national postdoctoral association. Retrieved from https://www.nationalpostdoc.org/page/Aboutflaher

National Postdoctoral Association. (n.d.). What is a postdoc? Retrieved from https://www.nationalpostdoc.org/page/What_is_a_postdoc

National Postdoctoral Association. (2019). *Overview of postdoc unionization*. Retrieved from https://cdn.ymaws.com/www.nationalpostdoc.org/resource/resmgr/2019_launch/resources/policy/pd_unionization_2019v1.pdf

National Research Council. (2005). *Bridges to independence: Fostering the independence of new investigators in biomedical research*. National Research Council (US) Committee on Bridges to Independence: Identifying opportunities for and challenges to fostering the independence of young investigators in the Life Sciences. Washington, DC: National Academies Press. https://doi.org/10.17226/11249

Negri, Luke Elliott. (2018). Wall to wall: Industrial unionism at the City University of New York, 19722017. In Kim Tolley (Ed.), *Professors in the gig economy: Unionizing adjunct faculty in America* (pp. 153–171). Baltimore: Johns Hopkins University Press.

Newfield, Christopher. (2003). *Ivy and industry: Business and the making of the American university, 1880–1930.* Durham, NC: Duke University Press.

Newfield, Christopher. (2008). *Unmaking the public university: The forty year assault on the middle class.* Cambridge, MA: Harvard University Press.

Newfield, Christopher. (2016). *The great mistake: How we wrecked public universities and how we can fix them.* Baltimore: Johns Hopkins University Press.

Nickel, David. (2020, August 29). At risk, all day, every day." *UCW Georgia.* Retrieved from https://ucwga.com/news/risk-all-day-every-day

Nissen, Bruce, & Churchill, Candi. (2020). Unionism in a right-to-work environment: United Faculty of Florida from stagnation to crisis mobilization to power building. *Labor Studies Journal, 45*(4), 370–393.

Noble, David F. (1977). *America by design: Science, technology, and the rise of corporate capitalism.* New York: Knopf.

Noble, Jason. (2017, February 17). Branstad signs controversial bargaining bill into law. *Des Moines Register.* Retrieved from http://www.desmoinesregister.com /story/news/politics/2017/02/17/branstad-signs-controversial-bargaining-bill -into-law

Nofacultyunion.blogspot.com. Blog of Nicholas Burbules and Joyce Tolliver.

NYSUT Community College Distance Education Committee. (2013). *Negotiating the distance and beyond: Bargaining contract and policy language for distance education and intellectual property.* Latham, NY: New York State United Teachers.

O'Brien, Rebecca. (2000). *Bread and roses.* UK: Lionsgate Films.

Ohio University. (2024, May 10). Ohio responds with brief to State Labor Board. *Ohio Today.* Retrieved from https://www.ohio.edu/news/2024/05/ohio-responds-brief -state-labor-board

Okolski, Gabriel. (2004, April 5). Kennedy backs student fight. *The GW Hatchet.* Retrieved from https://gwhatchet.com/2004/04/05/kennedy-backs-student -fight/

Oppenheim, James. (1911, December 11). Bread and roses. *American Magazine.*

Orphan, Cecilia. (2018). Public purpose under pressure: Examining the effects of neoliberal policy on regional comprehensive universities. *Journal of Higher Education Outreach and Engagement, 22*(2), 59–102.

Orphan, Cecilia. (2020, July 13). Why regional public universities are vulnerable during recessions and must be protected. *Third Way.* Retrieved from https://www.thirdway .org/report/why-regional-public-universities-are-vulnerable-during-recessions-and -must-be-protected

Pacific Lutheran University. (2014). *Contingent Faculty FAQ Compilation.* Retrieved from http://www.plu.edu/provost/wp-content/uploads/sites/217/2014/11 /contingent-faculty-faq-compilation.pdf

Park, Sangchun, Sine, Wesley D., & Tolbert, Pamela S. (2011). Professions, organizations, and institutions: Tenure systems in colleges and universities. *Work and Occupations, 38,* 340–371.

Patel, Pooja, Kanrar, Arpita, & Yumeen, Leena. (2022, March 10). SWC's contract: A win for student workers and the national labor movement. *Columbia Political Review.* Retrieved from http://www.cpreview.org/blog/2022/3/swcs-contract-a-win -for-student-workers-and-the-national-labor-movement

Pennington, Carolyn. (2009, November 19). Health Center faculty vote to unionize in tight election. *UConn Today.*

Perna, Laura W., & Finney, Joni E. (2014). *The attainment agenda: State policy leadership in higher education.* Baltimore: Johns Hopkins University Press.

262 • References

Phillips, Mike. (2007, October 4). Adjuncts struggle to afford the city. *The GW Hatchet.* Retrieved from https://gwhatchet.com/2007/10/04/adjuncts-struggle-to-afford-the-city/

Porter, Stephen R. (2013). The causal effects of faculty unions on institutional decision-making. *Industrial and Labor Relations Review, 66,* 1192–1211.

Pratt, Gregory. (2018). Adjunct faculty at Loyola University Chicago ratify first contract. *Chicago Tribune.* Retrieved from https://www.chicagotribune.com/news/local/breaking/ct-met-loyola-university-chicago-faculty-contract-02180427-story.html

Press, Alex. (2018, January 29). White-collar unionization is good for all workers. *The Nation.* Retrieved from https://www.thenation.com/article/white-collar-unionization-is-good-for-everybody/

Prochaska, David. (2014). A faculty union at UIUC, part 1. The public i: A paper of the people. Campus Faculty Association, University of Illinois, Urbana Champaign. June 2014. Publici.ucimc.org/a-faculty-union-at-uiuc-part-1/

Quilantan, Bianca. (2018, April 11). Union organizer at Penn State's grad school cites university's "veiled threat" to foreign students. *The Chronicle of Higher Education.* Retrieved from https://www.chronicle.com/article/Union-Organizer-at-Penn/243096

Quinn, Ryan. (2023, January 18). University of Illinois at Chicago faculty members strike. *InsideHigherEd.* Retrieved from https://www.insidehighered.com/news/2023/01/18/professors-university-illinois-chicago-begin-strike

Quinn, Ryan. (2023, March 1). Lacking collective bargaining rights, but organizing anyway. *InsideHigherEd.* Retrieved from https://www.insidehighered.com/news/2023/03/01/unions-organizing-states-lack-collective-bargaining

Quinn, Ryan. (2024, January 18). Washington State U student workers strike, get deal. *InsideHigherEd.* Retrieved from https://www.insidehighered.com/news/quick-takes/2024/01/18/washington-state-u-student-workers-strike-get-deal

Quinn, Ryan. (2024, March 1). Full-time, non-tenure track NYU faculty members unionize. *InsideHigherEd.* Retrieved from https://www.google.com/search?client=safari&rls=en&q=ryan+quinn+NYU+nontenure+track+lecturers+unioize&ie=UTF-8&oe=UTF-8

Quinn, Ryan. (2024, April 8). Nontenure track Harvard lecturers and researchers unionize. *InsideHigherEd.* Retrieved from https://www.insidehighered.com/news/quick-takes/2024/04/08/harvard-nontenure-track-lecturers-researchers-unionize

Quinn, Ryan. (2024, May 21). UC academic workers strike over pro-Palestinian protest arrests. *InsideHigherEd.* Retrieved from https://www.insidehighered.com/news/faculty-issues/labor-unionization/2024/05/21/uc-academic-workers-strike-over-pro-palestinian

Ramirez, Jameson. (2018). Bargaining for adjuncts: An assessment of adjunct union growth in the St. Louis region. *Journal of Collective Bargaining in the Academy, 10.* https://doi.org/10.58188/1941-8043.1739

Ran, Florence Xiaotao, & Xu, Di. (2018, May 4). Does contractual form matter? The impact of different types of non-tenure track faculty on college students' academic outcomes. *Journal of Human Resources, 54*(4). https://doi.org/10.3368/jhr.54.4.0117.8505R

Rein, Marcy, Ellinger, Mickey, & Legion, Vicki. (2020). Free City! Reclaiming City College of San Francisco and free education for all. *Labor Studies Journal, 45*(1), 56–73.

Rhoades, Gary. (1993). Retrenchment clauses in faculty union contracts: Faculty rights and administrative discretion. *The Journal of Higher Education, 64*(3), 312–347.

Rhoades, Gary. (1998a). *Managed professionals: Unionized faculty and restructuring academic labor.* Albany: State University of New York Press.

Rhoades, Gary. (1998b). Rethinking administrative costs. In John C. Smart (Ed.), *Higher education: Handbook of theory and research, Vol. XIII* (pp. 11–47). New York: Agathon Press.

Rhoades, Gary. (2007). Technology enhanced courses and a Mode III organization of instructional work. *Tertiary Education and Management, 13*(1), 1–17.

Rhoades, Gary. (2008). The centrality of contingent faculty to academe's future." *Academe, 94*(6), 12–15.

Rhoades, Gary. (2009a). Carnegie, DuPont Circle, and the AAUP: (Re)shaping a cosmopolitan, locally engaged professoriate. *Change, 41*(1), 8–15.

Rhoades, Gary. (2009b). From the general secretary: "Naaational." *Academe, 95*(5), 71.

Rhoades, Gary. (2012a). The incomplete completion agenda: Implications for academe and the academy. *Liberal Education, 98*(1), 18–25.

Rhoades, Gary. (2012b). *The plight of postdoctoral researchers: Putting UMass Amherst in perspective.* White Paper for United Autoworkers, Local 2322.

Rhoades, Gary. (2013a, September 25). Adjunct professors are the new working poor. *CNN.com.* Retrieved from https://www.cnn.com/2013/09/24/opinion/rhoades-adjunct-faculty/index.html

Rhoades, Gary. (2013b). Bargaining quality in part-time faculty working conditions: Beyond just-in-time employment and just-at-will non-renewal. *Journal of Collective Bargaining in the Academy, 4.* https://doi.org/10.58188/1941-8043.1274

Rhoades, Gary. (2013c). Disruptive innovations for adjunct faculty: Common sense for the common good. *Thought & Action, 29*(Fall), 71–86.

Rhoades, Gary. (2014a). The higher education we choose, collectively: Reembodying and repoliticizing choice. *The Journal of Higher Education, 85*(6), 917–930.

Rhoades, Gary. (2014b). We are all contingent: Re-organizing higher education and society. *On Campus, 33*(4), 2–4.

Rhoades, Gary. (2015a, April 20). *Bread and roses, and quality too: A new faculty majority negotiating a new academy.* Paper presented at the annual meeting of National Center for the Study of Collective Bargaining in Higher Education and the Professions, New York.

Rhoades, Gary. (2015b). Creative leveraging in contingent faculty organizing. *The Journal of Labor and Society, 18,* 435–45.

Rhoades, Gary. (2015c). What are we negotiating for? Public interest bargaining. *Journal of Collective Bargaining in the Academy, 7.* https://doi.org/10.58188/1941-8043.1463

Rhoades, Gary. (2017a). Bread and roses, and quality too: A new faculty majority negotiating the new academy. *The Journal of Higher Education, 88*(5), 645–671.

Rhoades, Gary. (2017b). Negotiating whose property it is, for the public good. In Samantha Bernstein-Sierra & Adrianna Kezar (Eds.), *Intellectual property, faculty rights, and the public good* (pp. 63–76). New Directions for Higher Education, Number 177. San Francisco: Jossey-Bass.

Rhoades, Gary. (2018). Choosing how, why, and to whom we profess: Negotiating professional neutrality in public scholarship. In Laura W. Perna (Ed.), *Taking it to the streets: The role of scholarship in advocacy and advocacy in scholarship* (pp. 58–64). Baltimore: Johns Hopkins University Press.

264 • References

Rhoades, Gary. (2020). Taking college teachers' working conditions seriously: Adjunct faculty and negotiating a labor-based conception of quality. *The Journal of Higher Education, 91*(3), 327–352.

Rhoades, Gary. (2021). Working in coalition and wall-to-wall. *Journal of Collective Bargaining in the Academy, 12.* https://doi.org/10.58188/1941-8043.1877

Rhoades, Gary. (2023). Postdoc identity, jurisdictional issues, ideologies, and unions: Considerations in organizing professionals. *Labor Studies Journal, 48*(2), 101–120.

Rhoades, Gary. (2024). From the margins to the center: Negotiating a new academy. In Eric Fure-Slocum & Claire Goldstene (Eds.). *Contingent faculty and the remaking of higher education: A labor history* (pp. 17–31). Urbana-Champaign: University of Illinois Press.

Rhoades, Gary, Berry, Joe, & Worthen, Helena. (2023). Power despite precarity: A conversation with the authors on strategies of and for the contingent faculty labor movement. *Journal of Collective Bargaining in the Academy, 14.* https://doi.org/10.58188/1941-8043.1907

Rhoades, Gary, Canton, Cecil, & Toombs, Charles. (2023). Centering anti-racism and social justice in a journey toward a more perfect union: A conversation with the authors. *Journal of Collective Bargaining in the Academy, 14.* https://doi.org/10.58188/1941-8043.1908

Rhoades, Gary, Castiello-Gutierrez, Santiago, Lee, Jenny J., Marei, Mahmoud Sayed, & O'Toole, Leslie C. (2019). Marketing to international students: Presentation of university self in geopolitical space. *The Review of Higher Education, 43*(2), 519–551.

Rhoades, Gary, & Rhoads, Robert A. (2003). The public discourse of U.S. graduate employee unions: Social movement identities, ideologies, and strategies. *The Review of Higher Education, 26*(1), 163–186.

Rhoades, Gary, & Sporn, Barbara. (2002). New models of management and shifting modes and costs of production: Europe and the United States. *Tertiary Education and Management, 8*(1), 3–28.

Rhoades, Gary, & Torres-Olave, Blanca M. (2015). Academic capitalism and (secondary) academic labor markets: Negotiating a new academy and research agenda. In Michael P. Paulsen (Ed.), *Higher education: Handbook of theory and research, Vol. 30* (pp. 383–430). New York: Springer.

Rhoads, Robert A., & Rhoades, Gary. (2005). Graduate employee unionization as symbol of and challenge to the corporatization of U.S. research universities. *The Journal of Higher Education, 76*(3), 243–275.

Rhodes, Dawn. (2017, March 16). Illinois regional universities toil through state budget standoff. *Chicago Tribune.* Retrieved from http://www.chicagotribune.com/news/local/breaking/ct-budget-crisis-regional-universities-20170316-story.html

Rhomberg, Chris. (2018). "$15 and a union": Searching for workers' power in the fight for $15 movement. In Janice Fine, Linda Burnham, Kati Griffith, Minsun Ji, Victor Narro, & Steven Pitts. (Eds.), *No one size fits all: Worker organization, policy, and movement in a new economic age* (pp. 251–270). Champaign, IL: Labor and Employment Relations Association.

Rinschler, John. (2010). Students or employees? The struggle over graduate student unions in America's private colleges and universities." *Journal of College and University Law, 36*(3), 615–640.

Roberts-Grmela, Julian. (2023, April 10). Rutgers' president threatened to take striking instructors to court. Then he walked it back. *The Chronicle of Higher Education.* Retrieved from https://www.chronicle.com/article/rutgers-president-threatened-to-take-striking-instructors-to-court-then-he-walked-it-back#:~:text=The%20standoff%20has%20put%20a,"return%20to%20normal%20activities

Rodich, David. (2017, March 26). Multi-institutional labor-management committees for contingent faculty. Presented at the annual conference of the National Center for the Study of Collective Bargaining in Higher Education and the Professions, New York.

Rodrigues, Marcela. (2022, August 26). After student walkout, American U agrees to new contract with striking staff. *The Chronicle of Higher Education*. Retrieved from https://www.chronicle.com/article/after-student-walkout-american-u-agrees-to-new -contract-with-striking-staff?cid2=gen_login_refresh&cid=gen_sign_in

Rogers, Sean E., Eaton, Adrienne E, & Voos, Paula P. (2013). The effects of unionization on graduate student employees: Faculty-student relations, academic freedom, and pay. *Industrial and Labor Relations Review, 66*(2), 487–510.

Rohn, Jennifer. (2011, March 2). Give postdocs a career, not empty promises. *Nature, 471*(7). Retrieved from http://www.nature.com/news/2011/110302/full/471007a.html

Rojas, Laura. (2015, March 10). Wear the letter "a" with pride not shame. *The Independent*. Retrieved from https://neiuindependent.org/3738/news/wear-the-letter -a-for-adjunct-with-pride-not-shame/

Rourke, Francis, & Brooks, Glenn. (1966). *The managerial revolution in higher education*. Baltimore: Johns Hopkins University Press.

Rutgers AAUP-AFT Academic Worker Union. [@ruaaup]. (2022, September 26). President Holloway to @RobScottAnthro & adjunct prof & long-time organizer Karen Thompson. [Post, video attached]. X. Retrieved from https://x.com/ruaaup /status/1574461165912166427

Saia, Toni, Nerlich, Andrea Perkins, & Johnston, Sarah P. (2021). Why not the "new flexible"? The argument for not returning to "normal" after COVID-19. *Rehabilitation Counselors and Education Journal*. https://doi.org/10.52017/001c.28332

Sainato, Michael. (2023, September 2). US labor movement celebrates new regulation to counter union-busting. *The Guardian*. Retrieved from https://www.theguardian .com/us-news/2023/sep/02/union-nlrb-decision-delays-busting

Saint Louis University. (n.d.) Adjunct faculty union information: Saint Louis University– SEIU collective bargaining agreement. Retrieved from https://www.slu.edu/provost /faculty-affairs/adjunct-faculty-union-information

Salazar, Karina G. (2022). Recruitment redlining by public research universities in the Los Angeles and Dallas Metropolitan areas. *The Journal of Higher Education, 93*(4), 585–621.

Salazar, Karina G., Jaquette, Ozan, & Han, Crystal. (2021). Coming to a neighborhood near you? Off-campus recruiting by public research universities. *American Educational Research Journal, 53*(4), 1–45.

Saltzman, Gregory M. (1998). Legal regulation of collective bargaining in colleges and universities." In Harold S. Wechsler (Ed.), *NEA 1998 almanac of higher education* (pp. 41–59). Washington, DC: National Education Association.

Saltzman, Gregory M. (2006). Rights revoked: Attacks on the right to organize and bargain." In Harold S. Wechsler (Ed.), *NEA 2006 almanac of higher education* (pp. 49–63). Washington, DC: National Education Association.

Saltzman, Gregory M. (2012). An anti-union tide: The 2011 attacks on public employees' bargaining rights. In Harold S. Wechsler (ed.), *NEA 2012 almanac of higher education* (pp. 35–46). Washington, DC: National Education Association.

Sam, C. (2012). Institutionalization of a positive work environment at a community college. In Adrianna Kezar (Ed.), *Embracing non-tenure track faculty: Changing campuses for the new faculty majority* (pp. 100–113). New York: Routledge.

Schackner, Bill. (2018, April 12). Is fear over visa status being used to derail Penn State unionization effort? *Pittsburgh Post-Gazette*. Retrieved from https://www.post

-gazette.com/news/education/2018/04/12/Penn-State-University-graduate-studnets-international-students-visas-labor-Pennsylvania-stories/201804120153

Schackner, Bill. (2019, April 18). Bid to organize Pitt faculty falls short, but union contests ruling. *Pittsburgh Post-Gazette*. Retrieved from https://www.post-gazette.com/news/education/2019/04/18/University-of-Pittsburgh-Pitt-Steelworkers-USW-union-labor-election-PLRB-faculty-adjuncts/stories/201904180131

Schackner, Bill. (2023a, October 9). Just shy four years ago, another graduate worker union drive has begun at the University of Pittsburgh. *TRIBLive*. Retrieved from https://triblive.com/business/just-shy-4-years-ago-another-graduate-worker-union-drive-has-begun-at-the-university-of-pittsburgh/#:~:text=9%2C%202023%209%3A46%20a.m

Schackner, Bill. (2023b, November 29). Faculty union files labor complaint against Pitt, alleging it is stalling contract talks. *TRIBLive*. Retrieved from https://triblive.com/news/faculty-union-files-labor-complaint-against-pitt-alleging-it-is-stalling-contract-talks/

Schillebeeckx, Maximiliaan, Maricque, Brett, & Lewis, Cory. (2013). The missing piece to changing the university culture. *Nature Biotechnology, 31*(10), 938–941.

Schlaerth, Christian A.I. (2022). Adjuncts units! The struggle to unionize, administrative response, and building a bigger movement. *Labor Studies Journal, 47*(1), 5–27.

Schrader, Adam. (2024, February 9). Philadelphia's University of the Arts faculty union reaches its first contract agreement. *Artnet*. Retrieved from https://news.artnet.com/art-world/philadelphia-university-of-the-arts-union-first-contract-agreement-2430891

Schudde, L. (2019). Short- and long-term impacts of engagement experiences with faculty and peers at community colleges. *The Review of Higher Education, 42*(2), 385–426.

Schuster, Jack H., & Finkelstein, Martin J. (2006). *The American faculty: The restructuring of academic work and careers*. Baltimore: Johns Hopkins University Press.

Schuster, Jack H., Smith, Daryl G., Corak, Kathleen A., & Yamada, Myrtle M. (1994). *Strategic governance: How to make big decisions better*. Phoenix: Oryx Press.

Scott, John Henry. (2017, March 29). United academics: Local adjuncts labor union seeks rights for non-tenured professors. *The Spirit of Penn's Garden*. Retrieved from http://spiritnews.org/articles/united-academics-local-adjuncts-labor-union-seeks-rights-for-non-tenured-professors/

Semuels, Alana. (2018, January 26). Organized labor's growing class divide. *The Atlantic*. Retrieved from https://www.theatlantic.com/business/archive/2018/01/union-organizing-media-white-collar/551453/

Sennett, Richard, & Cobb, Jonathan. (1972). *The hidden injuries of class*. New York: Vintage Books.

Service Employees International Union Local 500. (2012). GW contract highlights. Retrieved from http://www.seiu500.org/files/2012/11/GW-Contract-Summary-July-2012.pdf

Service Employees International Union Local 500. (2020). Unemployment Assistance. Retrieved from https://www.seiu500.org/covid19-resources

Shearer, Lee. (2020, July 1). Furloughs for UGA employees? None planned in 2020–21 budget. *Athens Banner-Herald*. Retrieved from https://www.onlineathens.com/news/20200701/furloughs-for-uga-employees-none-planned-in-2020-21-budget

Shin, Jung Cheol. (2010). Impacts of performance-based accountability on institutional performance in the U.S. *Higher Education, 60*(1), 47–68.

Silver, John. (2013). *Just a union . . . of nurses: The rise to political power of the California Nurses Association*. Winter Park, FL: Legacy Book Publishing.

Simpson, Ida Harper. (1989). The sociology of work; Where have the workers gone? *Social Forces, 67*, 563–581.

Sinclair, Upton. (Ed.). (1915). *The cry for justice: An anthology of the literature of social protest*. Philadelphia: John C. Winston.

Sitter, Phillip. (2020, May 27). Lincoln University faculty union offers plan to avoid layoffs. *News Tribune*. Retrieved from https://www.newstribune.com/news/local/story/2020/may/27/lincoln-university-faculty-union-offers-plan-avoid-layoffs/828719/

Sitter, Phillip. (2020, June 22). Lincoln University cuts employee pay, eliminates bowling program, *News Tribune*. Retrieved from https://www.newstribune.com/news/local/story/2020/jun/22/lincoln-university-cuts-employee-pay-eliminates-bowling-program/831735/

Sitter, Phillip. (2020, September 10). Lincoln University retracts pay cuts, *News Tribune*. Retrieved from https://www.newstribune.com/news/news/story/2020/sep/11/lincoln-university-restores-pay-cuts/840886/

Skelding, Conor. (2016, August 25). Muted reaction from Ivies after dramatic labor board decision on Columbia graduate students. *Politico*. Retrieved from https://www.politico.com/states/new-york/albany/story/2016/08/most-other-ivies-mum-after-nlrbs-decision-on-columbia-grad-students-104934

Slaughter, Sheila. (1993a). Academic freedom in the 1980s. In Philip G. Altbach, Robert O. Berdahl, & Patricia Gumport (Eds.), *Higher education in American society* (3rd ed., pp. 73–99). Buffalo: Prometheus.

Slaughter, Sheila. (1993b). Retrenchment in the 1980s: The politics of prestige and gender. *The Journal of Higher Education, 64*(3), 250–282.

Slaughter, Sheila, & Leslie, Larry L. (1997). *Academic capitalism: Politics, policies, and the entrepreneurial university*. Baltimore: Johns Hopkins University Press.

Slaughter, Sheila, & Rhoades, Gary. (2004). *Academic capitalism and the new economy: Markets, state, and higher education*. Baltimore: Johns Hopkins University Press.

Smile Politely. (2010, January 5). U of I announces furloughs: "At some point we will be unable to meet payroll." Retrieved from https://www.smilepolitely.com/splog/u_of_i_announces_furloughs_at_some_point_we_will_be_unable_to_meet_payroll/

Smith, Mark F., Rhoades, Gary, & Dougherty, Kristine A. (2011). Negotiating virtual space. *The NEA 2011 Almanac of Higher Education* (pp. 53–70). Washington, DC: National Education Association.

Smith, Vernon, & Rhoades, Gary. (2006). Community college faculty and web-based classes. *Thought & Action, 22*, 97–110.

Sneiderman, Marilyn, & McCartin, Joseph A. (2018). Bargaining for the common good: An emerging tool for rebuilding worker power. In Janice Fine, Linda Burnham, Kati Griffith, Minsun Ji, Victor Narro, & Steven Pitts. (Eds.), *No one size fits all: Worker organization, policy, and movement in a new economic age* (pp. 219–134). Champaign, IL: Labor and Employment Relations Association.

Snyder. Thomas D. (Ed.). (1993). *120 years of American education: A statistical portrait*. Washington, DC: U.S. Department of Education, Office of Educational Research and Improvement.

Southerland, Suzanne, & Kamara, Yusufu. (2023, March 17). *Community college strikes for adjunct pay*. Presented at the 2023 NEA Higher Education Conference, San Jose, CA.

Sproul, Curtis, Bucklew, Neil, & Houghton, Jeffrey D. (2014). Academic collective bargaining: Pattern and trends. *Journal of Collective Bargaining in the Academy, 14*. https://doi.org/10.58188/1941-8043.1315

St. Amour, Madeline. (2020, April 20). Vermont may close three campuses. *InsideHigherEd*. Retrieved from https://www.insidehighered.com/quicktakes/2020/04/20/vermont-may-close-3-campuses

Staff Editorial. (2006, January 17). Stop the foot-dragging with part-time union. *The GW Hatchet*. Retrieved from https://gwhatchet.com/2006/01//17/staff-editorial-stop-the-foot-dragging-with-part-time-union/

Stein, Sharon, & Oliveira de Andreotti, Vanessa. (2016). Cash, competition, or charity: International students and the global imaginary. *Higher Education, 72*, 225–239.

Stephan, Paula E. (2012). *How economics shapes science*. Cambridge, MA: Harvard University Press.

Stepan-Norris, Judith, & Southworth, Caleb. (2010). Rival unionism and membership growth in the United States, 1900–2005: A special case of inter-organizational competition. *American Sociological Review, 75*(2), 227–251.

Stern, Mark Joseph. (2021, January 22). Biden gave Trump's union busters a taste of their own medicine. *Slate*. Retrieved from https://slate.com/news-and-politics/2021/01/peter-robb-alice-stock-nlrb-fired.html

Stillman, Don. (2010). *Stronger together: The story of SEIU*. Washington, DC: Service Employees, International Union.

Straumsheim, Carl. (2013, October 11). Faculty pushback on online deal. *InsideHigherEd*. Retrieved from https://www.insidehighered.com/news/2013/10/11/rutgers-u-graduate-school-faculty-vote-block-pearson-partnership

Street, Steve, Maisto, Maria, Merves, Esther, & Rhoades, Gary. (2012). *Who is professor "staff," and how can this person teach so many classes?* (Policy Report No. 2). Center for the Future of Higher Education, Campaign for the Future of Higher Education.

Strunk, Katherine O., Cowen, Joshua M., Goldhaber, Dan, Marianno, Bradley D., Kilbride, Tara, & Theobald, Roddy. (2018). It is in the contract: How the policies set in teachers' unions collective bargaining agreements vary across states and districts. *Educational Policy, 32*(2), 280–312.

Tamayo, Ana M. Fores. (2013, October). Non-tenured faculty fight against their conditions. *People's Tribune*. Retrieved from http://peoplestribune.org/pt-news/2013/10/non-tenured-faculty-fight-conditions/

Tate, Emily. (2017, March 6). Northeastern Illinois students lose jobs. *InsideHigherEd*. Retrieved from https://www.insidehighered.com/quicktakes/2017/03/06/northeastern-illinois-students-lose-jobs

Temple Association of University Professors. (2020). Welcome back reminders for adjunct faculty. Retrieved from https://taup.org/welcome-back-reminders-for-adjunct-faculty/

Temple University. (2018, May 24). Viral international education campaign #youarewelcomehere unveils 2019 national scholarship program. Temple Now. Retrieved from https://news.temple.edu/news/2018-05-24/viral-international-education-campaign-youarewelcomehere-unveils-2019-national

Terkel, Studs. (2012). *Hope dies last: Keeping the faith in troubled times*. New York: New Press.

Terkel, Studs. (1974). *Working*. New York: Free Press.

Tiede, Hans-Jorg. (2020). Policies on academic freedom, dismissal for cause, financial exigency, and program discontinuance. Washington, DC: American Association of University Professors. Retrieved from https://www.aaup.org/report/policies-academic-freedom-dismissal-cause-financial-exigency-and-program-discontinuance

Tierney, William G., & Lechuga, Vicente M. (2004). *Restructuring shared governance in higher education: New directions for higher education, number 127*. San Francisco: Jossey-Bass.

Tierney, William G., & Minor, James T. (2003). *Challenges for governance: A report by the Center for Higher Education Policy Analysis*. Los Angeles: Center for Higher Education Policy Analysis, University of Southern California.

Tolley, Kim. (Ed.). (2018). *Professors in the gig economy: Unionizing adjunct faculty in America*. Baltimore: Johns Hopkins University Press.

Tolley, Kim, & Edwards, Kristen. (2018). Reflections on the possibilities and limitations of collective bargaining. In Kim Tolley (Ed.), *Professors in the gig economy: Unionizing adjunct faculty in America* (pp. 187–206). Baltimore: Johns Hopkins University Press.

Tope, Daniel, & Jacobs, David. (2009). The politics of union decline: The contingent determinants of union recognition elections and victories. *American Sociological Review, 74*(5), 842–864.

Trainor, Sean. (2022, March 19). *In the belly of the beast: Organizing at tier 1 research universities*. Presented at the NEA Higher Education Conference, Baltimore, MD.

UAW. (2024). NYU contract faculty win their union, form largest union of full-time, non-tenure track private university professors in the country. *UAW Featured, News*. Retrieved from https://uaw.org/nyu-contract-faculty-win-their-union-form-largest-union-of-full-time-non-tenure-track-private-university-professors-in-the-country/

UIC Joint Furlough March 8: A Day of Education in Support of Public Education. (2010). Retrieved from https://uicjointfurlough.wordpress.com/jointfurlough/

UIC United Faculty. (2020a, March 11). UIC United Faculty's official statement on UI policies issued March 11, 2020. Retrieved from http://uicunitedfaculty.org/wp-content/uploads/2020/03/UICUF-statement-on-UI-COVID-19-policy-3.pdf

UIC United Faculty. (2020b). University of Illinois Chicago United Faculty Press Releases. Retrieved from http://uicunitedfaculty.org/news/

UI University Senates Conference. (2010, February 10). Response to Bunsis report. Private document.

Umbach, P. (2007). How effective are they? Exploring the impact of contingent faculty on undergraduate education. *The Review of Higher Education, 30*(2), 91–123.

Umhoefer, Dave. (2016, November 11). For unions in Wisconsin, a fast and hard fall since Act 10. *Journal Sentinel*. Retrieved from https://projects.jsonline.com/news/2016/11/27/for-unions-in-wisconsin-fast-and-hard-fall-since-act-10.html

United Academics University of Oregon. (2020). Frequently asked questions for Spring, the COVID crisis, and summer bargaining. Retrieved from http://uauoregon.org/faq-spring-2020/

United Academics University of Oregon. (2021, September 20). Reopening update. *The Duck and Cover: The Voice of United Academics Since 2017*. Retrieved from https://newsletter.uauoregon.org

United Steelworkers. (2024). Pitt faculty reach tentative agreement with university administration. Retrieved from https://m.usw.org/news/media-center/releases/2024/pitt-faculty-reach-tentative-agreement-with-university-administration#:~:text=The%20more%20than%203%2C000%20Pitt,served%20on%20the%20bargaining%20committee

University of Oregon. (2016, November 10). *Dear ducks: You belong here* [Video file]. Retrieved from https://www.youtube.com/watch?v=Sl__CZp1Dkg&feature=youtu.be

University of Oregon. (2023, July 28). UO issues funds to Willamalane for expanded child care services. *Around the O*. Retrieved from https://around.uoregon.edu/content/uo-issues-funds-willamalane-expanded-child-care-services

UO Matters. (2020, April 16). Pres Schill offers faculty union a pay cut proposal and a threat: Take it or suffer the consequences. Retrieved from https://uomatters.com

270 • References

/2020/04/pres-schill-offers-union-a-wage-cut-proposal-and-threat-take-it-or-suffer
-the-consequences.html

U.S. Bureau of Labor Statistics. (2024, January 23). Economic news release: Union members summary. https://www.bls.gov/news.release/union2.nro.htm

UW Excellence. (n.d.). A momentous decision. Retrieved from see www.uexcellence.org /the-case-against-unionization.html

Valentine, Susan. (2008). The administration strikes back: Union busting at NYU. In Monika Krause, Mary Nolan, Michael Palm, & Andrew Ross (Eds.). *The university against itself: The NYU strike and the future of the academic workplace* (pp. 123–136). Philadelphia: Temple University Press.

Vallas, Steven Peter. (2004). Bread, roses, and resistance at work. *Contemporary Sociology, 33*(1), 13–15.

Vargas Llosa, Mario. (1989). *The storyteller.* New York: Farrar, Straus and Giroux.

Warner, Claire. (2020, July 20). Faculty union reaches tentative deal with UO administration over salary cuts, FTE restoration. *Daily Emerald.* Retrieved from https://www .dailyemerald.com/news/faculty-union-reaches-tentative-deal-with-uo-administration -over-salary-cuts-fte-restoration/article_05c5cf6c-d2ad-11ea-bea0-733854468ff75.html

Wasserman, Dale (Writer), Darion, Joe (Lyrics), & Leigh, Mitch (Music). (1966). *Man of La Mancha.* New York: Random House.

Watson, Bruce. (2005). *Bread and roses: Mills, migrants, and the struggle for the American dream.* New York: Viking Press.

Weissman, Jordan. (2015, April 13). Someone calculated how many adjunct professors are on public assistance, and the number is startling. *Slate.* Retrieved from https:// slate.com/business/2015/04/adjunct-pay-a-quarter-of-part-time-college-faculty -receive-public-assistance.html

Wertsch, Nicholas M., & McCartin, Joseph A. (2018). A just employment approach to adjunct unionization. In Kim Tolley (Ed.), *Professors in the gig economy: Unionizing adjunct faculty in America* (pp. 87–103). Baltimore: Johns Hopkins University Press.

Wickens, Christine M. (2008). The organizational impact of university labor unions. *Higher Education, 56*(5), 545–564.

Woolston, Chris. (2002, August 20). Perpetual postdocs. *Chronicle of Higher Education.* Retrieved from https://www.chronicle.com/article/perpetual-postdocs/

Worthen, H., & Berry, J. (2002). Bargaining for "quality" in higher education: A case study from the City Colleges of Chicago. *Labor Studies Journal, 27*(3), 1–23.

Wozobski, Lizzie. (2006, November 20). Web update: Court denies GW's appeal in adjunct faculty union suit. *The GW Hatchet.* Retrieved from https://www.gwhatchet .com/2006/11/20/web-update-court-denies-gws-appeal-in-adjunct-faculty-union-suit/

Wozobski, Lizzie. (2006, December 7). GW concedes defeat in part-time faculty union case. *The GW Hatchet.* Retrieved from https://www.gwhatchet.com/2006/12/07/gw -concedes-defeat--in-part-time-faculty-union-case/

WSUCASE. (2024). Before unionization vs. after first contract. *WSU Coalition of Academic Student Employees.* Retrieved from https://wsucase.org/before-and-after-union/

Xu, Di. (2019). Academic performance in community colleges: The influence of part-time and full-time instructors. *American Educational Research Journal, 56*(2), 368–406.

Zuboff, Shoshana. (1988). *In the Age of the Smart Machine: The Future of Work and Power.* New York: Basic Books.

Zumeta, William M. (1985). *Extending the educational ladder: The changing quality and value of postdoctoral study.* Boston: Lexington Books.

Zweig, Michael. (2012). *The working class majority: America's best kept secret* (2nd ed.). Ithaca, NY: Cornell University Press.

Index

Abbott, Andrew, 29–30, 42, 68–69, 89, 231n13
academic capitalism: and austerity practices, 125; critique by contingent academic employees, 117; failure of furloughs and, 142; general pattern and priorities, 19, 33, 147; intersecting with social (in)justice, 202, 207, 217; in new circuits of production, 170; regarding students, 98; social relations of, 201–202
academic freedom, 6, 58, 66, 178, 182, 238n7; for contingent faculty, 230n5; for graduate employees, 93–94, 98, 100, 103; for postdocs, 111, 114; in shared governance, 120, 127, 146, 148, 224n25, 235n3, 236n5
affect, importance in organizing, 203, 210
agency fee(s), 14, 15, 193
American Association of University Professors (AAUP): acknowledgement, 9, 200, 216; campaign at UCHC, 17–19, 222n11, 222n14, 222n16, 223n22, 224n25; campaign at UIC, 12, 20–24, 132–134, 145, 224n30, 236n9; campaign at UO, 24–26; campaign failures, 26–27, 49; chapters and conferences, 5, 9, 14, 133, 219n5; contingent faculty, 39, 227n3, 232n4; contracts, 148–152, 154, 158, 160–161, 164, 192, 238n11, 238n13, 238n15; as general secretary, 9, 219n5, 220n6, 222n9, 223n24, 225n31; graduate employees, 91, 93, 233n14; NFM members, 206; policy statements on

academic freedom, 236n3, 236n5; policy statements on distance education, 120, 169, 171; policy statements on financial exigency and retrenchment, 144–147, 150–154, 158; policy statements on graduate employees, 93; policy statements on shared governance, 120, 127–128, 131–132, 235n3; postdocs, 234n26; staff in government relations, 12; staff in relation to AFT, 225n31; staff in relation to NMSU campaign, 27; staff in relation to UCHC campaign, 18, 222n11, 222n16; staff in relation to UIC campaign, 22, 204, 224n30, 224n31; staff in relation to UO campaign, 25–26; staff on shared governance, 131
American Council on Education, 96, 233n15
American Federation of State, County, and Municipal Employees (AFSCME), 15, 17, 30, 222n11
American Federation of Teachers (AFT): acknowledgement, 216; contingent faculty at Temple, 228n22; contingent faculty numbers nationally, 229n23; at CUNY, 51; graduate employees, 89, 92, 103; identity as teachers union, 224n25; joint agreement with AAUP, 223n24, 224n25, 225n31; joint organizing numbers and tensions with AAUP, 53, 206, 224n30, 227n13, 241n9; joint organizing with AAUP at UIC, 12, 20–26, 132, 225n34, 225n39, 226n41, 236n9; membership gains despite Janus, 15; metro

271

272 • Index

American Federation of Teachers (Cont)
campaign, 48; NFM members, 52;
organizing at GW, 43, 223n21; staff, 43;
survey of contingent faculty, 54, 227n3;
Weingarten on common good bargaining,
209

apprentices, 7, 11, 36, 87–89, 94, 105, 116, 196,
233n16

arbitration, independent external as a
campaign issue, 5, 89, 98, 103–104,
110–111, 113, 115, 153, 197, 208; procedures,
97, 150, 157, 160, 228n17

assaults, on collective bargaining rights, 2,
12, 14–16, 216

Association of American Universities
(AAU), 17, 24–25, 107, 225n33, 225n34

Association of Governing Boards (AGB),
127–129, 235n2

austerity: management agenda and
discourse, 11, 58, 121, 125–126, 134,
189, 197; management practices, 7, 11,
121, 123–124, 142, 144–145, 192,
197–198

balance of power: between faculty and
management, 2, 6, 36, 76, 89, 116, 201; in
contracts, 173, 179, 194; shared governance, 127, 129

Berry, Joe: acknowledgement, 216, 240n5
(chap. 9); Berry and Savarese data, 7, 28,
68; Berry and Worthen, 47–51, 66, 202,
206, 220n7, 231n10, 232n17; best contracts
for adjunct faculty, 232n17; book title, 3;
competitive unionism, 73; effects of
graduate employees on labor movement,
104; faculty versus staff-run unions,
222n14; inside/outside strategy, 50–51;
metro strategy, 47–49; "professionals," 3,
223n23; respect, 67

Bowling Green State University, 17, 23, 26,
149, 223n22, 224n27, 236n10

bread and butter issues, 6, 31, 63, 97,
100–101, 106, 109–111, 116, 197

bread and roses, 7, 10, 41–42, 246, 261; issues
in campaigns, 46, 54, 58, 61–62, 66, 75,
85–86, 88, 195–196; textile workers strike,
36, 39–41, 195

Cain, Timothy Reese, 32, 90, 129, 132, 202,
232n5, 233n14, 237n2

California Faculty Association (CFA), 13,
202, 229n29, 232n17; before the metro
campaigns, 51–52; contracts, 66, 194,
231n10; social justice issues, 206, 208

Campaign for the Future of Higher
Education, 9, 205

card check: in campaigns, 26, 204, 224n30;
definition of, 224n30

circuits of production, new, 7, 11, 168–169,
173, 175, 179, 184, 189–190, 199

class cancellation fees, 8, 10, 55, 63, 65–67; in
contracts, 67–70, 72–75, 84–85, 196,
221n12

coalitions, 3, 17, 24, 45, 48, 54, 198, 203–207,
210, 212

Columbia University, 88, 91, 93, 95, 234n26

corporatization, as a union campaign issue,
19, 20, 95, 124, 126, 135, 140, 142, 198, 208

course management systems, 75, 172–173,
178–179, 190, 199

COVID-19. See pandemic

creative strategies/tactics: of adjunct faculty,
10, 42, 44–46, 49, 60–61, 195, 216;
regarding new circuits of production, 172

defensive approaches, strategies, and
posture: in furloughs, 136–137, 142, 198;
in general, 203, 212; in new circuits of
production, 11, 170, 183, 189–190, 197, 199,
239n2; in retrenchment, 160–161,
165–166, 169, 198, 236n5

deskilling, 40

disaster academic capitalism, 58, 61, 142, 145,
153, 197

discrimination: against international
students, 100, 104–105; against strikers,
43; by gender, racial, and marginalized
identities, 5, 36, 89, 98, 103–104, 110–111,
115–116, 192, 197, 208

distance education, 119–120, 169–171,
189–190, 199–200, 240n10; broadening
the script, 172; class size, 181–182;
compensation, 180–181; contracts,
172–174, 176, 178–180; the defensive
script, 170–171; displacement, 183–184;
evaluation and surveillance, 182–183;
flipping the script, 171–172; governance,
185–186; intellectual property, 186–189,
240n8; training, 184–185; voluntary,
180–181

enskilling, 170, 185

Faculty Forward, 10, 49–50, 229n24
financial exigency, 7, 11, 120, 120–121, 136,
    237n1, 237n6; in contracts, 136, 143, 144,
    146–149, 151–154, 167, 198, 238n7, 238n9,
    251, 268; AAUP definition, 146–147
funds of knowledge, 203, 210, 253, 257, 259;
    activist funds of knowledge, 11, 194, 203,
    204
furloughs, 7, 11, 17, 236n6; in contracts, 135,
    137–138, 197–198; in pandemic, 138–141;
    UIC campaign, 24, 123–134, 132–135,
    142–143, 146, 151

George Washington University (GW): class
    cancellation fee contractual clauses, 69,
    231n11; job security in contract, 155;
    management resistance to unionizing,
    44; metro strategy, 47; organizing of
    adjunct faculty, 41, 43–47, 60, 195, 223n21,
    227n11; quality bargained in contract,
    228n16; student support of adjunct
    faculty organizing, 45–46, 211, 228n14
graduate employees: academic literature on,
    32; affiliates, 48, 50, 139–140, 228n20,
    232n5; challenges to rights to collectively
    bargain, 13–15; contracts, 88, 100–105,
    234n25; issues, 36, 97–100, 208, 212,
    225n31, 232n4; numbers organizing, 2, 16,
    28, 195, 233n11; public discourse, 93–96;
    strategy, 91–92
grievance(s), 7, 15, 102, 109, 113, 115, 220n10

Herbert, William: acknowledgement, 217;
    certification votes, 17, 61, 233n13;
    bargaining social issues, 89, 98; faculty
    union density, 32, 56; faculty organizing
    in the 2000s, 2, 16, 41, 49, 53, 68, 92, 130,
    193, 195; graduate student organizing in
    the 2000s, 2, 16, 92, 193, 195, 233n11,
    233n12; growth in combined units, 205;
    postdoc organizing in the 2000s, 2, 92,
    106, 193, 195, 234n26; strikes, 17, 88, 92,
    197, 206; UAW members in higher
    education, 226n45; younger peoples' more
    favorable view of unions, 90
Higher Education Contract Analysis System
    (HECAS): acknowledgement, 215;
    content of data source, 7, 63, 100, 147, 174

Higher Education Labor United (HELU),
    10, 205
hybrid, 172–176, 181, 190, 240n8

identities: of AAUP and AFT, 22; author's,
    4–5; embodied in race/gender/orientation,
    60, 89, 104, 110, 201–202, 210; general, 2–3,
    6, 10–11, 89, 107, 116, 194, 224n25
inside/outside strategy, 50–52, 61, 195,
    204–205
instructional resources, 10, 36, 63, 74–78, 80,
    80–81, 83–86, 190, 196, 228n16
intellectual property: of curriculum, 169,
    173, 180, 186–188, 220n10, 240n7 (chap.
    8), 240n8, 240n11; postdocs, 111, 114
international employees, postdocs, 87, 89,
    110–111, 113, 115, 194
international students/employees: general
    information about, 233n18; graduate and
    postdoc employee support of, 37, 89, 98,
    100, 104–105, 115, 208, 234n20; manage-
    ment threats to unionizing despite
    #youarewelcomehere messaging, 99–100,
    234n20

Janus decision, 15, 193
jurisdiction(al), rights, claims, negotiation,
    6, 74, 89, 116, 194, 196, 201

Lane Community College, 70, 72, 179, 183,
    209
Lane Community College Education
    Association (LCCEA), 13
Layoff. See retrenchment

managed professionals, 1, 3–6, 11, 13, 33, 125,
    215, 217
management rights, 103, 152, 220n10
managerial discretion: in access to instruc-
    tional resources and professional
    development, 76–77, 196; in course
    assignment/class cancellation fees, 68–70,
    196; general, 1–2; in relation to graduate
    and postdoc employees, 89, 100, 103, 111;
    in retrenchment, 146–147, 153, 155,
    159–160, 163–164, 166, 173, 179, 189, 197
managerial disrespect, 56, 192, 210–211
managerial professionals, 220n6, 240n3
McLeer, Anne, 44–47, 60, 216, 227n12,
    230n39

274 • Index

metro campaigns: defined, p.48; of AFT, 48, 64, 74; of SEIU Local 500, 47, 155; of SEIU locals, 49–50, 54, 69, 73, 155, 193, 195, 196, 217, 226n42, 239n24; of USW, 48

National Association of Graduate-Professional Students (NAGPS), 94–95
National Center for the Study of Collective Bargaining in Higher Education and the Professions (NCSCBHEP), 10
National Education Association (NEA): acknowledgement, 215–216; affiliation of locals, 51–52, 234n26, 238n9; campaigns, 27; HECAS database, 7; higher education vs. K–12 members, 224n25; NFM members, 206
National Labor Relations Act (NLRA), 44, 88, 91, 96, 228n19, 230n36
National Labor Relations Board (NLRB): appointments to, 232n9; Biden's changes, 15, 92; briefs to NLRB, 93, 95–96, 233n15; (graduate) student employees' strategies towards, 91, 233n10; requirements for filing with, 43; rulings and shifts by federal administration on graduate assistants, 14, 30, 44, 88, 90–91, 232n6, 233n17; rulings on cases of contingent and tenure stream faculty, 44, 228n19; in Yeshiva ruling, 30
National Postdoctoral Association (NPA), 108–109, 234n32
National Research Council, 108
New Faculty Majority (NFM): acknowledgement, 216; described, 2, 10, 39, 40, 61, 87; faculty working conditions are students' learning conditions, 39, 208; inside/outside strategy of leveraging change, 41, 51–53, 56, 195, 206, 229n30; public advocacy and public purpose, 30, 39, 53, 57, 208

office hours, 74, 169, 172–178, 180, 190, 199
office visits, 19, 212, 223n18, 223n20

pandemic: amplifying and affecting issues, such as social justice, underlying organizing, 59–61, 91, 120, 140, 239n3, 240n10; bargaining about/amid, 169, 171–175, 186, 190, 200; connected to disaster academic capitalism, 197; as

"force majeure," 153; increasing solidarity between tenure stream and contingent faculty, and among all workers, 205, 230n38
pay parity, 10, 13, 56, 65–66, 85, 86, 196, 230n6
postdocs: academic literature, 32; background to organizing, 35, 105–106; identity of, 106–107, 109–110, 240n7 (chap. 9); issues underlying organizing, 88, 192; postdoc units' establishment, 16, 27, 205, 225n39; public discourse about, 106–109, 234n30; websites, campaigns, and contracts of, 57, 109–115, 232n4, 234n26, 234n29, 235n34, 235n36
privatization, as a union campaign issue, 18, 20, 24–26, 124, 142
proactive, strategies, posture, tactics, 11, 15, 169, 171–172, 183, 189–190, 197–198, 200, 209
professional(s): ideology of specialness and excellence as obstacle to unionizing, 21, 26–27, 46, 204, 225n40; book title, 3–4; getting over specialness and professional ideology in organizing, 21, 201, 204; in governance, 128, 130; managerial discourse and strategy about excellence and quality, 41, 46, 57, 83, 220n9; postdoc identity, 109; special relations between faculty and graduate students, 96–97
professional development, 11, 26, 46; contingent faculty, 56, 63, 74–75, 79–82, 84, 84–86, 89, 98, 196, 200, 228n16, 235n36; faculty control of, 185; graduate employees, 100, 102–103; metro strategy, 47; postdocs, 108, 110–111, 114
professional issues, in bargaining, 6, 100, 103, 108, 110–111, 179, 184
Professional Staff Congress (PSC), 51–52, 131, 195, 205–206, 216–217, 220n6, 223n23, 229n28
professorial stratification: between faculty, 2; in distance education contractual language, 189; in organizing campaigns, 20, 24, 56; in pay and contracts for contingent faculty, 65, 68–70, 74, 80, 85–86, 196; in retrenchment clauses in contracts, 146, 156, 158, 163–167, 199–200
program discontinuation/elimination, 146–147, 153–155, 166, 198

public interest, 5, 31, 36–37, 41, 57, 77, 89, 173, 179, 188; in contracts, 82, 84, 188, 190, 196, 200, 207–210, 241n12

quality, labor-based conception of: in campaigns, 10, 39, 54, 63, 74–75, 195–196, 220n9; in contingent faculty contracts, 78, 84–85; in distance education, 190; locally based, 47; in retrenchment clauses, 180, 210

reduction in force (RIF). *See* retrenchment resource mapping, 210–211
respect: basic thesis about respect as the basis of organizing, 6, 11, 29, 32, 41, 56, 212–213; contingent faculty and respect, 10, 40, 46, 53, 67, 226n2; contingent faculty and respect from tenure-track faculty, 78; for all workers, in coalition forming, 203; for meaningful faculty input/voice/shared governance, 5, 17, 20, 125, 127–128, 191; for public purposes of the academy, 125; graduate and postdoc employees demanding respect for full humanity, 89; how unions command respect, 4, 8, 215; roses as respect, 36, 40–42, 55–56, 61, 63, 195; strikes and, 200, 217, 226n2
retrenchment: contingent faculty involvement, 161; dominant management strategy, 138; faculty strategy, 236n5; general, 119–121, 197–199, 239n22; for financial exigency, 146–152; for other rationales, 153–166, 238n16, 239n29; key takeaways, 167; new circuits of production, 168, 173; SUNY case, 132
right to work, 14–15, 92, 109

SEIU Local 500, 41–44, 47–49, 52, 59, 195, 207, 216, 228n20
Service Employees International Union (SEIU), 7, 10, 27, 41, 52, 54, 59, 223n21, 226n42, 233n12, 234n26; class cancellation fees, 68, 68–69, 73, 86, 196; history, 31, 194; Local 500, 43–44; metro campaigns, 47–48; other organizing, 49, 92, 195, 197, 228n17; retrenchment, 155; staff, 8, 50, 215, 217, 227n12, 229n25; staff union, 207
sexual harassment, 5, 36, 100, 104, 109–111, 115–116, 197, 208

shared governance and faculty voice, 6, 11, 13, 142; AAUP, 93, 120–121, 127–128, 193–194, 224n25, 235n3, 236n5; academic literature, 32, 121, 125–127, 235n1; AGB, 128–129, 235n2; in campaigns, 18, 20, 23–27, 125, 127–135, 140, 236n10; for contingent faculty, 39, 51, 56, 77–79, 128–129, 156, 167, 199, 205; in financial exigency and retrenchment, 103, 124, 145–146, 154–156, 160–161, 167, 173, 197–199, 238n10; in technology-mediated education, 178–180, 182, 199–200; unions and, 129–132
social justice: in contingent employees' campaigns, 36–37, 58, 60, 66, 86, 89, 98; in contracts, 100–101, 103–104, 108–111, 116; in general in campaigns, 6–7, 13, 36, 191, 194, 208; in negotiating furloughs, 139, 197, 237n11; in negotiating new circuits of production, 172–173, 189; in negotiating retrenchment, 162, 169; in union governance, 206; new bread and butter, 197; UICUF, 24. *See also* workplace justice intersecting with social justice
social movements, 4–5, 59, 86, 208, 212
Sowards, Robin, 65, 85, 216, 223n23, 231n9
staff: AAUP model of building advocacy chapters first, 26; AAUP model of organizing, 22–23, 204, 223n22, 224n30; AAUP policy staff, 128; AAUP staff and reluctance to take risk, 17, 23, 222n11, 222n12, 225n31, 225n32, 233n14; AAUP staff and threats to collective bargaining, 12; acknowledging, 9, 10, 215–216; AFT, 223n24, 224n25, 224n30, 236n9; of locals, 222n14; NEA, 224n25; professor staff, 40, 67; relations among and between staff, leaders, members, 31, 83, 205, 224n29, 229n26; SEIU, 8, 217, 229n25; staff employee organizing and bargaining units, 50–51, 60, 124, 139–141, 207, 211, 219n3, 228n20, 230n4, 240n3; USW, 223n23, 231n9
strikes: before contract settlement, 26, 41, 98, 112, 210; of contingent academic employees, 37, 96, 115–116, 207; in 2020s, 17, 89–90, 204, 206, 210–211

timing, importance in organizing, 69, 72, 210, 238n11

276 • Index

UIC United Faculty (UICUF), 20–21, 24, 56, 59, 172, 205, 208–209, 224n30, 230n38
union governance, 13, 51, 131, 216
United Academics University of Oregon (UAUO), 15, 56, 141, 172
United Autoworkers (UAW): adjunct faculty organizing, 41, 43, 58, 86; graduate employee contracts, 100, 206, 233n12; graduate employee organizing, 57, 91–92, 233n17, 234n20; higher education membership, 226n45; postdocs, 106, 109–110; strategy for filing for an election, 227n9; strike, 206
United Campus Workers, Arizona (UCWAZ), 60, 141, 237n11
United Electrical, Radio, and Machine Workers of America (UE), 27, 92, 100, 197
United Steelworkers (USW): membership gains after Janus, 15; metro campaign of, 48; NFM members, 52, 206; organizing contingent faculty, 64, 67, 82, 225n34, 228n19, 229n25, 232n16
University of Connecticut Health Center (UCHC), 17–20, 23, 204, 222n12,

222n14, 222n15, 223n19, 223n22, 224n25, 225n35
University of Illinois, Chicago (UIC): organizing campaign, 20–24, 26, 223n24, 224n29, 227n13, 236n9; campaign issues, 124, 132; coalition between faculty, 59, 205, 209; contract of, 102; furloughs, 132–135, 142, 237n4; specialness of tenure track faculty at, 204, 225n35, 225n40, 236n10
University of Oregon (UO), 25, 26, 141, 204, 209, 225

wall-to-wall, 4, 41, 47, 59, 60, 219n3
workplace justice intersecting with social justice: in contingent academic employee campaigns, 89, 101, 104, 110; in general, 6, 201–203, 207, 217; in new circuits of production, 173; in retrenchment, 194
Worthen, Helena: acknowledgement, 240n5 (chap. 9); Berry and Worthen, 47–51, 66, 131, 202, 206, 220n7, 229n33, 231n10, 232n17; "professionals," 3; quality, 74–75

About the Author

GARY RHOADES is a professor of higher education at the University of Arizona's Center for the Study of Higher Education, of which he was director for nineteen years, and author of *Managed Professionals: Unionized Faculty and Restructuring Academic Labor* and (with Sheila Slaughter) *Academic Capitalism and the New Economy: Markets, State, and Higher Education*, as well as numerous articles on academic labor and academic restructuring. From January 2009 to June 2011, he was general secretary of the American Association of University Professors. Rhoades has been an active participant in the academic labor movement for three decades and is currently a member of United Campus Workers, Arizona, Local 7065 of the Communications Workers of America. His first direct experience of the power of a union was as a summer utility worker at Garden State Paper Company and a member of what was then the United Paperworkers International Union, which taught him in a visceral, material way about the union's role in shaping terms and conditions of employment like workplace safety and collective power vis-à-vis management and the foremen.